REPUBLIC
of DETOURS

REPUBLIC
of DETOURS

HOW THE NEW DEAL
PAID BROKE WRITERS
TO REDISCOVER AMERICA

———————◆———————

SCOTT BORCHERT

FARRAR, STRAUS AND GIROUX

NEW YORK

Farrar, Straus and Giroux
120 Broadway, New York 10271

Printed in the United States of America
First edition, 2021

Library of Congress Cataloging-in-Publication Data
Names: Borchert, Scott, 1986– author.
Title: Republic of detours : how the New Deal paid broke writers to rediscover
   America / Scott Borchert.
Description: First edition. | New York : Farrar, Straus and Giroux, 2021. |
   Includes bibliographical references and index. | Summary: "A literary history of the
   Federal Writers Project" —Provided by publisher.
Identifiers: LCCN 2020057978 | ISBN 9780374298456 (hardcover)
Subjects: LCSH: Federal Writers' Project. | American guide series. |
   United States—Intellectual life—20th century. | United States—Civilization—1918–1945.
Classification: LCC E175.4.W9 B67 2021 | DDC 973.917—dc23
LC record available at https://lccn.loc.gov/2020057978

Designed by Gretchen Achilles

Our books may be purchased in bulk for promotional, educational,
or business use. Please contact your local bookseller or the Macmillan Corporate
and Premium Sales Department at 1-800-221-7945, extension 5442, or by email at
MacmillanSpecialMarkets@macmillan.com.

www.fsgbooks.com
www.twitter.com/fsgbooks • www.facebook.com/fsgbooks

1   3   5   7   9   10   8   6   4   2

for Addie,

for my parents

More public good has come out of the bankruptcy of the economic order than ever came regularly out of its most flatulent prosperity.

—LEWIS MUMFORD, 1937

CONTENTS

———◆———

CONTENTS

REPUBLIC
of DETOURS

PROLOGUE

Imagine stopping someone on a Manhattan street and asking for directions to Times Square. If that person commenced a monologue beginning, "It is the district of glorified dancing girls and millionaire playboys and, on a different plane, of dime-a-dance hostesses and pleasure-seeking clerks. Here, too, in a permanent moralizing tableau, appear the extremes of success and failure characteristic of Broadway's spectacular professions: gangsters and racketeers, panhandlers and derelicts, youthful stage stars and aging burlesque comedians, world heavyweight champions and once-acclaimed beggars," and then that person recounted the histories of every theater and club, the development of the area's rapid public transit, and the origin of the phrase "the Great White Way" (coined, supposedly, in 1901 by the adman O. J. Gude), all in a tone both disdainful and celebratory of the famed intersection that "lights the clouds above Manhattan with a glow like that of a dry timber fire"—you would know what it was like to read the American Guides, a curious series of books that appeared during the last years of the Great Depression. Specifically, you'd know what it was like to read the *New York City Guide*, which was published in 1939. And you'd be no closer to Times Square.

Alongside New York City, there was a guide for every state (forty-eight of them then), plus the District of Columbia, the Alaska Territory, and Puerto Rico.

Other cities and towns—and locales such as Death Valley and routes such as US 1—got the guidebook treatment, too. The public bought them, expecting books in the popular Baedeker mode: travel companions that were concise, comprehensive, and functional. But the hefty American Guides were something else.

These books sprawled. They hoarded and gossiped and sat you down for a lecture. They seemed to address multiple readers at once from multiple perspectives. They ran to hundreds of pages. They contained a mélange of essays, historical tidbits, folklore, anecdotes, photographs, and social analysis—along with an abundance of driving directions thickened by tall tales, strange sites, and bygone characters. They were deeply researched on subjects of little use to a traveler—the structure of local government, a state's literary residents—while they barely mentioned diners, motels, and gas stations. They were rich and weird and frustrating.

Most of the state guides were divided into three sections. First, perplexed readers paged through essays on history, industry, folkways, and other subjects. Then came profiles of notable cities and towns, and, finally, a collection of automobile tours across the state. The tours highlighted scenic overlooks and recreation spots, but they were also dense with Indian massacres, labor strikes, witches, gunfighters, Continental Army spies, Confederate deserters, shipwrecks, slave rebellions, famous swindlers, and forgotten poets. They traveled through towns with bizarre names and towns founded by religious cults; they pointed out architectural curiosities, dubious monuments, and decayed trading posts. They paused for every old-timer's story that could be fastened to a patch of ground. They knew of ghosts on every road. They mentioned all the places where Washington ever slept and where Lincoln was ever born. They guided tourists across the land but also deep into the national character, into a past that was assembled from the mythic and the prosaic, the factual and the farcical. The tours seemed less accessories for motorists than rambling day trips through the unsorted mind of the Republic.

This shaggy opulence, this Americana maximalism, made the guides unusual. But their provenance made them remarkable. They weren't issued by some erratic publisher or obsessive-compulsive tourist association: they were in fact created by the federal government. They were researched, written, and edited by members of the Federal Writers' Project, a division of the Works Progress Administration. The WPA was a cornerstone of the New

Deal, one of several agencies tasked with delivering jobs to the jobless. The American Guides were among the unlikeliest weapons in the improvised arsenal that the Roosevelt administration brought to bear upon the Depression.

Launched with the WPA in 1935, the FWP provided work for unemployed writers, whether professional or aspiring, competent or otherwise. It wasn't a huge program, comparatively. The entire WPA employed more than 2 million people a month, on average, while the FWP averaged 4,500 to 5,200 people and peaked at 6,686. FWP workers were scattered in offices around the country: in each state's largest city and in satellite offices, and in the project's headquarters in Washington. Some of them worked mostly at home or in the field. Many federal writers were teachers, beat reporters, clerks, lawyers, librarians, people laid off from advertising firms or real estate agencies, members of the clergy—white-collar workers whose jobs had disappeared and who were better suited to desk labor than, say, draining malarial swampland. They worked alongside poets and novelists, including some significant writers whose fame had been eclipsed by the Depression and others who had yet to become famous. A handful of illustrious figures from the world of American letters collected an FWP paycheck at one time or another. (I'll skip the potted roster. We'll meet them.)

The FWP operated in tandem with the other WPA arts projects, for theater, visual art, and music; all were part of the same policy strategy that, through the Civilian Conservation Corps, sent young men to clear forest trails or, through the Public Works Administration, paid workers to build the Lincoln Tunnel. The FWP was a work relief program, and its primary mission was to keep writers from starving to death or killing themselves, while putting cash into circulation and contributing, however modestly, to the economic recovery. But it was also a literary endeavor of unprecedented scale. When the FWP was finally dissolved, along with the rest of the WPA, in 1943, *Time* magazine gave it the epitaph "the biggest literary project in history." That sounds like hyperbole. But the project's administrators and its defenders made this claim, too, and it does not seem to be disputed. "The work we do has one notable feature," wrote Henry G. Alsberg, the FWP's national director, to his friend the novelist and critic Waldo Frank. "It is a cooperative job, the first on such a great scale that has ever been attempted, I believe." Alsberg would know—he'd seen a good chunk of the world as a roving journalist, and he'd been to Soviet Russia, where they tried things like this. But, with the FWP, he sat at the helm of something truly new.

The project might have been a disaster. Many doubted that staffing an unwieldy government bureaucracy with temperamental and often desperate writers—not a few impaired by heavy drinking, professional jealousy, political sectarianism, or all three—could lead to any good outcome. (The journalist Dorothy Thompson remarked, "Project? For Writers? Absurd!" and the poet W. H. Auden, unknowingly echoing Thompson, later called the entire WPA arts program "one of the noblest and most absurd undertakings ever attempted by a state.") But from 1937, when the first guides appeared, to 1943, when the project was disbanded, the FWP managed to produce at least one thousand publications and gather reams of unused material. (Some of these manuscripts, especially individual life histories and the testimonials of formerly enslaved people, would be treasured and interrogated by future scholars.) Each successful publication chipped away at assumptions about the FWP, proving that it was no hopeless boondoggle for failed writers and unimaginative hacks. Reviewers were generally impressed, finding that the books far surpassed their expectations.

Among the most incisive of contemporary reviewers was Alfred Kazin, then in his late twenties. Kazin, the son of working-class Jewish immigrants, seemed to emerge from nowhere when his book reviews began appearing in *The New Republic*, *Scribner's*, and New York newspapers. (He had actually emerged from his family's cramped apartment in Brownsville, Brooklyn, and the City College of New York.) During the second half of the thirties, he supported himself by writing reviews and teaching classes. He also spent hours hunched over the long tables of the New York Public Library on Forty-second Street, researching and composing an ambitious study of American literature.

Kazin was just the sort of person—bookish, precariously employed, a child of immigrants—who might have worked for the FWP. Indeed, he nearly did. In his memoir of the thirties, he describes being offered an editorial job with the FWP in Washington; intrigued, he set out for an interview at the local Manhattan office—always the most turbulent, owing to politics and personalities, of all the FWP outposts.

I went down for my interview in the New York office, somewhere along the waterfront, to enter a room crowded with men and women lying face down on the floor, screaming that they were on strike. In order to get to the supervisor's office at the other end of the hall, I had to make my way over bodies stacked as if after a battle; and as I sat in the supervisor's office, he calmly discussed the job while shouts and screams came from the long hall outside.

Kazin left, stepping over the bodies of would-be colleagues. Such a scene, he implied in his memoir, was not for him. But, in reality, he had been quite eager for the job—as his application letter and anxious follow-up, now sitting in the FWP archives, reveal. Kazin was struggling to bundle the "lean pickings" that were available to him, job-wise, into some kind of sustainable living: as a freelance researcher and book reviewer, manuscript reader and editorial assistant, and "a ghost-writer for an Irish colonel, who was unfortunately illiterate." The FWP could offer the security and support he needed, while putting his talents to good use. Like so many young and aspiring writers, he coveted a job on the project. And like so many of them, he was turned away because there simply weren't enough positions.

Instead, he retreated to the New York Public Library and dedicated himself to that study of American literature. Whether he noticed or not, his book developed in perfect parallel with the FWP. He'd begun it in 1937, the year of the first American Guides, and he finished it in 1942, when the project was effectively ending. *On Native Grounds* was a tour through American prose literature, beginning with the realist novels of William Dean Howells and proceeding into the thirties, informed by Kazin's deep reading and marked by peppery judgments and a keen moral sensibility. And, whatever the actual circumstances of Kazin's encounter with the FWP, he saved a place in his book for an assessment of the American Guides.

Kazin ended *On Native Grounds* by taking up the "literature of nationhood" that emerged most forcefully after the crash of 1929—a literary trend of broad membership, involving novelists and sociologists and critics and folklorists and bureaucrats from the Farm Security Administration. As Kazin described it, the "literature of nationhood" comprised an upsurge of disparate writing "whose subject was the American scene and whose drive always was the need, born of the depression and the international crisis, to chart America and to possess it." These were books that turned away from the frivolous, the insular, the sharply modernist writing that dominated the twenties, and, spurred by the economic collapse and the growth of fascism, focused their attention on the American land, its people and their works, past and present. Edmund Wilson's book of reportage, *The American Jitters*, fit this pattern, and so did Van Wyck Brooks's literary study *The Flowering of New England*, and so did Carl Sandburg's biographies of Lincoln, and so did *You Have Seen Their Faces*, a documentary record of the southern poor with text by Erskine Caldwell and photographs by Margaret Bourke-White. Books such as these had literary ancestors in Emerson, struggling to conjure up a distinct and meaningful American spirit at his desk, and in Whitman, who chased that spirit down and sought to become possessed by it.

The American Guides sat at the heart of this new literature. Kazin singled them out for praise and insisted on their literary merit (the superior volumes, anyway), perhaps because he knew they had surpassed the low expectations of so many reviewers. In 1942, the books were still fresh—several had only just been published—but Kazin had a clear view of where they belonged in his story of American literature. His commentary was an artful summation of the general feeling among the FWP's contemporary admirers:

> The WPA state guides, seemingly only a makeshift, a stratagem of ad-ministrative relief policy to tide a few thousand people along and keep them working, a business of assigning individuals of assorted skills and interests to map the country, mile by mile, resulted in an extraordinary contemporary epic. Out of the need to find something to say about every community and the country around it, out of the vast storehouse of facts behind the guides—geological, geographic, meteorological, ethnological, historical, political, sociological, economic—there emerged an America unexampled in density and regional diversity . . . More than any other literary form in the thirties, the WPA writers' project, by illustrating how much so many collective skills could do to uncover the collective history of the country, set the tone of the period.

The American Guides, in other words, could not be dismissed as mere curiosities—or as evidence of the New Dealers' mania for spending tax dol-lars in creative ways. The books were key to understanding the historical moment, for the guides, as Kazin had it, "became a repository as well as a symbol of the reawakened American sense of its own history."

Most thoughtful reviewers shared this view, as did an impressive portion of the reading public. (The books sold well, sometimes exceptionally well.) Sanguine administrators even envisioned a permanent FWP that operated like the census, drawing on government resources to churn out a stream of useful and illuminating publications, year after year. This was not to be, of course. But even though the FWP was terminated—assailed by its critics, mortally wounded by Congress, and then dissolved into the war effort—the American Guides remained. Before and after Kazin, sympathetic reviewers suggested that the books would become ubiquitous, with a few volumes—if not the entire set—resting on the bookshelves of every American home. Soldiers would carry them overseas; students would pack them for college. Sets would be passed down from one generation to the next, bequeathed as family Bibles and copies of *The Pilgrim's Progress* had been in an older era. The guides—symbols and repositories of a distinct, vital Americanness—would occupy a place in the national cultural landscape that was both visible and honored, henceforth and forevermore, amen.

But things did not work out that way—not precisely. As the guides began falling out of print, they retained their fans through the postwar years. Authors—including John Steinbeck, William Least Heat-Moon, and even Thomas Pynchon—admitted their debts to the guides; scholars of the thirties certainly did not forget them. New editions were issued from time to time and some even remain in print. Many of them, scanned and digitized, now reside on the internet. But mostly, the American Guides sank into that twilight realm where cultural artifacts are neither dead nor truly living, where they lie inert between the present and the past, assigned a new value, transformed to fit a different purpose.

They became collector's items.

One of their collectors was a man named Frederick Board. In July 1942, Frederick walked into the John G. Kidd and Son bookstore in Cincinnati and picked up a copy of *Kentucky: A Guide to the Bluegrass State*. He was a twenty-five-year-old from New Jersey with a war deferment and disposable income. He found himself in Cincinnati on business. Perhaps he was planning a trip to Kentucky, or he knew that his company would send him there next. He bought the book for three dollars.

Frederick worked in sales and traveled often. When he landed in a new city, instead of camping out in a bar like many of his cohorts—he wasn't much of a drinker—he dug around in bookstores. It was only a matter of time before he noticed other state guides created by the nearly defunct Federal Writers' Project. By the end of 1942 he owned the guides to California, Colorado, New Mexico, Utah, and Pennsylvania. By the close of the decade he had acquired thirty-nine more. By 1955 the set was complete, aside from *Georgia: A Guide to Its Towns and Countryside.* That was also the year Frederick and his wife, Jane, moved into a rambling old house in Stamford, Connecticut. He filled the house with other, rarer FWP publications, hundreds of which existed in addition to the state guides. By then he was a full-blown book collector with expanding interests. He tracked down first editions of nineteenth-century writers and bought up biblio-curiosities: books of unusual construction and materials. He became smitten with miniature books and amassed a vast collection of those as well.

In 1964, he finally got ahold of the Georgia guide from a bookstore in Los Angeles, completing his set of American Guides.

Frederick rose through the ranks of business and eventually became a senior VP at Borden, Inc. He acquired fifty-odd brands for the company, including Wise potato chips and Cracker Jack. He continued to acquire books, too, but in an oddly secretive way. He invented a fake bookstore, the Book Board, and registered a PO box across the state line in New York. (That way, he could buy at the bookseller's discount—which he did.) He bought books under the name of his secretary. He bought duplicates—ten, twenty copies at once—and stuffed the boxes into drawers and closets. He kept track of his collection with index cards, reams of them, one for each book he acquired, all meticulously housed in metal filing drawers. Whenever he bought a new book, he took out a fresh index card and inscribed it with the essentials: author, title, edition, publisher, where he purchased it, when he purchased it, how many copies he purchased, and how much he paid. Like many collectors, he used a unique, ten-letter alphanumeric cipher to record the price. His code was FLEISCHMAN. The letters "INN" scrawled inside a book meant that it cost $4.00, which is what he paid for *A South Dakota Guide* in 1944, at a bookstore in Portland, Maine. Once the card was complete, he put it in a filing drawer. It didn't much matter where in his house the book ended up. Acquisition was the means and the end. The book existed on an index card and the index card was everything.

Frederick kept other sets of index cards, too. Some were in his study, hidden under the blotter on his desk. These cards began in 1955, the year he and Jane moved into the house in Stamford. One set recorded the dates of the year's first frost. Another recorded Frederick's height and weight on his birthday. Another recorded the general disposition of his financial assets, and another, his top one hundred books by value. He updated the cards annually until he died.

I knew Frederick Board by a different name: Old Uncle Fred. He was my great-uncle, my dad's mother's brother. After he died, his set of American Guides ended up with me. My dad had discovered them in an antique barrister bookcase in Old Uncle Fred's attic, pushed up against the chimney, cleaved off from the rest of Fred's massive book collection and stashed away, oddly. He and my mom decided that the guides—outdated enough to be useless and vaguely socialistic in origin—were just my style, and that I would make better use of them than the book dealers who were carving up Fred's collection into auction lots. So they dragged the American Guides out of the attic and brought them home. The books carried the smell of that attic when I opened them up and flipped the pages. They were intriguing, but I didn't know what to make of them and I likewise pushed them to the back of my mind. I was about to begin my second year in college; George W. Bush was entering his second term in office. Several years passed. Then, financial institutions began to implode and the economy sank into a recession. A Great Recession. The 1930s were on everyone's lips. We wondered if the new, charismatic Democrat in the White House would launch a New New Deal. The American Guides in their antique bookcase felt freshly relevant.

I cracked a few open once again. Musty relics, maybe, but they were crowded with beguiling wonders. They were overstuffed and ramshackle, as I remembered Old Uncle Fred's house to be, and they appeared to share his accumulative impulse. Where had these books come from? Who created them? I needed to find out.

As I delved into the story of the Federal Writers' Project, I found a bibliography that had belonged to Old Uncle Fred. Next to many of the entries was a small penciled X. Fred, in his neat hand, even added some entries of his own: *Hoosier Tall Tales*, *The Builders of Timberline Lodge*, *Gazetteer of Utah Localities and Altitudes*. This was Fred's guide to the American Guides and all the rest of the FWP's published work.

I tallied up the Xs. Fred's collection had consisted of 376 FWP publications—local and regional guides, pamphlets, books about specific rivers and mountains and ethnic groups—which meant that the American Guides in my possession represented about one seventh of the whole. The overwhelming majority of the collection had been packed up and auctioned off, returned to the world of the collectors, over a decade earlier. The American Guides were left with me.

I puzzled things over. Should it be my task to reassemble the rest of Old Uncle Fred's collection? Not that I had the money. But wasn't there something gratifying in the notion of chasing down the same books and circling the Xs on Fred's bibliography when I had recaptured one? Wouldn't I get closer to the story of the FWP, so rich and fascinating, by acquiring its books—and acquiring, and acquiring—even if it took years?

This seemed exactly wrong. The FWP wasn't created for the benefit of future book collectors. Embarking on a hunt for rare and expensive editions seemed like an easy way to lose sight of the project's true meaning. And yet I was drawn to these books and the story of how they came to be—how it was that the federal government ended up in the publishing business, with such a peculiar list of titles to show for it. That is what I found most striking about the American Guides. As a historical undertaking and a collective editorial project—created under conditions of enormous strain, at a scale never attempted, by workers grappling with the stresses of poverty and, often, their own inexperience—the American Guides were a triumph. But the books themselves are not triumphalist. They carry a whiff of New Deal optimism, sure, but for the most part they resist those signature American habits of boosterism and aggressive national mythologizing.

Another contemporary reviewer of the guides understood this well. In

1939, as the FWP's enemies in Congress and the press were sharpening their knives, the young novelist Robert Cantwell made his own assessment in *The New Republic*:

> It is doubtful if there has ever been assembled anywhere such a portrait, so laboriously and carefully documented, of such a fanciful, impulsive, childlike, absent-minded, capricious and ingenious people, or of a land in which so many prominent citizens built big houses (usually called somebody's folly) that promptly fell into ruins when the owner backed inventions that didn't work.

For Cantwell, the FWP's America was a country of secret rooms and of boundaries decided by the flip of a coin, a place built up by "builders of spite fences, spite churches, spite towns" and populated by harebrained inventors and the losers of duels. "It is a grand, melancholy, formless, democratic anthology of frustration and idiosyncrasy," he wrote, "a majestic roll call of national failure, a terrible and yet engaging corrective to the success stories that dominate our literature."

Cantwell was right. For books that are ostensibly travel guides, the FWP publications have a habit of wandering off—steering, more often than not, down forgotten back roads and toward the dead ends of American history. But that was the point. The guides do form "a majestic roll call of national failure," as Cantwell put it, and also more than that. They are melancholic at times, but they are exuberant, suggestive, slapdash, overdetailed, and over-confident, too. The spirit of the guides, in other words, is multitudinous and democratic—they have a fundamentally public orientation to match the public enterprise that created them. They don't offer one way of looking at a state but several. They contain many voices but, as books for travelers, they convey essentially a single invitation to explore, to roam, to inquire.

So, in that spirit, I launched an inquiry.

The Federal Writers' Project was a sprawling and heavily peopled thing. Every account of the project includes an obligatory mention of its well-known alumni. Some are among the boldest of the boldface names in the history of twentieth-century American literature. Some enjoyed a certain level of notoriety at the time, or maybe after the war, while others never quite escaped the pages of little magazines and obscure manifestos. These writers, whatever their relative renown, labored alongside thousands of others whose contributions are difficult to trace but who made up the vast majority of FWP workers, the ones who showed up to offices or issued field reports from everywhere in the country.

They experienced life on the project in different, and often totally opposing, ways. They loved the work; they felt like hacks. They saw the FWP as launching their careers; they saw it as a sad and bitter end. Black federal writers were grossly underrepresented, and yet a remarkable group of them coalesced around the FWP and its innovative studies of African American life. American Indians, also underrepresented as workers, appear in every guide, but are too often relegated to the past, bundled up with sections on archaeology, less present in essays on history or the contemporary scene. The guides themselves, meant to convey an argument about inclusion and pluralism, were sometimes undermined by their own creators—and the compromises involved in their creation.

By plucking its workers from all corners of the land, the FWP inevitably became a showcase for their ideas, aspirations, preoccupations, and prejudices. All the tensions of American society in the thirties were stuffed into the project's offices, into the words of its correspondence and memos, and between the lines of its books and pamphlets. It was a roiling and seething experiment, and even its participants could not agree on what it all meant. Was the FWP a noble vehicle for progressive patriotism, a fount of radical propaganda, or a bureaucratic instrument for managing social strife and whitewashing history? Was it all of these? The question of purpose, too, was fiercely debated. Was the FWP meant to be the "unfailing patron," as one official put it, of novelists and poets working individually at their own creations, an act of noblesse oblige from the country squire in the White House? Or was it meant to mobilize "brain workers" in the same way that the WPA did "muscle workers" (as radicals of the day put it), by treating writers as laborers whose job it was to construct texts, just as millions of other WPA laborers built roads and sewers? Critics inside and outside the government found both of these visions objectionable, even when they agreed with the FWP's pluralistic and expansive vision of America—and especially, emphatically, when they did not.

The story of the FWP—its unlikely birth, tumultuous life, and ignoble death—is the story of people who found themselves reckoning with these questions at a moment when all the old answers seemed to be dissolving. It involved many thousands of people from many backgrounds, living and working in every state of the Union. In telling this story, I've taken a cue from the American Guides, which, as biographies of the states, tend toward the longer view. (The geologic view, even.) I believe this is helpful: to understand the FWP and where it came from, you need to understand the federal writers and where *they* came from. Their journeys to the FWP can be as illuminating as the work they did once they got there. Of course, just as you might take many routes across a state, choosing where to stop and what to pass by, trading detours and dead ends, so there are many possible ways to tell this story.

Here is one of them.

———◆———

HENRY ALSBERG, WASHINGTON, DC

"A COMPLETELY DEBACLED INTELLECTUAL LIBERAL"

On December 26, 1933, Henry Alsberg sat at his typewriter and banged out a letter. He was fifty-two years old—four months older than President Franklin Roosevelt—and living in his mother's apartment on the Upper West Side of Manhattan. (Roosevelt was rounding out his first year in the White House.) For years, Alsberg had been bouncing between Europe and West Ninety-fifth Street and a small cottage in the Hudson Valley. Overseas, he'd been a roving correspondent, a diplomatic aid, and a relief worker. In Manhattan, he wrote feature articles and book reviews and kept up a parallel, albeit dwindling, career in the downtown theater scene. In his Hudson Valley shack, as he called it, he lived between relaxation and procrastination: writing letters, stabbing at an autobiographical novel, staring into the low, forested hills. He was a bearish man with dark eyes and a small mustache, affable and irascible, prone to melancholy and to fits of whimsy. On that late December day in New York, he sat and typed, already feeling the weight of another uncertain year bearing down on him. He'd written to this particular correspondent many times in the past decade, and once more, he unburdened himself.

Dear E.G.: I was sure you didn't want me to know about your coming, because you didn't breathe me a word about it in any letter. Of course I heard about it, and am waiting with "spannung" [great eagerness] to greet you . . . Do come along soon. I will not consider any other possibility. During the last year since I saw you I have fallen into complete moral and mental desuetude. Nobody loves me any more, except perhaps you, my dear E.G. I need some moral and mental support. So when you come, I shall immediately begin to lean on you.

His "dear E.G." was the world's best-known anarchist, Emma Goldman. They'd met in 1920, inside the Soviet Union—Alsberg as a reporter with Bolshevik sympathies, Goldman as an exile struggling to find a place in the new Russia, which she increasingly distrusted. Alsberg was tagging along with Bertrand Russell, who was part of a delegation from the UK, when they ran into Goldman. "He brought with him a whiff of the best that was in America—sincerity and easy joviality, directness and *camaraderie*," as she put it in her memoir, which, later, Alsberg would help her edit. He befriended Goldman and her companion, Alexander Berkman, whom everyone called Sasha.

During the twenties Alsberg grew close with the pair, visiting them in Europe when he could, writing when he couldn't. He noticed their ideas shaping his inchoate radicalism, seeping into his sensibility. "I am passionately interested in freedom as an abstract proposition," he wrote to Goldman in 1925, "and I am devoting my life to helping the acquirement of it along wherever I can"—but he was also "hopelessly christian in sentiment, although hopelessly sceptical" and "indolent in a sort of Buddhistic manner." Alsberg could admire Goldberg and Berkman for their certainty and militancy, for the clarity of their thinking, but he could never match them—so he believed, anyway.

Goldman was only twelve years older than Alsberg, but the emotional currents of their correspondence nudged her into a maternal role. To Goldman, Alsberg was "old grouch," "old lobster," "dear old Henry," sometimes "Hank"—even "old Hanky boy." Her fondness for him was inflected with amusement and a small bit of irritation. They discussed friends and comrades and adversaries. They conferred over apartments and compared their unsettled living situations. Both of them could be touchy and aggrieved—Goldman forthright as a soapbox speech, Alsberg self-pitying and sarcastic—but tension between them always dissipated. They seemed never to discuss the intensely private matter of Alsberg's sexuality, a fact held close for his entire, solitary life. Perhaps he felt they didn't need to. They talked about Gandhi and the Russian Revolution and *The Nation* ("as smug and comfortable as any oily middle class sheet," according to Goldman). For years they shared a running joke about gefilte fish.

As he composed his letter, Alsberg was excited by the thought of meeting his friend on Manhattan soil. Goldman hadn't set foot in New York since 1919, when she, Berkman, and 247 other alien radicals were loaded onto a ship and booted out of the country. (That happened in another December, at dawn, Goldman peering bitterly through a porthole at the Statue of Liberty as the buildings receded and the bay opened into the gray Atlantic.) Alsberg was a stranger to her then. Now he was a friend, but he'd only sat beside her in foreign places, usually briefly, and he was eager to welcome her to town.

That night, the Depression was also on Alsberg's mind. Their correspondence since 1929 hadn't much brought up the economic crisis. They usually discussed Goldman's manuscript—a commercial flop for Knopf when it finally appeared in 1931, another casualty of the 50 percent drop in sales that rocked the publishing industry in the years following the crash. In December 1933, as Alsberg wrote, the country was six months past the flurry of legislation known as the One Hundred Days, when the Roosevelt administration fed a compliant Congress a series of bills that sought to alleviate the Depression. In the short term, their efforts stopped the banking panic and boosted federal spending on unemployment relief. But the One Hundred Days also restructured the economy—agriculture, industry, labor, and banking—in ways that, six months later, were only beginning to be understood. Two new institutions, the Tennessee Valley Authority and the Public Works Administration, inaugurated planned regional development and public works construction on an unprecedented scale—and signaled policies to come.

And yet 1933 was still a dismal year, likely the worst of the entire Depression. Gone since 1929: three quarters of the value of all financial assets, $7 billion in bank deposits, half of the gross national product. Hundreds of thousands of homes were lost to foreclosure. A quarter of the total workforce was unemployed. Marriage, divorce, and childbirth rates all plummeted—consequences of the Depression's paralyzing effect on daily life. And even though Alsberg had been an intellectual adrift for years before the economic crisis—shuttling between continents, owning no real property, providing for no dependents, enjoying no steady employment—he felt the deepening misfortune around him acutely.

> This country is in a fearful mess, of course. Nobody knows which way he is going or coming. But we are all hoping that a mysterious providence which takes care of drunken sailors and Americans will do something about something. Otherwise these happy states will become a vast poorhouse in which we shall all try to live by taking in each others' washing—until there is no wash left, and then we shall simply run around in a state of nature.

He added, "With this result in view I have been trying to diet and conserve my beautiful figure." The remark was typical of the dark humor Alsberg brought to occasions of stress. And lately, his life had felt like one prolonged stressful occasion. He was deep into middle age with no fixed address, no consistent career path, no great literary achievement to his name. And, despite his friends and many acquaintances, he was painfully lonely. He was, to himself, a wretched figure.

> I don't see why you bother with me at all. I have been most neglectful and am certainly, in a practical way, no use to anyone any more, least of all to myself. I have fallen from even the modest imminences I may once have occupied. I am less than nothing, less than the ground you shall tread upon your triumphant return. Nobody pays any attention to me any more, and I don't pay attention to anybody. I am in complete retirement, mentally, physically (not altogether, however), and morally. A completely debacled intellectual liberal. Expect to find me in my intellectual rags and tatters, barefooted, brazen and unashamed. I am, as it were, a beachcomber, on this garbage-strewn strand that calls itself a metropolis.

He sent the letter and that grim year of 1933 came to a close. But soon Alsberg would face another disappointment. Emma Goldman did not arrive in New York as expected. (Her trip was delayed by visa issues.) After the New Year, he wrote to her again, soliciting advice. Should he give it all up and move to a friend's cooperative farm in Michigan? He could attend to his writing and do cultural work among the farmers—perhaps teaching classes—and handle some of the physical labor. "I am not such a terrible carpenter myself," he wrote, "and, as to farming, I can tell a cucumber from a strawberry, and lettuce from cabbage." He was willing, it seemed, to entertain any path that would give him purpose—"something productive and real and profitless."

He signed off, "Take care of your health, and don't forget your quite useless correspondent."

He had no inkling that, while he stewed in feelings of uselessness, the New Dealers transforming the country would soon find a use for him. Within months, he'd be in Washington, working alongside them, helping to address the "fearful mess" that had befallen the nation. And in a year and a half, he would be swept into the directorship of the most ambitious national literary project ever attempted anywhere.

"HAS THE BRAINS TRUST SWALLOWED YOU UP?"

Harry Hopkins made no secret of his love for horse racing. A top US diplomat once said he was a man possessed of "the purity of St. Francis of Assisi combined with the sharp shrewdness of a race track tout." It was barely a metaphor—Hopkins spent a lot of time at the track. He inherited the taste from his father, a small-time gambler with a fondness for bowling. (The St. Francis connection was more of a stretch, although his pious mother did instill in him a sense of Christian charity.) As Roosevelt's relief czar, charged with overseeing federal support for the swelling ranks of the poor, Hopkins occasionally gathered his aides in the racetrack stands—shouting over loudspeakers and the beating of hooves as they puzzled out the problems faced by the young administration.

Hopkins was a divisive figure: a hero of the New Deal or its most sinister plotter, depending on the beholder. He was unpretentious and forthright, irreverent in style but serious, even zealous, about his work. He liked playing devil's advocate to test the convictions of those around him. He was a lanky man with a high, wide forehead and an expressive face and a rapid way of speaking. He cursed. He felt an intense affiliation with the poor. He often said he was the son of a harness maker, which was not exactly true. (His father, after cycling through jobs around the Midwest, which may have included harness making, did eventually own a harness and sundries shop in Grinnell, Iowa.) His mother was a fervent supporter of the Methodist Missionary Society. When Hopkins left the Midwest after an unremarkable stint at Grinnell College, he threw himself into the world of East Coast social reformers and began rising through the ranks of private charities in New York.

He was ambitious and a little relentless. It was as though his concern for the poor was fused with a hard-nosed fixation on problem solving—and a sense of irritation when the solving didn't come easily. Poverty, for Hopkins, was a moral challenge but also a practical one, an obstacle that could be overcome by effort and reason and, crucially, by spending cash. He was a professional in a field that was newly professionalized—its traditional charities replaced by staff agencies, its assumptions reset on a sociological basis, its amateur enthusiasts pushed aside by trained caseworkers and experts. Hopkins was formed in that shift, even if he never achieved a polished, professional deportment. One colleague described him as "an ulcerous type" who would wear the same shirt days in a row and was often caught shaving in the office. He had a nervous demeanor fueled by black coffee and cigarettes. Every weekday, he'd descend on Manhattan from the suburbs to the north, where he lived with his wife and children, commuting by train into the city, reading Keats and Shelley and Amy Lowell amid the rustling newspapers of his fellow passengers, his thoughts slipping past the gray concerns of organizational administration. He was another rumpled commuter, perhaps more rumpled than most, soon to preside over a historic overhaul of the nation's paltry, antiquated relief system—as architect and overseer of its transformation.

"Relief," for most of the country's history, was a multisided thing. It could be a cash payment, a basket of food or a parcel of clothing or a bucket of coal, a voucher with a local merchant, a place in a poorhouse or in a veterans' home. Sometimes it was a job: "work relief." Politicians, social reformers, and many citizens preferred it when relief was distributed by private charities, secular or religious. But the alternative, public relief, was as old as the Republic, and older, administered by a patchwork of organizations at the state and local levels, typically at the smallest possible unit: the town or parish and, later, the county. Much of this relief was directed toward mothers with dependent children, the blind and others who could not care for themselves, and war veterans. Remarkably, aside from military pensions and bonuses, the federal government—from the ratification of the Constitution to the eve of the Depression—played almost no role in relief efforts. In 1854, Franklin Pierce vetoed a bill championed by the reformer Dorothea Dix that would have distributed land for the benefit of the indigent mentally ill. Pierce argued that the federal government had no duty to provide for the poor—a precedent that remained mostly intact until it was shattered by the Depression. It was true that for a time, the increasingly generous system of federal benefits for Civil War veterans and their dependents began to resemble a proto–welfare state—for those who wore the blue, anyway. But this system wasn't designed to deliver relief per se, and it waned as the old soldiers died off. (Many reformers also saw it as a Republican Party patronage apparatus, intended to siphon off the budget surpluses yielded by high tariffs.) Machinery for assisting the poor and unemployed, in a truly comprehensive and effective way, seemed unlikely ever to be assembled at the national level. By one account, between 1803 and 1931, the federal government spent only a little over $11 million on direct relief in the form of congressional appropriations, mostly for victims of disasters—floods, overwhelmingly, but also "grasshopper ravages" in 1875 and the San Francisco earthquake of 1906.

Then came the Depression. The localized and uneven relief system was quickly overwhelmed. Herbert Hoover confronted the crisis with monetary tinkering, protectionism, limited public works, bank bailouts, and heaps of optimistic exhortation. But when it came to direct relief for the jobless, he upheld the federal government's tradition of neglect. Private charities were exhausted. Public funds soon covered an unprecedented 90 percent of the relief being distributed. Around three quarters of the unemployed received no relief at all. Finally, in July 1932, during the last desperate months of his administration, Hoover signed the Emergency Relief and Construction Act, which offered states a meager $300 million in funds, hardly enough to meet the severity of the moment. In some counties, 80 or 90 percent of people were on relief. The effort failed, and Franklin Roosevelt was swept into office.

The new president brought Harry Hopkins with him. As governor of New York, Roosevelt had launched the Temporary Emergency Relief Administration, the first state agency to bolster and organize relief in the face of the Depression. Hopkins ran it. After Roosevelt's inauguration, Hopkins and another social worker pitched their plan for a massive federal relief program—New York state's TERA on a national scale. They tracked down Frances Perkins, the new labor secretary, at the Women's University Club in Washington, found a place to speak underneath a staircase, and hurriedly outlined a federal relief bill. She brought it to Roosevelt, he embraced it, Congress acted, and so appeared the Federal Emergency Relief Administration (FERA). Roosevelt put Hopkins in charge, with a $500 million appropriation to disburse to the states—half outright and half in matching funds.

On his second day in Washington, Hopkins met Roosevelt at the White House. The president promised his support and insisted that relief must be distributed fairly, without regard to political affiliation, a policy that was strictly adopted under all subsequent relief programs. From there, Hopkins arrived at FERA headquarters in the Walker-Johnson building on New York Avenue; finding that his office furniture hadn't yet been moved into his office, he sat down in the hallway and began to work. By the end of the day he'd funneled more than $5 million to eight states. When a jittery *Washington Post* article suggested that Hopkins was burning recklessly through his funds, he announced, "I'm not going to last six months here, so I'll do as I please."

The FERA didn't much change the existing relief structure—it just flooded the states with cash. Hopkins preferred a decentralized operation and he mostly left local administrators alone, although he did push for them to provide direct payments without stipulations, instead of relief "in kind," as much as possible. It was cleaner that way, and it helped preserve the dignity of people in need.

During this early phase of the FERA, there was little in the way of work relief—handing out jobs instead of checks or cash. But Hopkins believed that jobs were better than the dole. He'd watched during the spring of 1933 as the Civilian Conservation Corps plucked young men from cities, small towns, and farms and put them to work on federal lands: cutting trails and building shelters, planting trees and stocking fish, staving off floods and combating soil erosion. And yet the CCC, however popular, was limited. It was open only to men between eighteen and twenty-five who were unmarried and came from families on relief, and its crews performed only manual labor in designated areas. (It was limited in another sense: Black CCC workers were underrepresented and CCC camps, though initially integrated outside the South, were segregated in 1935.) The other major federal driver of employment, the Public Works Administration—headed by Interior Secretary Harold Ickes, a prickly but principled Republican—was slow to initiate its larger, capital-intensive projects. They would need to invent an entirely new agency, Hopkins realized, in order to establish work relief on a wide scale.

Roosevelt approved Hopkins's next plan. They created the Civil Works Administration, a temporary agency that hired the jobless directly and put them to work during the winter of 1933–34. The CWA triggered a frenzy of activity. Around a million workers signed up after two weeks. The Bureau of Printing and Engraving had to run three shifts just to print all the paychecks. By January 1934, the CWA employed more than 4 million workers—nearly as many as were mobilized during the First World War—and at its peak ran about 400,000 projects. CWA workers built or improved a half million miles of roads, forty thousand schools, and a thousand airports, along with parks, pools, sewers, and other public infrastructure.

The FERA and the CWA produced something else, too: a newfound appreciation for robust federal activity. Hopkins knew this thanks to the sixteen field investigators he'd sent into the country beginning in the summer of 1933. One of them was Martha Gellhorn, then a young reporter; another was Lorena Hickok, a more seasoned journalist for the Associated Press (and an increasingly close companion of Eleanor Roosevelt). Hickok's letters to Hopkins described grasshoppers chewing crops down to the ground and eating clothes off the line. Unemployed coal miners were too starved and exhausted to riot. Whole families were sharing single beds to keep warm. A local work relief project in West Virginia, where rates of illness had spiked among the poor, was paying the unemployed to build coffins. But as she witnessed one grim scene after another, Hickok also noticed a distinct upsurge in support for Roosevelt, thanks to these relief efforts. Some people posted his photograph in their homes like an icon; others spoke casually and intimately of him, as if they knew him personally. From Fergus Falls, Minnesota, she wrote to Hopkins about the general feeling in the upper Midwest: "I have witnessed close up—so close up, in fact, that I was hardly conscious of it at first—one of the swiftest and most complete changes in the public opinion that this part of the country has ever seen."

The CWA folded up at the end of March, leaving behind an array of improvements and infrastructure built from scratch. Hopkins refocused his efforts on the FERA and continued some work relief projects there. But the experience proved that the nation required a sustained, perhaps permanent, work relief program, and he and his aides began plotting.

In the wake of the CWA, Henry Alsberg arrived in Washington. He never did join that cooperative farm in Michigan, the one he described to Emma Goldman. He'd certainly been feeling desperate enough. But then—thanks, perhaps, to the "mysterious providence which takes care of drunken sailors and Americans" (as he put it in his letter to Goldman)—something unexpected happened. A government job fell into his lap. Jacob Baker, an old acquaintance, had become one of Harry Hopkins's closest aides. Baker knew Alsberg from the left edge of the Greenwich Village literary scene, and he offered Alsberg a place on the FERA staff. Alsberg's meandering career took yet another turn: he became a federal bureaucrat.

During the previous year Washington had been transformed by an influx of newcomers like Harry Hopkins and Jacob Baker—the New Dealers. These were men and women (although mostly men), economists and social workers and lawyers (mostly lawyers) who'd been stirred to action by Roosevelt and were taking up positions in his administration, or else angling for one. Ideologically, they represented all strains of early twentieth-century reformist attitudes: trustbusters and Bryanite agrarians and classical laissez-faire Democrats and progressive Republicans and assorted socialists, mingling with the usual careerists and patronage seekers. Their habits and manners— intellectual and informal, committed to hard work but comfortable with abstract ideas—made the southern city into the cosmopolitan center it had never been.

Such it was in the spring of 1934, when Alsberg arrived in DC and joined the Roosevelt administration. Edmund Wilson came to town at the same time and found it newly animated, as if it had shaken off the last administration "like a darkness, like an oppressive bad dream, in which one could neither speak nor act." Washington had awoken in a mood for action, its new energy personified by sharp young people graduated from eastern universities and familiar faces from intellectual circles in New York. "Everywhere in the streets and offices you run into old acquaintances," Wilson wrote, "the editors and writers of the liberal press, the 'progressive' young instructors from the colleges, the intelligent foundation workers, the practical idealists of settlement houses, the radicals who are not too radical not to conceive that there may be just a chance of turning the old order inside out and the Marxists who enjoy looking on and seeing how the half-baked liberals are falling victims to their inherent bourgeois contradictions." Alsberg—veteran of the liberal press, former foundation worker, not-too-radical radical—fit the profile. As he settled into his new environment, he did not find his milieu merely reflected in Washington, but effectively packed up, transported, and reconstituted on the banks of the Potomac.

Jacob Baker was one of the familiar figures Alsberg found there. In many ways, the two of them were quite different. Baker was bald and stout, a former agricultural and industrial engineer from Colorado who'd taught in college classrooms and rural high schools (despite never graduating from college himself), overseen miners and ranchers, sweated as a day laborer, and been a partner in a Chicago engineering firm. But, like Alsberg, he was a radical of sorts—although a registered Republican—with literary interests. During the twenties, Baker operated the left-leaning Garland Fund in New York and, on behalf of its board members, helped set up and manage the Vanguard Press. He was an admirer of the anarchist Peter Kropotkin and belonged to a group that promoted mutual aid societies among the poor and unemployed. (While reporting from Russia, Alsberg had actually visited the elderly Kropotkin at his home and smuggled documents out of the country for him; the next year, after Kropotkin died, Alsberg returned to march in the funeral procession with his new friends Emma Goldman and Sasha Berkman.) Baker the federal official was still keen on the cooperative movement and believed that society ought to be transformed along cooperative lines. Even if the New Deal was a step in the right direction, it wasn't nearly enough. Once he wore a black shirt to an event at the White House to signal this dissatisfaction (which may have contributed to his strained relationship with Eleanor Roosevelt). So when Baker described Alsberg as "an anarchistic sort of a fellow incapable of administration but one with a great deal of creative talent," it wasn't a total putdown. He and Alsberg were on the same anarchistic wavelength.

Alsberg took a desk in a FERA back office and threw himself into the job, so much so that Emma Goldman complained about his silence when she wrote for inside info about the New Deal. "Has the brains trust swallowed you up to the extent that you haven't time to sit ye down and answer my letter?" she asked. "Or have you grown lazzyer than you had always been?" His first assignment was to compile and edit *America Fights the Depression*, a kind of coffee-table book designed to promote the CWA's multitudinous efforts over the winter. It showed CWA workers laying brick sidewalks and cobblestones, draining mosquito swamps, surveying highways by plane and dogsled and motorcycle, hauling gravel, planting trees, blowing glass for sodium lights, chopping wood, repairing shoes and tools, sowing oyster seeds, making malaria kits, tearing up old trolley tracks, conducting aeronautical research—and building or refurbishing bridges, dams, schools, pools, incinerators, stadiums, aqueducts, zoos, levees, and airports. The point was not only to capture the CWA's activity but to emphasize the sheer variety of projects, all of them responsive to local needs, called into being at the grassroots level but executed by the federal government. Baker was extremely pleased with the result. (So was a reviewer for *The New York Times*, struck by the book's handsome quality and convinced that the CWA was "a program wholly new in all the history of civilization.") Baker asked Alsberg to stick around as the supervisor for reports and records, which involved promoting the FERA in an editorial capacity and editing two FERA magazines.

So Alsberg spent the spring and summer. By autumn, the New Deal relief apparatus was given a tremendous boost. The Democrats swept the 1934 midterm elections, gaining seats in the House and Senate that surpassed even their most optimistic forecasts. It was the kind of electoral triumph rarely seen in American politics. The editorialist William Allen White announced of Roosevelt: "He has been all but crowned by the people." Harry Hopkins—who deserved some of the credit for that victory—celebrated, naturally, with a trip to the racetrack. By now, he was in the front rank of New Dealers, a combative, press-savvy fighter who seemed to thrive on attention from his enemies—and could often skillfully anticipate and undercut their attacks. Hopkins loaded up a car with his closest aides and, as they barreled down some Maryland highway, he exhorted them to take advantage of the moment. For months, they'd been sketching out proposals for a new, robust work relief project to replace the short-lived CWA. Now was the time to make it happen. "Boys—this is our hour," he exclaimed. "Get your minds to work on developing a complete ticket to provide security for all the folks of this country up and down and across the board."

Hopkins understood that any new program would need to include a substantial white-collar component. By the spring of 1934, when Alsberg arrived in Washington, the administration had managed to avoid a total breakdown of the economic system. But the recovery was stalling. This meant that the makeup of the relief rolls was changing. The first to go on relief, the poorest, were eventually joined by the broader working class, who over time were joined by white-collar workers who'd exhausted their savings. Hopkins described the situation in an address to the National Conference of Social Work in Detroit. "We are now dealing with people of all classes," he said. "It is no longer a matter of unemployables and chronic dependents, but of your friends and mine who are involved in this." The lesson was clear: any new work relief program would need to include not just manual laborers but white-collar workers—including, perhaps, writers.

The FERA and the CWA established some work relief projects with a cultural bent, but these were scattered and limited. They tended toward the recreational and educational: roving theater groups, community symphonies, a smattering of public art projects, lessons for adults and children. "Both the quality of the work and the kind of work carried on were, with few exceptions, of exceedingly low grade," as Alsberg would put it later. He highlighted a few in his book *America Fights the Depression*. There were orchestras and sculpture classes and research projects. There was a Grant Wood mural celebrating veterinary medicine and a CWA-painted backdrop for the snake enclosure at a zoo. A researcher in Chicago's Field Museum repaired the wrappings of a mummy from Peru. There was even a photo of a CWA worker, a woman in a wide-brimmed hat, sitting with a family on their porch in rural Georgia, conducting an interview—a precursor to the federal writers who'd do the same. (Small-scale efforts to interview formerly enslaved people and collect folklore began around this time; both would become essential to the FWP's work.) Otherwise, the new dispensation didn't offer much for writers as such, other than jobs as researchers and clerks (or editors, like Alsberg) in the expanding New Deal bureaucracy. But one project in

Connecticut did show potential: a modest undertaking, initiated under the CWA and finished with FERA funds, to research, write, and publish a guide to the state. It employed only eleven relief workers and around a thousand volunteers, and it was a thin forerunner of the FWP's American Guides. But the experience showed that such a thing could be done, and the guide sold well, earning back all its costs in two months.

The most promising development along these lines, although outside of Hopkins's portfolio, was the Public Works of Art Project, launched in 1933. The PWAP crossed an important threshold: it was the very first stand-alone federal relief program dedicated to the arts. It hired 3,749 artists to create murals, sculptures, and visual art of all kinds to embellish and beautify public buildings in every state. This wasn't technically work relief: artists competed for the jobs and were hired according to their skill, not their need. The PWAP followed the traditional public works model, in the sense that its justification and ultimate purpose was to create something (in this case, artworks), not to shift the needy from relief rolls to public employment, to give out jobs instead of doles. But the precedent was established.

Hopkins was protective of cultural workers on relief, few as they were. "Hell!" he snapped at critics. "They've got to eat just like other people!" At a press conference in early 1935, as the FERA's successor was taking shape, Hopkins lost his composure. "They are damn good projects—excellent projects. That goes for all the projects up there. You know some people make fun of people who speak a foreign language, and dumb people criticize something they do not understand, and that is what is going on up there—God damn it!" He launched into a full defense of the projects that fell outside the realms of construction and engineering: "As soon as you begin doing anything for white collar people, there is a certain group of people who begin to throw bricks. I have no apologies to make. As a matter of fact, we have not done enough." For years, Hopkins would be haunted by a misquotation of these words, which had him say: "People are too damned dumb." But he was undaunted.

Pressure came from outside the administration, too. The Newspaper Guild and the Authors Guild demanded jobs for writers, although they had in mind veteran reporters and published authors. The Unemployed Writers Association, a new group agitating from the left, sought to represent the rest, the struggling and the aspiring. It had the backing of established names such as Theodore Dreiser, Ida Tarbell, and Sherwood Anderson, and, in 1934, it morphed into the more aggressive Writers Union. That same year, a groundbreaking strike at the Macauley Company, a Manhattan book publisher, drew wide support from writers, while workers from other publishing houses joined in solidarity—a sign of the simmering discontent and growing class-consciousness spreading throughout the industry. Together and separately, organized writers were demonstrating, lobbying federal officials, and calling for work relief. In late February 1935, the Writers Union launched picket lines across New York. The *Daily Mirror* reported that, in the absence of government intervention, the only work available was writing more protest signs.

This outside pressure likely ratified what was in the works already. Even before the midterm sweep, Roosevelt wanted to pivot from direct relief to a CWA-style work program. But the question remained: Who would run it? Roosevelt was acutely aware of the rivalry between Hopkins and Interior Secretary Harold Ickes and understood that, despite their overlapping responsibilities, they occupied very different places in the administration's volatile mix of personalities. Ickes was a progressive Republican, an old Bull Mooser—pugnacious and deeply sensitive, a political brawler who nursed private grievances and often threatened to resign. Roosevelt sometimes called him "Donald Duck" and lumped him among the administration "prima donnas." Ickes wasn't as even-keeled as the brain truster Rex Tugwell—or the ever-reliable Harry Hopkins.

But personalities alone weren't the issue. Ickes's Public Works Administration was cumbersome by nature. It initiated capital-intensive public works projects, such as dams and bridges and airports, and it typically didn't draw workers from the relief rolls but rather awarded contracts to existing firms. Ickes himself tended to slow the process down as he reviewed those contracts and blueprints as well, wallowing in the fine print, meticulously honoring his stewardship of billions of tax dollars. His cautious approach would make the PWA a resounding success: by 1939 it had helped construct 70 percent of new educational buildings; 65 percent of the courthouses and city halls and sewage plants; 35 percent of the hospitals and healthcare facilities; and 10 percent of the roads, bridges, and subways; along with naval warships and the Grand

Coulee Dam and the Triborough Bridge, and all without a hint of scandal or corruption. But it wasn't very flexible, and it didn't move as swiftly as the FERA and the CWA did under Hopkins.

Even as the new relief law began to take shape in Congress and details crept into the press, Roosevelt made no decision. Even when, on April 8, 1935, Congress passed the Emergency Relief Appropriation Act and designated $4.8 billion for work relief, Roosevelt made no decision. This was the largest single appropriation in American history—or in any nation—to date. Ickes and Hopkins were left anxiously wondering which of them would oversee it.

Finally, Roosevelt chose. "Ickes is a good administrator, but often too slow," he told a top advisor. "Harry gets things done. I am going to give this job to Harry."

After two years of argument, plotting, and experimentation, Hopkins finally had his work relief program on a grand scale: the Works Progress Administration. It arrived at a crucial moment. Widespread early support for the New Deal was beginning to falter as the Depression dragged on. Its critics grew bolder and more numerous; disaffected old-guard Democrats and conservative Republicans joined in a chorus of recrimination. The radical left was torn between cautious support for Roosevelt and outright hostility. A trio of figures—the pension-scheme promoter Francis E. Townsend, the radio priest Father Charles Coughlin, and Louisiana's governor-turned-senator Huey Long—collected masses of followers while short-circuiting conventional American politics. (Were they progressive firebrands or incipient fascists?) Meanwhile a deeper, less focused disgruntlement simmered among American workers and farmers, 20 percent of whom were still unemployed and many more of whom were being radicalized through months, and in some cases years, of deprivation.

And yet, for all the talk of boondoggling, and despite the exertions of the most hidebound Republicans, the idea of work relief had widespread support. In July 1935, as the WPA was coming into being, *Fortune* magazine conducted a survey with a simple question: "Do you believe that the government should see to it that every man who wants to work has a job?" A solid majority of upper-class respondents opposed this view. But, to the chagrin of *Fortune*'s editors, 81 percent of the lower-middle class, 89 percent of the poor, and 91 percent of African Americans agreed.

The WPA made this idea policy. And a portion of the WPA would be set aside for white-collar workers, with a slice of that earmarked for people in the arts, and a sliver of that reserved, specifically, for writers. But the question remained: Who would run it?

Henry Alsberg was wondering the same thing. By the spring of 1935, about a year after he left New York for Washington, Alsberg was growing bored with his FERA assignment. He needed the job too much to quit, but he worried that he'd be laid off, a casualty of the precarious relief structure. He wrote to Emma Goldman about his desire to return to Europe—to where, even still, his attention and affection pointed, more than to the United States.

The WPA was formally launched by executive order on May 6. A few months of bureaucratic jostling followed as the arts projects came together. Jacob Baker, who got Alsberg the FERA job, remained Harry Hopkins's assistant in the new setup and now supervised the white-collar division, including projects for visual art, theater, music, and writing—collectively named Federal Project Number One. Alsberg soon found himself in Baker's office, listening while Baker discussed Federal #1 with his own assistant, Arthur "Tex" Goldschmidt. They were talking about directors. Who could they find to direct the writers' project? Finally, Tex spoke: "Give it to Alsberg or he'll be disappointed." Baker looked at Alsberg and saw a particularly glum figure. The decision was made.

He was an unlikely choice. Outside of his FERA officemates, who in official Washington had ever heard of him? He was known to certain literary and dramatic circles in New York; middle-aged radicals may have recalled a younger, feistier Alsberg from the twenties. Worse, during his short career as a New Dealer, he'd developed a reputation as a poor administrator: he avoided making carbon copies and saved only the documents he thought were interesting—everything else went into the trash. Now Hopkins was placing him in charge of the FWP. From the WPA's roughly $5 billion appropriation, the directors of Federal #1 had slightly more than $27 million to spend on the arts projects; $6,288,000 of that was set aside for the FWP. Though a fraction of the massive WPA budget, it was still a lot of money.

Critics and supporters alike would have been forgiven for wondering, Who is Henry Alsberg?

He'd seemed destined for a life that was stable, predictable, respectable. His family were secular German Jews, highly educated professionals. (His father, a chemist, helped found the American Chemical Society; his eldest brother would become chief of the United States Bureau of Chemistry, forerunner to the Food and Drug Administration.) Henry Garfield, the youngest of four, was born in 1881, two days after his namesake, President James A. Garfield, succumbed to an assassin's wounds. He grew up on the Upper East Side as the nineteenth century waned and New York developed into a modern metropolis. He attended Columbia, nurtured literary ambitions, and graduated with the class of 1900—the "Naughty Naughtians." Next was Columbia Law School, and years of intermittent legal work while he fiddled with poems and short stories and essays and plays and was increasingly drawn to the bohemian world emerging downtown.

He was restless. He tried graduate studies at Harvard (with William James, one semester away from retirement) but returned to Manhattan a year later. He shuffled from his late twenties into his thirties, living with his mother (now on the Upper West Side, after his father's death), and finally gave up law for journalism. He got a job at the *New York Evening Post* and started writing for *The Nation*, both owned by the liberal Oswald Garrison Villard. He published in *The Masses*, the day's premier radical magazine. (His piece was a hammy satire, purported Roman newspaper clippings about Jesus of Nazareth and the hobo army he led on Jerusalem.) Alsberg was veering away from the genteel attitudes of his upbringing. He'd watched Greenwich Village become an enclave for artistic experimentation melded with all manner of radical thought. A spirit of nonconformity inspired by H. L. Mencken as much as Karl Marx animated discussions of labor strikes, free love, industrial sabotage, and birth control. Socialists squabbled with anarchists; Big Bill Haywood and Elizabeth Gurley Flynn of the militant Industrial Workers of the World hunkered down in salons alongside modernist poets. Emma Goldman was there, lecturing on anarchism and women's rights. In 1913, a year before Alsberg's *Masses* debut, this radical bohemian milieu announced itself through two highly publicized events: an epoch-making exhibition of modernist art at the Lexington Avenue Armory and a sold-out pageant at Madison

Square Garden to support the striking silk mill workers of Paterson, New Jersey. Alsberg found this world attractive, although he didn't throw himself into it with the violence and passion that others did. If a cultural scene has its major and minor figures, it also has its larger assembly of peripheral admirers and dabblers. Alsberg was one of those.

In 1916, there came another swerve, now into government service as the secretary and press attaché to the US ambassador to the Ottoman Empire, a family friend. In Constantinople and throughout the region, Alsberg made his debut as a relief worker, supervising the embassy's efforts to assist Armenians and Jews. After the United States entered the war, he was evacuated and returned to Washington, where he advised officials on the Ottoman situation. When he resumed his journalistic career, it was with an international bent. He sailed to Europe as a correspondent for *The Nation* and as a newspaper stringer, reporting from England and Ireland, then drifting gradually eastward: Paris, Prague, Budapest, Sofia, Bucharest, Odessa. The political landscape of postwar Europe was shifting daily, and Alsberg took down lucid chronicles of battling factions, parties, and nationalities. But he was disturbed by the violence remaking the continent: "I have now been three months and more in this seething caldron of hates and prejudices called Europe," he wrote from Budapest. His conscience wouldn't allow him to stay a mere observer. Unbeknownst to his readers, he began working for the Jewish Joint Distribution Committee, a relief organization he'd first encountered in Constantinople. Throughout Central and Eastern Europe he gathered information and distributed money on the JDC's behalf. He visited war refugees and children orphaned by pogroms; he conferred with officials and advocated for the displaced. For months he moved among some of Europe's most wretched and hopeless people—a world away from Manhattan and the affluent German Jewish immigrant milieu of his youth, where attitudes regarding their poorer coreligionists from Eastern Europe tended toward snobbish indifference, or worse.

Alsberg's travels entered a consequential phase in May 1920, when he crossed into the Soviet Union. He was thirty-eight, a dedicated leftist who admired the workers' revolutions erupting throughout Europe (in Hungary, he met the Communist leader Béla Kun and discovered they had mutual friends in the United States). But he was basically a pacifist, repelled by violence and hating the human suffering that flowed from even righteous struggles. And yet he despised the hypocrisy of the West for its hostile treatment of the Communist governments taking power. "When the history of this period comes to be written, Lenine, I am inclined to think, will be its greatest figure, with nobody a bad second," he'd written from Hungary. Now he was in the heart of the world revolution, staying in a Moscow hotel alongside delegates to the second congress of the Comintern. He was still a foreign correspondent but he continued his JDC work as well, gathering information in villages ravished by pogroms. It was dangerous—two of his JDC colleagues had been killed by Bolshevik soldiers who thought they were Polish officers.

After he met Emma Goldman and Sasha Berkman, he joined them that summer on an expedition to collect artifacts and documents for the Museum of the Revolution in Petrograd. For six weeks they traveled south from Moscow and into the Ukraine in a specially outfitted Pullman car. Alsberg was unsettled by scenes of poverty and suffering. Goldman compared it to something out of Dante. But he also saw evidence of improvements and was especially struck by the new cultural programs being organized by the revolutionary state. "The proletariat has the orchestra stalls now," he announced in *The Nation*, and he applauded the government's efforts to include common people "in workmen's and peasants' theaters, in choruses and orchestras and brass bands, in the painting of pictures and the making of literature."

> The participants in the drama not only act but also conduct the theater and do the stage carpentering and scene-painting and shifting themselves. How many manuscripts have already been submitted from every part of Russia in the competition for the new revolutionary international song—manuscripts by quite humble individuals, peasants and shepherds and carpenters!

Alsberg wouldn't forget such glimpses of a robust, state-supported public culture. But neither could he ignore the repressive aspects of daily life in Russia, which was still locked in a brutal civil war. He soon got a taste of that repression firsthand when he was detained by the Cheka and—despite Goldman and Berkman's personal entreaty to Lenin—ordered back to Moscow. He'd tell the story of what followed for years: He and his guard embarked on

a days-long train ride. He enticed the guard to share some vodka, and eventu- ⟡
ally the guard became so drunk—and then sick with pneumonia—that, when
they arrived in Moscow, Alsberg had to carry him into the Cheka station.
"Here is the man you sent out to find me," he said. It was a sour end to his first
Soviet trip. The following year, he made a second trip, this one coinciding
with the Kronstadt Rebellion, when revolutionary sailors on a naval base outside Petrograd launched an anti-Bolshevik uprising. They were crushed by
government forces. A few months later, Alsberg, increasingly disillusioned,
wrote "Russia: Smoked-Glass vs. Rose-Tint" for *The Nation*, summing up
his Soviet experience and diagnosing two "journalistic conspiracies." The
"smoked-glass" approach "insisted on seeing everything bolshevik in a dark-
ened and distorted form" and often peddled fabrications. "It committed
suicide some time ago by over-indulgence in lies," he wrote. But "rose-tint"
accounts were guilty of the opposite fault. "There has grown up an uneasy
feeling among liberal-minded onlookers, and even among western Communists, that Russia has been swallowed a little too whole, without any mastica-
tion whatsoever." Alsberg insisted simply that journalists and commentators
do more chewing.

Back in the United States, he turned forty. For the rest of the twenties,
instead of jumping between careers, he tried balancing several at once. He
continued to lecture and write for the JDC. With Emma Goldman, Sasha
Berkman, and Roger Baldwin of the ACLU, he helped form the International Committee for Political Prisoners and edited its first publication, *Letters from Russian Prisoners*. (He and Berkman had gathered the bulk of the
contents themselves.) Meanwhile, he got involved in the downtown theater
scene, mostly as a producer or director or publicist. In all three areas, he
found success mixed with failure and missed chances. He contracted with
the JDC to write a history of the organization. His nine-month deadline
came and went, and four years later, he presented the JDC with a massive
manuscript—his greatest literary accomplishment to date. The JDC couldn't
use it. (It was revised and scaled down but never published.) His work on
behalf of political prisoners won some acclaim but just as much recrimination
from those still sympathetic to the Soviet experiment. Alsberg lost friends
and writing opportunities. The theater delivered his highest moment of glory
when the Neighborhood Playhouse produced his adaptation and translation

of a Yiddish play, *The Dybbuk* by S. Ansky. The play was a success and it bestowed on Alsberg a little fame. But even this was spoiled: George Gershwin wanted to adapt it as his first opera (beating Arthur Hammerstein to it), with Alsberg as librettist, before they realized Alsberg did not possess the musical rights to the play—only the translation rights. The project imploded and Alsberg was left behind while Gershwin moved on to his second choice: *Porgy and Bess*.

Alsberg muddled through the final years of the twenties. He helped Emma Goldman edit her memoirs and half-heartedly worked on his own projects: a book about political prisoners around the world, a new play, an autobiographical novel. Goldman by now had a keen sense of his character. "Henry dear you are not very grown up at times," she wrote to him, "though at others you are as wise as Solomon." In 1931, the year of his fiftieth birthday, he moved in many circles and fit comfortably in none of them. He wrote to Goldman that summer in a sour mood and ended by paraphrasing a line from Hart Crane's "The Bridge": "Love is a dead cigarette butt floating in a urinal." (He was close; it was a "burnt match.") Goldman dismissed the cynicism of Crane and his generational cohorts. She reminded Alsberg that he was fundamentally of a different temperament. "Don't deceive yourself, old dear," she wrote. "You are not of them. You do have depth and intensity even if you pretend to be amused by the devil don't care attitude to life on the part of the Cranes. You are a Yid my dear, you'll never free yourself from the woe of the world."

This was the Henry Alsberg who eventually stepped off a train in Washington, DC, bound for a FERA desk job—forlorn, aimless, trailing a hodgepodge of a career. But when the new Federal Writers' Project needed a director, he made a better candidate than many might have guessed. He possessed an elite education and a law degree and experience in government service. He'd been a capable relief worker under treacherous conditions in multiple nations. He knew the writers' trade as a journalist, critic, editorialist, dramatist, translator, and editor, and he knew what it meant to struggle in all these roles, and, sometimes, to fail. His politics—anarchist-ish, tempered by age and doubt—put him in general sympathy with the New Deal, and the WPA in particular, while his public criticism of the Soviet Union inoculated him against red-baiting. (Or so it seemed.)

He wasn't the most adept administrator, although his conciliatory nature surely helped. But he proved to be the FWP's crucial visionary. The FWP put a tremendous amount of literary labor power at his command—and he knew it. What if he marshaled those resources toward creating high-quality books for the American people, composed by their fellow citizens, about their fellow citizens? It would be the work of a lifetime. And it would save him from the obscurity he dreaded, the fate of living and dying as the "completely debacled intellectual liberal" he described in his letter to Emma Goldman. The FWP offered him a different path. Alsberg, in retrospect, offered the FWP a creative spark that very well saved it from producing a series of forgettable, quickly outdated discursive road maps. That they found each other was historically fortunate.

Alsberg took his place among the other newly installed directors of the WPA's Federal #1. Hallie Flanagan would run the Federal Theater Project; Holger Cahill, the art project; Nikolai Sokoloff, music. As summer 1935 drifted into autumn, they worked to get their projects off the ground. They had the entire short history of Hopkins's relief apparatus on which to build, but Federal #1 represented a cultural undertaking of unprecedented scale and scope. There were the usual bureaucratic kinks and obstacles. The directors shared a sense of being somewhat out of joint with the WPA—transplants from artistic realms who never fit snugly into the New Deal machinery. But they also shared a fierce commitment to their projects. "We worked like mad, we cursed the delays, the postponements, the involved procedure," wrote Hallie Flanagan in her memoir of the theater project. "We criticized each other, our superiors, and ourselves; we laughed at each other, ourselves, and the W.P.A.; we went through fire for each other and the W.P.A. We were a violent lot, a thorn in the body bureaucratic."

As the pieces fell together, the directors as a group wanted to meet with Harry Hopkins. He obliged and listened to their complaints. Once the meeting had gone on for a bit, he noticed that Alsberg hadn't spoken.

"What about you, Henry?" Hopkins asked. "What is your gripe?"

Alsberg smiled. "I don't have any gripe, Harry," he said. "I haven't had as much fun since I had the measles."

"ONLY GOD CAN END THE GUIDE"

The FWP's first challenge was figuring out what, exactly, it was supposed to do. The project needed a grand, overarching task that would absorb a maximum number of jobless workers from the relief rolls—one that wouldn't attract controversy or invite charges of boondoggling, one that was inarguably useful. In late June, even before Alsberg was officially appointed, an internal WPA proposal laid out a mission. Its ancillary goals were predictably bland: a government encyclopedia, WPA progress reports, to-be-determined special studies. But the FWP's key task nicely fit the introspective mood of the moment. It would create a guidebook to the United States, issued in five volumes, with a sturdy and authoritative title: "The American Guide." Who would object to such a benign and practical idea? Who wouldn't feel soothed by a unifying survey of the American scene when, half a decade deep into the Depression, the country seemed always on the verge of unraveling? How exactly to compile such a guide was left up to the director and his national staff. Nothing quite like it—a vast national self-portrait assembled by thousands of destitute citizens, under the aegis of a wholly public institution, in response to an economic and social crisis of exceptional severity—had ever been attempted. There was no course to follow other than one of pure improvisation and experimentation. Henry Alsberg, the product of a fairly improvisational life, had just the right temperament to meet the task.

He would have felt at home in the FWP's first office: an old theater. It sat a few blocks west of the White House, a boxy, concrete structure nestled among drab government buildings. Anchored to the top of the façade were enormous letters that spelled out AUDITORIUM. In the twenties, when the building was new, those letters would have been illuminated, glaring down on the crowds that funneled through the doors for operas, lectures, movies, an Easter church service hosted by Calvin Coolidge, and Franklin Roosevelt's first inaugural ball. But by 1935—with the galas displaced by boxing matches and dog shows, and the building eventually leased by the FERA for staff offices—the tiny bulbs inside the letters were dark and the concrete façade was mottled from neglect.

The theater itself was dilapidated and dreary. Its enormous pipe organ, specially commissioned when the building was constructed, loomed inside the space like the remains of some extinct beast. Six thousand organ pipes clung to the walls. The climate was stifling. (So it was, too, in the main WPA building just down the block, where workers were beginning to call their agency the "Wet Pants Administration.") The rows of seats were cleared out for partitions and desks; the opera boxes were loaded with filing cabinets. When the journalist Ernie Pyle visited and looked for his regular seat—where he'd once sat and listened to Paul Robeson sing, Clarence Darrow debate, and Amelia Earhart describe her trans-Atlantic flight—he found instead a WPA official sitting at a desk and speaking into a Dictaphone. Behind the stage, on the third floor, was a dressing room that had been converted into Alsberg's office. From here he could peer down at the jumble of desks and cabinets and wonder what he'd gotten himself into.

Peering up at him were the project's first workers, wondering what to make of their director. He was a large man with a low, resonant voice; he spoke slowly, carefully, often meanderingly. He wore the dark mustache he'd grown three and a half decades before, as an undergraduate at Columbia. Now it was mildly yellowed by nicotine. One FWP worker said Alsberg resembled "some shaggy bear dressed in rumpled clothes," another saw "a lovable St. Bernard." He seemed fit for a directorship, with his stature and his voice, even if his sensibility was more bemused and scattershot than authoritative.

Alsberg settled into the theater and began assembling his key staff. He hired a new secretary, Dora Thea Hettwer—his twelfth, amazingly, since he began working for the Roosevelt administration. Hettwer was wary of a man who'd burned through secretaries at the rate of roughly one per month. But she came to appreciate Alsberg's amiable nature, his way with words, and his knowledge of German, which she also spoke. She grew devoted to him— perhaps in part because he so clearly needed her help.

He brought Reed Harris, his assistant from the FERA. Harris was a full generation younger than Alsberg and vastly more skilled in the administrative arts. When Alsberg had arrived in Washington, Jacob Baker knew him well enough to assign him a diligent and organized helper. Reed Harris was that person. He'd attended Columbia, as Alsberg did, although he'd been expelled for printing an exposé of the dining halls in the college newspaper (protests by faculty and the ACLU got him readmitted, but then Harris quit out of principle). Like Alsberg, he moved through a number of jobs:

journalist, editor, ghostwriter, advertising production manager. In 1932, as Alsberg fretted over his stalled career, Harris published *King Football*, an attack on the seamier side of the high-stakes collegiate game. In the FERA office, Harris was first to discern the basic principles of the Henry Alsberg filing system when his boss, pressed to produce some document, shouted, "Hell, I don't keep carbons!" It was said that, as Alsberg's assistant, Harris did 90 percent of the work—while Alsberg did 90 percent of the talking.

Alsberg and Harris constituted two parts of a shaky triumvirate, with George Cronyn, the associate director, as the third. Cronyn, another old friend of Jacob Baker's, was closer in age to Alsberg and had a résumé perhaps more diverse than Alsberg's own. Cronyn was a bestselling novelist who had also edited encyclopedias and magazines and an anthology of Native American songs and chants, *The Path of the Rainbow*; before that, he'd been a cowboy, a rancher in the Southwest, a movie scenarist, an apple grower in the Northeast, a stonemason, an English professor, and a plumber. He'd seen the country and was comfortable handling a wide range of obscure information and commenting on it with authority. Like Alsberg and Harris, he'd studied at Columbia; unlike them, he also studied and taught out west, at the University of Montana. Like Harris, he possessed the methodical touch that Alsberg lacked, and he became something of a managing editor for the office. But his prickly temperament left Harris to handle many personnel issues, especially relations with the mushrooming state offices.

The FWP didn't remain in the theater for long. All of Federal #1 was soon ushered into a new space just northeast of the White House. It was another emblem of twenties opulence repurposed after the crash: the McLean mansion, a faux-Renaissance pile occupying one third of a block on I Street. It belonged to Evalyn Walsh McLean, a Washington socialite whose other possessions included the Hope diamond. (Her husband's family owned *The Washington Post*.) When times were better, she would string the diamond around the neck of a Great Dane named Mike during the lavish parties she threw for the capital's elite. But, laid low by the Depression and in debt to many party caterers, she was forced to lease the mansion to the federal government in 1935.

Soon her mansion was occupied by the workers of Federal #1. They drifted through the mammoth rooms, gazing up at the chandeliers, admiring the woodwork, wandering among the gaudy statuary. They found a case of champagne in the basement and drained it. Some used the statues as coatracks. Rumor abounded: there was a ghost in the mansion's ballroom (now taken over by the FWP), the specter of a woman who plunged off the musicians' gallery during a long-ago ball; beneath the floor was a subterranean tunnel, once traveled by War- ren Harding and his mistress, that led to the White House. As in the FWP's pre- vious home, desks were clustered out in the open and filing cabinets stuffed into any available spot—including inside the fireplace. Again, the air was stifling, full of smoke from cigarettes and cigars. The McLeans' doorman remained with the building, and he looked upon the new tenants—harried men and women used to working for a living—with dismay. (Alsberg, coincidentally, was renting a room in a house attended to by another former servant of the McLeans, who likewise reminisced about her superior ex-employers.) The very idea of lowly New Deal bureaucrats occupying the mansion and despoiling it of grandeur drove Roos- evelt's upper-class enemies into a rage. Alsberg was likely tickled by it.

As the national office filled in around Alsberg, Reed, and Cronyn, the DC staff determined how best to fill the FWP's ranks around the country. This meant confronting a question that seemed simple but wasn't, not really: Who, precisely, deserved jobs set aside for writers? Jacob Baker grappled with this question even in the FERA days, when he noticed growing num- bers of white-collar workers in surveys of the unemployed. Teachers, college professors, librarians, and ecclesiastics were losing jobs alongside novelists and journalists—could they all be grouped into a single project for writers? A more selective approach would mean judging applicants on the quality of their writing, as the PWAP did for artists. But such aesthetic vetting contra- dicted the very mission of the WPA. Its aim was to reduce the relief rolls, put cash into hands and pockets, and alleviate the suffering wrought by the Depression. Harry Hopkins had made this clear. At a staff conference in June 1935, Hopkins—conveying Roosevelt's wishes—said that the WPA's first ob- jective was to take 3.5 million people off relief and put them to work. Human beings came first; the quality of the books and plays and paintings of Federal #1 came second. "Don't ever forget that first objective," he said, "and don't let me hear any of you apologizing for it because it is nothing to be ashamed of."

So the FWP threw open its doors to all writers, broadly defined, including—as Alsberg put it—"near writers" and "occasional writers." This meant that young aspirants would be working alongside professionals laid off in mid-career and older scribes whose livelihoods had crumbled long before the Depression, as well as clerks and recent college graduates and teachers— people who'd never published a thing and never planned to. Such an approach exposed the FWP to criticism and ridicule from hostile observers who saw the arts projects as epic boondoggles, havens for loafers and hacks. But the FWP's inclusivity carried an important, if subtle, philosophical argument. Instead of thinking about writers as uniquely inspired individual artists of exceptional talent, the FWP treated writing as a craft like any other—or, better yet, as a form of labor. And, as with any form of labor, some people excelled, some didn't, and a great many simply got the job done. The FWP would serve writers all along that spectrum of ability. Just as WPA construction projects weren't reserved for the most gifted pickax swingers but for anyone who could do the work and needed a job, so the FWP wouldn't cater only to solitary geniuses. What made someone a "writer," in the FWP's view, was their ability to carry out the tasks of the writers' project—no more, no less.

This approach was underpinned by a strict hiring quota: 90 percent of FWP workers had to come from the relief rolls. The remaining 10 percent were skilled writers and editors who were not on relief but could provide the necessary technical expertise. Such an arrangement had drawbacks. Becoming certified for relief meant submitting to a "means test," an invasive interview that confirmed the applicant's destitution. It was also called "swearing the pauper's oath." Many found it humiliating, and some worried that it would hurt their chances of future employment. One federal writer who'd lost his job in publishing described the ordeal: "I finally went on relief. It's an experience I don't want anybody to go through. It comes as close to crucifixion as . . ." (He didn't finish the thought.) "You sit in an auditorium and are given a number. The interview was utterly ridiculous and mortifying. In the middle of mine, a more dramatic guy than I dived from the second floor stairway, head first, to demonstrate he was gonna get on relief even if he had to go to the hospital to do it." O. Louis Guglielmi, an artist working for the Federal Art Project, captured the feeling in his painting *Relief Blues*: a family is being interviewed by a social worker in their shabby apartment, and all of them are struggling to contain feelings of great intensity beneath their uncomfortable, and discomfiting, demeanors—a portrait not of relief but of festering anxiety and plain old sadness.

But the quota system had a purpose. It ensured that the ranks were filled by those who most desperately needed work, and, as Roosevelt and Hopkins intended, it moved people off the relief rolls. Inevitably, though, the FWP attracted some dubious applicants. In New York, a mail carrier applied because he was "a man of letters." In Chicago, an elderly Egyptian man—who claimed to be 120 years old and was apparently illiterate—did nothing but produce ornate calling cards every three months. (They kept him on staff for amusement and perhaps out of mercy.) A story circulated about an overflowing toilet in a state office and the four editors—all plumbers by trade—who sprang up to fix it. In the Washington office, Reed Harris collected more examples: One was "a very chunky little man, somehow impressing one as would a little bantam rooster," who "came in one morning in a rush and announced breathlessly that he was a 'twenty-pound poet.'" The man meant, apparently, that he had a twenty-pound suitcase full of poetry and wanted the government to publish it. Some undermined their own claims of competence, such as the "author of a lot of output" who lamented that writing "cannot be very remunerative under present circumstances because of the deluge of output pouring in on the editors in general." Others weren't bashful about their qualifications: one gave his own as "fencing, swordsmanship, weapon repair, boating, boxing, stamp collecting, and fancy diving." The project also attracted its share of alcoholics—hard-drinking reporters, soused poets, even a family friend of the Roosevelts' with a habit of disappearing on benders. When Eleanor Roosevelt asked Alsberg to find this friend a job, one without too much responsibility, Alsberg reassured her. "Mrs. Roosevelt," he said, "if we made it a rule not to hire writers given to drink, we would probably not have a Writers' Project."

Soon enough, they had a workforce: flawed, diverse, desperate, promising. And they had an assignment, too: the American Guide, although the details were still vague. The idea for a guidebook, or a series of guides, wasn't entirely new. It had been percolating in various New Deal agencies and was even suggested to the CWA by the poet Marianne Moore, who saw it as a useful endeavor for out-of-work writers. Jacob Baker and his aides had fielded similar proposals. One journalist suggested that writers create "iconographies," assemblages of original source material—combinations of images and text, such as broadsides and handbills—that would essentially be sociohistorical scrapbooks. And then there was the slim Connecticut guide, published under CWA and FERA auspices, which provided that most valuable commodity in the bureaucratic world: a precedent.

So the timing was right when a staffer in the Resettlement Administration named Katharine Kellock cornered Tex Goldschmidt, Jacob Baker's assistant, at a cocktail party. The RA was a short-lived agency headed by Rex Tugwell that relocated distressed farmers and laid-off urban workers to cooperative farming communities and planned garden suburbs. Kellock's job was to visit these communities and report back to Washington. But she had an abiding interest in the nascent FWP, and when she encountered Goldschmidt, she pressed her idea: the FWP ought to create a series of guidebooks, American Baedekers, updating the popular German brand that was the standard for travelers. (She'd been making the rounds of DC cocktail parties with this pitch, trying to find a sympathetic ear in the right agency; before that, she'd presented the idea to commercial publishers.) Kellock was a convincing evangelist. Guidebooks, she argued, would require the work of many people—and therefore absorb more from the relief rolls—while naturally gaining support from the communities they covered. And there was a demand for such books. Leisure travel, ever since the late nineteenth century, was on a decades-long upswing that the Depression couldn't reverse; so was auto tourism and the prevalence of paid vacation time for workers. Auto sales were erratic in the thirties, but fuel sales and car registration rates actually went up. The situation was analogous to what was occurring in the world of books, where library membership rates soared while book sales plummeted. People were still eager to travel and to read, but they did so within their means.

Goldschmidt was convinced and brought the idea to Jacob Baker. "Iconography is for the birds," he exclaimed. "I've got the answer." Meanwhile, Kellock discussed the idea with another FERA official, who happened to be her husband's old college pal and a fellow Naughty Naughtian: Henry Alsberg. Soon she was collaborating on a plan with two FERA staffers, which led to a formal proposal for the FWP, submitted on June 25, 1935—the one calling for a guidebook as the project's main task.

Kellock left the Resettlement Administration and transferred to the FWP, even though it meant a pay cut. She was a decade younger than Alsberg, born in Pittsburgh to a middle-class family, but they had similar résumés. While

Alsberg was reporting on postwar revolutions in Europe and working for the JDC, Kellock was on the continent, too, undertaking famine relief with the American Friends Service Committee, the Quaker organization. In New York, she worked for the Henry Street Settlement on the Lower East Side and began writing for newspapers and magazines and the *Dictionary of American Biography*. Like Alsberg, Reed, and Cronyn, she had studied at Columbia, where she was profoundly influenced by the Progressive historian Charles Beard, who'd recently taught there. She arrived at the FWP possessed of staunch Progressive attitudes: eager for reform yet optimistic about the course of American industrial civilization, preoccupied with understanding how technological and economic trends shaped social life, and sensitive to the conditions of workers who were subject to those trends. If Alsberg represented one type of New Deal sensibility—creative, loose, conversant with the arts world, tinged with political radicalism—then Kellock represented its more grounded and technocratic complement.

Kellock, in other words, was more "brain trust" than Greenwich Village. She was focused and precise, tenacious in a way that occasionally irked her male colleagues—especially once she became the project's highest-ranking woman. One of them called her a "small tornado of a woman whose voice seemed to alternate between the sounds of scolding and laughter." She was not afraid to clash with her subordinates and did not seem particularly bothered when she did. "But," that colleague went on, "she was as honest as she was zealous and her devotion to her task emanated a pervasive aura of dedication that seeped into the bones of the rest of the staff."

As Alsberg and his team sketched out a vision for the American Guide and its five regional volumes, they began to see flaws in this approach. George Cronyn argued that regional boundaries are notoriously slippery; Katharine Kellock pointed out that state guides would elicit more support from legislators, who were, after all, the patrons of the FWP. So they chose a different tack: they would produce not one big guidebook, regionally divided, but separate guides to all of the states. (Alsberg and the DC staff never quite abandoned the goal of a single, massive guide to the nation and planned to someday produce one by condensing the finished state guides.) What these new guides would look like on the page was still unclear. Their ostensible model, the American Baedeker, was published in 1893 and last revised in 1909. It was written by a Scot with

European travelers in mind: the author warned of an "absence of deference or servility" from "social inferiors" and alerted readers to the American habit of spitting on floors. It wasn't going to be a template for the FWP, and neither would the drearily functional Blue Books and Green Books. (Victor H. Green's adaptation of these generic guides, *The Negro Motorist Green Book,* which he designed to help Black travelers avoid discrimination and danger on the road, appeared slightly later.) The American Guides, in form and content, would need to update and surpass their guidebook predecessors.

Through the fall of 1935, the project shuddered to life. Alsberg issued a burst of missives to college presidents, newspaper editors, chambers of commerce, head librarians, Kiwanians, and Rotarians around the country, explaining the mission of the FWP and the nature of the guides, and urging them to cooperate with the FWP field workers who would soon be visiting cities of ten thousand or more people and fanning outward from there. The replies were favorable.

Meanwhile, the DC editors compiled the FWP's bible: "The American Guide Manual." Federal writers in every state would study it—or were supposed to, anyway—and learn about the project's structure and mission. The manual contained commandments: "No pains should be spared to make the data reliable and inclusive" and "The literary style as a whole should be a model of precise, succinct excellence" and "The semi-colon should be used cautiously." It also explained how the guidebook-making process would unfold on the ground. Armed with questionnaires on various subjects—these made up the bulk of the manual—field workers would go into their communities and gather data. Through a combination of research (in libraries and museums and newspaper morgues and family records), interviews with locals, and firsthand observation, the field workers would fill in the questionnaires and then write up "Field Continuities," that is, their notes in unabridged prose form. Then they'd condense and polish the Field Continuities and convert these to Field Editorial Copy, which would then be converted to State Editorial Copy in the local offices, and absorbed into guidebook manuscripts. Then the states would ship the manuscripts off to DC for additional editing—manuscripts that were, by now, the collective products of many hands.

When the field workers fanned out across the country—often in their own hometowns and the surrounding countryside, or their own city neighborhoods and adjacent streets—their task was to catalog the American scene in all its aspects. Everything was relevant: the manual mentioned fish hatcheries, topography, lookout towers, polo grounds, church choirs, gold rushes, band shells, aquariums, famous ballads, soil conditions, homes for the aged, slum-clearance programs, plantation manors, navy yards, epidemics, folk customs, battlefields, floods, welfare associations, raids and wars and notable authors and on and on. Mostly, the manual asked for field workers to compile descriptive lists—all the railroads in a given area, or universities, or waterfalls of special beauty. But it also provided questions. "Are there interesting animal colonies such as colonies of beavers or prairie dog cities in your district?" "Are there any unusual instruments which were invented in your district?" "What deposits are there of marble, granite, clay, potash, etc.?" "Have 'Americanization' and intermarriage obliterated racial differences or are there sharply defined racial groups?"

Their approach, a hearty embrace of the American land and all that it contained, resembled something dreamed up by Walt Whitman—if he were handed a federal bureaucracy and a hefty budget. Its multitudinous potential may have seemed overwhelming. But the basic methodology laid out in the manual was all straightforward enough.

Then came the supplements. On the heels of the manual the DC office began issuing supplementary instructions. They sent at least eighteen of them, well into the fall of 1937, after several guides had already been published. Early supplements clarified the staff hierarchy; others explained the procedures for consulting outside specialists and volunteers. One provided subject codes for field workers to affix to their notes (S-202 meant a state's "entrance into the Union," S-503 meant "Notable roadhouses, dude ranches, resorts, etc."). Exasperated state editors complained that keeping track of the supplements was a job in itself. (Imagine finding this in your mail: "Supplementary Instructions 11B, Appendix 1 (Revised) to the American Guide Manual.") The barrage of supplements were proof that, week by week, manuscript by manuscript, Alsberg and his team were shaping and adjusting the FWP's methods even while those methods were being carried out. It was a dynamic and deeply improvisatory process—and it was often messy.

The manual and its supplements were intended to steer FWP activities on the ground. It was left to the DC editors, meanwhile, to decide what the

American Guides would actually look like. Katharine Kellock, who helped think up the very idea of the guidebooks, was also pivotal in shaping them—but not before she was ensnared in a scandal that nearly ended her career and might have sunk the entire project. When she first transferred from the Resettlement Administration to the FWP, Alsberg made her a field representative. This meant that she was a liaison between DC and the state offices, charged with explaining directives and keeping the work on track. Kellock had this job until February 1936, when she was hit with a sudden and furious wave of red-baiting. The William Randolph Hearst papers—rabidly anti-communist—ran an editorial naming Kellock as the sinister figure behind a taxpayer-funded "Red 'Baedeker.'" She was using thousands of relief workers, it alleged, to compile information on American industrial and agricultural resources, along with highway and railway maps, with the purpose of funneling this information to the Soviet Union. The charge would have seemed ridiculous to anyone who knew Kellock—except that her husband, Alsberg's college friend, did in fact work for the Soviet embassy, which had been newly recognized by the Roosevelt administration. Harold Kellock was a journalist and publicist who'd worked for Robert M. La Follette's Progressive Party presidential campaign in 1924, and then for a private group that provided information about Russia to American businesses; after Roosevelt recognized the Soviet Union, Harold was offered a job handling press materials for the embassy—that is, *incoming* clippings and reports from the US media—and he took it. As Reed Harris wrote at the time, "He is known to be somewhat anti-communistic in his views and keeps his job chiefly because he is a good publicity man willing to present the actual facts in an attractive way."

But to the Hearst press, he was a spy and a traitor. When they attacked his wife—and by extension, the FWP—they set off a wave of criticism. For months, petitions organized by a Republican group arrived in stacks, protesting the appointment of "a woman whose husband, because of his office, must necessarily be pro-communistic, when there are plenty of American women, imbued with American principles and ideals, who need the work." They called for Kellock to be fired. Anxious senators and representatives contacted WPA officials and forwarded outraged letters from their constituents. One private citizen wrote from Atlanta: "In the name of common hard

horse sense, have the officials in Washington gone mad? Are there not sufficient real patriots (descendants of such) left to fill positions of responsibility
in the government without calling in this horde of foreigners?" Jacob Baker
quickly worked up a form letter refuting the charges, explaining Kellock's
qualifications, and emphasizing that she belonged to no foreign horde: she
was a US citizen and came from a well-established family. (Her maternal
grandfather was a cousin of Rutherford B. Hayes.) WPA officials regretted
the controversy—not in sympathy with Kellock, but wishing someone less
controversial had been hired in her place. And yet they were determined not
to fire her. Instead, Kellock was transferred to a new role in the DC office as
the editor in charge of tour copy—a less visible job than field supervisor, but
one vastly more important in allowing her to shape the American Guides.
She'd join a select group of national editors who were responsible for specific
subject areas: the renowned but controversial song collector John Lomax, for
instance, was brought on to handle folklore.

In her new position as tours editor, Kellock didn't hold back while her colleagues wrestled with the design of the American Guides. The DC staff knew
that, like the Baedekers, the guides would combine essays with descriptions
of routes and cities. But would these books be functional items for travelers?
Or would they be more reflective and digressive, literary compendiums that
delved into the history and culture of each and every state? Alsberg tended toward the latter idea. Kellock, however, was firmly in the first camp. In a blunt
memo, "Differences in Form and Content of Different Types of Books"—so
precise it was somewhat condescending—Kellock defined various types of
publications, including an atlas, a dictionary, a gazetteer, and a geography
book. These, she explained, are all reference works, and their information is
arranged topically or alphabetically, and they are intended for libraries or for
the home. A guidebook, however, presents its information in the order that
travelers will need it as they follow along a route, and is intended for the field.
"It is a major error to try to <u>combine</u> a reference volume and a guidebook," she
insisted. And yet Alsberg was intent on making just that "error." The result
was a kind of hybrid, a book that could rest in your car's glove compartment
or on your nightstand, something that would meet Kellock's expectations for
functionality while fulfilling Alsberg's desire for literary quality. This formal
compromise would draw jeers from some critics: "It isn't a guidebook if you

have to leave it in the car," according to Bernard DeVoto. But others appreciated that these books had room to stretch, to ramble a bit, and perhaps to suggest something more about the land they charted than simply what was around the next bend.

Kellock accepted this decision and turned to her work with gusto. The tours—dense collages of the mundane and the remarkable, of reported fact and alluring hearsay, whose juxtapositions were sometimes odd and frequently surprising—would become the signature aesthetic achievement of the American Guides. "The tour form is a difficult form," Alsberg once said. "It is like a sonnet; but, if you can learn it, you can be more interesting in the description of a tour than in any novel." Kellock, as national editor of the tours, their engineer and philosopher, sought to bear this out. From her desk in DC she envisioned a network of routes crisscrossing the United States, an invisible webbing that held all the guides together. She thought about how to join one to another and how to account for the flow of traffic. She thought about their placement on the page, the typography and the headings. She thought about the real-life experiences of the human beings who would be navigating these tours by car, hour after hour—and she thought about the places they'd pass through, the sites they would see. "THE PURPOSE OF A GUIDE IS TO LEAD SOMEWHERE," she reminded Alsberg in a memo. So why not saturate the tours with destinations? This meant expanding them to include everything that wouldn't fit neatly into the city profiles. It also meant, naturally, more work for her: as the tours editor, she was responsible for massive amounts of copy, with the help of only one and a half assistants and two secretaries. (The half assistant didn't work on tours exclusively.) But she had a vision and she wanted to see it fulfilled.

She was meticulous and sophisticated, but sometimes her zealousness got the better of her. At one point, Reed Harris sent an unusually fierce memo on Alsberg's behalf to Kellock and the tour section, criticizing them for writing brusque letters to the state offices that made the DC staff seem "as if we were posing as little tin gods."

There has been a definite school-teacherish method of expression used . . . It immediately antagonizes the reader. It makes every line of your letter, or editorial comment, sound like a slap. There are very few times when it is necessary to use this type of language in dealing with state directors. It must be assumed that they are intelligent human beings, and in many cases they have long experience in the writing and editorial fields, and that they will not stand for being treated like school children.

Kellock had a habit of writing terse and pointed memos when she was addressing an important issue. She certainly may have neglected to embroider her letters to the states with anything but the directions she meant to convey. But she was, after all, a national editor of the highest rank. And it's hard to imagine any other such national editor, all of whom were men, being compared to a schoolteacher mistreating her pupils.

Even so, Kellock's authority inside the project was fairly secure. Outside the project, the red-baiting frenzy had dissipated, at least for the moment. Kellock and the entire staff had reason to be optimistic. They'd improvised their way toward a foundation for the largest literary project ever attempted, and, so far, it seemed to be working. George Cronyn wrote to Jacob Baker and another WPA official: "There is no escaping the conclusion that this will be a permanent government function, similar in certain respects to the census. It will be one of the most important perpetual sources of information the government can offer." Reed Harris believed they needed to foster "snob appeal"—the kind of hype that would make readers believe they *needed* to read these books. That the books, once published, would be able to garner a few select strong reviews, or that they would even *appear* in the first place, were foregone conclusions.

At the center of it all was Alsberg, chain-smoking, dictating a letter or discoursing into a phone or hunched over documents. He still struggled with administrative tasks, sometimes jumbling up who was on what phone and which state office he was instructing to do what task. When he hired the state director for Louisiana, Alsberg promised him one salary and then sent a letter offering a larger one. George Cronyn caught the mistake, but Alsberg replied, "Oh, I forgot. Unfortunately, must pay 2600—don't see what you could do about it." He could be absentminded and aloof when it came to such details. But his dedication to the work never flagged. He rarely took breaks, although he did occasionally steal into a movie theater for a nap. He usually brought work back to his home and toiled into the night. Despite his missteps and fallow periods, he had never quite lost the drive that once propelled him across war-torn Europe, into shtetls and through the Soviet gates. Some project workers knew his history but many didn't, and they might have been surprised to learn the story of a man whom they occasionally saw shuffling from his office into the nearby women's restroom (more conveniently located than the men's room downstairs), leaving his secretary to guard the door.

After moving to Washington, Alsberg didn't correspond much with Emma Goldman. But she did write in October 1935, as the FWP was getting off the ground. "Indeed I never would have believed that you would display such sticktoitiveness to organizational work. I take off my hat to you, old dear." Goldman's position was that if someone were to helm such an instrument of the state—to which she was opposed in principle—it might as well be Alsberg and not "some corrupt person." She was clearly glad to see her friend's life take this unexpected and promising turn.

And so the copy flowed into Washington, revisions and telegrams and supplementary instructions flowed out. Every single sentence in every manuscript, Harry Hopkins informed the president, would be read and edited in the DC office. In a way, the FWP had all the problems of a major publishing house, a newspaper with far-flung bureaus, a large relief agency, and a government bureaucracy that lived or died by the whims of distant legislators. It was attempting a project of unprecedented scope and scale for which there was no blueprint. It was employing thousands of people at a task for which most had no real training or experience. It was operating at a perilous moment, when the very assumptions of American life and the democratic experiment were in question. And its core base—writers—were a group not particularly known for comfortably inhabiting large institutions, working cooperatively, or obeying orders. George Cronyn, who received weekly progress reports from the DC staff, knew this well. One particularly insouciant report carried the subject line "What I have been doing thru the week" and concluded: "Friday—in bed all day, not working, but certainly thinking of God and the Writers' Projects."

And far from Washington, another editor, Miriam Allen deFord of the

San Francisco office, expressed her feelings in verse (with apologies to Joyce Kilmer):

> *I think that I have never tried*
> *A job as painful as the guide.*
> *A guide which changes every day*
> *Because our betters feel that way.*
> *A guide whose deadlines come so fast*
> *Yet no one lives to see the last.*
> *A guide to which we give our best*
> *To hear: "This stinks like all the rest!"*
> *There's no way out but suicide*
> *For only God can end the Guide.*

VARDIS FISHER,
IDAHO

"TO SAVE AMERICA FROM THE AMERICANS"

Henry Alsberg spent the first phase of his career facing overseas. His great literary accomplishments—the book on Russian political prisoners, the history of the Joint Distribution Committee, the translation of a Yiddish play—were Eurocentric efforts. This was hardly unusual for the intellectuals and writers of his time, who tended to be preoccupied, on a grand level, with Europe. "He was so representative of his generation, the generation of John Reed and Dos Passos," recalled an FWP editor who became close with Alsberg. "They liked the big thing. They liked to spread out over the world. And Henry had done it."

But while Alsberg and other American writers were setting sail for Europe or merely looking overseas for inspiration, a countervailing trend was emerging. The first decades of the twentieth century saw a surge of interest in American themes: the nation's literature and history, especially, but also its vernacular culture, its folktales and ballads and handicrafts. This trend didn't arise from nothing; its roots stretched to the aftermath of the Civil War, when Americans, for a variety of reasons, were becoming more tradition-oriented than earlier generations. (Up until that period, civic discourse in America had been dominated by forward-looking attitudes that valued progress and novelty over memory and tradition—attitudes, it was believed, fit for a young republican society in the process of making the world over. "I like the dreams of the future better than the history of the past," wrote Thomas Jefferson, a sentiment reiterated ad nauseam by politicians and wrought into a literary trope by Ralph Waldo Emerson, among others.) From roughly the 1870s to the turn of the century, an unprecedented vogue for historical commemoration and preservation led to an eruption of monuments, shrines, and civic pageants, as well as a frenzy of genealogical research and a newfound appreciation for the decorative arts of the colonial era. The mood of the time tended toward the nostalgic and antiquarian, though it had its darker aspects, too, in Lost Cause monuments and ancestor-worshipping genealogies designed to validate the prevailing racial order. The emphasis was on majesty and eminence—figures of power and esteem (like a US president), artifacts with grand associations (like a president's desk), items of exceptional beauty (like a pewter candlestick holder in the restored home of a president).

This trend, the Americana turn, continued apace into the 1910s and accelerated through the twenties and thirties. But it was changing, too, morphing into a more capacious fascination with the everyday *stuff* of American life and the idea of a distinctive American culture. Its permutations were visible in the collection and study of folk materials, in historical highway markers and the preservation of old village districts, in the Metropolitan Museum of Art's American Wing and Henry Ford's Americana collecting spree and J. D. Rockefeller's yearslong restoration of colonial Williamsburg that began in 1928—and, especially, as a pervasive theme in the arts. "I have fallen in love with American names," began a poem by Stephen Vincent Benét: "The sharp names that never get fat, / The snakeskin-titles of mining-claims, / The plumed war-bonnet of Medicine Hat, / Tucson and Deadwood and Lost Mule Flat." Writers of all sorts, working in diverse forms, were similarly lovestruck, even while their methods and conclusions differed. They weren't simply flinging off nationalist paeans: Claude McKay, a Jamaican immigrant, revolutionary socialist, and future federal writer, offered one variation in his poem "America": "Although she feeds me bread of bitterness, / And sinks into my throat her tiger's tooth, / Stealing my breath of life, I will confess / I love this cultured hell that tests my youth." (If the Americana turn, following Benét and McKay, was a form of love, then it involved an irresistible attraction that could never obscure, and might even illuminate, the flaws of the beloved.) This literary moment, in all its diversity of form and style, boiled down to a simple idea: that a writer could find sustenance and purpose—morally, socially, and aesthetically—in the act of discovering, or *rediscovering*, some essential truths about America.

The books and poems energized by this idea formed the "literature of nationhood" that Alfred Kazin described in *On Native Grounds*—itself emblematic of the Americana turn. Appraisals like Kazin's had been appearing since at least the 1910s—Van Wyck Brooks's and Lewis Mumford's literary studies set the tone early, as did Waldo Frank's *Our America* and Randolph Bourne's social criticism. In 1923, there was D. H. Lawrence's cryptic and freewheeling *Studies in Classic American Literature*, and two years later, William Carlos Williams's wordy and restless collection of portraits *In the American Grain*. Constance Rourke's *American Humor*, her resplendent excavation of the national culture, appeared in 1931. There were more books by Van Wyck Brooks, including his vastly popular *The Flowering of New England* (which won the Pulitzer Prize *and* the National Book Award), biographies by Carl Van Doren and Carl Sandburg, V. L. Parrington's intellectual history *Main Currents in American Thought* (another Pulitzer winner), new editions of H. L. Mencken's influential *American Language*, and an effusion of treatises and essays. In 1941, F. O. Matthiessen published his landmark analysis of nineteenth-century writers, *American Renaissance*, and Kazin's *On Native Grounds* followed the next year, effectively capping off a period that had overthrown the old ideas about the thinness of American culture (and would blossom into the academic field of American studies).

Books such as these—cerebral, scholarly, and inclined toward the American past—were gradually joined by another type of book, one that was more journalistic and fixated on the Depression-ravaged present. Some appeared as reportage or nonfiction meditations by the likes of Edmund Wilson and Theodore Dreiser, James Rorty and John Dos Passos. Others fused text with stark and evocative photographs, such as Dorothea Lange and Paul S. Taylor's *An American Exodus*, Erskine Caldwell and Margaret Bourke-White's *You Have Seen Their Faces*, and James Agee and Walker Evans's nervy and profound *Let Us Now Praise Famous Men*. At a time when everything seemed thrown into question, these books were groping for answers in the hard truth of the documentary form. Whether they added up to a portrait of resilience or captured the first glimpses of an American death spiral, their authors and readers did not know. But all of them—the documentary books and the literary studies, the collections of folk materials and the novels and poems that sponged up vernacular culture—shared an unshakable feeling that something valuable and meaningful was out there, waiting, squirreled away in the forgotten corners of the American land.

At the same time, another force—related but distinct—was reshaping the literary landscape. Since the onset of the Depression, more and more writers were becoming radicalized in their thought, their rhetoric, and their actions. They were trading in the stances of the twenties—art for art's sake, modernist obfuscation, contempt for cultural philistines—for a new, unstable set of ideas about revolutionary commitment and class struggle.

This shift in attitudes had a prologue: the 1927 execution of Sacco and Vanzetti. For six years, only the radical left much cared about the two imprisoned anarchists. But in the months before Sacco and Vanzetti went to the electric chair, writers and intellectuals took up their cause—and failed. (Alsberg, in Paris at the time, spoke at a rally alongside Vanzetti's sister.) From that failure emerged poems and plays and novels as liberal writers found their assumptions shaken by the whole sordid experience. Two years later, the Depression triggered an even greater reappraisal of ideas and commitments. The previous decade's pervasive irreverence began to feel hollow; the rottenness of American society was becoming visible in repressed strikes around the Midwest and the South, the ordeal of the Scottsboro Boys, lynchings, evictions. Disturbing headlines had writers pivoting from self-exploration to social analysis; where once they were fixated on sex and the soul and unfocused rebelliousness, now they mulled over economic conditions and the revolutionary transformation of society.

The decisive moment arrived during the run-up to the 1932 presidential election, when fifty-three writers, artists, and intellectuals issued a statement urging a vote for the Communists William Z. Foster and his running mate, the African American James W. Ford. The signatories—a group of novelists, critics, poets, dramatists, biographers, and philosophers, including Edmund Wilson, John Dos Passos, Theodore Dreiser, and Sidney Hook—rejected both the promises of Roosevelt's Democratic Party and what they saw as the tepid reformism of Norman Thomas's Socialist Party. They launched an organization, the League of Professional Groups for Foster and Ford, that gathered support for the candidates while struggling to overcome the traditional division between, as they put it, "brain workers" and "muscle workers."

Radicalized writers had different attitudes toward the party and (although this was a separate question) the Soviet Union—some joined the party, some moved in sync with it, some rejected it outright, and some experienced all three states. It wasn't a clean process. (The party, meanwhile, didn't entirely trust outside writers and artists, no matter how sympathetic, and frowned at their bohemian tendencies—for the moment, anyway.) Many who signed the statement backing Foster and Ford considered it a protest vote, a way of emphasizing the severity of the crisis—only the equally severe Communist Party platform fit the urgency of the moment. But their statement signaled a new reality. The sturdy trope of the writer who toiled individually in pursuit of art was being replaced by the idea that writers, as a group, belonged to a social movement of all laboring classes.

Malcolm Cowley, the literary editor of *The New Republic*, signed the Foster and Ford statement and worked for the short-lived league once he could no longer ignore the class struggle erupting on the pages of his magazine. "As the months passed I began to feel that there was no refuge from the storm, that the profession I loved was involved in the fate of everything else, and that everything, including literature, would have to be changed," he wrote. Cowley was busy chronicling another literary trend in his 1934 book *Exile's Return*, which told the story of how writers and artists of his generation had journeyed to Europe after the World War, pursued lives of creative indulgence, and then gradually moved back to the United States. (Alsberg, though slightly older, had followed a similar trajectory.) When these former exiles made their homecoming, they discovered a stateside literary scene that no longer resembled the one from which they'd sailed away. Writers, including Cowley, who were now reorienting themselves toward their native country did so in an atmosphere of increasing deprivation and radicalization. Cowley even found himself running a miniature, pre-WPA model of work relief from his desk at *The New Republic*: when he couldn't hand out assignments to all the hungry book reviewers who piled into his office, he at least gave them review copies to sell for cash at secondhand bookstores so they could buy a meal.

All of these literary trends—the Americana turn, the documentary impulse, and the radical commitment—converged in one perfectly representative book: Sherwood Anderson's *Puzzled America*. When it appeared in 1935, Anderson, nearly sixty years old, was well known as a master of regionalist Americana, thanks to his 1919 story collection *Winesburg, Ohio*. His work that followed was uneven (critics decided that he'd never quite developed a knack for novel-writing) but he was intermittently successful and consistently productive, even when he took up the life of a small-town newspaper editor in Virginia. The Depression nudged him into a radical phase, and he traded his old populist sympathies for a more explicit anti-capitalism; he, too, signed the statement for Foster and Ford. ("I found Sherwood Anderson all full of Communism," Edmund Wilson wrote to John Dos Passos. "He doesn't know much about it, but the idea has given him a powerful afflatus.") His radical fervor ebbed, though, as he came to admire the New Deal's practicality and effectiveness. A new magazine, *Today*—an unabashed house organ for the administration, edited by the original brain truster, Raymond Moley—commissioned Anderson to travel the country and report on the real-life impacts of New Deal policies, and these pieces formed the basis of *Puzzled America*.

It was a road-trip book, confined mostly to the South and Midwest, with Anderson as aimless guide: visiting mining camps and mill towns and union meetings, picking up hitchhikers and chatting with local informants. As with other books in this genre, his aim was descriptive rather than prescriptive; he was simply documenting the American scene as he saw it, using clean, at times incantatory, prose and abundant quotations to give it the feel of "real life" (even though he made a little bit up). The book reads this way, at least. But cutting through Anderson's folksy perplexity is a persistent refrain, that America is a rich land and that everyone deserves to share in its riches, to own it and improve it. Over and over, Anderson is reminded of this idea and he sees it, especially, in signs of the New Deal: a CCC camp, TVA dams, a CWA archaeological dig. Hitchhikers he picks up feel the same. "Everywhere I go people crying out, not first of all for food, clothes, comforts—but for work, work, work," says a young woman, a cotton mill worker fired for leading a strike. "I guess it will have to be government; but it will have to be a different notion of government from what we have had," says a middle-aged farmer who lost his land. "It means something what they call the New Deal. It means that people have got to be made to quit cutting each other's throats. Individualism means that—the devil take the hindermost. We're the hindermost," says a news-hungry tobacco grower who keeps an ear to his radio at night. "Suppose what is going on here is but a beginning," says Anderson.

> It is an interesting idea that this thing that has now begun in America—government having a thought of the land, men in Washington, in government, daring to say—"We'll begin trying it."
>
> Trying what?
>
> Suppose it should come down to this, that there is a plot on foot in America—men actually serious about it—a plot, let's say, to save America from the Americans.

Puzzled America appeared in the early spring of 1935, just a few months before the creation of the WPA. The FWP would pick up where the book left off. The same preoccupations and attitudes that were swirling within the American literary scene and that had converged in Anderson's book inevitably ended up in the project's DNA. The focus on a distinctly American culture and its regional shadings, the desire to document the words and experiences of common people, the notion that hard times and uncertainty invited a wandering survey of the land, the unsteady interplay between New Deal activism and forces to its left—all would profoundly shape the FWP's internal culture and its mission. The FWP even echoed Anderson's idea about saving America from Americans but chose to put a more reassuring spin on it: introducing America to Americans.

And yet, by the fall of 1935, when the FWP was new, its territorial footprint was still tiny. Federal writers had surveyed and explored only the interior of the McLean mansion ballroom, and the old Washington Auditorium before that. There was nothing more to the project than Henry Alsberg and his national staff, their desks and supplies, and a presidential authorization. To carry out its grand and somewhat romantic endeavor of national rediscovery, the FWP needed to unfurl into the American land.

"THE PLANE OF PERMANENT LITERATURE"

One Friday morning in October, the associate director George Cronyn gathered the staff and announced plans to begin the unfurling. They'd just hired the first fifteen state directors, he said, and were sending instructions by airmail. The state directors were to report to their local WPA headquarters on Monday and begin putting the jobless to work: schoolteachers, discouraged poets, news stringers, and others taken from the relief rolls would become field workers, researchers, stenographers, secretaries, and editors. Each director would set up a central project office, usually in their state's largest city, and then, in more populous states, a network of small satellite offices. For the moment, building this human infrastructure was their top priority—and it represented the FWP's crucial first steps toward exploring and documenting a weary, puzzled nation.

A few days later, Alsberg wrote to the first batch of state directors. He wished to emphasize a key idea. "The first and primary object of our organization is to take people from the relief rolls and set them to work," he wrote. "Our projects, themselves, no matter how important and interesting, come second." This was the official line, promoted by Franklin Roosevelt and Harry Hopkins on down. Alsberg agreed, sort of. It was never a secret that he disdained literary leaf-raking and sought, instead, for the FWP to create high-quality work of lasting value. But he recognized that, to do this, the FWP needed to fulfill its primary purpose and focus on employment. He also knew that their success would build support for the New Deal and, in a circular way, reinforce the security of the project itself. (Alsberg's political savvy was often lost on those who couldn't see past his amiable befuddlement.) He encouraged the state directors to keep up a steady flow of information to local newspapers—even the anti–New Deal papers, he insisted, would look favorably on the FWP's efforts to move people from direct relief to honest, productive work. He signed off with a characteristically optimistic if muddled sentiment: "It has often been said that every 'knock is a boost' and we will convert many 'knocks' into boomerangs, if we carry out the ideals set before us."

Alsberg, with an eye toward the FWP's official launch date of November 1, spent the rest of October hiring state directors. He needed to fill positions in all forty-eight states, plus a stand-alone office in New York City. As he and Jacob Baker, Hopkins's aide, sought out candidates, Alsberg found himself preferring novelists who had an attachment to their home state. But he kept an open mind. On the phone with a WPA administrator in Virginia, he described, not very precisely, the type of candidate he sought: "An editor, or journalist or someone who wrote novels, somebody with some reputation and somebody not entirely helpless or whom you would have to nurse along, someone who can stand on his own feet without bothering you too much."

At least 116 people cycled through the directorships during the life of the project, plus "acting directors" with brief tenures. Most were men who'd worked as editors, journalists, and academics. But nearly a quarter of the directors were women, fourteen of them appointed during the project's early months. (Their rate of survival was "far higher," Katharine Kellock would observe, than that of the men.) Twenty-one directors were writers well-known enough to appear in the literature essays of various American Guides. A few were in their seventies when they signed up with the FWP; a handful were only in their twenties. All of them were white.

Some directors served their offices with aplomb. From Arizona, Ross Santee—illustrator, novelist, cowboy—wrote to Alsberg: "Anyone who can wet-nurse a hundred and fifty saddle horses, know where they run, and know all the quirks of each particular horse, ought to be able to wrangle a bunch of writers." In his case, he was right. The best directors proved, like Santee, to be nimble and resourceful stewards of their projects.

Inevitably, some fell short. More than one state director was fired or removed for drunkenness. Another was accused of trading employment for sex. Certain offices faced political interference: the Missouri project was run by a creature of Kansas City's Pendergast machine, while in Nebraska, the director was said to be a former mistress of a powerful friend of her state's senator—incompetent and unfireable, she was transferred, complete with desk and secretary, to "direct" the project from home. Washington State's director was a pulp fiction writer who allegedly told his workers simply to make things up—perhaps finding the state too boring to describe factually. One southern office was run by the aunt of a sitting US senator. She ignored the instructions to prepare a guidebook and instead came up with her own assignment. When someone from the national staff checked in, she led him to a room of workers pounding away at typewriters and said, "Have you ever seen such an inspiring sight? Seventeen poets, all in one room, writing poetry seven hours a day."

As the first directors took their places, the FWP still planned to create a single "American Guide," divided into regional volumes. But when that book morphed into a series of discrete American Guides, one for every state, the directors became even more central to the project's work. They were no longer simply funneling copy to DC but were now responsible for distinct portions of the FWP's emerging self-portrait of the nation. And yet their role carried even more significance than that. In a practical sense, the FWP's mission to "rediscover America" meant engaging with the writers who would carry out that mission on the ground: most crucially, the professors from rural colleges, the editors of provincial newspapers, and the semi-successful regional novelists who directed the state projects. These people weren't simply low-level administrators; they were the roots by which the FWP seeped up attitudes and feelings and styles from the thirties literary landscape. Their relationships with DC gave concrete expression to the FWP's lofty notions about introducing America to Americans—a task that began, after all, with making the acquaintance of the writers who were running operations in each and every state.

One of those writers, far from DC, overseeing a state that the national staff would have considered an afterthought, was destined to enter FWP lore in an outsize way. He came to Alsberg, as did so many others, by way of recommendation—in this case, from Harold Merriam, director of the Montana project. Merriam ran his project from the University of Montana campus, where he was chair of the English department. A few years earlier, during the summer session, he'd hired a novelist and sometime professor from Idaho named Vardis Fisher. He would have recalled a lean man in his late thirties, hard-featured, with a prominent nose and receding hairline and dark eyes that tended to settle into an unnerving stare. Since those days, Fisher had published a few more novels to some acclaim but with little financial reward. And yet Merriam believed that Fisher was in the forefront of novelists working in the northwestern United States. If they were looking for a director in Idaho, Merriam insisted, Vardis Fisher was the one.

Fisher was a logical choice. He was a born Idahoan and the author of five novels—two gritty pastorals, rich with the speech and habits of Idaho's homesteaders, and three ferociously introspective confessionals—that had earned him a national reputation. He had a PhD in literature from the University of Chicago and a scholarly disposition. He seemed to match nicely Alsberg's description of an ideal candidate—a productive writer with some stature in the literary world, a strong connection to his home state, and a self-sufficient temperament.

But Vardis Fisher on paper was not the man in full. That man grew up on a riverbottom homestead in southeastern Idaho, where desolate plains crumpled into mountains and gorges and the deadly Snake River cut through the middle. He was dually motivated by pride and fear, fiercely independent, arrogant, and relentlessly self-scrutinizing—marks of the driven scholar and the homesteader, both. He read voraciously and drank heavily. He flaunted his distaste for Christianity—especially the Mormonism of his youth—and cast aspersions on the niceties of modern living. The wagon train, not the welfare state or the business corporation, had a place of honor in his political philosophy. He was an intense teacher who, according to his student Wallace Stegner, made it his mission to blow the minds of young Mormon yokels who entered his classroom. (Fisher encouraged Stegner but would later appear in his short story "The View from the Balcony" as a pugnacious and inebriated professor: "His face was like the face of a predatory bird, beaked, grim-lipped; because of some eye trouble he always wore dark glasses, and his prying, intent, hidden stare was an agony to encounter. His mouth was hooked back in a constant sardonic smile.") In his personal relationships, Fisher could be both generous and cruel, intensely present and coldly remote. "I have friends scattered over the country," he wrote, "who have seen the ape in me rise to the surface and show his simian features." He possessed an intransigence that, in many writers, fosters either greatness or folly. In Fisher—as Alsberg and the DC staff would learn—it generated handfuls of both.

Cronyn offered him the job. Fisher accepted. He asked if instructions would be waiting for him at the WPA office in Pocatello. "I'm laying aside my writing to get this job moving and I don't want to be caught twiddling my thumbs and wondering precisely what I'm supposed to do," he said. From Montana, Harold Merriam, pleased that his recommendation had stuck, telegrammed Fisher his congratulations. Don't take the directorship too seriously, Merriam insisted. They weren't expected to achieve anything, he joshed, aside from handing out jobs and getting people to vote for Roosevelt.

Fisher could have taken Merriam's advice. He could have treated the job as hack work, cashed the checks, finished his novels. It wasn't as if the DC office expected grand things from the sparsely populated, unglamorous state of Idaho. (The guide would report a population of 445,000 persons—315,000 of them on farms.) But Fisher had a habit of applying himself intensely to his tasks—homesteading, writing, researching, drinking—and this would be no different.

He set up the Idaho project and, as copy began to flow into the Washington office, three things became clear.

First, the writing was superior to what anyone had expected, especially coming from a half-forgotten western state. "To be quite frank, I didn't expect any real literature from our Directors," Alsberg admitted in a letter to Fisher. "Therefore, your piece came as an unexpected windfall." Cronyn went even further: "Mr. Alsberg and I both agree that you have succeeded in raising Guide writing to the plane of permanent literature."

Then something else became clear. Fisher had written nearly the entire guide himself, jettisoning the cooperative spirit of the project.

And finally, to Alsberg's dismay, Fisher announced that he was on track to finish the guide, far in advance of any others. Alsberg wanted the inaugural volume to be the guide to Washington, DC. But Fisher had already made arrangements with a local Idaho publisher to release his guide. And if Alsberg and the national office felt that the DC guide should—*must*—come first? Fisher didn't give a damn.

"A DEFEATED EGOTIST"

Idaho, tucked into the northwestern interior, did not feel the effects of the Depression right away. But the crisis got there soon enough. In late 1931 and into 1932, as industrial demand fell, the state's mining and timber industries began to shrink. Farmers, many of whom had struggled through the twenties, faced an especially bad harvest. Agricultural prices continued to slide. Mortgage foreclosures and delinquent taxes peaked. Bank holdings plummeted.

In 1930, Idaho had a bit more than six thousand officially unemployed workers. Two years later, there were twenty thousand.

When the slump reached Idaho, Vardis Fisher seemed able, barely, to
float above it. He was a full-time novelist—not unemployed, but not quite
gainfully employed either. And yet, among professional writers, he was in a
better position than most. He lived with his wife, children, and parents on
a ranch in the southeast of the state, nestled along the Snake River, a mountain range away from the Wyoming border. It was so remote that he drove
forty miles once a week just to pick up the mail. But the ranch allowed for
some measure of self-sufficiency. He and his family knew that during hard
times they could depend on what they grew and what they could gather
from the land. Those times had come and Fisher's novels weren't making
anyone rich.

Idaho was not ground zero for the architects of Federal #1. Jobless writers
were demanding work and picketing in the streets of Manhattan, not Boise.
And yet Fisher was precisely the sort of struggling professional writer for
whom the FWP was designed. His five novels, though they sold modestly,
were generally well regarded by critics. The first two, *Toilers of the Hills* and
Dark Bridwell, were set in Fisher's home territory and drew from the experiences of relatives and acquaintances. The next three were installments
in a planned tetralogy, a minutely observed and intensely autobiographical
portrait of a character named Vridrar Hunter. These novels showed Fisher
working within a few of the day's common literary currents. He was a regionalist: he delved and charted his native Antelope Hills as had Sherwood
Anderson in Winesburg and William Faulkner in Yoknapatawpha County
and any number of less visible writers who surveyed their local provinces. He
was an elegist for the pioneer experience, as Willa Cather had been more than
a decade earlier. And, when he turned his imaginative power toward himself,
he resembled Thomas Wolfe writing his novels of inward sprawl. But Fisher
was no mere imitator. He knew Wolfe—they taught together, briefly, at New
York University—and his admiration was mixed with scorn for Wolfe's sentimentality, his lack of cold self-criticism. He dismissed Willa Cather and popular writers such as Edna Ferber (unfairly, perhaps) as woefully sanitized.
And he spurned the Faulknerian path; he'd build no literary monument on
his native patch of land. "The reviewers never understood that I detested the

Antelope country and was trying to come to some kind of terms with it, so that I could proceed to a more sunlit area," he wrote later. His novels carried a distinctive voice and vision, but Fisher was still broadly and identifiably a writer of his time.

He was also generally (although not decisively) in tune with the political temper of the moment. His first two novels, about uncouth, determined folk wrenching a living out of the Idaho hills, reflected the growing determination among writers to represent the lives of working people, who toiled in both urban and agrarian settings. His autobiographical novels carried traces of his own ideas, although his politics were hard to pin down. As a young man in the twenties he'd been a socialist, absorbing *The New Republic* and *The Nation* (where he likely encountered Alsberg's dispatches). When he taught at the University of Utah, he formed something called the Radical Club, whose members discussed risqué topics such as birth control and invited controversial speakers, including the socialist Scott Nearing. By the thirties he was cautiously optimistic about Roosevelt's efforts to fight the Depression—especially anything that would benefit wheat farmers such as his father—although he feared that the entire New Deal would fail unless it moved in a more aggressive direction. He also believed, as did many others during these years, that, one way or another, an uprising among desperate farmers was imminent—and justified. In 1934, a year before the birth of the FWP, he contributed to a symposium on literary criticism in *New Masses*, admitting to a "deep but quite unreasonable sympathy" with "the Marxian point of view," although he rejected revolutionary class struggle for the "ruthless application of the scientific point of view to ourselves" in order to overcome our true oppressor: the habit of self-evasion, inculcated by our basic animal nature and centuries of superstition and benighted traditions. "While I am not sure that its adolescent idealism does me any good," he concluded of the Marxist position, "I do find in it both earnestness and vitality; and that is a hell of a lot more than I can say for certain Olympian and empty aestheticism that still endures in and around New York." Fisher didn't share the explicit radical commitments that motivated many other federal writers (and would soon draw the ire of the project's enemies), but he felt loosely aligned with them in a shared antagonism with the literary establishment. At bottom, he was a gleeful iconoclast from out of the American West.

Rocky Mountain iconoclasts—and cowboy novelists and bayou raconteurs—were just the sorts of writers the FWP needed to draw into its ranks if it meant to create a portrait of the nation from the ground up; it needed to be geographically inclusive, with outposts everywhere, including in the cultural peripheries. Few places were as culturally peripheral (or, at least, appeared to be) as Fisher's homestead on the bank of the Snake River. And yet even there, Alsberg found an experienced, capable, and nearly impoverished writer—someone who would never have cause to assemble a guidebook but, if put to the task, might produce a book worth noticing. This was the FWP's key proposition, one it sought to test through Vardis Fisher and many others who shared his profile.

But, again—Fisher on paper was not the man in full. His journey to the FWP was entirely his own.

When Brigham Young led the Mormons into the Utah Territory, Vardis Fisher's paternal grandfather (then a boy of twelve) followed in the caravan, driving a team of oxen, and watched his mother die of cholera. When Joseph Smith was killed in Illinois, Fisher's maternal grandparents were among the acolytes who scattered into the hinterlands. The two families converged west of the Rockies and carved modest lives out of the land. Fisher held fast to that pioneer experience. It was his virtuous inheritance: a tradition of self-sufficiency in thought and deed, of mental and physical toughness. "I'm glad I knew them," he wrote of the frontier realms later in life, "no matter what their terrors for neurotic children; for in having known them, I am better able to understand the world that is being built out of them." Fisher had no illusions about the brutality and crudeness of pioneer life, but he admired its hard simplicity. "It was the kind of life that destroyed the weak, and added the meaning of their death to the strong."

By 1895, when Fisher was born, that world was dissolving. (Even the name of the settlement in southeastern Idaho where his parents made their home was changing: Poole's Island, then Annie's Place, then Annis.) Five years earlier, the census of 1890 had officially declared the close of the frontier. Whether in some measurable way or only in perception, frontier life as a historical experience was nearing its end. Fisher appeared in one of its remaining pockets. When he was six, his family left Annis for a homestead thirty miles to the east. For two days they traveled by wagon in almost complete silence—Vardis, his parents, his brother and baby sister—until they came upon a cottonwood shack with an earth floor and an earth roof, sitting on four cleared acres bounded by the Snake River. Vardis wouldn't leave the riverbottom for about five years. (This was the homestead to which he would return, as an adult, in the early days of the Depression.) His father planted hay and grain and raised livestock; at night he worked the fields by lantern. His mother made cheese and sold it in distant settlements. The children called her Mater and she raised them, ostensibly, as Mormons. But they were so far on the fringes of organized religious life that their real instruction was a kind of ad hoc backwoods Puritanism.

Fisher grew up fearful. He was afraid of blood and of beasts lurking outside the cabin and of the dead eyes of slaughtered livestock. He was afraid of his mother's talk of the devil and he was afraid of his father in general. He was afraid of the violent Snake River. When the spring runoff was strong, the river would rush through its course so powerfully that the cupboards rattled. People drowned in it—including Fisher and his brother, nearly. He was afraid to walk into the surrounding hills at twilight to round up the cattle. And he was afraid of the Bible, which was all the literature they owned aside from a few cheap novels and a book of Mormon doctrine. But, starved for intellectual nourishment, he read it more than once, first page to last. The religion didn't stick—as an adult, he'd become an outspoken atheist—but he discovered a deep connection with the written word. He began to write poetry, inspired by an uncle who recited his homespun verse to visitors, and found that he had a natural facility for meter and rhyme.

His long march out of the riverbottom began when he was twelve. He and his brother, Vivian, left for formal schooling. By the time they entered high school in Rigby, back in the direction of their hometown, Annis, they were living like a pair of old bachelors in a hut their father had built for them. They were socially aloof—Vivian was cross-eyed, Vardis grim and withdrawn— and they dressed like they had wandered out of the previous century. But academically, they excelled. Their mother's tutoring had prepared them well, not because she'd taught them much, but because she insisted that they become powerfully educated. Vardis continued writing poems, which he marked with a rubber stamp: "By Vardis A. Fisher, Amateur Poet—Rigby,

Idaho." He also commandeered the school's typewriter and wrote a novel, the first of many that he would compose and then burn.

After high school—he graduated in a class of nine—Fisher made two great leaps away from the Idaho backcountry. He enrolled at the University of Utah, in the bewildering metropolitan hub of Salt Lake City, and he married a girl from Annis, Leona McMurtrey. It was 1917; he was twenty-two, she was eighteen. The townspeople considered her popular, intelligent, and beautiful. But Vardis and Leona's life together was vexed. In Salt Lake City, Leona felt uprooted and stifled. She watched with dismay as her husband disappeared into his studies, leaving her to fill the hours with domestic tasks. The pattern continued over the next half-dozen years. They had children, two boys, while Vardis pursued his degrees: a BA from Utah, the first in his family, then graduate work at the University of Chicago. (He'd write a master's thesis on Daniel Defoe and a dissertation on George Meredith.) In Chicago, he fiddled with plays and more novels and he gorged himself on books, staring at page after page for so long, with such intensity, that he temporarily went blind. Leona read to him, so he wouldn't falter in his progress.

In the summer of 1924, their relationship hit a terminal point. Fisher revealed that he'd met another woman, Margaret Trusler, a fellow graduate student. She made Leona look like a rube. He announced that he was leaving Leona and the children, that he'd never become a great writer trapped in a mismatched marriage, that he'd be a coward not to leave. His parents were aghast; his mother thought he'd gone mad. But Fisher insisted that Leona would be better off. She might even be improved by the suffering, the struggle. She was the type who would recover easily, forget him, and move on.

That summer, Leona suffered. She wrote from Chicago to her sister-in-law: "Be careful, Irene, and don't say yes to some guy in a lonesome moment and then become his slave for the rest of your life; even after he has tired of you and gone off with a fresh woman." On the last day of August, Leona wrote to the Fisher family again. "Just a line to say we are still in the land of the living, if we do wish we were dead most of the time." One afternoon, a week later, Fisher and Leona argued. He made a cruel remark about her parenting and stormed out into the backyard. Leona followed. She stepped out the door and called his name—he turned—and then she raised a glass and drank it and collapsed. Lysol. She made it to the hospital and then she died.

Fisher telegrammed his family back in Idaho: "LEONA IS DEAD. COME AT ONCE FOR CHILDREN. VARDIS."

For months, he wore her ring around his neck and churned out guilt-racked and maudlin poetry that he'd occasionally mail home. It was all he could think to do, aside from pushing on with his career—which he did. He spent the rest of the twenties as an academic, first at the University of Utah (where he taught Wallace Stegner) and then at Washington Square College of New York University. Margaret accompanied him and taught in both places as well, and they married. Manhattan was a world away from the riverbottom, and Fisher grew optimistic about his life's trajectory. Even the stock market crash, a year after he arrived in New York, did not deter him. Neither did the visible signs of the Depression. "I see all around me people so much worse off than I am," he wrote to his family. "Unemployment is growing. There are six million men in this country out of work; and thousands of men who were wealthy a year ago are in breadlines now. So I can't complain."

He was establishing himself as a novelist. *Toilers of the Hills* appeared to mostly strong reviews while he was settling down in New York. (In Utah, he'd written four or five manuscripts, all duds and rejects.) His next novel of the Antelope Hills, *Dark Bridwell*, was in the pipeline. At NYU, he befriended another fiction writer, a hulking and unkempt figure whom he'd spied in the faculty office—Thomas Wolfe. When Wolfe's *Look Homeward, Angel* appeared, Fisher comforted him as he sobbed and raged at poor reviews and angry letters from his hometown. Fisher, meanwhile, was trying to sell a new manuscript, a fictional retelling of his early years—not unlike Wolfe's own literary project—but publishers weren't interested. Eventually, Wolfe went abroad, and left Fisher with a parting exhortation: "Vardis, don't let the sons of bitches lick you. Keep fighting." Fisher decided to keep fighting on his own terms, from his home territory.

In 1931 he returned to Idaho with Margaret. It was as if his tether, reaching across the country to Manhattan, had stretched far enough—and now snapped him back to the lonely benchland and the shadowy gorges. They joined Fisher's parents and his two sons on the homestead where he'd spent his youth. He quit academia and began a regime that would last for his entire life: mental labor in the morning, pounding away at a typewriter, and physical labor in the afternoon. When *Dark Bridwell* appeared, his publisher, Houghton Mifflin, concerned by the coarseness of the material, insisted that Fisher receive no royalties on the first two thousand copies. It sold less than half that amount. His next novel, *In Tragic Life*, inaugurated the Vridar Hunter tetralogy. Ostensibly fictional—as Fisher insisted, despite his protagonist's silly name—the books were a confession and an exorcism and a manifesto all at once. Into them he poured his frontier traumas, Leona's suicide, frank ideas about sex and philosophy and literature. He altered certain details but not the basic shape of his life. People who knew Fisher said that Vridar Hunter reflected his behavior and attitudes.

Over the next few years, it seemed as though Fisher was outrunning the economic calamity engulfing the rest of the literary world. *In Tragic Life* was published by Caxton Printers, a regional press, but garnered such strong reviews that Doubleday, Doran worked out a co-publication deal for the tetralogy. Doubleday even commissioned the painter Grant Wood—recently acclaimed for *American Gothic* and other works—to create the jacket art for the first two novels. Fisher's rising success also landed him a literary agent, Elizabeth Nowell, who represented his old colleague Thomas Wolfe. But despite the good reviews, the Manhattan agent, and the Grant Wood jacket art, Fisher continued to struggle. His chosen profession was precarious even in the best of circumstances. Now the situation was alarming. In 1933, his Doubleday editor wrote from New York and described "publishing houses curling up and falling off like autumn leaves." (That year, instead of buying its usual 250,000 books, the New York Public Library bought only 50,000, mostly replacement copies of older titles.) By 1935, Fisher's publisher at Caxton reported that conditions in the publishing industry were getting even worse.

When he learned about the FWP job, his most recent book, *We Are Betrayed*, the third installment of the tetralogy, had sold only 2,285 copies between both publishers. "I'm getting ready to throw my typewriter away and hike to the South Seas," he told Harold Merriam in Montana. "Is that a good asylum for a defeated egotist?" When the FWP's telegram arrived, it offered him a salary of $2,600 a year. Then the offer was adjusted to $2,300, ostensibly because Idaho had fewer people on relief. Fisher later admitted that he would have done it for $1,500. Over the last several years, he'd been living on half that amount.

Up to that point, he'd observed the New Deal with a mix of cautious optimism and jaded cynicism. (He still identified, loosely, with the left, but would soon begin sliding toward an ornery libertarianism.) The time had come to exchange observation for participation. "Yes, I'm a Roosevelt man now!" he told Merriam after taking the job. He was less sanguine writing to Elizabeth Nowell in New York: "I feel absurd in going into this work but when a man is financially against a wall and has two sons soon ready for college he does absurd things."

"SCOURING THE HINTERLANDS FOR ROOSEVELT"

When Vardis Fisher became director of the Idaho project, New Deal policies were already reshaping the West. A bevy of federal agencies, especially ones attached to the Departments of Agriculture and the Interior, attempted to stabilize and improve the region. They fought soil erosion, converted marginal farmland for grazing, built new irrigation systems and recreation areas, expanded electrification in the countryside, resettled entire farming communities, reformed how natural resources and public rangelands were managed, and took initial steps toward conserving pristine areas and wildlife populations. CCC and WPA crews took up light construction and improvements while the PWA provided grants for bigger projects. The Office of Indian Affairs, under the directorship of John Collier, implemented an "Indian New Deal" that sought to reverse decades of "cruel and stupid laws" (as Collier put it) designed to parcel out tribal land and repress Native cultures. His office overturned that legacy by working to pass the Indian Reorganization Act, which consolidated land holdings, provided some economic assistance, and encouraged tribal self-government, while Collier rejected policies of forced assimilation and pushed for expanded access to public services, including New Deal programs (such as the CCC's Indian Division). For farmers across the Great Plains—harried by dust storms and locusts after years of overproduction and diminishing soil quality—New Deal policies meant life or death.

Their hired hands and tenants often found work on CCC or WPA crews. Farther west, ranchers, grown accustomed to watching thin cattle roam the land, were bailed out, too. For a time, many farmers and ranchers throughout the region relied on the federal government as their only source of income.

So it was in Idaho, a traditionally Republican state whose leadership flipped with the Democratic sweep of 1932. The AAA, before it was overturned by the Supreme Court, increased crop production and the PWA constructed sewers, schools, and irrigation systems. Federal loans were issued for homeowners and bankrupt farmers. The New Deal's most visible success in the heavily forested state was perhaps the CCC, which employed more than 18,000 young men and paid nearly $7 million to their dependents. Along with the usual light construction, the CCC treated around 2 million acres of trees for blister rust fungus. The WPA employed 22,000 people on 510 projects in the state. On top of all this, the Roosevelt administration's generous policies toward silver—half-heartedly endorsed by the president and other officials but pushed by the "Silver Bloc" in Congress—meant that the US Treasury purchased most output from silver mines in the west, which especially benefited Idaho, the nation's leading silver producer.

The myths of an individualistic, hardscrabble West had always concealed the reality of an active state—activity that most of all appeared in the form of land grants to railroads and homesteaders, and military forces deployed against Native inhabitants and restive laborers. The New Deal just made that arrangement more visible, even though the details changed. Now, to its roster of activist policies west of the Mississippi—shocking interventions, perhaps, for those still beholden to the myths—was added the Idaho writers' project.

Its director, Vardis Fisher, resigned in a huff one week after he started. The resignation didn't stick, but it wouldn't be the last time he threatened to pack it up and walk away.

From the start he was frustrated by the WPA apparatus itself. Nationwide, the WPA was organized on three levels—federal, state, and district. Fisher initially reported at a district WPA office in Pocatello, in southeast Idaho. The Pocatello administrator had never heard of him. So he traveled across the state to Boise, headquarters of the Idaho WPA, and met with its top administrator, J. L. Hood, who was similarly bewildered. Hood's response was typical: the relationship between state WPA administrators and the state writers' projects was murky. Alsberg and the DC staff hired state directors such as Fisher and gave them orders, even though the state writers' projects belonged to that state's WPA machinery. Fisher, in other words, would work *with* J. L. Hood in Idaho, but not *for* him. That suited Fisher fine. Hood wouldn't actually oversee the project, but he was expected to keep an eye on Fisher and report anything objectionable back to the federal WPA, while providing secretarial staff, office space and equipment, and whatever else was needed. But, like quite a few state administrators, Hood was angry that he wasn't allowed to appoint the writers' project director himself.

So the Idaho WPA took it out on Fisher. For the first ten days, Hood's administration essentially ignored him. They claimed that they could spare no office space or stenographic help. Fisher finally wrote to DC: "Damn it, I want an office (I'm weary of standing around in the halls like a fellow hunting a job) and I want some competent help and I want some typewriters and filing cabinets. Without these, how can I be expected to do anything?" Alsberg, and later Jacob Baker, intervened on Fisher's behalf. By Thanksgiving he had a place to work—"a dirty little hole"—with one typewriter, one real desk, and one homemade thing cast aside by other WPA workers. He paid for incidentals out of pocket. Staffing the office became a headache. Hood's secretary told him to hire only "worthy Democrats"—advice Fisher rejected—and the labor assignment office stonewalled him until, again, Hopkins's office had to intervene. Fisher was furious—but conflict only fueled him. He became more committed to making the project work.

He and Margaret moved to an apartment close to downtown Boise, a brisk fifteen-minute walk from the office. On paper, Margaret had no official position—WPA regulations allowed for only one job per household. But Vardis's letters to DC and to his parents suggest that she was just as busy as he was. Margaret, after all, was equally qualified to be the director: she was a Barnard alumna with a PhD from the University of Chicago (her dissertation was on English medieval mystery plays), she'd lectured in college classrooms, and she'd published poems and scholarly articles.

The couple exhausted themselves during those first few weeks. "I was an enormous ass to take the job," Fisher admitted to a friend. But his private misgivings were balanced by optimism and a touch of arrogance. "I'm out in the lead of the pack now and my gang will be putting their nose to the cultural scent while in some other states they are still dickering with Alsberg," he said. "Besides, I cut through a lot of red tape and am still unhanged for it."

Forming that "gang," though, was difficult. "Idaho is not, of course, a state of unemployed writers," he reminded DC. In the twenties and thirties, working writers were clustered in the Northeast and Mid-Atlantic, around Chicago, and in California. Most directors in the less-populated states had trouble hiring workers for their projects. As the Idaho project took shape, Fisher began referring to himself as the only unemployed writer in the entire state. He meant it literally. He often couldn't even find people competent enough to handle stenography and basic research. Still, he maintained a staff that hovered between fifteen and twenty people. He kept some of the workers busy by asking them to copy passages from library books, which he had no intention of using. After less than a year on the job, he fired off an ornery letter to Alsberg. "The preparation of a book like this demands persons trained in research and with the point of view of a scholar who knows that a thing is either right or wrong and that there can be no argument about it," he wrote. "Such persons are not available in this state."

Fisher instead turned to the person who *was* available—himself. Like Sherwood Anderson writing *Puzzled America*, like Lorena Hickok scribbling dispatches to Harry Hopkins, Fisher became a roving observer. He bought a Nash automobile and set out to log around eight thousand miles of Idaho's roadways, and write the tour copy for the guide, alone. Sometimes, he scouted out routes by plane. During these trips, Margaret would wait at home or else visit relatives in California. Once, before leaving for a few weeks, he wrote to his agent, "I'm scouring the hinterlands for Roosevelt to see if any unsung Miltons are out in the Idaho sagebrush."

He found no Miltons but he did find plenty else. After rambling all day, he'd choose a place to stop and then he'd write until midnight, stitching together what he'd seen and heard until he had a portrait of Idaho as glimpsed from one particular route—for instance, the guide's Tour One, a 244.9-mile journey from the Montana border, across the southeastern quadrant of the state (his home territory), to the Utah line. Fisher drove through the thin air of the Targhee Pass, 7,078 feet above sea level, and down through forests of lodgepole pine and Douglas fir and Englemann spruce, land that was an explosion of wildflowers in summer and heaped with so much snow in winter that you could ski over hidden buildings—then to Henry's Lake, known for marshy islands that rose and sank, legendary Native American burial grounds that "vanished and reappeared with their cargo of dead"—and on through a swath of resorts, cabins and campgrounds and dance halls and streams thick with trout—glimpsing, as he drove, the peaks of the Tetons and the Upper and Lower Mesa Falls tumbling over their escarpments—past Ashton, whose famous dog-sled derby was once nearly won by a bulldog—through the Idaho sand dunes, which put him in a lyrical mood: "their soft and shimmering loveliness is to be seen most impressively under a gorgeous sunset, when the flame of the sky falls to the burning gold of the dunes, and the whole earth here rolls away in soft mists of fire"—past the site of Fort Henry, built in 1810 and forgotten until 1927, when someone found a rock carved with the words "Al the cook, but nothing to cook"—then to Driggs, beneath which sat an estimated 11 million tons of unexploited coal—and to Teton Basin, beneath which sat a litter of arrowheads and spearheads and tomahawks from an iniquitous attack on a band of Gros Ventre by white men and allied Indians—through Idaho Falls, where the municipally owned hydroelectric plant makes it "Idaho's most socialistic city, and promises to become in consequence eventually tax-free and the most prosperous one in the State"—through a lava field where, until 1928, stood an ancient juniper that began growing in the year 310—and into Shelley, where Spud Day is celebrated "with choice potatoes on display and with baked potatoes served to passengers on every train and motor coach going through town"—and through Fort Hall, an Indian agency, where the Bannock, Shoshone, and other tribes would hold the Sun Dance, the War Dance, the Owl Dance, the Rabbit Dance, the Grass Dance, and the Warm Dance in winter and the Easter Dance in spring, nearby old Fort Hall, built in 1834, where westering white migrants once looked for the "H.B.C." flag above its ramparts, standing for "Hudson's Bay Company, but meaning, old trappers said, Here Before Christ"—past the Malad River, "named by French-Canadian trappers, though whether they were made ill from drinking the water or from overgorging on the flesh of beaver seems not to be known"—and on to Preston, where, in 1863, US forces attacked the Bannock Indians, who were "so badly defeated that Franklin settlers who visited the battleground the next day declared that 'you could walk on dead Indians for quite a distance without touching ground'"—and finally into Franklin, "the first permanent white settlement in Idaho," founded by Mormons in 1860, where a 10,000-pound steam engine (shipped by Brigham Young up the Missouri River and hundreds of miles overland) once sat discarded on the roadside after years of use, until the people of Franklin reclaimed it as a historic relic and put it on display, which is where Vardis Fisher, pulling into town in his dusty and overheated Nash, saw it, presumably.

These sites accounted for just a handful of stops in Tour One, and Fisher was busy assembling ten more tours. Together, they'd form a portrait of Idaho that was fragmentary, piecemeal, but revealing in ways that an essay could never be. The conquest of the frontier was there, alongside the old myths of rugged settlers and doomed races and the bloody roots of civilization. But it was all chopped up and jumbled up, its narrative encasement broken, the pieces spilled and left to mingle with images and anecdotes from ten or twenty years ago, or that day. The tours showed the wreckage and glories of the past piled up in the present, there for you to explore and make sense of on your own. The tours were invitations, and federal writers were busy composing them in every state.

"THE RUBRIC OF THE EAST WIND"

Vardis Fisher's domination of the Idaho project was, he claimed, a solution to the problem of local scarcity. But it was also an expression of his personality. In the man who took up such a task—crisscrossing the state, composing every tour, writing page upon page of essays—it was easy to see the child who read and reread the Bible, or the student whom one professor called "a book drunkard" and who studied himself into a half-blind stupor. Fisher's directorship was, in a sense, an act of literary homesteading: he cleared the land, raised the buildings, planted the crops, tended the livestock, and stood to reap the rewards.

His approach was unusual. But it was productive and, over the course of the FWP's first full year, autumn 1935 to autumn 1936, Fisher made enviable progress toward finishing a manuscript. By that time, most of the other guides poised for early publication came from New England. This was perhaps appropriate. New England's place in the national mythology was well understood: it was the realm of Pilgrim fathers and patriot graves, its town meetings were the incubators of American democracy, its mills the first engines of American industry (or so the feeling went). But the myths of New England were also coming under increased scrutiny, especially with regard to Puritanism and its legacy. For most of the nineteenth century, writers and civic leaders treated the Puritan model as a gift bestowed by history: a lesson in self-restraint, hard work, moral rectitude, self-government, and community spirit, one learned by each passing generation. Some writers took a more ambivalent view (think Hawthorne and Emerson), but it wasn't until the 1880s that Puritanism, as both trope and historical practice, was the target of sustained criticism. By the twenties, that criticism had flowered into a full-on backlash—which, of course, was itself contested. Writers, varying in purpose and seriousness, sought to tear down the Puritan mystique by flinging charges of tyranny, theocracy, censoriousness, and repression—H. L. Mencken leveled all these charges and more in his searing essay "Puritanism: A Literary Force," from *A Book of Prefaces*. The Puritan legacy, no longer a gift, was declared a fetter on the development of the American personality, or perhaps a gloomy burden that weighed too heavily on the modern spirit.

The Massachusetts project was born into this context. It would have been clear to its workers, as well as to the national editors in DC, that the Bay State had a *meaning* in a sense that many states did not, and that this meaning was, in the thirties, very much in play. Katharine Kellock understood this, as she explained to an editor in Boston: "The story of how the people of a key State have made their livings for three centuries, the aspirations expressed in their buildings, clubs, libraries, monuments, the religious, patriotic and social squabbles that have moved them—that is a picture of the rise of Massachusetts civilization, which, to some extent, is that of the United States." A guide to Massachusetts, with its lofty place in the nation's history and mythology, was inevitably a book about the fundamentals of the American character.

The project's workers, meanwhile, were more consumed by the immediate challenges of getting it up and running. Massachusetts was among the larger projects, beginning with roughly 350 workers and, for the rest of the decade, fluctuating at around 200. (Only California, Illinois, Pennsylvania, and New York City were larger.) The choice of director was crucial. The first, an historian and archivist from Harvard, turned out to be a dud. Advisors to the project, such as the historian Arthur Schlesinger, Sr., and future Supreme Court justice (and Henry Alsberg's friend) Felix Frankfurter, paid close attention. Eventually, they hired another Harvard-educated historian: Ray Billington, a young professor at Clark University who'd done his dissertation under Schlesinger. Billington was destined for eminence as a scholar of the American West, but in 1936 he was in his early thirties and a few years into his first teaching gig. Unlike Fisher, who attempted to run the project himself, Billington delegated with ease. He didn't even work in the office full time.

The scene that confronted Billington when he first arrived in Boston— "a roaring maelstrom," he called it—was typical of the FWP's early days:

> All reason and order seemed to have fled as writers converted reams of copy paper into the manuscripts that would justify their continued employment, as each day's mail from Washington brought orders that contradicted those of the day before, as district supervisors shouted their opposition to each procedural change and the state director helped keep the telephone company alive by relaying their invective to his superiors in Washington.

For Billington, it was not administrative maneuvering that he found most difficult about the job. He was deeply affected by the destitute figures who shuffled in and applied for spots on the project. "To watch their bleak, downcast eyes, their broken spirit, their air of sullen defiance, was a heart-rending experience," he wrote. (Compare that with Vardis Fisher, who coldly informed Alsberg that "most of the college graduates on relief in Idaho are incompetents either because of stupidity or age.") But Billington found his reward in the sight of workers transformed by their jobs: he saw it in their expressions and their postures, and also in their new shoes and winter coats.

As *Massachusetts: A Guide to Its Places and People* took shape, it addressed squarely Kellock's suggestion. "Clues to Its Character," the opening essay, avoids homilies on Plymouth Rock and the spirit of 1776. Instead, it admits to groping for a symbol that would capture the contradictory nature of the Bay Stater: "He has been pictured as a kind of dormant volcano, the red-hot lava from one eruption hardening into a crater which impedes the next; as a river, with two main currents of transcendental metaphysics and catchpenny opportunism running side by side; as an asocial discord consisting mainly of overtones and undertones; as a petrified backbone, 'that unblossoming stalk.'" (The last phrase is borrowed from Van Wyck Brooks, whose literary history *The Flowering of New England*—emblematic of the heightened interest in the region and the Americana turn in general, and a revision of his earlier anti-Puritan writings—had just appeared.) All of these symbols were inadequate, the guide suggests, before offering its own: "the rubric of the east wind." It was the east wind that blew English ships and their cargoes of religious rebels to Provincetown and then to Plymouth harbor, and it was the wind that intermittently returned to shake things up: a symbol for spiritual dissenters and utopian communities, the Minutemen and Daniel Shays, agitators for women's rights and abolition and educational reform, striking millworkers and mutinous whalers, all forming an inevitable pattern of rebellion and conformity and rebellion again. "It is a State of tradition, but part of its tradition is its history of revolt. Its people are fiercely individualistic, yet they have fierce group loyalties. It is noted for conservatism, yet it exports not only shoes and textiles but rebels to all corners of the earth." This theme spreads across the other essays, in the idea that the Massachusetts story is primarily a history of the American experiment in self-government, and that the revolution of 1776 was reborn around 1830—when restive laborers, organizing for workplace rights and political representation, fought to expand the promises of democracy. And while the guide doesn't skimp on the stuff of traditional histories, it boldly celebrates the changing face of the state: "Many new strands have been added to Anglo-Saxon culture," it says. "Slavic, Semitic, and Celtic influences have permeated Massachusetts thought, enriching folkways, enlivening speech, and giving a new perspective to graphic art, music and literature." Sometimes forcefully and often subtly, the Massachusetts guide projects a democratic, pluralistic sensibility that would have appealed to New Dealers and those further to the left who, as the Depression held on, were becoming increasingly preoccupied with the idea of a usable and *revolutionary* American past.

The guide did contain one conspicuous fault line. It ran between two essays, printed side by side: "Literature," by the poet Conrad Aiken, and "Literary Groups and Movements," by radical federal writers who were appalled by Aiken's individualistic—and therefore inherently suspect—analysis.

Aiken was recruited to the Massachusetts project by Alsberg himself; though his *Selected Poems* had won the Pulitzer Prize several years earlier, he badly needed the money. As a poet, he was known for a diverse body of work that, while well regarded, drifted across many forms and styles. His poems, like those of his friend and contemporary T. S. Eliot, were often demanding. He never tried to be fashionable, and he found more support among critics than from the reading public, so he needed to supplement his verse with short fiction and criticism—and, eventually, a federal paycheck. For a writer uncomfortable with the political mood of the time, one who wrote in *The New Republic* in defense of complete autonomy for the individual artist, it was not a welcome development.

He worked on the project for only five months, doing his writing at home, before he quit, put off by the "Commies" and "hopelessly incompetent" with whom he was forced to work. Billington included both literature essays in the guide as a compromise; he didn't want to alter a single word of Aiken's "literary gem" but feared antagonizing "our communist and near-communist friends" on the project. Aiken made other contributions, too, including the description of Deerfield, one of forty-seven town profiles from Amherst to Worcester. Aiken's weird and lyrical portrait invoked King Philip's War and represented the best of the guidebooks' convention-shattering style: this "ghost of a town, its dimness almost transparent, its quiet almost a cessation . . . is saying, 'I dared to be beautiful, even in the shadow of the wilderness'; but it is also saying, 'And the wilderness haunts me, the ghosts of a slain race are in my doorways and clapboards, like a kind of death.'" (What tourists and sightseers were meant to do with this description of Deerfield was anybody's guess.)

The editors in DC grew frustrated as reams and reams of tour copy arrived from Massachusetts. They drew their pencils through the interminable town halls and war monuments and private schools—"dull and inconsequential padding," as Joseph Gaer put it. Gaer was a field representative who'd become editor-in-chief of the New England guides, a job that stuck him uncomfortably between DC and the state projects. He found himself acting as an advocate for the local offices, especially as DC fiddled with the smallest details. "I do not see how Washington can begin requesting now that we should lasso or Shanghai some professor on his vacation to read, verify and prove that drunkenness in Maine long ago did not carry the same 'immoral' connotation," he wrote in a huff. (Alsberg sympathized. "I know you are having a deuce of a time with this job," he told Gaer. "The details that have to be watched are countless, but I am sure you will put the books over successfully.") The epic task of editing the Massachusetts tours fell to Katharine Kellock and one assistant. Together they checked and condensed the 200,000 words of copy that arrived in DC, and eventually wrestled it down to half. Kellock believed that the material was shaping up wonderfully—although, by her typically exacting standards, it could always be better.

Follow those tours and you'll come upon the expected: Indian trails and village greens, Thoreau's beanfield, Harriet Beecher Stowe's grave, old churches, old homes, old taverns. But also the less expected: a Cape Cod movie theater, Cape Cinema, among the country's smallest and decorated with murals by Rockwell Kent; a spot in Northborough, where, in 1884, the earth gave up the bones and teeth of a mastodon; "Beartown Mountain, for years the home of a hermit known as Beartown Beebe, whose weather predictions were published in many metropolitan dailies"; a church in Ipswich standing beside a rock with a cloven hoofprint left there by the devil; a piece of the Neponset River outside Walpole, where, during King Philip's War, British troops crossing a bridge witnessed a lunar eclipse and were struck by terrifying visions of "Indians and dripping scalps"; a fish-freezing plant where "the freezer is able to freeze everything—except the smell of fish"; a monument near Plainville marking the site of a boundary tree that once separated the Massachusetts Bay and Plymouth Colonies, and on which hung a sign: "Beyond this line Roger Williams may not goe."

And yet Massachusetts, for all the weighty cargo of meaning it carried, would not be the first American Guide presented to the public. That distinction, Alsberg believed, should belong to Washington, DC. There, in the national office, a team of twenty workers was scrambling to assemble *Washington: City and Capital*. The book was going to be massive. As they heaped notes upon notes, draft upon draft, tapping the resources of offices scattered across the federal government, they found themselves looking at a manuscript of roughly a million words. Some exuberant editing brought it down to about 450,000. The guide took on a unique shape: there were essays and tours and points of interest described in detail (the White House, the Folger Shakespeare Library, the Colonial Dames of America headquarters), followed by a hefty roster of federal departments, agencies, bureaus, commissions, boards, courts, authorities, administrations, and military installations, from the Procurement Division to the Naval Observatory to the Central Heating Plant. It was, in a sense, a performance—an overwhelming display of the FWP's ability to publish something substantive and valuable. And surely there was another motive at work in the exhaustive coverage: to firm up support for the FWP from various officeholders through flattery and attention to their offices.

The editors responsible for *Washington: City and Capital* faced a peculiar challenge. As they worked on the manuscript, they were bombarded by incoming copy from the states. The DC guidebook, they would explain in its preface, became a "training ground" as they prepared to tackle the rest of the American Guides. "The book had to be written while material for State guides, pouring into the Washington office sometimes at the rate of 50,000 words a day, was edited," they explained. "As a matter of fact, the central staff itself had to search for and find the necessary technique, a combination of painstaking accuracy and a lively appreciation of the colorful and interesting in the American scene, before it could presume to issue correct and effective instructions to the State staffs." Writing the DC guide, in other words, meant inventing both a product and a procedure.

They understood that the guide would have a national audience, and not only because readers would be intrigued by the FWP's novelty. The District of Columbia loomed in the American mind like no other site in the nation; it was the seat of an emotional magnetism that drew attention to its symbols and proceedings from everywhere in the country. It drew the people themselves, of course, too. Tourists who disembarked from their trains in Union Station discovered a deeply familiar scene, one they seemed to know as well as they knew their own communities. "They are thoroughly at home here in a historic and political atmosphere which they have breathed vicariously since childhood, and amid surroundings which they have seen pictured countless times," as the guide put it. This desire to experience the capital, which compelled its nearly 2 million yearly visitors, would likewise inspire a more distant audience to take an immersive, textual journey through the guidebook—from an easy chair in Nebraska, say, or a train car in Oregon. They'd heave the guide onto their laps and read the essays, which hit the usual notes (historical development, climate, architecture) but also topics particular to the city, such as the L'Enfant plan for the layout of its streets and "The Negro in Washington," a trenchant and sympathetic account of its African American citizens "who, from the start, exerted a profound influence upon the city's destiny"— even in the face of that grave and persistent contradiction between democracy and slavery, and then democracy and segregation. (Whether this essay would be a template for future guides or an outlier, the editors did not yet know.) Readers would peruse the points of interest which followed the essays and enjoy a lively, granular view of contemporary Washington. And while the tours were a little heavy on bronze statues and eminent residences—these were citywide, not statewide, jaunts, after all—they contained the FWP's distinct, temporally layered mix of the strange and the mundane, the brilliant and the ugly: a block off Pennsylvania Avenue, recently "obliterated" by the expansion of the mall, where, in 1932, protesting Bonus Army veterans were driven out by US troops, and where, sixty-eight years earlier, Walt Whitman "occupied a wretched third-floor bedroom"; a house in Georgetown, "scarcely 11 feet wide and hardly two complete stories high," wedged flush between two other homes, "said to have been built a century ago as 'spite work' to cut off a neighbor's light"; an old brick building, once the site of a nineteenth-century fire brigade, where now stands "a memorial plaque to Bush, a beloved mascot dog killed by poison"—the victim, perhaps, of a rival brigade.

Local variations on these tours were taking shape in every state office as federal writers prepared their guidebook manuscripts. Progress was uneven, certainly, but still, there was progress. And while the American Guides remained the central task, as Alsberg repeatedly stressed, the FWP was tentatively pushing into new areas that might serve as the basis for stand-alone publications: collecting folklore and individual life histories, conducting studies of ethnic groups, and seeking out the testimonials of formerly enslaved people. All these undertakings would ramp up in subsequent years. Meanwhile, the FWP's cousin project, the WPA Historical Records Survey, was sending its own workers into the archives of every single county, in an ambitious attempt to locate, assess, and preserve vital documents and then publish detailed inventories of what they found there. (The HRS was awkwardly stuffed into the FWP's portfolio and overseen by a young academic, Luther Evans. Alsberg, ostensibly in charge, had little interest, and after a confusing year, the HRS was broken off into a separate project under Evans's control, as the fifth component of Federal #1.) By the end of the decade, its workers were assessing, organizing, and indexing all manner of state and local archives, manuscript collections, church records, early American books and pamphlets and broadsides, and even painted portraits. They made original discoveries as well. As one federal writer put it, HRS workers were exploring "courthouse lofts and library cellars, where only the pigeons and mice had been before them, and have brought out records of which historians had no knowledge"—including forgotten letters from Lincoln and "the divorce proceedings of Alexander Hamilton's mother."

With this swirl of activity under his command, Alsberg fixed upon an immediate goal: he and the national editors would push *Washington: City and Capital* over the finish line and hold it up as the inaugural American Guide. It would be a grand statement of the FWP's capability and value, and a thundering rejoinder to its critics. The New England guides, and specifically Massachusetts, crucible of the nation, would appropriately come next. The Idaho guide, being busily assembled by an exasperated Vardis Fisher, out there somewhere over the western horizon, could come along whenever.

"THE WRATH OF IDAHO"

By the time George Cronyn received a telegram from Boise with a single sentence—"WHY THE DEVIL DON'T YOU SEND THAT PAGE PROOF BACK"—relations between Vardis Fisher and DC had bottomed out. The closer Fisher came to finishing the guide, the more he clashed with the editors. By letter and telegram and phone, they argued over issues large and small. DC insisted that Fisher remove digs at the city of Pocatello (the "ugliest of the larger Idaho cities"), the popular western novelist Zane Grey, and the state of Wyoming. They argued over Fisher's description of the bombing assassination of the former governor Frank Steunenberg and his comparison of Mount Borah with the senator it was named for (both "fat and flabby"). Fisher was perpetually incensed over what he thought were unclear, conflicting directions. After he took the job, he'd made himself plain to George Cronyn: "What I want is explicit and irrevocable orders to go ahead as I was first instructed to or an invitation to resign." But Fisher found that many orders were neither explicit nor irrevocable. Eventually, whenever he received a new message from Washington, he just shoved it into the furnace, unread.

The tours were a major flashpoint. Fisher balked at instructions to make the main tours—ones that connected to routes in neighboring states—flow in uniform directions: north to south and east to west. He thought this was "absurd" in a state where much of the traffic on major highways flowed from south to north, and he said so. (On this point, he wasn't alone. The Massachusetts editors would join Fisher's crusade against uniform tour directions—an east-to-west tour that began in Provincetown, they pointed out, required travelers to drive up the Cape, turn around, and retrace their route.) But Alsberg and Katharine Kellock were adamant, for matters not only practical but philosophical: the guides were intended to be a uniform, repeatable container for material about each state. Fisher tried recruiting some of Idaho's leading citizens to protest the decision, to no avail. When Fisher finally relented, he telegrammed Cronyn: "WE WILL DO ALL OF THEM FROM NORTH TO SOUTH AND THE WRATH OF IDAHO AND THE ILLOGIC OF THE DIRECTION CAN BE ON YOUR HEAD."

Fisher eventually described himself as a man who'd made a huge mistake but was too proud to quit. The hectic schedule and exhausting weeks of travel for the tours were bad enough; he also worried that he was wasting tax dollars and enabling graft. He fumed after each showdown with DC. And as he gathered material for the guide, he struggled to sift facts from masses of dubious information. On the eve of yet another road trip, he wrote to a friend:

> This poor fool who ought to have remained in isolation up among the beaver is not only at the end of his wits. He has no wits left. All night I breathe in my sleep, "Don doggle that bon, don't doggle that boon, ton't boggle that doon," and all day I race around to discover that what I thought was a fact is only a fiction. Of 4,326 facts which I had compiled a month ago, only six remain, and one of them is that there are no facts in Idaho.

But he couldn't deny the sheer pleasure of the work. He boasted to his parents that, by the time the guide was finished, he'd know more about Idaho than anyone. He was almost becoming a tall tale himself, the man who could talk for ten hours about Idaho and never tell everything he knew.

In DC, Alsberg left most of the skirmishing to Cronyn and other editors. He seemed to regard Fisher with amusement and irritation. Alsberg, it was said, divided people who worked for him into two categories: the amusing and the boring. Fisher, though he was many things, was not a bore. Once, Alsberg wrote to Fisher to remind him that it was unacceptable for the guide-book to point out which towns were ugly, even if it was true. "After all, the inhabitants of these towns are going to have to put up the money for the pub-lication of the Idaho Guide and, no matter how ugly the home towns, they are going to object to telling the world that," Alsberg wrote. He then added mis-chievously: "It may be possible to get in your criticisms indirectly—perhaps by praising the towns that have endeavored to improve their appearances." In general, though, Alsberg drew a firm line against overly opinionated, per-sonalized copy. Vardis Fisher, in this context, was not a private writer but a government employee; his job was to serve the project and not vice versa. (Under no circumstances, Alsberg announced, could Fisher reproduce in the guide, verbatim, an essay that he'd published in a recent issue of *Esquire*— and he certainly couldn't include a permission credit for the author, Vardis Fisher.) This didn't mean that Alsberg wanted writers to denude their prose of what made it vibrant and distinctive. He admired Fisher precisely because his writing had verve and personality. And, in perhaps the ultimate test of a guidebook, it inspired in Alsberg, who'd likely never set foot in Idaho, a desire to travel there.

Soon Fisher had something to show for his labors in the Idaho sagebrush. The project issued a pamphlet, *Tours in Eastern Idaho*, a sampling of the guidebook material. It was proof that the FWP was making progress, one of a handful of small, local publications released in 1936—the first items pub-lished by the FWP. Among them was a guide to Matawan, New Jersey; Penn-sylvania's *3 Hikes Thru the Wissahickon* (which sold five thousand copies); and a guide to North Little Rock, Arkansas. Alsberg regarded the latter as "a very poor little thing" but nonetheless presented it to the WPA administrator in New York City, an army colonel who happened to be from Arkansas. The colonel replied, "Who in the hell wants a guide to North Little Rock? Don't you know it's the asshole of the world?"

Alsberg, undaunted, pushed ahead toward the real prize: the first of the American Guides, beginning with Washington, DC. But then came news from Idaho. Fisher had already made arrangements with the local publisher Caxton Printers and delivered his manuscript to them. That was in September 1936, and the guide would be off press on January 2, beating DC and all the rest. Alsberg was taken aback, and before long the DC office began bombarding Fisher with corrections. They insisted that he'd included mistakes, ignored editorial instructions, and hadn't conformed to the most recent tour format. Fisher thought this was bunk and said so. On one occasion, the staff of the Idaho project gathered around the phone while Fisher delivered a profane reply to Alsberg that at least one federal writer thought would get them all fired. DC was delaying him, Fisher charged, so that *Washington: City and Capital* could appear first. Eventually, Alsberg admitted that he was right.

Fisher's surprise arrangement with Caxton wasn't a simple matter. By law—or the DC office's understanding of it, at least—publications created by a federal agency such as the FWP needed to be printed by the Government Printing Office. But the GPO was hardly set up for trade books, aesthetically or practically, and it had no marketing or distribution apparatus. Instead, Fisher devised a neat workaround. He persuaded the Idaho secretary of state to act as the guide's "sponsor" and then sign a contract directly with Caxton, along with an agreement to transfer any royalties to the US Treasury. Fisher surely was thinking of getting his guide out as quickly as possible, by whatever means necessary. But he created the model, perhaps inadvertently, that was adopted by the project in every state. The sponsors were typically agencies or officials at the state or municipal level, or sometimes state historical societies. In a few instances, such as in New Jersey and New York City, private citizens formed a "guild" to act as the sponsor. Alsberg meanwhile hired a young national coordinating editor, Jerre Mangione, to handle all matters involving the various sponsors and publishers. (Mangione, like Katharine Kellock, came to the FWP by way of the Resettlement Administration. He happened to share a rented house with other New Deal bureaucrats, including Henry Alsberg, who urged him to join the writers' project. "Let some yokel worry about the destitute farmers," Alsberg said. "You'll do better worrying about destitute writers.") If the FWP was the collective author of the American Guides, then Mangione was its literary agent.

The wisdom of Fisher's deal with Caxton wasn't enough to mollify Alsberg and the DC staff, who were still unwilling to accept Idaho as the very first guide. But Fisher held firm. "Halting this book now will shake this state from end to end with angry criticism," he promised. He was proud of his work and insisted that the guide would "be ready to shove under the noses of Congressmen" in time for the next session in January. "I repeat again that it will be a book that they will have some difficulty in sniffing at, even though some of the gentlemen may be most extraordinary sniffers," he told Alsberg.

DC pressed for more and more corrections and accused Fisher of ignoring previous ones. He erupted in a six-page letter, insisting that many of their changes were wrong, that he was hopelessly overworked, that George Cronyn was thin-skinned, and that they were spiking his book with grammatical and stylistic travesties. "I have taught advanced composition in four American universities and I fancied that I had some knowledge of these matters of grammar and emphasis and style," he wrote. "It appears that I have not." Then he threatened to resign.

Finally, on November 7, Alsberg took decisive action and dispatched George Cronyn, in the flesh, to Idaho. Cronyn carried with him a powerful weapon: a briefcase containing nearly two thousand corrections. Meanwhile, Fisher contacted J. H. Gipson, the publisher of Caxton Printers, and they cooked up a plan. When Cronyn arrived, Fisher brought him to Gipson's house, where they were to have dinner, go over the changes, and decide which photographs to use in the guide. Fisher and Gipson set their plan in motion: they drank water colored to look like whiskey while serving Cronyn—an avid drinker—the real deal. They calmly agreed to work out a compromise. Meanwhile, Cronyn got drunk. Then he got drunker. As they went over the photographs, Cronyn began flinging them around the room, discarding Fisher and Gipson's choices and insisting—he was adamant on this point—that the guide contain no photos of potatoes. At the end of the night, Fisher bundled Cronyn into a car, sped to the train station, and put him on an eastbound train. Then he and Gipson went ahead with the guide, more or less as they planned.

Both DC and Boise fired a few more salvos. But *Idaho: A Guide in Word and Picture* appeared on schedule in January 1937—the first of the American Guides, as Fisher intended.

He had written nearly the entire thing. Two of the essays—"History of Idaho Indians" and "Anthropology of Idaho Indians"—Fisher assigned to his indispensable secretary, Ruth Lyon. The description of Pocatello was written by "the businessmen of that city," according to the foreword (which did not explain, of course, that Alsberg had rejected Fisher's earlier, disparaging draft). Otherwise, the rest was his.

It showed. The guide begins with a strangely pugnacious essay on Idaho history and mythmaking. Here it is—the first paragraph of the first of the American Guides, the opening salvo of the FWP's signature achievement—in full:

> After three centuries of adventurous seeking, the American continent has been explored and settled, and the last frontier is gone. The lusty and profane extremes of it still live nebulously in the gaudy imbecilities of newsstand pulp magazines and in cheap novels, wherein to appease the hunger of human beings for drama and spectacle, heroines distressingly invulnerable are fought over by villains and heroes and restored to their rich properties of mine or cattle ranch; and the villain, if left unslain, passes out of the story sulking darkly; and the hero, without cracking a smile, stands up with the heroine clinging to his breast and addresses the reader with platitudes that would slay any ordinary man. But these villains with their Wild Bill mustaches, these apple-cheeked heroines agog with virtue, and these broad adolescent heroes who say "gosh ding it" and shoot with deadly accuracy from either hand are remote in both temper and character from the persons who built the West. They are shoddy sawdust counterfeits who would have been as much out of place in the old West as Chief Nampuh with his huge feet would have been among the theatrical ineptitudes of a Victorian tea.

And so it continues through the guide's 431 pages, a mosaic portrait of Idaho assembled from historical anecdotes and contemporary data and finely wrought descriptions of the state's natural wonders, narrated by a voice that is by turns sardonic and invigorated, occasionally somber, but rarely flat. The guide is crisscrossed by the footsteps of white trappers and missionaries and prospectors, of the Shoshone and Nez Percé and Bannock nations, of pious Mormons and whiskey-drunk murderers, of Chief Joseph and Captain Bonneville. It is full of massacre sites and ranches accessible only by foot or hoof. There is an abundance of hot springs and lava fields and waterfalls and caves, caves, caves—every major cave gets its own long, lyrical passage, evoked with more attentive detail than anything else in the state. There is no separate section profiling cities and towns, unlike in subsequent American Guides (such descriptions are absorbed into the tours). But there are essays unique to it: on the state's remote "primitive area," buried treasure, ghost towns, and tall tales, and a closing piece on Idaho place-names and their origins, all derived from Indians and white settlers, a fraught encounter that forms the basis of the state's identity.

Compared with later guides, this one is curiously unpeopled—its portrait of Idaho is dominated by natural wonders and stories of the dead. During revisions, an editor in DC chided Fisher for skimping on the preceding thirty years: "But what has happened in Idaho since Theodore Roosevelt was President?" It was a flaw he never quite remedied. Living Idahoans, the guide implies, consisted of Indians emasculated by the reservation system, far-flung and isolated ethnic groups such as Basques, and white descendants of pioneers puzzling out how to live in the modern era. Details on contemporary life in the state—its workplaces, transportation, cultural scenes, local government—are conspicuously meager.

When copies of *Idaho: A Guide in Word and Picture* arrived in DC, Henry Alsberg sent one to Harry Hopkins with a note. The rest of the American Guides would be somewhat different, he explained, in part because Idaho was the first and in part because Fisher was so obstinate. "We had a constant struggle with him to make him adhere, even to the extent he has, to our prescribed forms," Alsberg said. But he couldn't argue with the finished product. "The compensation for sins of omission and commission in the text is to be found in the vivid style in which the book is written. In this respect this State Guide Book will be unique, since it bears throughout the stamp of Vardis Fisher's unusual personality."

The guide was marked by Fisher's personality, or maybe his ego, in another way: a larger trim size. All the subsequent guides would measure 5.5 by 8.25 inches, a standard maintained by different publishers. But Fisher's guide was 6 by 9.25 inches. Placed on a shelf alongside the rest—as the books inevitably were, in homes and libraries and government offices—the Idaho guide stood out ever so slightly.

Its publication was met with a wave of favorable reviews from around the country. The popular historians Bernard DeVoto and Bruce Catton each wrote a glowing appraisal that took the guide as proof of the FWP's potential for greatness. (Eventually, there would appear more than two hundred reviews in magazines and newspapers—all of them positive.) Alsberg sent Fisher his own assessment: "It is a swell book and has already received favorable comment from officials here in the Works Progress Administration." He invited Fisher to visit Washington to discuss his plans—a truce. Fisher arrived in April. Alsberg, in his playful and conciliatory way, started calling him "the bad boy of the Project." Cronyn, whom Fisher had last seen while shoving him onto an eastbound train, drunk and disoriented, threw a party for his foe at his own home. Among the guests was Katharine Kellock, who had clashed with Fisher as much as anyone, especially over the tours. In fact, her reputation for stubbornness and tenacity rivaled Fisher's own. Of the core DC staff, she was less admiring of Fisher's idiosyncratic guidebook— she thought it was self-indulgent. When Kellock arrived at the party, she saw Cronyn standing beside a man she didn't recognize. "There she is," Cronyn said to the man, and then turned to Kellock. "Here's Fisher." For a brief moment, the two regarded each other. Then Fisher gave her a hug and kissed her and said, "Now do you forgive me?"

"THE GOVERNMENT OF THE FUTURE"

In April 1937, the same month that Vardis Fisher journeyed to Washington, the FWP's guide to the District of Columbia appeared. So began a furious publicity operation. Alsberg sent copies of *Washington: City and Capital* to every senator and representative, cabinet member, and governor, plus the WPA administrators and major newspapers. This was no mean feat: the guide was 1,141 pages long and weighed more than five pounds. The Government Printing Office, its ostensible publisher, was responsible for the bulky format, the heavy coated paper, and the thick, black cloth binding. (As it rushed the guide into print, the DC office was still grappling with the Vardis Fisher model of contracting with commercial publishers through sponsors.) The first copies arrived at WPA headquarters and Harry Hopkins made the obligatory doorstop joke. Franklin Roosevelt gazed at the book thoughtfully and then asked if it came with a steamer trunk. And yet the overall response from government offices, as well as from the press, was positive.

The guide's imposing bulk may have screamed bureaucratic dullness, which no doubt caused some readers to avoid disabusing themselves of this impression. But *Washington: City and Capital* contained a subtle argument in favor of the New Deal apparatus that created it. Here and there, it mentions creative ways the administration had put people to work: artists employed by the PWAP and the Treasury Section to decorate government buildings, WPA workers creating enclosures for alligators and crocodiles in the National Zoo, relief workers paid by the PWA to remodel the White House kitchen. And as the guide proceeds through its final section, that long roster of government bodies beginning with the venerable executive departments, it begins to resemble a New Deal greatest-hits collection. In 1937, when the guide appeared, many of these offices were new and still controversial: the Tennessee Valley Authority, the Securities and Exchange Commission, the Social Security Board. And yet they appear here as normal, reasonable, beneficial elements of the federal machinery like any others. The roster concludes with a chapter on the "Emergency Administrations," a mini-history of how the New Deal had revolutionized public works and relief through its arsenal of acronyms, culminating in the WPA. Readers who made it that far, to page 1037, were likely either cheered or startled by this sentence: "Thus the emergency organizations which are here described (as they were functioning on December 15, 1936) have far more than a historical interest; they show the Government of the future in the making." Here was the true meaning of the guide: it was a portrait of the national government during a vast and unprecedented expansion of federal power. For those who welcomed such an expansion, the hefty guide was a fitting symbol of its boldness and comprehensiveness. But for those opposed, the guide was a different type of symbol: an overstuffed and overwhelming waste of money, and a weighty burden for the individual citizen, attempting to navigate their relationship with the state, to lug around.

With its first two American Guides completed, the DC staff threw themselves a party. They gathered at the rambling old house on Wisconsin Avenue where Henry Alsberg, the national coordinating editor Jerre Mangione, and two of Harry Hopkins's aides were living. Alsberg was out of town but the staff got on well enough without him. The party drifted from celebration into mild debauchery, fueled by martinis served out of a punch bowl. Jacob Baker, Alsberg's old friend who'd been instrumental in launching the FWP and the rest of Federal #1, was there—although he'd just been forced out of his position. His relationship with Eleanor Roosevelt had always been strained, and it finally triggered a reassignment. Hopkins planned to send Baker to Europe to study cooperatives while one of his subordinates, Ellen Woodward, a friend of the First Lady's, took his place. Baker thought it was a stab in the back—he believed Hopkins chose loyalty to the Roosevelts over loyalty to him—but he accepted the decision. At the party, he got roaring drunk and eventually jumped into his car to get Chinese food. When he insisted that others join him, a few people entered the back seat of the car through one door and then fled through the other, leaving Baker to speed off into the night, alone—and away from the FWP for good.

Ellen Woodward kept her distance from Baker during the party and took the opportunity to meet the DC staff. She'd emerged from Democratic politics in Mississippi to become one of the highest-ranking women in the Roosevelts' inner circle, second perhaps only to Labor Secretary Frances Perkins. Now, she oversaw all Women's and Professional Projects for the WPA and was, essentially, Alsberg's boss—the link between him and Hopkins. She drifted through the gathering wearing an orchid, a veteran of political schmoozes, and chatted with FWP workers, including the few African Americans on staff. Eventually, word of the integrated party reached Theodore Bilbo, the senator of her home state. On the Senate floor, in the middle of a speech that was very long and, even for the time, staggeringly racist, Bilbo sprang to Woodward's defense and insisted that she'd been tricked, "thrust into this motley melee of miscegenated mongrels and full-blooded Ethiopians," this "off-colored party of mental prostitutes," by her hosts—chiefly "Henry Alsberg, a white man." Bilbo didn't realize that Alsberg hadn't been at home, but still he continued: "If this deception had been practiced in her native State, Mississippi, those who perpetrated it would have decorated the tallest magnolia tree available nearby before the sound of revelry from the party had died out upon the midnight air. Thus would have been avenged the honor and the good name of southern womanhood." It was a chilling reminder that the most reactionary forces arrayed against the FWP, those opposed to any kind of inclusive portrait of America, were not just hiding behind white hoods or lurking in German American Bund camps but were perched, like Bilbo, in the highest ranks of the government. (In the aftermath, the New York City project director wrote to Alsberg, "I am pleased to learn that you really are a white man!")

As the DC office prepared the next raft of American Guides, Alsberg opened the bidding to commercial and university publishers, sending letters to around fifty of them. The response was encouraging. Simon and Schuster was interested in picking up the entire series, but the list was ultimately carved up among several publishers. Houghton Mifflin acquired all six New England guides. Random House and Viking split the mid-Atlantic states, while the former took New York City and the latter a handful more states in the South and West. Oxford University Press and Hastings House bought up many of the rest. In the scramble for contracts, the president of Random House, Bennett Cerf, wrote to the president of the United States asking him to put in a good word—with Henry Alsberg. The private houses understood that, while guidebooks were nothing new, the scale and scope of the FWP's work was unprecedented. As an undertaking involving thousands, it could never have been approached except as a vigorous public effort.

Houghton Mifflin published four of the New England guides in the second half of 1937, to roundly favorable reviews; Connecticut and New Hampshire followed in 1938. With these books, the FWP settled on the American Guide template: essays, city and town profiles, tours. *Massachusetts: A Guide to Its Places and People* seemed more than capable of meeting the high expectations set for it. The first review, in a sense, came from a professional copy marker at Houghton Mifflin: as he prepared the text for the printer, he couldn't help himself from pausing to read the material. Eventually, eminent critics such as Lewis Mumford and Bernard DeVoto seconded his appraisal. On certain points, DeVoto's review was mixed. But the tours, which were becoming recognized as the FWP's signature aesthetic innovation, he judged an "unquestionable triumph"—superbly edited, rich and intelligent, easy to use (even backward), far superior to anything else in the guides. "It is a rich, various and rewarding spectacle that the tours compose, a heartening reminder of how complex the current scene is and on what a variegated and fascinating base it rests," he wrote.

But the guide's warm reception was nearly wrecked from the outset. Within twenty-four hours of publication, conservative commentators in the press started picking the book apart. The essay on labor—an unvarnished celebration of the state's workers and their struggles to organize—was especially offensive. They were outraged that the guide devoted more space to the controversial execution of the anarchists Sacco and Vanzetti than to either the Boston Tea Party or the Boston Massacre—and far more than Louis Brandeis or Oliver Wendell Holmes received. Worse, it quoted the left-wing journalist Heywood Broun on Sacco-Vanzetti, saying, "Though the tomb is sealed, the dry bones still rattle." Governor Charles Hurley—who had approved the guide and even provided a glowing foreword—quickly disowned it; a former governor declared that the books should be burned on Boston Common (although he later claimed to mean this rhetorically).

Shoved to the center of the controversy was the director, Ray Billington, and his two assistant directors, Bert Loewenberg and Merle Colby. All three were attacked by name in the press. Loewenberg, a history PhD from Harvard, was on the cusp of leaving Massachusetts for a job at the University of South Dakota, so he was accused of being a foreigner to the state (he was not). Colby, a novelist and another recent Harvard graduate, was condemned for being a radical (he was). (Colby also knew a thing or two about Boston: when he applied for a job on the project, he scrawled "take care of Merle Colby" on a note, signed it with a made-up Irish name, and passed it ahead to the interviewer. He got the job.) *The Boston Globe* outed Colby as the writer behind the labor essay and accused him of being a member of the Communist Party. He denied it. Massachusetts conservatives demanded his head; Alsberg instead transferred him to DC and made him the territorial editor, responsible for assembling guides to Alaska and Puerto Rico, which had no projects of their own.

Since the backlash over Katharine Kellock's appointment, charges that the FWP was developing a "Red Baedeker"—or something more sinister— never totally abated. The Massachusetts incident was the most dramatic and potentially damaging flare-up. But soon the threat subsided. From Harvard,

Arthur M. Schlesinger, Sr., defended the guide's treatment of Sacco and Vanzetti. At the head of the WPA, Harry Hopkins downplayed the controversy and suggested that it may have all been a publicity stunt. (This was unlikely, but the book did go into multiple printings.) Even Roosevelt was unfazed. On a rare tour of the FWP office, he visited Alsberg, poked the Massachusetts guide with his cane, and deadpanned, "I understand you had quite a bit of trouble over this book"—and then threw back his head and laughed. He seemed to relish it.

"GOOD PUBLICITY FOR A NOVELIST"

With their guide published, workers on the Idaho project took up new tasks: a 350,000-word *Idaho Encyclopedia*, and *Idaho Lore*, a compilation of yarns, customs, omens ("If you drop a dishrag, the act portends the arrival of someone dirtier than yourself"), and dubious cures ("Insanity: The only remedy reported is generous application of hot mustard to the stomach and loins"). The small staff completed the encyclopedia manuscript, including sixty maps, in an astounding ten months. Like the guide, both were published by Caxton Printers. But this time, relations between DC and Boise were civil. Fisher had proved himself; now he ran a model writers' project. The only dustup involved someone outside the FWP: a meddling Idaho WPA official named Harold Pugmire who tried to force the project under his purview. Fisher, exasperated, sent a warning to DC: "One of these days I will go over and pop Mr. Pugmire right in his eye and you will be looking for another director out here in Idaho!"

Fisher hadn't neglected his other work during these years. DC gave him permission to work in the office from 11 a.m. to 6 p.m., which freed up mornings for writing. In 1936, he completed the Vridar Hunter tetralogy with *No Villain Need Be*. *The New York Times* called him a "Modern Rousseau" and celebrated the confessional opus while acknowledging the flaws that divided critics (some of whom, such as the poet John Peale Bishop, saw Fisher's art deteriorating into artless confession). The next year, he published *April: A Fable of Love*, a whimsical story of "the homeliest girl in Antelope, the most unloved little squab in ten counties," whose identity dissolves into a fictional self, derived from reading novels, named April. Reviews were generally good and, of all his books, it was his favorite. But he was irritated that the Idaho guide got a better reception. Perhaps he shouldn't have been: few of the American Guides were as fulsomely and widely praised, and no state director was so individually associated with the publications created on their watch.

Alongside these, he published a collection of essays, *The Neurotic Nightingale*, and a didactic novel about neuroses, *Forgive Us Our Virtues*, widely considered a misfire (including by the author). His old student Wallace Stegner respectfully dispatched the latter in a long, perceptive review, admitting that critics and readers increasingly wished to dismiss or ignore him—"Fisher, digging under the dirty fingernails of human self-deception, is a nuisance"—but that he deserved to be taken seriously. One critic, David Rein, took him seriously enough to bestow a peculiar honor of the times: he wrote a book-length Marxist polemic exposing the deficiencies of Fisher's work. *Vardis Fisher: Challenge to Evasion* carried a nine-page preface, "In Defense of the Obvious," from an unlikely contributor: Vardis Fisher. Although he was drifting further away from the "deep but quite unreasonable sympathy" he'd described feeling toward Marxism in *New Masses* several years earlier, Fisher was hardly one to shut out his critics. Instead, as that preface showed, he embraced the fight and went in swinging.

Fisher meanwhile began a sweeping historical epic about the Mormon exodus, *Children of God*. It was a private effort but the FWP left its mark on the book in several ways—most obviously, by giving Fisher an income while he wrote it. His research also benefited from the labor of federal writers who had uncovered diaries of Mormon pioneers during their fieldwork. Stylistically, too, it was as if the FWP had nudged Fisher into a different mode: his earlier novels were tightly focused and at times claustrophobic, but *Children of God* had a scope and heft that more resembled the Idaho guide or the encyclopedia. It also had an advantageous effect on Fisher's career, which had nearly been extinguished by the Depression. In the summer of 1939, before Fisher left the project, the book would win the biannual Harper Prize—and sell more copies than all his other novels combined.

But if the late thirties was a moment of professional productivity, it was also one of personal deterioration. Vardis and Margaret had a son in 1937 (she'd been hoping for one since 1935, when Vardis took the FWP job). Vardis was a reluctant father. He already struggled to support the two sons he had with Leona. "Well, Margaret will soon have a son to add to the confusion of the world," he wrote to friends, "and I'm supposed to give cigars and strut but I may on the contrary hide out for a month." By then, their marriage was crumbling, interrupted by frequent separations and undermined by Vardis's determination to spurn the academic world, a decision that thwarted Margaret's own scholarly ambitions. She was religious, too, and Vardis, hostile as ever to Christian dogma, tried to chip away at her piety. By the fall of 1938, she was living in Indiana and teaching at a college. She and Vardis exchanged letters and discussed divorce—as well as Vardis's new love interest, Opal Laurel Holmes, who'd begun working for the Idaho writers' project two years earlier. Margaret revealed that she'd felt suicidal during their separation. "In that period of chaos and dark, I looked toward the last unknown and found its surcease an irresistible magnet," she wrote. "I understood Neloa completely"—not Leona, the wife Vardis had driven to suicide, but Neloa, the character in his confessional tetralogy. They divorced the following year.

At the height of Fisher's battle with the DC staff—when he was stuffing their directives into the furnace and sending threatening telegrams—no one would have guessed how much they would come to rely on him. But such was the unpredictability of the FWP. Alsberg eventually deployed Fisher as an editor to Nevada and Utah, states that were struggling to complete their guidebooks. Then he asked if Fisher would be interested in a promotion to become their new regional director for the Rocky Mountain states: Idaho, Montana, Colorado, Wyoming, Utah, and New Mexico.

WPA officials in Idaho quashed the idea. Fisher, it seemed, was still living up to Alsberg's nickname for him, "the bad boy of the Project," by becoming a public nuisance. One night, he was arrested for speeding through the town of Nampa and tossed in jail. Then he wrote a smarmy column in the *Idaho Statesman* about Nampa's overzealous police force and its bedbug-infested amenities. (The *Statesman* afterward printed the police's account: "He protested considerably, took off his trousers and paraded around the cell in his shirt tail. Then we found out he was Idaho's famous dime novelist, and we put him in the ladies' cell. In a falsetto voice he explained Idaho's traffic laws in detail. Then he would shake the bars. After about four hours of this he produced a $10 bond, which he had with him all the time.") The new WPA state administrator, O. K. Hine, was deeply embarrassed. "This may be good publicity for a novelist but I do not think it helps the WPA program in Idaho," he wrote. Alsberg insisted that the episode was blown out of proportion and continued to back Fisher.

So they proceeded in a way that perfectly suited the FWP's improvisatory style. They compromised and made up a new title. Fisher would be a technical consulting editor for the Rocky Mountain states instead of a regional director—in other words, an editorial troubleshooter who could still go out and do the work, sparing the WPA the embarrassment of granting him a more eminent position. In a sense, it didn't matter. Fisher agreed and hit the road. They were giving him a raise, and that's all he really wanted from the beginning.

———◆———

NELSON ALGREN,
CHICAGO

"PERSONALLY HELPING TO ACCELERATE
THE DESTRUCTION OF CAPITALISM"

In 1933, Nelson Algren, twenty-four years old, was riding a Southern Pacific boxcar through West Texas. The railroad bulls got him in Sanderson and dumped him trackside. It wasn't the first time. He was, by then, a full citizen of the transient nation sliding around the nation's rails during the Depression, the ones who'd been knocked loose and sent spinning, the ones looking for work or refuge or simply motion. He knew the hazards and attractions of this world—he knew what it was to cower before a swinging nightstick, to pray that the door of a refrigerated boxcar didn't lock behind you, to watch the doomed tumble under wheels of steel. But there was thrill and freedom, too, speeding over the American land, for free. He'd been triangulating between his home in Chicago, the borderlands of the Southwest, and the old Confederacy, learning the lingo of his fellow hoboes and taking it down on scraps of paper. He was, by outward appearances, one of them. But he also had a journalism degree and a novel under contract with a prestigious Manhattan publisher, and his rambling had a purpose: he was going to document it in his fiction. From the train, before he was kicked off, he'd seen a town, so he headed back in that direction. The town was called Alpine and it seemed like a good place to rest and finish his novel.

He spent several months there, hanging around a teachers college, spreading the gospel of proletarian literature, using the school's typewriters. Into the manuscript went the scraps, the images and impressions, he'd gathered during his trips across the American underbelly. A man in shock who knows that he is dying. A kid whose arm is sliced off by a boxcar, so close you can smell the blood. Sex workers on a New Orleans street. A nation of people just milling around. The experience broke apart his notions about life in the United States and it gave him purpose as a writer. "All these scenes, one after another, piled up into something that made me not just want to write but to really say it, to find out that this thing was all upside down," he recalled years later. "Everything I'd been told was wrong." People across the country, standing outside foreclosed homes and shuttered factories, were reaching the same conclusion—they were beginning to question their beliefs about the course of progress, the nature of prosperity, the value of the old ideas. Algren's task as a writer, he believed, was to burrow deep into that unraveling mess, look at it without blinking, and then tell the world what he saw.

Autumn became winter, and by late January he was ready to return to Chicago. He said goodbye to Alpine and hopped back on a train—but not before stealing a typewriter, boxing it up, and mailing it to his parents' house. He needed one, after all, and the school had so many. The sheriff caught up with him in Sanderson, where the bulls had nabbed him months earlier. His booking statement spoke for all the writers in 1934, before the creation of the FWP, who found themselves separated from their means of production: "A typewriter is the only means I had to complete a book which means either a few dollars or utter destitution. There is nothing that is more vital to my mere existence as a typewriter, it is the only means I have to earn a living."

Algren lingered in jail for a month, waiting for a circuit judge to hear his case. A guilty verdict meant Huntsville. He'd seen some grim sights on his travels, and even back home in Chicago, but the jail in Sanderson was harrowing—his fellow prisoners included a murderer and a sadist; another died on the floor from a gunshot wound after he allegedly tried to escape. (Less menacing was a deserter from the Civilian Conservation Corps.) Finally, he was brought to trial, and his court-appointed lawyer took up the idea from Algren's statement that writing was a livelihood like any other. What Algren had done, he argued, was no different from another laborer stealing the tools on which their survival depended. The times demanded it. Algren got a suspended sentence and beat it back to Chicago, saved by the hobbled economy and, surely, by his own white skin.

Over the next year—while Henry Alsberg settled into his FERA job, Harry Hopkins sketched out a new work-relief agency, and Vardis Fisher wondered how long he could hide from the Depression—Algren focused on his writing. His career was ascendant. His novel was under contract with Vanguard Press, the respected radical house in New York—the same one that Jacob Baker, Hopkins's assistant and Alsberg's boss, helped to set up. Algren had won the contract on the strength of his first published piece, "So Help Me," which appeared in *Story* magazine alongside William Faulkner and another future federal writer, Zora Neale Hurston. (Encouraged by a form inquiry letter from Vanguard, Algren had hitchhiked to New York, showed up at the office, improvised his way through a meeting with the president, James Henle, and walked out with a contract: one hundred dollars for expenses and another hundred if they accepted the manuscript. Henle pulled a ten-dollar bill out of his wallet and handed Algren the first installment of his advance.) From early spring of 1934 through the fall, Algren published something almost monthly: in literary magazines (*Story, The American Mercury*) and harder-edged radical ones (*The Anvil, New Masses, Partisan Review*). That summer, he finished his novel. *Somebody in Boots* followed a dispossessed young man on a bleak excursion through Depression America, down some of the same roads and railroad tracks Algren had traveled. The "somebodies" in boots—authority figures and vicious men—were symbols of the ambient oppression to which Algren was becoming finely attuned. Boots swung through the protagonist's nightmares and pressed into his stomach when he was hungry. "Whenever he thought of one man robbed by another," Algren wrote, "he thought of somebody in boots."

The world of the novel was grim and often squalid; it was heavy on texture, less concerned with plot. Later, reflecting on its many dismemberments and decapitations (both human and animal), Algren said, "In every chapter some child had her head cut off, and you know I was really laying it on." But his writing was charged with an unmistakable partisanship for the poor and oppressed. Algren's style and sympathies aligned him with the writers who spent the first half of the thirties churning out proletarian literature—a varied body of work that shared a commitment to portraying the lives of working people and promoting the revolutionary cause. In an eruption of short stories, novels, poems, plays, reportage, confessions, and manifestos, young proletarian writers forged a new avant-garde that briefly became the focal point of US literature. Their writing could be artful or tedious, stirring or laughably contrived. They seldom agreed on what, precisely, proletarian literature meant. But everyone—the writers, editors, critics, publishers, and readers who made up the movement—got the gist. They were motivated by a profound disenchantment with the state of things and a desire to pay close attention to the lives of workers in a way that few writers had before. Their sensibility overlapped with the hard-boiled style that found widespread expression in detective novels and pulp magazines, although the proletarians were more overtly political, often romantic rather than cynical, and treated crime and violence as symptoms of a sick social order, not sources of narrative titillation. They had a network of little magazines, "mushroom mags," that sprang up with the onset of the Depression, some fusing modernist aesthetics with radicalism and some emphasizing plainspoken dispatches from the class war. Before the end of 1935, there would appear a hefty anthology, *Proletarian Literature in the United States*.

Alfred Kazin, no fan of the movement, described them as writers who "delighted in hitting back at life in their books as violently as life had hit them." His description fit Algren, whose characters were seized by this very idea. "She wanted to strike out at something, to hurt something as she had been hurt," he wrote of a sex worker in *Somebody in Boots*. Algren was, in many ways, a typical proletarian writer: descended from recent immigrants, born into the lower middle class, driven by a heap of political conviction and a little firsthand experience. But Algren mostly avoided the clumsy didacticism and clichéd characters and red-banner-waving "conversion" endings that appealed to some of his cohorts. And he was less interested in the lives of factory workers and struggling craftsmen—workers like his father, back in Chicago—than he was in prisoners, thieves, and drifters. It was the lumpenproletariat who had his attention.

In January 1935, as Algren waited for his novel's publication, *New Masses* printed a "Call for an American Writers' Congress." It began:

The capitalist system crumbles so rapidly before our eyes that, whereas ten years ago scarcely more than a handful of writers were sufficiently far-sighted and courageous to take a stand for proletarian revolution, today hundreds of poets, novelists, dramatists, critics, short story writers and journalists recognize the necessity of personally helping to accelerate the destruction of capitalism and the establishment of a workers' government.

The call was a mouthful—and overly optimistic—but it was broadly accurate. A significant chunk of writers and intellectuals had moved left since the crash (such as Sherwood Anderson and the fifty-two others who signed the statement supporting the Communist presidential candidates). The call itself was drafted by Granville Hicks, a liberal professor who was radicalized in the wake of Sacco and Vanzetti, joined the Communist Party, and became one of the leading Marxist voices of the thirties. The Writers' Congress would be the most visible, organized expression of this trend. It was also a striking rejection of Franklin Roosevelt's vision for a new work-relief program, the WPA, which he'd floated to a joint session of Congress earlier that month. "Work must be found for able-bodied but destitute workers," he said. "We must preserve not only the bodies of the unemployed from destitution but also their self-respect, their self-reliance, and courage and determination." Such a program, he believed, would carry the nation through the Depression until things returned to normal. But this begged the question of whether normalcy was worth returning to. The organizers of the American Writers' Congress thought otherwise. They sought instead a radical restructuring of the economic and political order, one that went far beyond the seemingly limited aims of the WPA, or any other ideas that emerged from the Roosevelt White House. Their immediate goal, however, was more modest. They would form a body, the League of American Writers, that would oppose fascism and war while working out the particularities of revolutionary art in an American context. (One area it sought to explore was "relations between revolutionary writers and bourgeois publishers and editors.") The Communist Party played a central role, but that was no secret—writers signed on because they agreed with the principles of the program, whether they were party members or not. (And yet radicals who were critical of the party, such as Max Eastman, were pointedly excluded.) Sixty-two writers signed the call, including Theodore Dreiser, Langston Hughes, James T. Farrell, Erskine Caldwell, Lincoln Steffens, and Malcolm Cowley. John Dos Passos contributed an essay to the proceedings, but he did not sign the call or attend the congress—a mark of his growing detachment from the left. The list of signatories also included Earl Browder, general secretary of the Communist Party, and Alexander Trachtenberg, who oversaw the party's publishing operation. At the top of the list—albeit by alphabetical accident—was the name Nelson Algren.

Algren would have been known only to keen observers of the literary left, if at all. But he was poised on the brink of writerly glory. He'd survived the rails and a month behind bars. He could claim an impressive portfolio of stories, one of which would appear in that year's O. Henry Prize collection. And the freshly published *Somebody in Boots*, if successful, would propel him into the congress, triumphant in the eyes of his comrades.

It didn't happen that way. The publication date—less than two weeks before the creation of the WPA—came and went. *Somebody in Boots* was not a hit, nor was it a total failure. The reviews were good but sparse. Sales were low. Algren had hoped for angry denunciations in the bourgeois press, but the response was more like scattered applause from a small, sympathetic audience. He was devastated. He became depressed. He attempted suicide—a girlfriend caught him with his mouth on the apartment's gas line. He was placed into the care of friends. By the time he arrived in Manhattan for the Writers' Congress, he was a wreck. A month earlier, he'd been emblematic of the rising young writers carrying the banner of proletarian fiction. Now he was just another creative casualty of the Depression.

The Writers' Congress convened on April 26 at the Mecca Temple in midtown, a theater between Times Square and Central Park, around the corner from Carnegie Hall. It was the first such gathering of writers ever held in the United States. Algren and more than two hundred other delegates took their places in rows of folding chairs arranged on the stage. (If the radical movement of the thirties needed a symbol, said Malcolm Cowley, who addressed the congress that night, it would be rows of folding chairs set up on a bare floor.) The theater was packed, although no one could say what ratio obtained between sympathetic onlookers and party members. Friedrich Wolf, a German novelist and playwright, spoke first and set an anti-fascist tone by telling of German writers who were being harassed, jailed, and killed by the Nazis. The novelist Waldo Frank, an old friend of Henry Alsberg's and the first elected secretary of the league, argued against schematic writing and simplistic thinking. "A story of middle-class or intellectual life," he insisted, "or even of mythological figures, if it is alight with revolutionary vision, is more effective proletarian art—and more effective art for proletarians—than a shelf-full of dull novels about stereotyped workers." Earl Browder, general secretary of the Communist Party, appeared during the opening session, too, and struck a reassuring note. "We do not want to take good writers and make bad strike leaders of them," he told the delegates. Anyone concerned about the dead hand of communist didacticism might have felt a bit of relief.

Still, disharmony and sectarianism lurked just below the surface—as an incident involving the literary theorist Kenneth Burke demonstrated. Burke, an old friend of Malcolm Cowley's, had likewise moved to the left with the onset of the Depression, but his writing and thinking was idiosyncratic, more aligned with the avant-garde of an earlier era. His opponents saw him as a petit-bourgeois bohemian, and Burke—sensitive and conflict-averse—knew it. But he was impressed by the call for the congress and wanted to play a helpful role. "Particularly to those of us who had been taught to think of a literary renaissance as six men assembled in the back room of a saloon to discuss the need of a new magazine," he reflected afterward in *The Nation*, "it was a revolution in itself to behold four thousand people packing the pit, balcony, gallery, and stage of Mecca Temple to consider the problems of literature." To this groundbreaking assembly Burke presented a paper, "Revolutionary Symbolism in America." His talk was a bit of knotty philosophizing about myths as social tools and why revolutionary propaganda needed to align with the cultural heritage. But it boiled down to the sensible suggestion that, in its rhetoric, the league ought to replace "the workers" with "the people." The audience applauded, at first—but then Burke watched with dread as party members rose to denounce him. One of them, "throbbing like a locomotive," shouted, "We have a snob among us!" Friedrich Wolf, the German writer whose chilling speech had opened the congress, compared Burke's proposal to Hitler's invocation of the *Volk*. When the ordeal was over and the meeting ended, Burke found himself walking behind two young women and realized they were discussing his transgression. "Yet he *seemed* so honest!" one said.

That night, as he tried to fall asleep, he was jolted awake over and over by the memory of his name cast forth accusatorially: *Burke! Burke!*

The next day, though, Burke's critics apologized. Soon he was on the league's executive committee. Burke excused the "internal sectarian distinctions" that fueled attacks on him as proof of a broader unity—the league, he insisted, was drawing together writers not as isolated artists but as engaged citizens, who necessarily argued over the tasks at hand. That appraisal might have been wishful thinking. (The FWP, not the league, would come to stand as the preeminent effort of the thirties to fuse the writer's vocation with purposeful citizenship.) But, with his proposal and his analysis, Burke inadvertently anticipated a major shift in Communist Party policy. Since the late twenties, the party had operated in a mode of sectarian nastiness, reflecting the stance of the Comintern's "Third Period," when social democrats and socialists, labeled "social fascists," were its prime enemies—a policy with especially tragic consequences in Germany. But by 1933 or so, that stance was moderating, aside from an inglorious incident in 1934, when party members disrupted a socialist meeting at Madison Square Garden. After 1935, the party made a remarkable pivot toward the more inclusive, less dogmatic, and somewhat ideologically fuzzy Popular Front policy. Now the party that once derided the New Deal as tentative fascism was gathering up the old chestnuts of American patriotic rhetoric—Washington and Lincoln were drafted for the cause, "the people" became the progressive actors of history (à la Burke), and a new slogan was deployed, "Communism Is Twentieth Century Americanism." Granville Hicks, who drafted the combative call for the Writers' Congress, published a book with the difficult-to-misinterpret title *I Like America.* A *New Masses* profile of General Secretary Earl Browder noted with pride that if Browder were sent "back where he came from," he'd end up in Kansas, "somewhere near the exact geographical center of the United States." The two great cultural trends of the Depression era—the Americana turn and political radicalization—were converging. To outside observers, the Communist Party had begun rolling out its own program, following the FWP's slogan, of "Introducing America to Americans."

The Popular Front was designed to appeal to people like Nelson Algren. He was energized by the revolutionary left but he wasn't much for theory—he saw the world as a conflict between those who owned property and those who didn't, between property rights and human rights, and that was that. He admired bourgeois figures like Lincoln and Thoreau, and socialists and anarchists like Eugene Debs and the Haymarket Martyrs, and he drew inspiration from the ragged, visceral radicalism that permeated the Midwest, comprising the ghost of defeated Populism, strands of Jefferson and Jackson, Christian socialism and municipal reformism, agrarian protest and industrial syndicalism. At any other time, the party would have viewed him as utterly undependable, a muddle of ideological deviations. After 1935, though, people like Algren became its target constituency.

Algren was elected to the league's national council, the larger assemblage below the executive committee. (So was Merle Colby, the future FWP editor in Boston and, later, Washington.) But his appearance at the congress was a disaster. During sessions at the New School, Algren spoke on a panel with Jack Conroy and Meridel Le Sueur (both future federal writers), along with the *New Masses* editor Michael Gold. It was a friendly bunch: Conroy had become something of a mentor to Algren, and Le Sueur praised Algren's work during her remarks. But Algren was emotionally wasted and physically near the point of collapse. Le Sueur and Gold propped him up while he mumbled about his book and then pleaded with the audience to buy it. He seemed to be unraveling.

By the time Algren returned to Chicago, he hadn't much improved. Eventually he was hospitalized. After that, he shuffled through the months. He managed to publish a few short pieces and he met a woman, Amanda Kontowicz, whom he'd eventually marry. They moved in together and rented one fleabag apartment after another. Sometimes their parents gave them food to eat; at other times, Algren stole bottles from milk wagons. He briefly worked at an elite health club, hosing down the clients after they exercised. (No Jews were admitted to the club, and Algren suspected that anti-Semitism had steered him into that particular role.) Then he found a job in a warehouse.

His dream of becoming a self-sustaining writer seemed more and more out of reach. And for thousands of aspiring writers like him, the situation was the same. Between 1929 and 1933, the number of new books printed fell by 60 percent. That decline was hard enough for the established writers, authors like Vardis Fisher. But for those who had no reputation to trade on, the Depression was a forced hiatus. How many of them watched as that hiatus persisted, for months and then years, until it finally curdled into an ending? Algren was a college graduate with a journalism degree who'd left home and searched for a job and watched the economy fall apart around him. No one was hiring, so he invented his own assignment and went to the front lines of the catastrophe and looked into the eyes of its first victims, the people who'd never known the prosperity of the twenties and were hit hardest by the crisis of the thirties. He wrote a novel inspired by what he saw. He met the situation with optimism, force of will, and talent. And then he was crushed by it.

"SIZZLING FROM THE GRIDDLE OF EXPERIENCE"

"You'll know it's the place built out of Man's ceaseless failure to overcome himself," Algren wrote, years later, of Chicago. Anyone who saw the city during the Depression, in all its faltering grandeur, would agree. The industrial colossus of the Midwest, an engine of unceasing production, a hub of vast distribution, was hobbled. The city's manufacturing workforce contracted by 50 percent. Payrolls fell by 75 percent. Black and Mexican workers, fired before whites and hired after them, were hit hardest. Informal networks of support, and then ethnic and religious charities, were quickly exhausted. Public relief existed, administered by the county, but before the New Deal it was mostly available to needy mothers, the blind, and veterans. In the sprawling reaches beyond the downtown Loop—Black and immigrant neighborhoods like the ones where Algren grew up—small, undercapitalized ethnic banks were obliterated by the banking panic. Only 16 percent of them survived the Depression. Some of the city's dominant firms—US Steel, International Harvester, and Western Electric—tentatively attempted to support their laid-off workers before scaling the programs back.

The crisis radiated out from the city's industrial base and its paralyzed banks and, as everywhere, touched all sectors of society, including white-collar workers, including writers. They staggered into the Illinois writers' project, facing some version of the situation that Algren had described in his booking statement before he was tossed in a Texas jail: their typewriters in hock, their newsrooms shuttered, their livelihoods denied by a withering market.

The project's first home was in a WPA office on South Michigan Avenue, just below the downtown Loop. Algren applied early, in November 1935, when he was still floundering within the wreckage of his young career and looking for a lifeline. But he ran into problems with his relief status and couldn't get hired. It was as though, after not being able to succeed as a writer, he couldn't properly fail as one. Literary friends pestered the WPA for him, and he interviewed more than once, with no luck. The project moved north, to 19 South Wells Street, before relocating again, northeast to 433 East Erie Street, a block from Lake Michigan, where its offices sat alongside the rest of Federal #1 in Chicago. Finally, the director of the New York City project (Orrick Johns, a *New Masses* editor and member of the League of American Writers) sent DC an effusive recommendation and called Algren "one of the most promising young novelists in the country," even though he couldn't remember the name of Algren's novel, which he nevertheless enjoyed. It was enough—Algren clearly benefited from his connections in the world of literary radicalism. The DC office backed his quest for a job. By the fall of 1936, he had one. When he walked into the office on East Erie Street, he'd been trying to join the project for a year, even though he was a qualified writer and plainly in need. Critics who attacked the FWP as a dumping ground for shiftless pencil leaners didn't recognize how difficult it could be to get hired.

Algren saw his fellow workers transformed by their new jobs. He was witnessing the same revitalizing effect that others, such as the Massachusetts director Ray Billington, were seeing around the country. "To such people the WPA provided a place where they began to communicate with people again," Algren said. "They got a little self-respect back." He was, of course, speaking about himself, too. In later years, he would credit the FWP with keeping the suicide rate down. (He was thinking anecdotally, but an observed correlation between suicide and economic recession backs him up.) He never let on that, before he arrived at the Illinois project, he'd had a near-fatal encounter with a gas pipe—that he was one of those potential suicides.

If Vardis Fisher was one type of federal writer—a solitary, established author whose income was drying up—then Algren was another. He was young and ambitious, still settling into a voice and groping for a form, testing out poetry and fiction and reportage. He was descended from recent immigrants, the rank and file of the new, multiethnic working class who, along with their children, filled the unions of the CIO, formed a critical bloc of the New Deal coalition, and shaped the cultural politics of the era. He was a radical, convinced that capitalism was a dying system and deserved to be swept away, but that, in the meantime, the WPA looked pretty good and was worth defending. And his career was being extinguished before it even really started. Federal writers who resembled Algren almost undoubtedly outnumbered those who resembled Fisher—to a great degree. The FWP not only kept them alive but kept them in the writer's trade; it harnessed their energies and, whatever their individual life stories, put them to work as surveyors of the places that formed them.

Algren's particular story, as he told it, began with a grandfather he never knew. He was named for the old man—Nels, or Nils, Ahlgren, an eccentric Swede who converted to Judaism, renamed himself Isaac Ben Abraham, and left Stockholm for Minnesota. His grandfather was part dreamer, part charlatan, and Algren knew him only through family stories, the sort of dubious tales that, one day, federal writers would collect and sow throughout the American Guides—that Isaac Ben Abraham narrowly escaped an attack on his trading post by the Sioux, that he made his own coins from tin, that he mounted his shack on wheels and rolled it back and forth across the county line to avoid paying taxes. When Nelson Algren Abraham was born in 1909, he inherited the old man's name (minus the "h"), his looks, and a measure of his disposition. "Can pseudo-intellectualism be inherited?" Algren mused years later.

He was pleased to claim an odd ancestor, but his story really began in Chicago. That city formed him. He grew up in Park Manor, a South Side neighborhood dotted with vegetable gardens and livestock and scraps of prairie, and then in Albany Park on the North Side, a busier, Jewish neighborhood. Algren and the other kids played in the streets and lit bonfires in vacant lots and pretended they were doughboys dying in the trenches of Europe. He thrilled over the White Sox and was heartbroken when they threw the 1919 World Series. He wrote his own newspaper and sold real ones around the neighborhood from a makeshift wagon. He was a child of the lowest fringe of the lower middle class and these years were basically pleasant. But the brutality of the city was always visible. Chicago—full of migrants, Black and white, drawn to its factories and stockyards, working alongside immigrants from overseas—was a simmering cauldron. Algren saw brawls on the street and heard his classmates toss around ethnic slurs. The summer before the disgraceful World Series, a spasm of racist violence left thirty-eight people dead and more than five hundred injured, most of them Black. Algren absorbed the distressing aspects of this world—from petty crime and random bloodshed to racial oppression and harrowing poverty—but he did not shrink from them. His mother once took him to see the hundreds of bodies laid out from the wreck of the *Eastland*, a pleasure cruiser that rolled over in the Chicago River, and he never forgot it. The same fascination would steer him into gambling rooms and pool halls, places where gangsters and lowlifes congregated. He was, fully, a product of the city—unlike his father, who'd grown up on a farm in Indiana and worked as a mechanic in the huge clanking factories of Detroit and Chicago, and later opened a tire-and-battery shop. By the time Algren was a teenager, he began to see his father as a dull and complacent figure, a rube floundering in the industrial metropolis. But he, the son, was determined to know Chicago from the bottom up and the inside out.

Algren's freethinking middle sister, Bernice, exposed him to novels, poems, plays, movies. She became his great benefactor and helped pay for tuition at the University of Illinois in Urbana. He matriculated in 1927, as the stock market bubble swelled and Calvin Coolidge informed the nation that he did not choose to run again as president, clearing the path for Herbert Hoover. Algren did not pay much attention to the outside world. Like Vardis Fisher at the University of Utah a decade earlier, he plunged into an intense study of classic literature: Shakespeare, Chaucer, Dickens, the Romantic poets, the Stoics. He memorized couplets and read and worked and rarely interacted with other students except when he waited on their tables and sold them sandwiches. He was interested in the new fields of sociology and criminology, but he majored in journalism and reported on courts and jails for the school paper. He wrote his first serious fiction: short stories and character sketches of the forlorn and downtrodden, the subjects that would become the focus of his life's work.

While Algren studied, another influence was gathering force. In New York, Michael Gold (Algren's future co-panelist at the Writers' Congress) had become editor of *New Masses*. Gold was pushing the magazine further from its bohemian-radical roots and toward a more hard-line communist stance. He'd been chasing the dream of proletarian literature since the early twenties, and he opened the July 1928 issue with the editorial "Write for Us!" announcing a new orientation:

WE WANT TO PRINT:

Confessions—diaries—documents—

The concrete—

Letters from hoboes, peddlers, small town atheists, unfrocked
    clergymen and schoolteachers—

Revelations by rebel chambermaids and night club waiters—

The sobs of driven stenographers—

The poetry of steel workers—

The wrath of miners—the laughter of sailors—

Strike stories, prison stories, work stories—

Stories by Communist, I.W.W. and other revolutionary workers.

Gold doubled down the following January with "Go Left, Young Writers!," a call for aspiring, working-class writers to align with the communist movement. "When I say 'go leftward,' I don't mean the temperamental bohemian left, the stale old Paris posing, the professional poetizing etc. No, the real thing; a knowledge of working-class life in America gained from first hand contacts, and a hard precise philosophy of 1929 based on economics, not verbalisms." (Soon after, Gold took his own advice and published the autobiographical novel *Jews Without Money*. He was on to something, apparently: the novel went through eleven printings in less than a year.) Algren may or may not have read these pieces. But when the Depression amplified Gold's message, he would, like so many others, take up the call.

The Depression nearly knocked Algren out of college, but he got a loan and, in 1931, graduated with a journalism degree and a certificate from the

Illinois Press Association. (He wasn't alone: college enrollment stayed steady during these years, as students hoped that jobs requiring more training and education would be insulated from the crisis.) Algren looked for work at a newspaper, spiraling out from Chicago into the Midwest, but no one was hiring. The best he could find was a temporary gig in Minneapolis that paid in experience, not dollars. He went home, frustrated and broke, and then set out again, this time heading south, one of many thousands shaken loose by the Depression and sent wandering, temporarily or permanently, in search of work. He still carried his journalism certificate, though its power grew suspect as he was turned away from office after office. He could not even find work selling papers at a newsstand, let alone a job in a newsroom. He wrote to the director of his journalism school, someone who had urged him to stay when times were hard, asking for advice. The director said he could return to the university and wash dishes.

So Algren chose a different path. If no one was hiring, then he'd write what he wanted, on his own terms. His travels within the transient nation gave him material and helped him to gain a sense of mission. He was jostling against all sorts of striving, discouraged, confused people. (The time he spent with two con artists, who claimed they were both named Luther, cast a long shadow over his fiction and formed the basis for his first published story, "So Help Me.") When Algren wrote *Somebody in Boots*, he chose a protagonist who resembled the young drifters he'd met in flophouses and boxcars. But he wasn't simply trying to capture a type. Cass McKay, the protagonist, represented a specific line of inquiry into the American character. He was a descendant of the Kentucky hunter who owned no slaves and worked for no bosses, who hid out from armies blue and gray and who, in the postwar reorganization, was pushed down into the border region. Jackson and Lincoln belonged to this lineage, Algren believed, but Cass was a "Final Descendent," the product of a long historical process that ended about as far from Jackson and Lincoln as possible, born into a place of utter dispossession, with little insight into his situation other than a pervasive sense that somehow, every day, he was being cheated. He was "a man representing the desolation of the hinterland as well as the disorder of the great city, exiled from himself and expatriated within his own frontiers," Algren put it later. "A man who felt no responsibility even toward himself." Cass was a citizen whose nation had failed him but who hadn't, like Algren, developed a revolutionary consciousness—the type of arrested lumpen that the Depression created in droves.

Algren, in other words, was engaged in an intellectual project situated within the long arc of American history. He wasn't simply a discouraged journalism major who decided to write a novel. But his work was halted by the Depression and it would likely have fizzled out were it not for the FWP. His new job on the federal payroll put Algren on a different track, for sure—he wasn't being paid to create proletarian novels. But it kept him writing and put him in close contact with his city, beloved and sometimes feared, forcing him to train his eye on his native ground, alongside hundreds of other Illinoisans assembling a collective self-portrait of their state.

When Algren joined the Illinois project, the director was Clark Slover, a specialist in early Irish literature at the University of Chicago. Initially, DC heard good reports about his administration. But then came rumors of drunkenness. Slover blamed his enemies in the office and troubles with his wife at home. Eventually, he was fired. (He died in 1939, on Christmas Eve, after a night in the taverns, when he was found on the sidewalk in front of his apartment with a cracked skull—whether from a fall or an assault, the police could not say.)

DC next installed a temporary director and the project staggered along. Finally, an exasperated editor, James Phelan, wrote directly to Alsberg and complained of the acting director's habit of listening to a problem in silence, nodding gravely, and admitting that it was indeed a headache—and then doing nothing. "I have a sincere feeling of pity for the man, because he is suffering from as terrible a case of meticulosity as I have ever seen," Phelan wrote. But this state of paralysis jeopardized the entire operation. "The idea of this letter is repugnant to me, but the present functioning of this project has achieved a nightmarish quality that is unbelievable." Phelan thought they could still get the guidebook manuscript into shape in four months—but "only if those four months are spent under a hardboiled and efficient director."

Alsberg didn't act right away. (He asked Jay Du Von, the director of the Iowa project and a Midwest field representative, to expand his portfolio and temporarily direct the Illinois project.) By August 1937, Alsberg appointed John T. Frederick—whom no one would call hard-boiled, but who had earned a reputation for efficiency nonetheless. Frederick, a professor and editor, was actually DC's first choice for director but, at the time, couldn't forgo his teaching responsibilities at Northwestern. Of all the directors in charge of projects in literary hubs—Chicago, New York, Boston, San Francisco—Frederick was considered the most effective.

He was best known for editing *The Midland: A Magazine of the Middle West*, an important venue for early twentieth-century literary regionalism. He was its driving force for nearly twenty years. In an era marked by a literary "revolt from the village"—typified by Sherwood Anderson, Edgar Lee Masters, Sinclair Lewis—Frederick was more of a village loyalist. *The Midland* folded in 1933, a casualty of the Depression, and merged with *The Frontier*, under the editorship of Harold Merriam at the University of Montana—future director of the Montana project and friend of Vardis Fisher.

More than most state directors, Frederick developed a keen understanding of the FWP's mission. Something was changing, he argued, in the way that Americans thought about American life. The old ideas about the nation, in a material sense—that it was a thing "to get," to grab hold of and recklessly exploit—were being pushed aside by a new emphasis on stewardship and conservation. The WPA was the highest expression to date of that thinking. "It is part of the government's job to see that we appreciate what we have, and that we conserve and use what we have, rather than destroy it," he put it in a speech. This stance extended to the realm of culture: just as New Deal programs were conserving arable land in the Dust Bowl region and timber forests in the west, the FWP was uncovering and protecting the histories of small hamlets and the creations of overlooked regional poets. In other words, it was presenting an alternative to both the fashionable contempt for small-town America and the dead end of provincialism. "If we can, in dealing with Galena or Dubuque, or any other small town, or small city of the middle west, help the people who are living there, and growing up there to see that they have something in their own home town that is special and intrinsically worthy, not something to get away from, but something to foster and appreciate, I think that is a pretty good job for us to try to do," he said. The FWP, he believed, would be the catalyst for a renewed appreciation of the American cultural inheritance.

There was an echo of this attitude in Algren's fiction—that literary riches could be found in overlooked, and even contemptible, places. But Frederick's point had broader implications. Federal writers weren't only digging for "special and intrinsically worthy" material out there in the land. *They* belonged to that material; *they* were part of the cultural inheritance, as its creators and shapers. Their talents needed to be conserved against the deleterious threat of the Depression, too. Clair Laning, a FERA official who became one of Alsberg's closest aides in DC, had a term for this. He called it "brain erosion." And Federal #1 was designed to tackle it, just as the CCC and other New Deal agencies were busy mobilizing thousands of workers to fight against its agronomical counterpart.

As with soil erosion, the cure for brain erosion was hard work. Algren eventually put his own writing aside and devoted most of his energy to the FWP. (He did keep up his note-taking habit, scribbling down impressions and scenes and storing them away for future stories and novels.) The Illinois project made him a field worker, responsible for churning out the raw material that formed the basis of the American Guides and all other FWP publications. Some of that material was based on firsthand reporting; other pieces were more like essays derived from a mix of secondhand research and interviews. Algren's work hit across the spectrum. For instance, he visited the Calumet Baking Powder Company on Fillmore Street and wrote up a one-page profile. It wasn't exciting work, but it was part of the exhaustive indexing of the American scene that federal writers were conducting in every state. Eventually, he took on heftier assignments, writing long, historically rich essays on topics such as "Chicago's Mail Order Industry" (forty-seven pages) and "The Dutch in Illinois" (forty pages). Sometimes he was able to stretch out and put his imaginative powers to work. For instance, he wrote an essay, unpublished and perhaps unfinished, titled "Midwestern Literature: Its Origins and Tendencies, 1848–1865," which begins, confusingly, with Nathaniel Hawthorne. Then it slips off the rails and keeps right on going, touching on Melville's genius and his money troubles and his fraught relationship with Hawthorne, *Moby-Dick* (a "symbolic attack on all property and all privilege"), the Fugitive Slave Law and John Brown in Europe and Harriet

Beecher Stowe, political titans of the antebellum age and how the Civil War cleared the way for "the rival imperialisms of eastern capitalism and western agrarianism," and much else—all except midwestern literature. It's an unfocused and intriguing hodgepodge, written with a supple power. From the project's standpoint, it was totally useless. But it kept Algren typing and thinking and typing. The fight against brain erosion was a messy business.

Algren had little to do with the Illinois guide itself. If Vardis Fisher's experience was dominated by his struggle to create the Idaho guide, then Algren's was dedicated to the FWP's auxiliary undertakings, its more granular methods of documenting the nation. Every state took up these tasks as the American Guides developed: guides to cities, counties, and regions; pamphlets on hyperlocal history; recreational and educational instruction booklets; bibliographies and social-ethnic studies and folklore compendiums and individual testimonials. Because the Illinois project was among the largest, at most times second only to New York City's, it had room to expand far afield. Its workers spun off into topics including "Navigable Streams in Illinois," "The Romance of Clark Street," "Chicago in Periodical Literature," "History of Chicago Churches," "Encyclopedia of Illinois," "History of Camp Grant," "Annals of Sports," "Special Schools in Chicago," "Humor in Illinois," "Civil Liberties in Illinois," "A History of Aviation," "A Chicago Almanac." There was a weather unit that compiled the state's meteorological data for the US Weather Bureau; there was a Chicago Park District Unit, which created booklets and bulletins for the municipal parks. Other workers were indexing newspaper archives for the State Historical Library. Only some of this material would be published during the lifespan of the FWP, but a catalog of items that *did* appear included more than 150 entries, such as *Gone to Blazes* ("episodes in verse about the Great Chicago Fire," thirty-six pages); *Manual for Caddies* ("gives the 'ten commandments for a caddy,' and enlarges upon same," forty-eight pages); and, naturally, *Boondoggling* ("making useful articles from waste materials," sixty pages).

Algren's most important contribution to this auxiliary work was a local guidebook. With each of these, the FWP was further modifying Alsberg's original vision of a single, all-encompassing "American Guide"—a heavy, authoritative tome that presented the nation as a unified text. The proliferating local guides instead suggested a decentralized and fine-grained alternative.

Taken as a body of literature, they implied that the United States was better described as a composite, an expanding collection of particular portraits, an unfolding *process*, even—and not as an overarching abstraction that you could fit between two covers.

In Algren's case, it was a guide to Galena in far northwest Illinois. The city was once a frontier boomtown and then a wealthy commercial center, thanks to some nearby lead mines and its position on the Galena River, a tributary of the Mississippi. It was also the home of U. S. Grant, "A Middle-Aged Clerk in a Faded Army Coat," as the guide would call him. (Grant, you might say, was the patron saint of local guides: in 1876, he urged Americans to celebrate the centennial by writing the histories of their towns, counties, and states, which many, apparently, did.) The book was mostly made up of short essays, packed into a slim ninety-six pages, with photographs and woodcut illustrations by the Federal Art Project. Galena, it suggested, was something of a town lost in time and poised for a rebirth.

Algren had never been there. He didn't exactly write the guide, either. Vardis Fisher notwithstanding, hardly any FWP publication can be traced back to a single hand. It was the FWP's method, and indeed its mission, to link field workers, writers, and editors in a single process of collective authorship. This sprawling collaboration made possible the FWP's immense scope and, perhaps counterintuitively, was more efficient than assigning whole books to individual authors. Even when this process seemed overly loose or duplicative, corralling half a dozen writers and editors when one or two would have sufficed, it reinforced the FWP's first and primary aim: to put people to work in a setting that retained their skills and got cash into circulation.

The Galena guide was a perfect example. The process began with field workers who gathered information on-site and from historical records. Then, an editor in Rockford, Sam Cousley, composed the first draft. (Meanwhile, the Illinois project was planning guides to Chicago, Cairo, Decatur, Elgin, East St. Louis, Joliet, Aurora, Alton, Peoria, and Springfield. Galena was going to be first.) Cousley's initial draft arrived in DC, and then his second, but the national editors kept discovering their ultimate bugbear: boosterism. "Its chief fault is a tendency to lose a picture of the real Galena and try to make it a civic promoter's dream come true," one wrote. "This is the kind of boosting that

Chicago and New York reviewers love to wise-crack about and we try to give them as little opportunity for that kind of thing as possible." The point, the editor insisted, was to capture "the inherent dignity of a small town bravely fighting a losing battle with modern industrialism, while it keeps intact its place in American history."

So, back in Chicago, the state editors tossed the assignment to Algren, who rewrote the manuscript with DC's comments in mind. When his draft was ready, they mailed it east along with yet one more draft by Cousley, who insisted on giving it another shot. Both versions arrived in DC, and George Cronyn subjected them to close scrutiny. (As he read, someone from the brand-new Social Security Administration wandered into the office and mentioned that he'd just driven through Galena, but all he could recall was a sign outside town warning about rattlesnakes—a walking demonstration that the guidebooks had a waiting audience.) Alsberg read both versions and likely weighed in, too. Each had its own strengths and weaknesses; together they were among the best local copy submitted all year, from any state. Cronyn wrote back to Chicago, "It seems at first glance that Illinois had wished on Washington a judicial headache of the kind that only one man in history so far, has ever been able to handle—and Solomon has been dead a good many years." In the absence of Solomon, Cronyn managed to come up with a solution. He chose Algren's draft because it represented the best work of both authors, and he even suggested ways the two versions could be further combined. It was collective work from top to bottom.

When the Galena guide appeared that summer—a prelude to the state guide—it was a success. Illinois's governor, Henry Horner, raved to WPA officials; the mayor of Galena told Alsberg that he and city officials were pleased. ("You can read a dozen biographies of Grant and get less insight into his early career than is supplied by a history of Galena," Robert Cantwell, with this book in mind, would argue in his essay on the American Guides.) The guide sold 1,500 copies the day it was published, roughly twice the number that *Somebody in Boots* had sold in a year. The name Nelson Algren appeared nowhere on it. But for an author who'd so despaired knowing that his novel had done nothing to raise the blood pressure of the bourgeoisie, that was probably all right.

Algren was promoted at the end of the summer. By now he was settling into life on the project. He joined the union's shop committee, a local of the CIO. "We move in a world of petitions, pleas, bulletins, protests, indignation meetings and partisan sharpshooting," he told a friend. Aside from handling the usual workplace matters and agitating against cuts to the WPA, the union communicated with Alsberg directly as it sought a voice in the basic functioning of the office.

Algren took the politics of the job seriously. Even after his disastrous appearance at the American Writers' Congress in New York, he'd stuck with the new League of American Writers and become the chapter secretary for Chicago. He knew a handful of comrades on the project who'd likewise been formed in Chicago's radical milieu, a scene with a long, rich history that emanated from the struggles of the city's industrial workers. It was in Chicago, in a 1919 emergency convention, that the Socialist Party fractured, leaving elements of its former left wing to eventually coalesce into the Communist Party. By the thirties, when the Communist Party was approaching peak membership, its presence in the city was strong—there were 408 demonstrations in 1931, and 566 the next year. Algren had a sense of this history and grew to appreciate it. "For it was here" in Chicago, he wrote later, "that those arrangements more convenient to owners of property than to the propertyless were most consistently protested by the American conscience." He had been interested in socialist ideas since high school—his grandfather and namesake passed through a socialist phase of his own—and he had done some haphazard reading of radical thinkers. By the time he joined the project, he'd been absorbing *New Masses* and *The Anvil*, Jack Conroy's magazine of proletarian fiction and poetry. Conroy, an editor and novelist whom *New Masses* praised as "the new man, the agrarian-industrial Ulysses of brutalized roadlife in America," had just become a federal writer himself in Missouri.

Algren and Conroy had been corresponding for several years, and it was Conroy who steered Algren toward the John Reed Club, an organization devoted to radicalism and the arts through which quite a few future federal writers passed. The first John Reed Club was spun off from *New Masses* in 1929, and, like the magazine, it was formally independent of the Communist Party, although that distance closed over time. The club was an unusual overture toward intellectuals and artists from a party that, at the moment, tended to disdain them. This was still the Third Period, when the party kept a narrowly revolutionary course, assailed Roosevelt and the New Deal, and opposed any leftists and reformists outside its ranks as "social fascists." They adhered to a classical Marxist-Leninist view of the working class: that the proletariat, the workers who were separated from the means of production and compelled to sell their labor power to capitalists, would be the crucial agent of any revolutionary transformation, and that the party vanguard existed to direct and focus the proletariat's struggle to take power. More concretely, this meant organizing factory workers, miners, laborers, the newly unemployed—not writers or artists. In 1933, the party leadership issued an open letter that grappled with their failure to become a mass movement, despite the unprecedented shock of the Depression. They were sticking to their approach; the letter called for a renewed commitment to organizing industrial workers inside factories and trade unions, while promoting an openly revolutionary agenda. But even then, this attitude was beginning to shift, and intellectuals, however unreliable and petit bourgeois, seemed like a prize worth pursuing. By the middle of the thirties, with the advent of the Popular Front, a more moderate party had reversed itself entirely: it eagerly pursued the endorsements of intellectuals and sought influence in cultural circles, even while it was busily organizing within the CIO.

The John Reed Club was the first real instance of this cultural outreach. And yet the party was always a little aloof, skeptical of the club's bohemian tendencies and the ideological deviations of its members: writers and visual artists, mostly young and unknown, some from the middle class but many from the working class, loosely committed to creating and debating art in a revolutionary context. Most chapters issued their own publications—in New York, it was the first incarnation of *Partisan Review*, unabashedly a party organ. Five years after the first club appeared, there were thirty chapters with 1,200 members.

A typical member was Jerre Mangione, future national coordinating editor of the FWP. Mangione didn't consider himself a Marxist or communist, but he was passionately anti-fascist and sympathetic to the left. He attended meetings of the New York chapter and found a welcoming atmosphere for aspiring writers whose hopes had been dashed by the Depression. (The novelist Edward Dahlberg, another future federal writer, planned to introduce him to the group—but Dahlberg walked in, engaged in a ferocious argument

with someone else, and stormed out. It was a typical scene.) "I listened to poets and critics orate with an eloquence more characteristic of barristers than
writers, which alternatively impressed and bewildered less erudite members
of their audience like myself," Mangione recalled. Between earnest debate
and predictable bloviating, members also found a purpose discussing actions:
"distributing leaflets, performing on public soapboxes, taking part in picketing and antifascist demonstrations and, inevitably, agitating for a government-
sponsored agency that would give jobs to needy artists and writers." Malcolm
Cowley visited the same New York clubhouse. (He was summoned by the
editors of *Partisan Review*, who intended to call him on the carpet for the
petit bourgeois deficiencies of something he wrote in *The New Republic*.) He
found himself on the second floor of a loft in Greenwich Village, crowded with
figures smoking, arguing, milling around, and nursing paper cups of coffee.
Most but not all of them were young, most but not all were white, and all of
them were men. The room had a certain psychic gravity—a sense of meaning
seeping through all the posturing and rhetoric—and Cowley decided that, for
the rising generation, the John Reed Club was "the place."

So it was for Algren, drawn to the political ferment and the stimulating
company. Like Mangione, he probably realized that he stood a better chance
of getting published in radical magazines, which, in that economic climate,
were almost alone in seeking out new writers. Through the John Reed Club,
Algren fell in with a group of aspiring literary radicals, several of whom
would also end up on the Illinois project. One was Abe Aaron, a writer and
activist from the coal mining country of Pennsylvania. Before the FWP,
he'd been working at the post office while putting himself through the University of Chicago. Another was Richard Wright. Like Algren, he'd been
published in Jack Conroy's magazine *The Anvil*—of the many unknowns
Conroy published, Wright would make arguably the biggest impact. At the
JRC, he edited the chapter's magazine, *Left Front*. To Algren, Wright was
shrewd and occasionally remote, but the two formed a strong friendship.
(It was Wright who organized a party to celebrate *Somebody in Boots* when
Algren was feeling creatively demolished.)

Abe Aaron, Richard Wright, and Algren all joined the Illinois project,
along with the poet Lawrence Lipton (a future beatnik who'd likewise helped
Algren out during his emotional nadir) and a few other JRC alumni. So did

Algren's buddy Dave Peltz, who got a job there after stints at the Illinois Theater Project and as a WPA rat poisoner. Dorothy Farrell, by then separated from her husband, James T. Farrell, author of the Studs Lonigan trilogy, was also on the project, researching Jewish life in the state. And Algren met someone who'd actually taken his name from those James T. Farrell novels: Louis Terkel, an ebullient member of the project's radio division, who went by "Studs."

Terkel was a law school graduate who didn't want to practice law—he'd been more concerned with jazz and blues 78s than torts. On his way to the FWP, he passed through several federal jobs, did a little amateur acting, and voiced gangsters for radio soap operas. The project's radio division consisted of Terkel and five others who toiled at home but met in the office once a week to critique one another's work. Some of Terkel's scripts dealt with slums and New Deal labor laws; others were historical ("Neither Would I Be a Master," which dramatized the young Lincoln's encounter with slavery); some were tales sponsored by the postal clerks' union ("The Amazing Mister Nutmeg," which was "the story of a timid, little postman who had a suppressed desire"—to be a barber, it turned out). Terkel also gained a quick education in art appreciation by working on broadcasts about famous artists, produced in collaboration with the Chicago Art Institute. These were quite popular—even the *Chicago Tribune*'s notoriously anti–New Deal publisher, Colonel Robert McCormick, loved them. But Terkel was convinced that the Colonel—who hated Roosevelt and hated Harry Hopkins even more—always fell asleep before the closing credits and never realized the shows were products of the infernal WPA.

Terkel had read *Somebody in Boots* and he and Algren became friends, chatting in the office and ducking out to go bowling down the street. Sometimes he'd go to Algren's place for a poker game, where he'd find Algren wearing a visor and garters on his arms, as if he were in a movie, laying cards out on green felt. Around the table were con men, bohemians, armed shopkeepers, small-time gangsters, but also "dull guys" who were simply there to play. "The dull guys won all the time because they were careful; they were accountants at heart," Terkel said. "Nelson and I lost *all* the time." Algren wasn't entirely reckless, though. Another project worker noticed him cashing his paycheck, filling an envelope with enough to cover his rent, and mailing it to himself. That way, he'd have enough for the landlord. The rest he could freely gamble away.

Algren also got to know Arna Bontemps, the project's second Black supervisor. (The first was Richard Wright, who left Chicago with the intention of rejoining the project in New York City.) Bontemps's literary credentials were among the most diverse and impressive in the Chicago office: he began as a poet in Harlem during the twenties; he collaborated with Langston Hughes on a children's book; he wrote the historical novels *God Sends Sunday* (about a Black jockey) and *Black Thunder* (about Gabriel's Rebellion in slavery-era Virginia); he worked as a school principal and pursued a master's degree; and he did some ghostwriting for W. C. Handy. In Chicago, he was writing a third novel, *Drums at Dusk*, about the Haitian Revolution. Sometimes Bontemps would sit at his desk and watch Algren flirt with the office typists. ("Women liked him, despite his caddishness and boorishness," Terkel confirmed.) But he otherwise found that Algren was a hard worker—when he wanted to be.

Bontemps was one of several gifted Black writers on the Illinois project. Their number hovered around ten, which, for a project that employed anywhere from 185 to 395 people, meant that Black workers were greatly underrepresented. But few project offices fared better, and most were worse.

There was Richard Durham, a Northwestern graduate, who, like Studs Terkel, worked in the radio division. The FWP was his first real writing job. He wrote forty scripts for the Chicago Art Institute programs, among other tasks, and it launched him on a groundbreaking career in radio.

There was Fenton Johnson, an older poet and magazine editor who'd withdrawn from the literary scene years earlier, only to reemerge on the project, where he was both a fellow worker and source of information about the city's cultural heritage. When he left the project, he dropped a stack of forty-two poems he'd written about the WPA on a desk and walked out; Arna Bontemps eventually prepared a manuscript, but the collection was never published.

There was Willard Motley, who, when he was young, wrote the *Chicago Defender*'s "Bud Billiken" children's column, then became a travel writer while striving to do more literary work. After his time on the project, he wrote *Knock On Any Door*, which became a bestseller, and then a movie starring Humphrey Bogart.

There was Frank Yerby, who worked on the project for only nine months while he studied for a doctorate at the University of Chicago, but later said the FWP gave him the best literary training he could have received. He became a novelist and sold more than 62 million books, mostly historical romances of the South that he called "costume novels," but also more serious work—far beyond what any Black author had ever attained.

And there was Katherine Dunham, a dancer and choreographer who was pursuing graduate studies in anthropology at the University of Chicago. Dunham supervised a small team of researchers (including Yerby) who investigated the city's Black religious groups; along the way, she had a pleasant meeting with Elijah Muhammad. (Decades later, a supervisor would look back on his time on the Illinois project and recall, "Katherine Dunham tried to teach me to rumba.")

Algren didn't socialize with everyone, of course. He paid no heed to Saul Bellow, who was fresh out of college, compiling a bibliography of Chicago newspapers and writing biographies of midwestern literary figures, bored by the work and grateful for it. Among Bellow's assignments was a critical portrait of Sherwood Anderson that ends with a consideration of *Puzzled America*: "Fundamentally his approach to all social problems is still through the individual," Bellow wrote. "He thinks of what happens to a woman in a cotton mill instead of generalizing about the conditions of cotton mill workers. He has begun to treat radical ideologies with more kindness but that has, alas, not been accompanied by anything like analysis." (Bellow, at that time, was a tough critic, but he'd come around to Anderson's individuated approach to fiction later.)

Missing from the office was someone who'd played an increasingly important role in Algren's life: Jack Conroy, the proletarian novelist and editor of *The Anvil*. For Algren, Conroy began as an idol, then became a mentor and a correspondent and, finally, a friend. He'd praised *Somebody in Boots* in *New Masses*, calling the novel an antidote to the romanticized, picturesque takes on hobo life churned out by Hollywood. "It is a story of American *bezprizorni*, cheap criminals, bums, whores, perverts, jailbirds, and scum of the earth," he wrote approvingly. (Conroy's review was perhaps even more validating than one a week earlier in *The New York Times*, by H. W. Boynton, which recognized that Algren—"fresh and sizzling from the griddle of experience"—offered a sensitive and unvarnished look at life in the hobo jungles and boxcars and dives, marred only by some "straight tub-thumping.")

Conroy was working on the project in his home state, Missouri, which was turning out to be among the FWP's most troubled outposts. The office in St. Louis was riven with conflict—fueled by political corruption, radical commitments, and disagreements over the very purpose of the FWP. For a time, it looked as if the entire project might explode.

And then it did.

"THE WILD AND WOOLY WESTERNERS"

When Algren, a discouraged journalism major, hopped a boxcar and joined the transient nation, he made a conscious decision to do so. That doesn't mean it was a game to him, that he was a voyeur gone slumming. He was truly broke; he faced the same risks as any hobo. But he could always go back home. And although he was, at first, an economic refuge like so many others, scrounging for a hot meal, a day's work, and a dry place to sleep, his rambling evolved into a kind of literary quest. He was after raw material to feed his writing, sights he'd never see and voices he'd never hear back in Chicago, working in his father's shop or buried in the newsroom of a small-town paper. His days of roaming became a means to a literary end.

Not all proletarian writers enjoyed that ability to choose. Many simply chronicled the lives of toil that would have been theirs if they'd never put pen to paper at all. Like Michael Gold's idealized contributors to *New Masses*—scribbling down "the sobs of driven stenographers" and "the poetry of steel workers"—they wrote about what they knew and, because they were poor, had no choice *but* to know. Their poems, stories, and novels, like lathe scars and stooped backs and battered eardrums, were essentially the byproducts of their working conditions. Their writing was especially prized by radicals—it was considered more authentic, and therefore charged with greater revolutionary potential. For a time, one writer was celebrated as king of them all.

Jack Conroy was born in a place called Monkey Nest. It was a ramshackle camp heaped up around a coal mine outside Moberly, Missouri. When Conroy was a child, his father and the other miners still used axes and shovels to dislodge the coal and mules to haul it from the pit. Underground, they dodged loose rocks and tried not to suck black damp into their lungs. Aboveground, their families lived in a collective state of tension. They shared every deprivation and disaster, every strike—and there were plenty of strikes. Conroy's father was a leader in the United Mine Workers local. In 1898, the year of Jack's birth, the UMW led 260 separate strike actions. They fought for better pay, safer conditions, and the eight-hour workday. The mine operators fought back. In Monkey Nest, as in other mining camps, class antagonism was laid bare. There were workers, sharing a plain common interest, and there were bosses. Conroy breathed that struggle in with the Missouri dust.

Like all the men around him, he seemed to have but one destination: the damp and dark of the coal pit. But death intervened. Both his half brothers perished in the mine. (Their father, Jack's mother's first husband, also died that way.) Then Jack's own father was killed in a blasting accident. His mother, who lost two sons and two husbands to the mine, vowed to send no more. She took Jack, now thirteen years old, and they walked the two miles into Moberly, to the Wabash Railroad machine shop, where he became an apprentice.

He worked there for ten years and came out the other side, perhaps surprisingly, a writer. Thank his parents, who kept a literary home in Monkey Nest; thank the union, which published his first pieces in the *Railway Carmen's Journal*; thank the Moberly library, where he stocked up on the classics, Jack London, and Upton Sinclair; thank the IWW, whose slogans he found carved inside boxcars like messages from some distant battlefront. Thank, too, the bosses and the National Guard, who smashed the 400,000-strong railroad strike of 1922, ending Conroy's career in the machine shop and dispersing him and his fellow strikers into the uprooted and drifting proletariat, the unseen labor force of the Jazz Age. "The Depression started early for me," he would say.

He was still a laborer through the twenties and into the thirties—a bricklayer and a surveyor's assistant and a ditch digger and a drift miner, chasing jobs around the Midwest. He worked in steel mills and auto plants and rubber factories and briefly ran a grocery shop. His wife was a factory worker, too. But once Conroy discovered the little magazines sprouting up around the interior of the country, the mushroom mags, he began to make his name. Through the mail he met various oddballs, iconoclasts, freethinkers, and radicals of all persuasions. He began to publish poetry (romantic and derivative, a hangover from the books of his youth) and then essays and labor narratives and character sketches. Eventually he was reaching a national audience through *New Masses* and H. L. Mencken's *The American Mercury.* He'd also become an editor himself, first by running the magazine of Rebel Poets, an umbrella group for writers of the American hinterlands, and then his own magazine, *The Anvil.* "We prefer crude vigor to polished banality," went *The Anvil*'s slogan, which captured Conroy's sensibility well. He admired the Communist Party's discipline and commitment but was allergic to sectarianism and party lines. He belonged, quite consciously, to a midwestern tradition of native radicalism—less theoretical, more democratic and ecumenical, cruder and more humorous than the prevailing style inspired by European ideologies. When his first novel, *The Disinherited*, appeared in 1933, Conroy became a key figure in the burgeoning proletarian literature movement (although, still, no one could agree on what precisely that meant). The novel was really thirteen stories and sketches rolled into a lumpy, disjointed portrait of working-class life, but it was precisely the kind of authentic literature that activists like Michael Gold were clamoring for, and aspiring writers like Nelson Algren were attempting to emulate.

Over the next couple of years, Conroy enjoyed his eminence. He became a mentor to young writers that he published in *The Anvil,* including Algren and Richard Wright. (Algren admired Conroy and secretly wanted to displace him as king of the proletarian writers; as a stylist, he'd soon surpass Conroy, whose prose was sturdy but faintly archaic.) He won a Guggenheim Fellowship to interview workers in Detroit and Akron, and he published a second novel, *A World to Win,* though it was more conventional than his first and not as well received. He was pleased to see Russian, French, and German editions of *The Disinherited.* But then things began to unravel. He lost *The Anvil* in a messy arrangement when it was effectively absorbed by *Partisan Review,* under pressure from the Communist Party. In Alabama, he and a group of activists tested a state law banning the sale of "seditious" literature by picketing in front of the state house with copies of *New Masses* and they were shot at for their trouble. His Guggenheim money ran out. Writing for *New Masses*—or *Midland Left* or *Labor Defender* or *Young Worker*—didn't pay the bills. When Conroy's wife, Gladys, finally lost her job at the shoe factory, the next step was to go on relief.

Conroy joined the Missouri writers' project in the summer of 1936. He moved to St. Louis and roomed in a decrepit mansion that had been split into apartments, the hub of the local radical and bohemian community. They called it the Kremlin. The project office was downtown in "a section of venerable, high, and smoke-smudged buildings," as Conroy described it. "Narrow streets slope down to old and odorous warehouses on the riverfront. There are taverns once the rendezvous of such Mississippi River pilots as Samuel Clemens. Brisk men of finance, smart stenographers, frugally neat filing clerks, swarm in and out of the buildings." On a floor high above the scrum, Conroy encountered a familiar face: Jack Balch, a writer in his mid-twenties who'd been on the *Anvil* editorial staff and was now the project's assistant director.

Conroy was actually Henry Alsberg's first choice for state director. Like Vardis Fisher, Conroy was an established novelist who'd written perceptively about life in his home state. He didn't have Fisher's academic credentials, but he did have years of editorial experience and a Guggenheim Fellowship to boot. But he also had a reputation as a radical activist in the orbit of the Communist Party. So the directorship instead went to Geraldine Parker, an amateur writer installed by the Pendergast political machine. The Pendergast operation was based out of Kansas City and stretched back to the late nineteenth century, when the saloon owner "Alderman Jim" Pendergast fashioned himself into the city's first Democratic boss. By the thirties, control passed to his younger brother, Tom, and the machine's influence reached across the entire state, propelled by licit and illicit business interests. It was their machine that plucked Harry Truman from a failing haberdashery and set him on a political career, with the result that, in Washington, he was known as the "Senator from Pendergast." When Truman was elected in the Democratic sweep of 1934, Pendergast was among the most powerful political bosses—perhaps *the* most powerful—anywhere in the nation, and a valuable supporter of the Roosevelt administration. Alsberg was uncomfortable knowing that Pendergast's influence reached into the Missouri project, but the presence of Conroy and Balch, both of whom had been hired on his recommendation, gave him some reassurance. "I think these people are very able and, if given the opportunity, will turn out a very creditable work," Alsberg wrote to Parker.

Before Conroy and Balch got very far, though, the project began to falter. Parker revealed herself to be a blatant stooge of the Pendergast machine.

Her single aim for the Missouri guidebook was to fashion a boosterish thing that would be acceptable to her political cronies. She stuffed the office full of men and women who were politically "in the picture" (a phrase she used) regardless of their capabilities. All of those hires except one were white. Balch was outraged when Parker passed over qualified Black candidates, including some with advanced degrees. Equally enraging was her brazenness—she gave all manuscripts to the state WPA administrator, a Pendergast man, for approval before sending them to DC. This meant deleting material about silicosis poisoning and even Missouri's native son, the painter Thomas Hart Benton. "I wouldn't hang him on my shithouse wall," the WPA administrator said. He told them to write about the roads instead.

Tensions finally exploded when a federal writer named Wayne Barker was fired. The details were somewhat murky: Parker accused Barker of being uncooperative and inefficient, then insisted that he'd been selling pornographic postcards. For his part, Barker accused the director of misappropriating funds, then claimed that he was being punished for organizing a union. When the DC office did not immediately intervene on Barker's behalf, seventeen workers went out on strike. Conroy was one of the leaders. The strike was triggered by a single incident, but it raised questions that got to the heart of the FWP's purpose. In *New Masses*, Conroy put it bluntly. "Does the administration, through the Federal Writers' Projects, intend to stimulate and foster writers, or is its purpose to stifle and emasculate them, close their mouths, keep them in intellectual bondage and submission twenty-four hours a day?" In other words, was the point of Federal #1 simply to provide work or to nurture the creative energies of the people it employed? The answer was up for grabs. "Those of us," he concluded, "who went at the job of writing the American Guide with the determination to make it a full-bodied, rich, and recognizable picture of life in the United States—the land, its people, their customs, their folk-lore—would like to know."

Even though Conroy was a strike leader, privately, he had misgivings. Perhaps he was thinking of the Great Railroad Strike of 1922 that forever changed his life. Or perhaps it was the distinctly fraught matter of striking against federal work relief. In a novel that Jack Balch would write about the Missouri project, *Lamps at High Noon*, a Conroy character distinguishes between a strike against private industry and one in the public sector. In the former, the strikers withhold profits from the owners. In the latter, they mainly withhold their own wages. "The government saves the money," he says. "The state balances its budget. The reactionary press hollers, 'Look at the dirty bastards! They won't even take relief, let alone work!'" He had a point.

The dispute had no clear solution. Barker, who'd apparently stolen documents to make his case and spread misinformation, wasn't entirely blameless. Alsberg sent his assistant director, the reliable Reed Harris, to Missouri while a delegation—including Conroy, Barker, and several union representatives—traveled to DC. The meeting did not go well. When someone suggested that Alsberg ordered Barker to be fired, he exploded: "That is an absolute lie. I knew nothing of Barker's dismissal until I got the first telegram. Whoever told you that is telling you an absolute lie. It is a damning lie, and you should tell me who said it." But when they pressed Alsberg to say if he could reinstate Barker that instant, he turned cagey and evasive. Alsberg was sympathetic to the strikers, especially Conroy and Balch. But Barker was plainly a liability (Reed Harris concluded that he should indeed have been fired) and Parker was plainly a hack. The DC office, the union, and the Missouri WPA administrator negotiated a sloppy ending. Barker's firing stood but Parker was forced to resign. Some of the strikers, including Conroy and Balch, were allowed to return.

Conroy stayed with the project half-heartedly and there was more talk of making him director, a notion quickly ruled out, again, because of his politics. Parker's replacement was not much better, and the office remained stagnant, no closer to delivering viable guidebook copy. On one research trip to Kansas City, Conroy spent his time visiting with Thomas Hart Benton and drinking bourbon—that Benton-hating WPA administrator and his shithouse be damned.

Otherwise, Conroy was drafting guidebook copy that won him few fans among the DC editors. His writing was lively but a little slapdash and oddly truculent; it belonged to the pages of *The Anvil* and *New Masses* but not inside a Baedeker. Take his essay on literature: "Not only did the wild and wooly westerners behave in a most unorthodox manner, but their speech was barbaric," he wrote, describing popular authors such as Artemus Ward and Petroleum V. Nasby. "Dialect was still frowned upon by the effete eastern arbiters of literature, so the embattled westerners, goaded to more violent revolt against the stylistic straightjackets imposed by those cloistered in the library and classroom, deliberately scorned grammar and encouraged misspelling." The editors in DC were growing frustrated. And Balch fared even worse: they found his contributions nearly incoherent.

By the fall of 1937, Conroy quit. He was feeling dejected and drinking heavily. Then came an invitation from Algren. What did Conroy think of relocating to Chicago, taking a job on the Illinois project, and reviving *The Anvil*? In March 1938, Conroy arrived at Nelson and Amanda's apartment, a derelict storefront that was once part of an arcade built for the 1893 World's Fair. Bohemians and radicals formed an enclave there and called it "Rat Alley." Conroy began sleeping in the Algrens' bed, while Nelson and Amanda, their young marriage already failing, took separate couches.

"YOU'VE BECOME A LANDMARK"

After Conroy left, the Missouri project essentially collapsed. Alsberg installed a new director who began the guide over from scratch, assisted by a skeleton staff and an editor sent from DC: Harold Rosenberg, the future art critic. The Missouri guide did eventually appear, but the project itself was one of the FWP's more conspicuous disasters.

The fiasco might have made Conroy radioactive but Algren had no trouble convincing John T. Frederick to hire him. The two men seemed like foils—Conroy, the boozing, gregarious radical, and Frederick, the buttoned-down scholar—but they knew each other from their days of editing little midwestern magazines. Frederick's nurturing and expansive style as editor of *The Midland* set an example for Conroy when he was building an epistolary network through *The Rebel Poet* and *The Anvil*. In 1933, when Frederick admitted that *The Midland* was in danger of folding, Conroy offered to send him money. Frederick didn't forget the gesture.

Now united in Chicago, Algren and Conroy used their spare time to get *The New Anvil* up and running. It lasted for seven issues and printed stories by the federal writers Frank Yerby from Illinois (his first), Jack Balch from Missouri, and Meridel Le Sueur from Minnesota, as well as Frank Marshall

Davis and William Carlos Williams. (The editors rejected submissions from two young writers: Tennessee Williams, who coincidentally had been passed over for a job on the Illinois project, and J. D. Salinger.) Meanwhile, in New York, *Partisan Review*, once *The Anvil*'s partner in a forced marriage arranged by the Communist Party, had reemerged with a stance that was fiercely critical of the party and the Soviet Union and Popular Front aesthetics in general.

There was nothing especially new about *The New Anvil*. Magazines like it, dedicated to stories and sketches that dealt with working life and radical ideas, had been appearing around the country since the twenties. By the late thirties, they were dying off, and it was not long before *The New Anvil* followed. For Algren and Conroy, the work of a small, radical magazine was familiar. Less familiar—and perhaps more innovative and meaningful—was their new assignment at the FWP. They'd paired up at an opportune moment. The FWP was expanding its portfolio and sending more field workers out to collect individual life histories, testimonials of formerly enslaved people and contemporary laborers, and folklore that emerged from present-day experiences, not just the misty past. This had always been part of the FWP's procedure: field workers relied on living informants as much as newspaper morgues and town records. ("If you're stopped by a stranger who wants to know your racial background and how many of your ancestors fell at Ticonderoga don't be ruffled," the NYC project director announced. "It will simply mean that you've become a landmark and are to be preserved for posterity.") As the FWP matured, filing cabinets in every state swelled with testimonials, spoken by people who were far from the levers of power—and taken down by such people, too. These interviews were edited, of course, and some were worked up into character sketches. The better writers could take a testimonial and nudge it and shape it until it glowed with a subtle poetry of heightened meaning. But, in another sense, there was no implied meaning to interpret, except: here are the thoughts and experiences, conveyed in the actual language, of Americans who don't get quoted in newspapers and don't issue press releases and don't broadcast over the airwaves, but who are important nonetheless.

Algren and Conroy were familiar with the appeal of taking down raw testimonials because proletarian writers had done it for years. It was the stuff Michael Gold called for in the late twenties. Shop-floor stories and straight-from-the-gutter monologues were arguably the most revered forms in the proletarian writer's arsenal, and often the most successfully executed, too. If the FWP wanted dispatches from the lives of ordinary Americans— who were, overwhelmingly, workers—then Algren and Conroy and their comrades were one step ahead.

Not that the proletarian writers, or the FWP, invented the testimonial approach. Henry Mayhew, an English journalist and founder of *Punch*, published *London Labour and the London Poor* in 1851, which documented the lives and captured the voices of the city's workers. By the 1920s, pulp magazines were stuffed with "true confessions" of every type. The form was so popular that confessions began appearing in respectable magazines and were repurposed by social scientists, who did little more than ornament stories of thieves and delinquents with their own learned conclusions.

In 1937, around the same time that the FWP was ramping up these efforts, the Mass Observation movement appeared in Britain, propelled by a similar impulse. Its founders set out to exhaustively document the minutiae of daily life in a way that ended up being part guerrilla anthropology and part Surrealist performance art. Investigators, like the FWP's field workers, canvassed homes and pubs and workplaces, while thousands of volunteers mailed in daily diaries and responded to questionnaires. There was no real organizing purpose, no theoretical underpinning, other than to show, in overwhelming detail, how ordinary Britons lived. Unlike the FWP, Mass Observation was an independent effort; it had nothing to do with relief or public employment (although it did help gauge morale for the government during the Second World War). And, unlike the FWP, it was focused on tabulation and (dubious) statistics, not narrative. But they both mobilized ordinary people in the documentation of ordinary life, and they both believed that the results could reveal something valuable about art and citizenship—even if the details were fuzzy.

The FWP's efforts were forward-looking, too: an important prelude to what would be called oral history. They predated by a decade the formal founding of the academic discipline in 1948, when the historian Allan Nevins established the Center for Oral History Research at Columbia University. But the FWP operated too far from scholarly circles to have much influence on contemporary historians and sociologists. It was different, after all. The FWP, like Mass Observation in the UK and like amateur folklore collectors, made no effort to be "scientific" as it selected informants and analyzed data. The testimonials weren't even really data, anyway. They were more like documentary prose poems. Accuracy was important, but so were readability and even publishability. In a sense, the testimonials were a literary end in themselves. More than that, the *process* by which they were created was just as important as the information they conveyed. Overlooked people became the narrators of their own lives and guides to their own tiny bit of the country. There was dignity in that. And even though FWP field workers and editors shaped the testimonials, they weren't simply mining informants for experiences and hauling away the words. The finished life histories were collaborations; the process was participatory. Everyone involved—the maid pausing to narrate her life story, the field worker taking it down, the editor lending it a touch of artful clarity—was together carrying out the FWP's vast, collective self-portrait of the nation.

The fullest expression of this effort was in the South, where W. T. Couch was regional director. (This was the position, created a few years into the FWP's life, that Vardis Fisher nearly attained for the mountain states but then was denied after his antics in a Nampa jail.) Couch organized a multistate effort to take down the life histories of ordinary southerners. They sent out field workers, guided by a simple outline: ask about family, diet, if they felt pride or shame in their work, if they vote. The field workers were free to improvise, too. "The criteria to be observed are those of accuracy, human interest, social importance, literary excellence," the instructions said. If it wasn't possible to achieve all four, accuracy and literary excellence were the minimum. The copy piled up. Couch planned a series of volumes, but he ended up publishing only one: *These Are Our Lives: As Told by the People and Written by Members of the Federal Writers' Project of the Works Progress Administration in North Carolina, Tennessee, Georgia.* "The people, all the people, must be known, they must be heard," Couch wrote in the preface. "Somehow they must be given representation, somehow they must be given voice and allowed to speak, in their essential character." Books of life histories weren't sufficient to reach this goal, he admitted. But they could help. *These Are Our*

Lives presented the words—mediated, of course, by federal writers—of men and women, white and Black, who worked on farms, in mills and factories, in service jobs, and who were on relief. That last category, people on relief, lent the book a somewhat meta quality, as if the WPA were reflecting on itself. Spoke a "Young white man in charge of WPA supply room":

> I'll admit there's some don't deserve a nickel of the government's money. Lot of them that comes here, why I'd sooner give them a kick in the pants than shove 'em out supplies. But you got to take the good with the bad. Or bad with the good, whichever way you've a mind to put it. Most that comes here are poor and can't help it. Needs help. Needs it just same I need this job. Always going to be more poor folks than them that ain't poor. Now take me. I've always been poor and I guess I always will be. I ain't saying that's the government's fault. It's just a downright truth, that's all.

The Illinois project applied this task to an urban setting. It was the perfect assignment for Algren, who, since his days of scribbling notes inside a hobo jungle or a Texas jail cell, never lost the habit. Conroy likewise had been working in this mode for his entire career. Sometimes together and sometimes alone, they went out into the Chicago streets, into taverns and pool halls and other places where workers gathered, and they listened, and they took it down hot.

> You see the way my head cocks up to'rd the ceiling every time I take my mind off it a minute? Well, sir, I got that way from cleaning wall paper in one of them old places on North Dearborn.

> Hell, you can't tell me about panics, man! Ain't I lived through three and ain't we right in the middle of one right now?

> A typesetter can get a good education because he has to comprehend at least something of the stuff he's putting into type. That's the way I first read Shakespeare, setting up a one-volume edition of his plays. I still know a lot of the best lines by heart.

Conroy collected a testimonial from his own nephew, Fred Harrison, who was only three years younger. (This seemed, somehow, like nepotism, so Conroy didn't mention it at the project.) They were close—after the defeat of the railroad strike, they moved from town to town, often by boxcar, looking for work. Conroy even based a major character in *The Disinherited* on Harrison. Now he turned to his nephew again as Harrison spoke about the mines and revealed a detailed, technical knowledge of the job that comes only through hours and hours of labor. The testimonial was suffused with the miners' lingo and their subterranean culture, including its more harrowing aspects:

> Some of the waste material is thrown into the places just mined out, and this part of the mine is known as the "gob." Miners throw scraps from their lunches into the gob and the place is always overrun by rats that fight and squeal in the dark. When I first went into the mine I was terrified at the thought of the rats, and so were other boys beginning in the mine. One of the standard threats of veterans to green boys is: "Look alive, or I'll throw you in the gob with the rats."

Algren's friend from the John Reed Club, Abe Aaron, was at it too: he spoke with tavern dwellers, sign painters, cab drivers, and newsboys, and he returned to his old workplace, the Chicago post office, to interview mail carriers and discuss the peculiar hazards of the Roosevelt era.

> One day I tore a woman's blouse right off her. It wasn't my fault; it was hers. She wanted her WPA check. I had it all right, but she couldn't wait. She sees a government envelope sticking out of the pouch and she says, "That's my check," and she reaches right over my shoulder and grabs it. I grab it right back. She snatches it again and when I go to take it from her she steps back and I grab hold of her blouse instead and it tears in my hand. I got a complaint on that, but I talked my way out of it all right.
>
> The fellows believe so many guys commit suicide because of the pressure of the work; they're bein' pushed around. Let's talk about somethin' else, huh?

With these narratives, Algren's project work was syncing up with the spirit of his own writing. He'd never needed an excuse to mingle with criminals and bums, but now he was given official license and a paycheck to do so. He hung out around grimy boxing rings and gangsterish social clubs and the city night court; he observed inveterate gamblers and exhausted dance marathoners and denizens of the racetrack. One testimonial, from a Chicago sex worker named Ellen O'Connor, could have been spoken by a character out of Algren's fiction:

> When a girl got nobody who cares and she got to quit school like I done, it don't matter much what line she goes into, she ends up pretty much the same way every time. Whether she hires out to cook some college-dame's meals and scrub her toilet or run a twenty-six game in a bar or tap tacks in a shoe factory, she's bound to take a beating in the end. The smartest just take it lying down. You last longer that way.

Another was a young Jewish boxer named Davey Day, whom Algren interviewed in a luggage store owned by Day's father.

> Yep, I'm him, Davey Day, that fast-stepping Jewboy on his way up, all fight and fancy footwork.
> Say, a dame wrote me a fan latter. I looked like George Raft she said. He used to be a pug too. I guess somebody must of told her I was punchy awready, I would believe anything. Say, I don't look like no George Raft.

As Algren collected such testimonials, he wasn't only honing a mood and a method that he'd repurpose in his fiction. Pieces of Ellen O'Connor's statement found their way into *Never Come Morning*, the novel he began writing after he was reinvigorated by his project job. And he'd name-check Davey Day in the story "Million-Dollar Brainstorm," which would appear eight years later in his collection *The Neon Wilderness*.

Conroy excelled at the task. Five of his testimonials were selected for "Men at Work," a compilation of labor sketches and industrial tall tales that was being planned in the DC office. Alongside "Logging in the Rain" (from Oregon) and "Organ Builder's Soliloquy" (from Illinois), there were contributions from two federal writers at the beginnings of their careers: "'Snake'

Magee and the Rotary Boiler" by Jim Thompson in Oklahoma, and "The Shipyards Get a Welder" by Chester Himes in Ohio. Conroy also had a few slated for *Nobody with Sense*, a collection of humorous tales and yarns.

Algren seems to have benefited from Conroy's industriousness, too: he turned in at least two narratives that were likely written by Conroy. (Both were later published under Algren's name in books compiled after the FWP.) One of them, "Highpockets," is a western tall tale repurposed for an industrial setting, about a factory worker, "a hillbilly from way back at the fork of the crick" who walked like "a man stepping over cornstalks." To the dismay of his fellow workers, Highpockets always obliges when the time-study man asks him to speed up or increase his labor. By the end of the tale, Highpockets is working the machines with both arms, both legs, and an apparatus rigged up between his teeth. When the time-study man asks if it's possible to squeeze out a little more work, he replies, "Sure, if you want to stick a broom someplace, I think I could be sweeping the floor!"

The federal writer who, in later years, would make the most of this approach—who would even epitomize it in the eyes of the country—wasn't gathering testimonials or life histories or industrial folklore at all. Studs Terkel was a member of the radio division, which meant that he was divorced from everyday office life: he was at home, working on scripts, and only occasionally conferencing with the rest of his division. He found the job both exhilarating and liberating—it offered him an alternative route, as he saw it, away from a secure but deadening life as a lawyer—but it's difficult to trace a direct line from the FWP to his first book of oral history, *Division Street: America*, which he didn't publish until 1967. (As he followed it up with *Hard Times*, *Working*, and *The Good War*, which won him a Pulitzer Prize, Terkel cemented his reputation as the nation's preeminent popular oral historian.) That work seems to have grown out of Terkel's years of experience as an interviewer on the radio and local television. And yet those books could have come straight from the files of the FWP, if it had continued into the postwar era. In other words, the project may not have given him the training, but it presented him with a trajectory. Terkel understood this and, for decades to come, was a tireless advocate for the FWP's legacy. "Lucky," he said, near the very end of his life. "I was lucky to be alive at that moment." He was one of its proudest alumni.

Algren, however, was not. In later years, his take on the FWP was a little salty. ("I was an editor," he told an interviewer. "I guess I was an editor.") He stuck up for the WPA but he downplayed his own experience. He was always getting fired, he suggested, and the work he did wasn't all that important anyway. He liked to tell a story about getting a free bag of moldy potatoes whenever he went back on relief—as if that summed up his whole connection to the FWP. "The truth is that that time is so remote I lost interest in it long ago," he wrote in 1964, turning down an invitation to contribute to a symposium on the thirties. (He was likely stung by critics who'd pigeonholed him as a Depression relic, a washed-up proletarian whose time had passed.) Algren insisted that he hadn't done much writing before the war, that his better work came later.

Perhaps it was true—but that was the point. Without the FWP, there may have been no later, better work. And the work that did appear, later, carried heavy traces of his time at 433 East Erie Street. His greatest achievements— *Never Come Morning* (which he wrote, on and off, while he was on and off the project), *The Man with the Golden Arm*, and the story collection *The Neon Wilderness*—were suffused with the sights and smells and speech of the city that Algren had learned to observe so carefully. It isn't hard to imagine these novels and stories being assembled from the notes of a field worker who'd been peeking into bars and back rooms and chatting up the characters who dwelled there—and that's because they were. Even Algren's other masterpiece, the prose poem *Chicago: City on the Make*, reads like a 100-proof distillation of the American Guides, a place-portrait that is barely able to contain itself. The FWP didn't hand him these books. Algren showed up with his own talents, his tenacity, and his humane instincts. But the project kept his brain from eroding and, in the process, shaped the work that was yet to come. It gave him more than sacks of moldy potatoes.

Algren himself knew this, back in the thirties, and he said so. After he'd been on the project for more than a year, he wrote a piece for a magazine published by the Artists Union of Chicago. It was an advertisement for the FWP, the kind of thing Alsberg sometimes contributed to national publications. But, unlike Alsberg when he wrote such pieces, Algren was essentially describing himself. "Men who may otherwise have become too demoralized by poverty to do creative work, or would be frying hamburgers or turning out ad copy or running a roulette wheel, are now assisting both themselves and the nation's cultural life through the federal writers projects," wrote the aspiring writer who once ran a carnival roulette wheel (or, more accurately, shilled for a crooked one). Algren rattled off an impressive roster of federal writers—Conrad Aiken, Jack Conroy, and Vardis Fisher among them—and added, "such names are supplemented by dozens of young unknowns with genuine creative impulses who no longer have to sell Realsilk hose or Herald and Examiner life insurance from door to door in order to meet their rent." He also knew what it was like to have doors slammed in your face while your box of wares grew heavier—he'd done it in New Orleans.

At the end of the piece, he turned, again, to Herman Melville, although with a bit more relevance than in his "Midwestern Literature" essay. Melville was "harassed by economic fear," Algren wrote, as were generations of American writers after him. If Melville could have worked in ease, *Moby-Dick* would have been a better book and Melville would have written more books like it. "But he did not and, in the end, gave over the struggle to become a customhouse clerk; for two decades he never put pen to paper. The loss to American culture was not only immeasurable: it was typical." There but for fortune and the FWP went Algren. Without it, he would have been forced to find his customhouse: a factory, a gambling den, a tire shop like his father's. That's if he found work at all. Otherwise, it might have been a suicide's grave or jail, again.

At the FWP, he found a different path. And even if Algren wasn't above a little double-dealing, borrowing Conroy's pieces as his own, he did good work. In 1939, during the height of the project's efforts to collect industrial lore, they held a staff meeting. Algren—who, with Conroy, was eventually promoted to supervisor—discussed the idea of a new book along the lines of *These Are Our Lives* but gathered from industrial settings. He pointed to work being done by federal writers in New York that had a straight documentary flavor, and had someone read from a particularly surreal and oddly appealing example:

Listen to what I'm gonna say to you now, carefully—the bacteria of primordial times is today the bacteriologist. Sh! Don't talk. Think that over . . . Now. Look at me. I look like a dirt monkey. True. I'm among the world of missing men. I'm so insignificant if they sent out a radio call for me a hundred years nobody would find me. I could write my whole will on a postage stamp. Tell me, then, why should I sing my country tis of thee or welcome sweet springtime I greet you in song. Economically I'm collapsed, not a single coin of the realm you'll find in my pocket, I ain't got enough real estate to put in a flower pot. And yet, my friend, you can never tell the way you stand by the way you're sitting down. I'm a could-have-been.

Algren suggested to the group that this unadorned, freewheeling, slangy anti-narrative was the most modern form of the folktale and, at the same time, a potentially significant kind of proletarian literature. "They are the same thing," he said. Something in it resonated with him. (*My friend, you can never tell the way you stand by the way you're sitting down.*) These were the words of a jobless man on the streets of Manhattan, rambling to someone, a federal writer, who was being paid by the government to listen. And it was pure literature. But, even so, Algren cautioned the group about leaving their transcriptions raw. "This may be naturalism," he said, "but we aren't working here as individuals: we're working in a group observed by the society about it, and what appears to be 'naturalism' may not be at all worth the cost." In other words, they were public workers, paid with tax dollars and under constant scrutiny from critics of the FWP who would like nothing more than to see them booted off the job. They needed to be cautious. "Let's not stick our necks out for a fetish," he said. There would be plenty of opportunities, later, back at his own work and standing up, for him to stick his neck out.

◆

ZORA NEALE HURSTON, FLORIDA

"THE HELL OF A WAY TO MAKE UP A GUIDE-BOOK"

In January 1936—before she was the project's highest-ranking woman, before she was the national tours editor, before she was compiling a "Red Baedeker" on behalf of the Soviets (according to the Hearst newspapers, anyway)—Katharine Kellock was an FWP field representative. As a liaison between the national staff in DC and the project offices in the states, she was something of an all-purpose troubleshooter, and a little bit of a spy. She'd done similar work as a staffer in the Resettlement Administration, under the direction of Rex Tugwell. Then, she had traveled to the new cooperative communities that the RA was setting up for farmers whose land was rotten and for urban workers whose factories were shuttered. Now, for the FWP, Henry Alsberg was dispatching her to the writers' project offices in the southeastern states. Other field representatives were out roaming the rest of the country, delivering and clarifying instructions from DC and reporting back on production of the American Guides—an idea Kellock had half invented. That January, she set out from Washington, southbound, to survey the offices and measure their progress.

Kellock was dismayed by what she found. She discovered incompetent editors and incorrect filing systems and improper spending. Some workers were turning in useless copy. Others weren't entirely sure what the FWP was supposed to be doing. Alsberg and the national staff had anticipated that the southeastern offices would be thin on expertise and experience; the density of writers in, say, Georgia, did not compare with that in New York or Illinois. But now Kellock could see how this disadvantage looked in practice. A federal writer on the North Carolina project described her colleagues this way: "A skilled city editor, victim of retrenchment—and a newsroom hanger-on to be described only as a moderate drunk. A man who had been good at his craft, in his day, but was simply too old to adapt. And housewives, some college women, some widows with only high school, or less. There were former teachers set adrift by cuts in staff. We had a few boys and girls who had really had no jobs at all."

Kellock wondered if they had it all wrong. At that moment, field workers were writing up their notes into brief narratives, the raw copy they called "field continuities." Maybe, she thought, they ought to be filling out index cards instead, and then handing the cards over to competent editors who would do the actual writing. Their current approach seemed like a colossal waste of time. And the instructions emanating from DC—the American Guide Manual and its ever-multiplying supplements—weren't helping. Federal writers *were* treating them like holy writ, but not in the intended sense. As a district supervisor in Charleston told her, "The Manuals are like the Bible—anyone can interpret them in any way."

Alsberg knew they were going to be leaning on competent writers. He wrote to Kellock—betraying his desire to create works of literary value over and above the FWP's relief mission—and said, "One person of writing and editorial ability will be worth 50 people without writing experience." But Kellock was concerned about the pace. She figured that, under present conditions and at the present rate, the southern guidebooks would be done in 1990.

The FWP's architects understood that the American South, since the fall of the Confederacy, was impoverished in a deep, structural way. Here was a region where investment capital was scarce, where workers tended to be poorly educated and unskilled, where ownership of everything aside from agricultural land—manufacturing, finance, transportation, communications—was concentrated in the Northeast, where segregation made a bad situation worse, where the formerly enslaved and their children and grandchildren lived in a state of superexploitation. Roosevelt, during his second term, commissioned a study to measure these exceptionally dismal social conditions. *Report on Economic Conditions of the South* was a portrait of appalling lows and disturbing highs. The South was far behind the rest of the country in per capita and gross incomes, tax collections, public services, basic education, sanitation infrastructure, and access to running water. It surpassed other regions in farm tenancy and share-cropping, illiteracy, water-borne diseases, catastrophic flooding, and malnutrition. The report concluded that the southern poor resembled "the poorest peasants in Europe"—though it did not address the racial hierarchy that generated and helped to perpetuate such widespread impoverishment. (The report was controversial, although not because it overlooked Jim Crow. Roosevelt's southern critics were predictably enraged when, speaking about the report, he called the region "the Nation's No. 1 economic problem." It didn't help that half a million copies of the report were distributed, or that it was reprinted by various public and private agencies.)

Florida was no exception to this grim pattern, despite the state's popularity as a tourist destination. Before the Depression, it saw 1.5 million annual vacationers, a trend spurred by a rising national income, new train lines linking the Northeast to southern Florida, more cars on the road, and more paid vacations for workers. ("Throughout more than four centuries," as *Florida: A Guide to the Southernmost State* would put it, "from Ponce de Leon in his caravels to the latest Pennsylvanian in his Buick, Florida has been invaded by seekers of gold or of sunshine.") But Florida's economy was vulnerable, weakened by a burst real estate bubble in 1926, followed by two destructive hurricanes and an infestation of fruit flies. Then came the Great Crash. By September 1933, Florida had the highest percentage of people on relief in the entire country.

The WPA in Florida got off to a tragic start. On Labor Day 1935, another massive hurricane tore through the Florida Keys, where hundreds of destitute army veterans—many of whom had participated in the Bonus Army march on Washington—were building a road through the islands. (It was a FERA project that was being transferred to the WPA.) As the storm bore down on the Keys, a train set out from Miami to evacuate the veterans and their families. But it was too late—seventeen-foot swells rose out of the sea and swept the entire train, except for the engine, off the tracks. The Florida guide described what happened next: "Wind and waves crushed the frail wooden shacks of the veterans. Many tied themselves to boats at anchor in an effort to survive. Miles of railroad embankment were washed away. Entire towns were obliterated; more than 500 bodies were recovered immediately after the storm subsided, and for months unidentified corpses were found in the mangrove swamps." An irate Ernest Hemingway visited the scene and wrote a dispatch for *New Masses* that described bodies strewn across the landscape: "You found them everywhere and in the sun all of them were beginning to be too big for their blue jeans and jackets that they could never fill when they were on the bum and hungry." The federal government, he concluded, was guilty of manslaughter.

Less than five months later, Kellock embarked on her tour of the South, finally arriving in downtown Jacksonville, home of the Florida project's main office. She had visited the office once before, when she was still working for the Resettlement Administration but anticipating a transfer to the FWP, and she'd sent Alsberg favorable reports. She believed, perhaps optimistically, that Florida's pool of writing talent more resembled New York City's than those in other southern states. But she had no illusions about the obstacles they faced, including deeply held ideas about states' rights and widespread regional hostility to the New Deal. ("I heard gruesome details in R.A.," she confided to Alsberg.) She surveyed the Jacksonville office and then made a long-distance call to DC.

"Can I talk to you freely?" Alsberg asked.

"Yes."

"Is the situation very bad?"

"Yes, it is."

"Well, then don't leave until it is straightened out."

She examined their manuscripts, the raw stuff of the future Florida guide. One piece took someone seven weeks to write, even though Kellock suspected that she could have done it, research *and* writing, in a single day. The prose was terrible. She mailed Alsberg some copy turned in by a Pensacola field worker: "Broken bluffs beribboned with many colored clays, semiphore their challenge to the restless waves, laving their banks with rainbow and sunset colors."

Back at her hotel, wearing her fur coat to keep off the January chill, she wrote to her husband. "Well, the ladies' club at its worst never did anything quite so flowery," she said. But the real problem with the Florida office, she realized, wasn't the infelicitous prose. It ran much deeper than that. Kellock believed that the FWP had been designed for conditions that obtained in big cities like New York and not for rural parts of the country, especially the South, where qualified writers and editors were scarce and there was little access to decent libraries and expert consultants. "What these dreamers in Washington did was assign a wide range of topics from history of the country to paleontology and anthropology and appraisals of local architecture and bid all 'writers' turn in 1500 words a week," she wrote. "That's the hell of a way to make up a guide-book."

By the end of her trip, though, Kellock again felt optimistic. The obstacles they faced, while real, were not insurmountable. She called Alsberg from North Carolina. "Henry, don't feel too worried about the states down here, or this part of the country," she said. "They are coming along nicely. It won't be a perfect job, but you won't have to be ashamed of them."

Over the next year and a half, the guides to the southern states did come together—with a certain amount of prodding and ample frustration all around. (The very first copy delivered to DC, in fact, was by Achmed H. Mundo, a journalist and former mercenary in the Alabama office.) But Kellock's remark—that the FWP risked being ashamed of the southern guides—had a deeper meaning. Their anxiety wasn't just about unqualified writers and meager resources and bad prose. It was about Jim Crow.

The DC staff understood that their project couldn't simply float above the southern social order. For all the control they imposed from Washington, the bulk of the work was being done from below, by writers and editors in local offices and field workers scattered across the forty-eight states. The FWP was inevitably shaped by conditions on the ground. In the South, that meant racial exclusion and white supremacy. And as an editorial matter, it meant that the FWP's portrait of America would be shaped by clashing attitudes about slavery, the Civil War and Reconstruction, and the contributions and status of African Americans. More tangibly, it meant splitting federal writers into segregated units.

These divisions, called "Negro Units," existed in some of the northern offices, but as loose subprojects designated for Black workers gathering material on Black life. In the southern states, Negro Units, if they existed at all, were formally segregated. There were three of them: first in Louisiana, and then in Florida and Virginia.

When Katharine Kellock visited the Florida project, she saw that qualified Black workers were available: "Ph.D's doing ditch-digging or little better," she wrote to Alsberg in a field report. She also knew that African American groups were applying pressure and hoping to secure jobs on the project. She urged Alsberg to support the creation of a Negro Unit. "There is a whole world within a world in each state," she wrote. "One can not leave out whole sections of the pop. in making up a nat. guide." Alsberg agreed—a version of the American Guides that left out African Americans would be factually incomplete, morally suspect, and, by failing to mobilize Black writers in charting their own communities, a betrayal of the FWP's inclusive, participatory method. Florida's state director, a teacher and historian named Carita Corse, felt the same—she'd been pushing for a Negro Unit from the very start. Corse arranged the support of Mary McLeod Bethune, the eminent Florida educator and civil rights activist, who was becoming one of the Roosevelts' closest African American advisors. But everyone—Corse, Kellock, Alsberg, even and perhaps especially Bethune—took it for granted that the Negro Unit would be segregated.

Corse believed that Black Floridians had an especially accomplished history, one that was hardly known outside the state and underappreciated within it. The work of an FWP Negro Unit could change that situation. "This knowledge would do much to remedy the feeling between the two races in Florida," she wrote to Alsberg, "a feeling which is not as good now as it was thirty years ago." She even had someone in mind to run it: the novelist, folklorist, dramatist, essayist, social scientist, and Florida native Zora Neale Hurston. This may have been wishful thinking on Corse's part. Five months later, Hurston, who was too busy to join the project, offered only a promise to someday help edit the Black material, and then moved on to other tasks.

In the meantime, they set up the Negro Unit. When Alsberg gave Corse permission to begin hiring, he made a decision that was subtle but significant: he denied her request to expand the state's overall quota. Expanding the quota would have meant tacking the unit on to an existing number of jobs that were, in practice, set aside for whites. Instead, the project had to make room for the unit—an implicit statement of support for Black writers on relief, at the expense of whites who would have benefited from an expanded quota.

The unit's task was to assemble a manuscript, "The Florida Negro." Federal writers in several states were following this same template; "The Negro in Illinois," for instance, was being compiled under the supervision of Arna Bontemps and Jack Conroy. Their version was sponsored by the philanthropic Rosenwald Foundation, which gave Bontemps and Conroy's team space in its headquarters, the former Rosenwald mansion. Bontemps and Conroy each had an office in one of the mansion's bedrooms—an echo of the DC staff occupying the McLean ballroom—and together they worked over the reams of material collected by the Illinois project. Sometimes they had visitors. Eleanor Roosevelt, whom Conroy found "toothy and gracious and utterly charming," stopped by. So did W. E. B. Du Bois, who told Conroy that he used to read *The Anvil*. ("The Negro in Illinois" was never published, but the team of Bontemps and Conroy would outlast the project; they used some of the material in their 1945 book on the Great Migration, *They Seek a City*.)

The Florida unit—segregated and lacking support from any eminent foundation—was unlikely to be visited by the First Lady. For the next two years, its workers gathered material on the lives and customs of Black Floridians, past and present. The staffing quota initially allowed for ten workers; because of cutbacks, it was usually half that. Around sixteen individuals joined the unit during the life of the project; more contributed only a piece or two. Nine of the core contributors, a majority, were women. A few workers were college educated, including one professor. Their office was in Jacksonville's Black neighborhood, half a mile from the main office, inside the Clara White Mission, a soup kitchen and charitable center. As they went over their field notes and typed up draft copy, the mission thrummed with activity: there were homeless people seeking food and shelter, babies and caretakers in a nursery, children in a music school, and adults in Bible classes or receiving medical services. WPA arts and sewing projects were crammed in there, too. Some of the mission's older residents had been born into slavery. Spirituals were sung before every meal.

The Florida project's white workers saw none of this. They were downtown, compiling the guidebook, ensconced in their own office. The only signs of the Negro Unit were packets of copy delivered to their doorstep and, every two weeks, a messenger who picked up their Black colleagues' checks and then turned back out into the humid streets.

One day, in the downtown office, Carita Corse appeared before the white staff. She had an announcement. They were going to be joined by a Black woman writer, a Floridian who'd lived in New York and moved in literary circles and was used to being praised by those circles. Her name, Corse said, was Zora Neale Hurston, and she would arrive with certain expectations. The staff should be prepared to make allowances. Corse was not complaining so much as putting them on notice. The message was clear. Zora Neale might even smoke in front of you, Corse warned. And when Hurston arrived, that is exactly what she did.

"A TOE-HOLD ON THE WORLD"

If you pick up *Florida: A Guide to the Southernmost State* and follow Tour 2— down Route 17 from the Georgia border, through the piney woods and into the citrus region, and go a breath over thirty-two miles—you'll reach Maitland, a town founded by Union army veterans in the 1880s. The population back then was sparse and the veterans invited Black workers from the citrus groves to fill out the ranks. So they did. Soon Maitland had a Black mayor and Black marshal and its Black citizens thought of forming their own town. So they did that, too. Some of Maitland's white founders sold them the land and from the rich loam of central Florida sprung Eatonville—likely the first Black, self-governing, incorporated town in America.

When the guide reaches Eatonville, it hands the tour over, unusually, to the words of a local author. "Maitland is Maitland until it gets to Hurst's corner, and then it is Eatonville," Zora Neale Hurston wrote. "Right in front of Willie Sewell's yellow-painted house the hard road quits being the hard road for a generous mile and becomes the heart of Eatonville. Or from a stranger's point of view, you could say that the road just bursts through on its way from US 17 to US 441, scattering Eatonville left and right."

Scattered there: a general store, a Methodist church, a school, Widow Dash and her new husband, orange groves and shady oaks, a Baptist church,

small neat homes, and another school, all of them owned or operated or inhabited by Black citizens, though Hurston doesn't spell this out. Finally, you
reach Lake Belle, where lives "Eatonville's most celebrated resident"—the
biggest alligator in the world.

> This legendary alligator, it is said, is no other than a slave who escaped
> from a Georgia plantation and joined the Indians during the Seminole
> War. When the Indians retreated, he did not follow but instead made
> "big medicine" on the lake shore, for he had been a celebrated conjuring
> man in Africa. He transformed himself into an alligator, the god of his
> tribe, and slipped into the water. Now and then he resumes human form,
> so people say, and roams the country about Eatonville. At such times all
> the alligators in the surrounding lakes bellow loudly all night long. "The
> big one has gone back home," whisper the villagers.

These villagers were Zora Neale Hurston's parents, her siblings, her
neighbors, herself. Eatonville was her village. And it was she, not a mythical
alligator, who was really Eatonville's most celebrated resident.

In early 1938, Hurston was back in Florida after many years of living
mostly elsewhere and building a career as a writer, scholar, and freelance
folklorist. She was forty-seven, though she claimed to be around a decade
younger. She was exhausted. She'd just finished a grueling trip through Haiti
and Jamaica, where, supported by a Guggenheim Fellowship, she collected
material for her second book of folklore. The journey had been exhilarating
and disquieting. Hurston already believed in the power of hoodoo, African
American folk magic, from her experiences studying it years earlier, when
she'd interviewed several conjurers, participated in their rituals, and become
an initiate of their ways. But her encounter with Haitian Vodou (and, she
claimed, an actual zombie) left her shaken. When she was struck by intense
stomach problems, she wondered if they were supernatural in origin, if she
had gotten too close to powers she did not understand. At the same time,
she was aware of another force at work on her—she'd just fled a passionate
and volatile relationship back in New York, and breaking it off had nearly
wrecked her. (She'd been forced to choose: him or her career.) In Haiti, she
gathered up all the sorrow and regret and poured it into a novel, her second.

She finished *Their Eyes Were Watching God* in a matter of weeks. It was her masterpiece.

Now, home in Eatonville, she basked in the novel's fine reviews and reckoned with the mountain of notes she'd lugged back from the Caribbean. Just to see the orange trees bloom was a pleasure. "The bees are humming in the trees all day and the mocking birds sing all night in the moonlight," she wrote to Carl Van Vechten, her friend and supporter back in drab, frigid New York. (She'd dedicate the forthcoming book to him.) She found a house for rent on the outskirts of Eatonville, by the edge of a small lake, near the crossroads known as "Tuxedo Junction." The house had once been a barn, and after that, a juke joint. It was weatherboarded and spacious and comfortable; around the yard she arranged a badminton net and a croquet set and a few putting holes. The lake was ringed with mossy oaks and cypress, and there was an old dock, perfect for fishing or diving into the placid water or watching turtles glide by. "The stillness on a calm day spells peace, but when the wind is high the ripples play tag with each other," wrote a member of the Negro Unit who visited Hurston there, eager to document the home of the noted Floridian. She'd found an idyll, and she got to work. But her lakeside cottage, remote and pleasant as it was, couldn't protect her from the Depression—just as Vardis Fisher found no refuge, ultimately, in his Idaho homestead. She'd always struggled to put together a living, and now, with each passing year, doing so became only more difficult. A finished book would mean another payout; after that, who knew?

Hurston's life was more than half lived by the time she returned to Eatonville. Her hometown retained a powerful hold on her mind. She still shared the amazement that her father, John, a carpenter from Alabama, had felt when he wandered through the settlement soon after it was established. He and Lucy, Zora's mother, raised a family there, in a sturdy home with plenty of space. John became a Baptist preacher and eventually served as mayor of Eatonville; Lucy, who was regarded as the smarter and tougher one, endured spells of John's philandering, but not always quietly. Zora—all of whose grandparents had been enslaved—grew up in a self-governing Black community, where the great rift was between the Baptists and Methodists, not between racial castes. Their campaigns and quarrels were of individuals living, working, relaxing, loving, and fighting freely among themselves.

Hurston knew this just as she knew Eatonville's gardenia and scrub palm and citrus trees with heavy branches, the chickens and rattlesnakes and roving hogs, the shape of tiny lakes and the twisty road to Orlando that ran past her gatepost. She absorbed her piece of the American land, as Vardis Fisher did Idaho's Antelope Hills and Nelson Algren did Chicago's sprawl of ethnic neighborhoods, and like them, she'd devise methods of returning there, again and again, in her writing.

As a child Hurston adored classic novels, Norse tales, Greek myths. But even more enticing, she realized, was the lively tableau right there in Eatonville. Hurston's neighbors mingled at Joe Clarke's general store, and the men arranged themselves on the porch and exchanged rumors and worries, boasts and challenges. Women were mostly excluded but Hurston would creep close and listen. "There were no discrete nuances of life on Joe Clarke's porch," she wrote later. "There was open kindnesses, anger, hate, love, envy and its kinfolks, but all emotions were naked, and nakedly arrived at." It was life ritualistically laid bare, the process and product of an oral culture. Threaded through the conversation were "lying sessions," as Hurston called them, when the old folk tales were whipped out and given a particular stamp by the teller: God and the Devil and a menagerie of animals, speaking and scheming like the human citizens of Eatonville. She was captivated. Between the books she read and the lying sessions she overheard, Hurston had discovered her life's work.

Eatonville in Hurston's remembering seemed idyllic and perhaps it was. But it had an end, fixed and devastating. Hurston's mother, Lucy, fell ill. She was bedridden. Eventually she summoned Zora and discussed the traditional folk rituals that the townspeople expected to administer. They would turn her bed to the east. They would remove the pillow from beneath her head, to hasten the dying. They would cover the clock and the mirror. But Lucy wanted none of this and asked Zora to prevent it. Her daughter agreed. When the time came, Zora protested, but it did not matter. The bed was turned, the pillow removed, the clock and mirror covered. Lucy tried to speak—to reprimand? to forgive?—but the words were faint. And then she died. "It seemed as she died that the sun went down on purpose to flee away from me," Zora wrote. She knew that she had failed, and that her failure was entwined with the folkways of her people in a knotty and ambiguous way. And yet those rituals became only more fascinating and powerful to her.

At Lucy's funeral, the Hurston children gathered together for the last time, ever. Then they scattered. Hurston's middle teens to her middle twenties were years of drifting. After a stint in a Jacksonville boarding school, she lived with relatives and friends and took jobs in domestic service, cleaning white homes and minding white children and dodging the advances of her white employers. Eventually she heard that the soprano in a traveling Gilbert and Sullivan troupe needed a lady's maid. Hurston got the job and left the next day, her suitcase stuffed with newspaper so her few belongings wouldn't rattle.

Her travels with the troupe were as formative as Eatonville. The performers, all white, were kind but condescending. They lent her books and told her their secrets and treated her like a pet. Hurston studied them, and as the troupe approached the Mason-Dixon Line, and then crossed it, she developed a keener sense of herself as a Black southerner. It was not just the lore she knew but the idioms and rhythms of her speech, the manner and substance, form and content—a discursive mode that was also a living art form, honed and sustained, as she would someday put it, by "the Negro farthest down." It was a cultural realm that was just as legitimate and sophisticated, in its way, as the troupe's Victorian repertoire.

She was also developing a personal philosophy of race relations. She was not naïve but neither did she dwell on the troupe's slights and teasing, which she saw as thoughtless, benign. "I found out too that you are bound to be jostled in the 'crowded street of life,'" she wrote. "That in itself need not be dangerous unless you have the open razors of personal vanity in your pants pocket. The passers-by don't hurt you, but if you go around like that, they make you hurt yourself." This was the attitude, perhaps, of someone who'd been spared the worst kind of racial violence and discrimination. But it was a powerful component of Hurston's developing worldview, a combination of race pride and individualism that flowed, she well understood, from Booker T. Washington's tradition of self-improvement. (Washington, whose students had founded Hurston's childhood school in Eatonville, would become a touchstone in her writing, fiction and nonfiction. In *Their Eyes Were Watching God*, for instance, a spiteful, color-prejudiced woman bad-mouths Washington—which Hurston clearly intends to be a shocking and foolish display.) Other figures, such as W. E. B. Du Bois and Marcus Garvey, she viewed with suspicion, at best. It was an attitude that would put her at odds with many of her friends and rivals and collaborators, including future federal writers, who were drawn to the more adversarial ideas of the left—and it would contribute to her own ambivalent feelings about joining the project in the first place.

Hurston returned to formal schooling: night classes and some high school in Baltimore, then Howard University in Washington. She worked as a maid, a server at the elite Cosmos Club, and a manicurist in a Black barbershop that catered only to white customers. (Some of these customers held lofty positions in the political world and, like the troupe members, confided things to Hurston with an ease that depended on her social insignificance.) At Howard she began to write seriously and joined the campus literary club, overseen by Alain Locke, the first Black Rhodes scholar and Howard's philosophy chair. She published her first short story, "John Redding Goes to Sea," in the group's journal; next, "Drenched in Light" appeared in *Opportunity*, the magazine of the National Urban League. Hurston drew freely from her life in Florida to form these stories; "Drenched in Light" described Hurston's childhood habit of sitting on the gatepost and hailing travelers on the road to Orlando, Black and white, while her grandmother, who had known slavery, reprimanded her for being so trusting. It was a story of her archetypical self: optimistic, independent, restless, proud.

In 1925, Hurston left Howard and arrived in New York, where she found, at last, the intellectual and artistic milieu to match her aspirations. She announced herself by winning two second-place prizes and two honorable mentions at an *Opportunity* magazine awards ceremony. (Arna Bontemps, the future federal writer, considered these gatherings the center of the Harlem Renaissance.) "Spunk," her winning story, showed a meaningful development in her writing—it dramatized the swirl of chatter, superstition, and analysis that prevailed on Joe Clarke's store porch by making oral communication a kind of protagonist, and the organizing force of the narrative.

Her Harlem years were an apprenticeship, not her most important or productive—those years came later. But New York was where Hurston learned to sweat as a writer. "My typewriter is clicking away till all hours of the night," she wrote to a benefactor, Annie Nathan Meyer. "I am striving desperately for a toe-hold on the world." Meyer was a founder of Barnard College and she arranged a scholarship that allowed Hurston to enroll there, the first Black student. To observers such as Meyer or the novelist Fannie Hurst (who hired Hurston as a secretary and befriended her), she seemed to have come from nowhere: a young woman catapulted from a student club to New York's most vibrant and significant literary scene. She was in fact a woman in her mid-thirties who'd fought for every inch.

At Barnard she studied under the groundbreaking anthropologist Franz Boas. From his position at Columbia, Boas was overturning assumptions about racial hierarchies and the linear progression of human groups from savagery to civilization. He was a German émigré with a thick accent and a face scarred by sabre wounds he'd collected on dueling grounds as a university student; he was intense but generous and devoted to his students, who called him, as Hurston did, Papa Franz. (The year Hurston arrived in New York, one of those students, Margaret Mead, was conducting research for what would become her influential *Coming of Age in Samoa*.) Hurston got to know this circle, including Boas's teaching-assistant-turned-colleague Ruth Benedict, and she absorbed their evidence-driven approach to understanding human culture, which was spreading to universities everywhere through a kind of Boasian dispersal. By the mid-thirties, Boas's thinking would have a major influence on the liberal intellectuals in the FWP and help to shape the pluralistic aspirations of the American Guides; he and Ruth Benedict, whose monumental *Patterns of Culture* appeared in 1934, were among the FWP's many volunteer advisors, and briefly oversaw field research on American Indian tribes before the effort was defunded.

Boas, along with his colleague Melville Herskovits (another former student), sent Hurston into the Harlem streets to measure the crania of passersby and amass empirical evidence that undermined phrenological theories of inferiority. (Boas had carried out similar, pioneering research early in his career, showing that the children of immigrants physically tended to resemble US-born children, not older generations of their purported racial group.) Then he helped arrange a fellowship grant and a field research trip to study the lore, mannerisms, and cultural practices of Black southerners. It was the first in a series of trips that Hurston would take over the next decade and more, under different auspices. When Hurston returned, Boas wasn't satisfied with the results—he thought she hadn't done enough to uncover original material, and said so, and she was mortified to find herself crying in his office. But she was learning to fuse her deep interest in Black folkways with systematic, scholarly contemplation—what she would call "the spy-glass of Anthropology."

From 1927, when she left New York on her first collecting trip, to the opening years of the Depression, Hurston faced obstacles and setbacks. Money was always tight. Her artistic and scholarly impulses rarely worked in harmony—even Boas wondered if she was cut out for the academy. She nearly tanked her career by publishing a heavily plagiarized article in *The Journal of Negro History* (although, at the time, no one noticed). She earned a BA from Barnard but her graduate studies at Columbia faltered. Most of her subsequent field research was independently sponsored by Charlotte Osgood Mason, an elderly white patron of other Harlem Renaissance figures. Mason's support was essential but she was controlling and possessive—contractually, Hurston was Mason's agent and Mason owned the rights to the material she collected. Meanwhile, Hurston's friendship with Langston Hughes, another of Mason's beneficiaries, imploded over a play, *Mule Bone*, that they were working on together. It was just one of several painful breakups. Hurston's marriage to Howard Sheen, a medical student with whom she shared a protracted, long-distance relationship, collapsed within a year. Another relationship, the one that propelled her to Haiti and Jamaica, left her wounded and regretful. Through it all, she was sporadically beset by health problems.

But Hurston was making gains, too. After "The Gilded Six-Bits" appeared in *Story* magazine—the same issue that contained Nelson Algren's first story—the publisher J. B. Lippincott and Co. asked her for a novel. The next year it released *Jonah's Gourd Vine*, a fictional portrait of Hurston's parents. As a novel, it was tentative and undercooked, but it was a dazzling statement of Hurston's ability to replicate and artfully arrange the idioms and speech patterns of her Eatonville neighbors. Her next book, *Mules and Men*, was a showcase of folktales and hoodoo practices she'd collected throughout the South, wrapped up in a subtle memoir. It carried a brief but warm foreword by Papa Franz Boas himself, a gesture of professional recognition that Hurston well deserved. She was by now a member of the American Folklore Society, the American Ethnological Society, and the American Anthropological Association—and one of the best-trained, most knowledgeable authorities on Black folklore alive.

But Hurston's patchwork income—fellowships, grants, private patronage, the odd check from a publisher or magazine—was not sustainable, especially as the Depression years piled up. (Her advance for *Jonah's Gourd Vine* was less than half of what another Boas protégé, Margaret Mead, had received six years earlier for *her* first book, *Coming of Age in Samoa*.) So, in 1935, Hurston joined the WPA—but not yet the FWP. She took a job with the Federal Theater Project. As a portion of Federal #1, it employed more people than the FWP but it was less expansive geographically. (At its peak, the FTP had 14,010 workers—roughly double the FWP—but operated in only twenty-eight states, plus New York City and DC.) For Hurston, it was a natural fit. She'd written dramatic and comedic plays, contributed to vaudeville revues, and staged her own showcase of Black folk song and dance, *The Great Day*, which she later revived under other names. Her brief or tentative affiliations with colleges all involved teaching drama. It was true that none of these teaching gigs panned out and that her productions barely made any money. But, conceptually, performance was crucial to Hurston's understanding of Black art. In her 1934 essay "Characteristics of Negro Expression"—a sort of checklist of observable features in African American aesthetics and folk culture—"drama" was the key characteristic: "Every phase of Negro life is highly dramatised. No matter how joyful or how sad the case there is sufficient poise for drama. Everything is acted out." Hurston saw this impulse at work not just in cultural patterns like mimicry and posing but in the very language she examined and collected: an abundance of similes and metaphors, action words, concrete imagery over abstraction. The theater, then, was where she needed to be.

With the FTP, she found a job alongside people who'd worked onstage and off: actors, dramatists, stagehands, technicians, set builders, publicists. The project was also intended to build up the community theater infrastructure around the country, especially in underserved areas. (The Roosevelts were particularly keen on its potential for cultural outreach.) Hallie Flanagan, the FTP's director, believed the project could unleash new creative forces in American theater as well. Flanagan didn't come from a commercial background; at the time of her appointment, she was director of the Vassar Experimental Theater. She'd been a playwright and critic, one of the four women who in 1926 were the first to win a Guggenheim Fellowship. Flanagan used hers for a study of the modern European theater and, like Henry Alsberg, found things to admire in the cultural experimentation of Soviet Russia. She was acquainted with Harry Hopkins; they both grew up in Grinnell and attended college there together. When she accepted Hopkins's invitation to run the FTP, an admiring profile in *The New York Times* described her as "a small, quietly decisive woman of extraordinary executive and artistic ability"—and "a soft-spoken slave driver."

Under Flanagan's direction, the FTP staged a wide array of productions: classical and modern dramas, musical comedies, vaudeville routines and circuses, hand puppet and marionette shows, radio programs, some dance, and a smattering of foreign-language plays. It cooperated with the Civilian Conservation Corps and sent performers into its camps, where they even staged an original work, *CCC Murder Mystery*. *The Swing Mikado*, an all-Black, jazzified version of the Gilbert and Sullivan operetta, was the project's biggest hit; an adaptation of Sinclair Lewis's anti-fascist novel *It Can't Happen Here* made headlines by opening with twenty-one simultaneous performances, including one in Yiddish. The Living Newspaper productions, perhaps the FTP's most innovative, dramatized pressing social and political issues—although critics derided these as New Deal propaganda pieces, or worse. (More controversial was *Revolt of the Beavers*, a children's play about a group of worker-beavers who organize themselves and then overthrow—with guns!—the beaver capitalist class. "The newest adventure of the WPA theatre ought to improve our diplomatic relations with Soviet Russia," groused one critic.) More than two thirds of all productions didn't charge admission and the ones that did kept prices low. FTP units avoided plays that required royalty payments, but some playwrights—including George Bernard Shaw and Eugene O'Neill—gamely agreed to reduce their rates.

The FTP's center was in New York, and here Hurston joined the Negro Unit in Harlem. The unit's first director, the celebrated Black actor Rose McClendon, died from pneumonia soon after it was established, and left behind her co-director, the producer John Houseman (who was just embarking on a momentous collaboration with a twenty-year-old Orson Welles). Houseman was an odd choice to help run the unit: not only was he *not* Black, he was British and living illegally in the United States under a false name. But McClendon had believed that she needed a partner who'd face no racial barriers while dealing with the broader theater world. Now Houseman, alone, faced the task of running a highly visible and culturally fraught undertaking that also happened to be the largest employer in all of Harlem.

He considered Hurston, who was hired as a "dramatic coach," the most talented writer on the unit. He wanted to stage her proposed adaptation of *Lysistrata*, which was set in a Florida fishing village and depicted a strike against a canning company (as in the original, the women withhold sex until the battle is won). But his hopes were dashed. "It scandalized both Left and Right by its saltiness, which was considered injurious to the serious Negro image they both, in their different ways, desired to create," he wrote of it later. "So I had to give that one up."

In fact, the FTP produced none of Hurston's work. After about six months, she was getting restless. "New York is not a good place to think in," she wrote to a friend. "I can do hack work here, but I need quiet to really work." She dreamed of returning to Florida. Instead, she found something better: a Guggenheim Fellowship to study Vodou in Jamaica and Haiti. The Harlem Negro Unit was just about to stage its most celebrated production, a Vodou-infused *Macbeth* set in Haiti during the revolution, directed by Orson Welles. Hurston, though, was less interested in set dressing than in documenting the beliefs and rituals of the real, living religion, so she didn't stick around. She quit the FTP and left New York.

In the Caribbean, she delved into social customs and sacred rites and tried to understand what they shared with hoodoo, the African American folk magic that she'd studied so closely in the field. It was the last phase of a journey that brought her back, again, to Eatonville. By now, Hurston was at her creative peak. She had ideas for other books and plays—there was always another project—but no steady income. Her six months with the Federal Theater Project was the first time she'd drawn a steady salary for creative work (not counting the stipend Charlotte Osgood Mason paid her to collect folklore). But her options were limited.

While she finished the Caribbean book, titled *Tell My Horse*, she heard from the local outpost of the Federal Writers' Project. They offered her a job but she turned them down. Once the book was done, they asked again. A job with the FWP meant that Hurston had to go on relief. (They didn't offer one of the non-relief editorial and technical jobs that, in every state, were set aside as a percentage of the whole staff.) That meant being subjected to the means test—publicly affirming that she had no job, no money, no property, no prospects. Hurston was used to scraping by on very little, but this was something new. She was proud. She was a child of Eatonville, daughter of the pastor and mayor, highly educated, an accomplished writer. She was not afraid of having too little money; she was afraid of the way poverty ate away at people and killed their aspirations. "There is something about poverty that smells like death," she wrote a few years later. "Dead dreams dropping off the heart like leaves in a dry season and rotting around the feet; impulses smothered too long in the fetid air of underground caves. The soul lives in a sickly air. People can be slave-ships in shoes."

She agreed to join the project. An FWP field representative told Henry Alsberg the news. "When I left Florida machinery had been put in operation to add Zora Neale Hurston to the Project on a security wage basis," he wrote. "She is greatly interested in all the project is doing, and will probably furnish us with valuable new Florida folklore." A caseworker came around to her house on the lake and interviewed her. Then Hurston swore the pauper's oath. At the time, she was likely the most published Black woman in the United States.

"THE MARK OF ZORA"

When Carita Corse, Florida's state director, watched Hurston walk into the Jacksonville office, she saw a robust woman with a pleasant, open face, someone who laughed easily and often and charged the air around her with a sense of activity. (Project workers would describe the smiling, spirited Corse in a similar way.) She recognized that they were about the same age—they shared a birth year, in fact, even though Hurston claimed to be a decade younger.

Corse had directed the Florida project from the start. She had the right background: she taught in a private school and wrote books about early Florida history, along with a traveler's guide published by the Florida State Hotel Commission. She was a daughter of the old and connected Doggett family, which allowed her to move easily through the state political landscape; Florida's senator Claude Pepper was a personal friend. She'd gone north for her education, to Vassar and then for graduate work at Columbia (she earned an

MA almost ten years before Hurston enrolled at Barnard). The University of the South had given her an honorary doctorate and she used the title with pride. As director, she drummed up enthusiasm for Floridiana while delegating the editorial heavy lifting to others.

That she was a woman running the project didn't much make difference, except when it did. She once faced a minor rebellion from district supervisors who were tired of working for a "skirt" and wanted to replace her with a man. Another time, she met with a state official, a man, to discuss a manuscript. The official's secretary happened to be away at lunch, so he locked the door and chased Corse around the office until she fended him off. (The manuscript was never published.)

The DC office had faith in her, mostly. "Her point of view is absolutely modern," Katharine Kellock told Alsberg after their first meeting in 1935, "and when she found that you really wanted the local aged-in-the-wood scandals, she was no-end excited." But when Kellock visited the office again, during her January 1936 tour of the southern states, she fumed over Corse's lax approach to finances—and that the director was nowhere to be seen. (According to one worker, Corse was motoring around the state on a joyride with her secretary; Corse insisted that she was recruiting volunteer consultants and setting up the other offices.) Kellock griped to Alsberg, "Mrs. Corse is a Florida 'lady,' with no idea of arithmetic or expenses." But as guidebook copy began flowing into DC, the editors were generally pleased. Kellock admired Corse's prose style and encouraged her to set an example for her workers who were struggling to find a voice between advertising copy and dry description. Alsberg, meanwhile, regarded Corse as a fine historian, even if he doubted some of her specific claims. (Corse once insisted that "Florida" had been the original name for the entire continent and wouldn't let it go until Alsberg consulted the chief of the map division at the Library of Congress, who refuted the idea.) Her biggest problem, he thought, was that she hewed too closely to "the Chamber of Commerce line." The DC editors were allergic to such writing, a situation that Nelson Algren knew well, after he was ordered to excise it from the guide to Galena, Illinois. But keeping profit-motivated boosterism out of a guide to Florida—a tourist destination that, in the midst of the Depression, was desperate to stimulate tourism—was a thornier proposition.

The Florida project initially employed more than one hundred workers, thirty of them alongside Corse in the central Jacksonville office and the rest scattered among eight district offices. Many were white-collar workers with no professional experience as writers per se: lawyers and architects, librarians and court reporters, laid-off teachers. There were publicists and copywriters who had been drawn to Florida during the twenties real estate boom and then cast loose by the bust. There were stringers whose rural weeklies disappeared with the Depression, and at least one AP reporter. There was a former pulp story writer, a ward heeler putting himself through law school, someone who edited a magazine for the state chapter of the Daughters of the American Revolution and another who edited the *Southern Lumber Journal.* More than half of them were women. Only Corse and two others had a job before they joined the FWP.

Hurston stood apart, career-wise. No other workers on the Florida project had published a book, aside from Corse and maybe one or two more. Hurston had published three books, with a fourth in the works. She had a national profile. FWP editors in DC cited her as an authority on folklore when they reviewed the Florida copy. She could even say that Franklin and Eleanor Roosevelt, who'd become close with Hurston's longtime confidant Fannie Hurst, were truly friends of a friend. She was no doubt qualified to direct the Florida project herself. (Whether she would have been an effective administrator, or if she'd even have wanted the job, is open to question.) But the FWP had no Black state directors anywhere, let alone in Jim Crow Florida.

She and Corse struck up a cordial relationship anyway. Corse invited Hurston to visit her home and meet her husband and four children, an unusually intimate gesture. Hurston, meanwhile, invited Corse to visit a Black storefront church. They arrived around ten at night—after working hours—and took their seats. The congregation was tranquil and the preaching subdued. Hurston was unimpressed with the service and whispered to Corse, "I'm gonna get 'em on their feet." She stood and began to clap and murmur. Others joined in. Soon Corse saw people rolling on the floor. She'd never witnessed such a scene and felt uneasy, and she asked Hurston if they could leave. But Hurston had made her point, or points—about the emotional power of Black vernacular culture and her own relationship to it. Hurston would write about such churches for the FWP and commend them for revitalizing Black musical expression and worship: "It is putting back into Negro religion those elements which were brought over from Africa and grafted onto Christianity as soon as the Negro came in contact with it, but which are being rooted out as the American Negro approaches white concepts." That night in the church, Hurston demonstrated that her writing didn't emerge from mere observation. She was both analyst and instigator: she hadn't revealed the scene so much as staged it.

There remained the question of Hurston's role on the project. Soon after she was hired, she and a group of singers traveled to DC for the National Folklore Festival. She dropped in at the FWP office and met Alsberg, who was impressed enough to write to Corse and ask her to put Hurston in charge of "The Florida Negro," which was being prepared by the Negro Unit, in addition to her work on the guide. That would mean a raise and a title change. Corse said that Hurston was already "acting as supervisor" but to make it official would exceed their quota. Whatever her private feelings, Corse knew that such a promotion was impossible. State WPA officials would block the appointment of a Black supervisor, and Corse was not one to upset the system. Instead, she gave Hurston an additional travel allowance, which raised her salary close to the editorial level but left her rank intact. It was a sly maneuver, emblematic of Corse's liberal and accommodationist racial politics. In correspondence, Hurston was sometimes referred to as the "Negro editor," but this was an informal designation. Her true title was "junior interviewer." It meant that she had no desk in the Jacksonville office and that she would work from the field—which meant she was free to spend time on her own writing.

So Hurston went home. Then she disappeared. Weeks would go by without a word. Corse frequently found herself querying the office: "Anybody heard from Zora?" No one had. She'd order a young project worker, Stetson Kennedy, to fire off a letter. Then they waited. Eventually, a thick manila envelope would arrive, stuffed with material on Florida folkways. When Kennedy saw the Eatonville postmark, he called it "the Mark of Zora." He knew there were exciting things inside.

Hurston wasn't spending much time in the field, though. "Folk-lore is not as easy to collect as it sounds," she wrote a few years earlier in *Mules and Men*—and she would know. Instead, she ransacked her files for tales, sayings, and songs she'd accumulated over the past decade. They suspected this in

Jacksonville but didn't much care—the material was excellent. For Hurston, paging through her notes and transcripts would have conjured up memories of her first trips across the South, when she rode in a car named Sassy Susie and passed whites-only hotels and restaurants and slept in Black boarding-houses and private homes. She had trouble, at first, speaking with strangers who were put off by her formal manner and direct questions—her "carefully accented Barnardese," she called it. But eventually she let her true accent unfurl and she eased into the interviews and sometimes told people she was a bootlegger. She carried a pistol. One night, in a juke near a sawmill camp, a woman rushed her with a knife and nearly sliced her open—jealous of the attention Hurston was paying to her former lover, maybe, or just out for trou-ble. Hurston was saved by Big Sweet, the toughest woman in the camp, and she fled for Alabama and then New Orleans, which was where she became an initiate in hoodoo rituals, lying facedown for days, boiling a black cat in a cauldron to yield a talismanic bone, casting a death spell through an intri-cate dance ceremony. She was an aspiring anthropologist then—but she was too alive to the art in the customs and the songs and the tales she observed, and couldn't approach them as mere bits of social data. So she improvised another path, one she could walk as an anthropologist or a novelist or a dra-matist, depending on her mood. By 1938, flipping through her notes again, she felt comfortable as that kind of hybrid writer. Maybe it was not the theater project but the FWP, with its capacious and improvisatory approach, that better fit her style.

Hurston, separated from the Jacksonville office, was not lonely. She had friends nearby and, for a time, took in two of her nieces, one and then the other: Wilhelmina, who married and left, and then Winifred. They adored their freewheeling aunt. Winifred would watch Hurston carry a card table out into the yard, set it up, place a typewriter on top, and then sit in her overalls and type while the sun shone down through the massive oaks and Spanish moss. On these days no one bothered her and she spoke to no one. (Winifred told inquisitive relatives that Aunt Zora didn't need a husband—her writing came first and there was plenty of it.) Sometimes Hurston would leave—she'd tell her nieces that she needed to go to New York, and then she would take a bus and disappear, just briefly. They never realized that a bus trip to Manhattan would have taken much longer. They didn't know what their aunt was really up to. She never told them about her work for the FWP, that she was on relief. It was a secret.

"NEXT YEAR'S CROP AND THE DEMOCRATIC PARTY"

Despite her accomplishments and obvious talent, Hurston was stuck in a lower rank. The Florida Negro Unit was segregated. These things were true but they were not failures specific to the FWP. They were local expressions of a national problem, a flaw designed into the edifice of the entire New Deal.

If the New Deal rested on three visible pillars—immediate economic recovery, deeper social and economic reform, and a realignment of the political landscape—then collaboration with the racial structure of the South was a shadowy fourth pillar. The reason for this was simple math: New Deal legislation depended on the votes of southern Democrats. (As a bloc, they possessed many leadership positions and committee chairs.) And southern Democrats, more than those in other factions of the party, were willing to break ranks when their sectional interests were threatened. So they were appeased: Roosevelt accepted this cold calculus and allowed, even recruited, prominent segregationists in and around his administration. (For every Harold Ickes, former president of the Chicago NAACP, there was a John Nance Garner, vice president and segregationist Texan.) Roosevelt conspicuously failed to back a federal anti-lynching bill, fearing that it would trigger open rebellion among the southern Democrats. Less visibly and perhaps more significantly, the administration won southern support through mechanisms built into New Deal programs: regional wage scales, local administrative control, and outright segregation on undertakings such as the Civilian Conservation Corps and some WPA units. Reforms initiated by the Agricultural Adjustment Administration and the Tennessee Valley Authority tended to benefit landowners, who were overwhelmingly white, and not tenant farmers or sharecroppers. Discriminatory practices touched nearly every agency, from housing to the National Youth Administration. In perhaps the administration's most consequential decision, domestic and agricultural workers were excluded from landmark legislation: the National Industrial Recovery Act, the Social Security Act, the Wagner Act (which secured the right to organize), and the Fair Labor Standards Act (which set minimum wage and overtime rules). Most Black workers in the South fell into two categories: domestic and agricultural workers.

Southern Democrats were enthusiastic partners when they knew the racial order was secure. Many of them embraced the robust reforms that, they believed, were redistributing power from Yankee capitalists to the disproportionately impoverished, rural, and underindustrialized South. They backed Roosevelt in the legislature and, at election time, with votes. In 1936, Roosevelt won with sweeping support across the South. In certain states, his victories were staggering: 97 percent in Mississippi and 99 percent in South Carolina.

For a symbol of this collaboration (and you could take your pick) there was Senator Theodore Bilbo of Mississippi —the very same legislator who stood on the Senate floor and said that Henry Alsberg deserved to be lynched for hosting an integrated party at his home. Bilbo was a fierce, almost mystical, segregationist, and a proud Klansman. (He was such a prominent racist that his 1947 demise inspired a song—"Bilbo Is Dead"—by the blues musician Andrew Tibbs.) But he was also a staunch Roosevelt supporter who backed the New Deal 100 percent—as long as it didn't impinge on white supremacy.

At the same time, the New Deal wasn't purely an instrument of the prevailing racial order. Civil rights groups (along with the radical left and CIO activists) lobbied and protested the Roosevelt administration because they knew that there were gains to be made. Not since Reconstruction had the federal government so actively and so directly sought to improve the conditions of African Americans. Much of that impact came by way of the relief projects, despite their shortcomings: the Civilian Conservation Corps, the National Youth Administration, the Public Works Administration, and the WPA provided badly needed wages and training to those hit hardest by the Depression. But alongside the failures, such as the eventual segregation of the CCC, there were promising developments. At the PWA, Harold Ickes targeted Black communities for improvement and imposed an effective labor quota system that actually favored Black workers more than proportionally. At the WPA, Harry Hopkins pushed back against local segregation, while hundreds of thousands of African Americans benefited from WPA vocational and literacy classes. The NYA had the most Black administrators of any New

Deal agency. Together with other New Deal programs, they brought more Black workers into skilled and semiskilled occupations, shrank the gap between Black and white median family income, reduced Black infant and maternal mortality, and boosted Black life expectancy.

Inside the government, Roosevelt vastly expanded the number of Black administrators and political appointees—his informal "Black Cabinet"—and deracialized the Civil Service application process. He appointed the first Black federal judge and first Black brigadier general. (His Supreme Court appointees were all white, but they delivered significant decisions that promoted civil rights and laid the groundwork for momentous decisions to come.) During the 1936 campaign, the Democratic convention had its first accredited Black delegates, first Black reporters in the press box, and several Black speakers, including the minister who delivered the invocation. Prominent officials, most importantly Eleanor Roosevelt, were outspoken in their defense of civil rights. The message of all this was clear: even while the Roosevelt administration refused to confront the political power of the segregationist South, it made "the race problem" a subject for public discussion and democratic politics in a way that no previous administration had dared to. This, along with the material benefits delivered by New Deal policies, explains why Black voters shifted their support so decisively from Hoover and the Republicans to the new Roosevelt coalition of Democrats.

In other words, it was complicated. Federal #1 was no different. The arts projects were unprecedented in the support and visibility they gave to Black creative work, but they were also deeply flawed. At the FWP, even the smallest decisions might carry traces of this contradiction. DC editors quibbled over every matter of usage and style, and imposed uniform standards across the far-flung offices—forcing Vardis Fisher's Idaho tours to flow in the proper direction, for instance. And yet Alsberg allowed the southern guides, and them alone, to use a potent and divisive phrase. As the Florida chapter of the United Daughters of the Confederacy told Carita Corse in a terse letter, "the term 'Civil War' would be <u>very</u> prejudicial to the popularity of the publications in Florida or anywhere in the South." The UDC and other neo-Confederates wanted "War Between the States." Alsberg gave it to them.

The FWP's race problem was more fundamentally a labor issue. Its Black employment record was dismal. Some of the most talented Black writers in the country were concentrated in the New York City and Chicago offices, it was true. But of roughly 4,500 FWP workers in February 1937, only 106 were Black. A survey taken a year later showed that fourteen state projects had no Black workers on the payroll. Qualified Black candidates were often passed over. (This was one factor that sparked the confrontation in Missouri between white radicals, including Jack Conroy and Jack Balch, and the state director.) Black workers who *were* hired faced open discrimination, subtle harassment on the job, and unfair treatment by white editors.

Alsberg and the DC editors weren't entirely acquiescent to these conditions. From the start, when they still planned to create a multivolume national guidebook, they envisioned a section called "Negro Culture in America," entirely researched and written by a special group of Black workers and expert advisors. They also agreed with outside groups who were pushing the FWP to hire a national "Negro Affairs" editor. But Alsberg seemed to believe he couldn't act unilaterally. "I feel that it would be only just that one able negro writer be given a position here in Washington, so that the American Guide will do justice to negroes," he wrote to Aubrey Williams, director of the WPA's National Youth Administration. "However, I must have special permission from Mr. Hopkins to appoint such a person." While Alsberg waited, he planned to push for greater Black employment in the southern projects— although he insisted on being "tactful." As for the north, he blithely assumed that racism was not an issue and that low Black employment numbers reflected a lack of qualified candidates, and nothing more.

Eventually, permission was granted, and they hired the poet, critic, and university professor Sterling A. Brown to oversee the "Negro Affairs" division. It made him the highest-ranking African American in all of Federal #1. Brown was in his midthirties and teaching at Howard University; a few months earlier, he and a group of Black intellectuals had thrown a banquet at Howard for Alsberg and the associate director George Cronyn, so they could make the case for the FWP to create just such a position. Brown turned out to be the person to fill it—and to shoulder the accompanying responsibility, stress, and attention.

Brown, like Hurston, was interested in fusing Black vernacular culture with his creative work. As a student, he read Robert Frost and Carl Sandburg and Edgar Lee Masters, white poets who imbued their verse with the distinctive speech of white farmers and provincials. Brown was inspired to do the same, using Black idiom, and began to write poems somewhat in parallel with Langston Hughes, who was taking a similar approach. He spent most of the twenties teaching at Black universities in the South before settling at Howard in 1929. (It was a homecoming for Brown, who was reared on the university campus. His father, Sterling N. Brown, who'd been born into slavery three years before the firing on Fort Sumter, was a professor and minister at Howard when his son was born in 1901.) Brown was known to Harlem literary circles but was not of them. He looked askance at a scene that involved a little too much partying and far too much posturing for the benefit of white patrons. He also clashed with Fannie Hurst and utterly disdained Carl Van Vechten—two of Hurston's closest white companions.

He and Hurston may have met when they were students, or at an *Opportunity* awards ceremony in New York; they certainly met, face-to-face, in the fall of 1932. Brown admired Hurston as a fine storyteller and a talented performer. He traveled from Washington to New York to see *The Great Day*, her musical folk showcase. Hurston, for her part, found him to be an impressive figure. But Brown knew that Hurston could be combative, especially if she felt that someone had slighted her work. When he reviewed *Mules and Men* in *New Masses* (a mostly positive review), he faulted her for overlooking the "exploitation and terrorism" that shaped Black life in the South. "Her characters are naïve, quaint, complaisant, bad enough to kill each other in jooks, but meek otherwise, socially unconscious," he wrote. "Their life is made to appear easy-going and carefree." Brown spoke for other Black intellectuals who felt the same about Hurston's work, but Hurston bristled against this line of thinking. When they ran into each other again, she warned Brown that he wasn't going to make a communist out of her and walked away.

Brown took the FWP job in April 1936, a part-time addition to his full-time position at Howard. He and a small editorial team were immediately overwhelmed by the immensity of their task. They were responsible for personnel issues—advocating for more Black hires and intervening in cases of discrimination—along with substantial editorial work. Rough copy from northern and southern offices was lousy with stereotypes and generalizations. Brown was astounded by conspicuous gaps, such as a description of Nashville that left out Fisk University. He and his team had to fill in the blanks, so they found themselves generating heaps of original material, on top of their other responsibilities. (It was Brown, for instance, who wrote the unflinching essay, "The Negro in Washington," that appeared in the DC guide.) Their job required tremendous improvisational skill and more hours than the day contained.

Some state editors, particularly in the South, resented Brown's interventions. In Alabama, the state director Myrtle Miles accused Brown of bias (missing the point, perhaps, that his job as Negro Affairs editor required him to be biased). She insisted that their guidebook copy was "no apologia for slavery, which is naturally indefensible," but that they were correct to describe the institution in what they considered to be a balanced way. They stuck by their conclusion: "that the Negro, in three or four decades before the Civil War, was economically and spiritually better off than in the 20 years after the war." In North Carolina, where the project was headed by two ostensible liberals—including W. T. Couch, architect of the southern life histories and *These Are Our Lives*—Brown addressed their dismal employment record and pushed them to expand coverage of Black Carolinians. In return, he got excuses about how "special conditions" in the state made his requests impossible. Disgruntled white project workers, tired of seeing Brown's initials SAB attached to his comments, began calling him "SOB Brown."

Mississippi was his most trying case. After the guide was published, Brown realized that nearly all his edits had been ignored. He wrote Alsberg a memo to lodge a formal complaint. *A Guide to the Magnolia State* was unabashedly a book for white readers. You need only compare two of the opening essays, on white and Black folkways, for proof.

The white essay, written in the first-person plural: "Our faith is in God, next year's crop, and the Democratic Party."

The Black essay: "Those who know him well enough to understand something of his psychology, his character, and his needs, and like him well enough to accept his deficiencies, find him to be wise but credulous—a superstitious paradox."

Later: "The Mississippi folk Negro neither lays up monetary treasures nor invests in things of tangible value. He spends money for medical and legal advice, a virtue that undoubtably would bring him praise but for the fact that he has never been known to take anyone's advice about anything."

And toward the end: "As for the so-called Negro Question—that, too, is just another problem he has left for the white man to cope with."

While Brown vetted incoming copy for the American Guides—to mixed results—he thought about stand-alone publications. One, a massive social history titled "The Portrait of the Negro as American," would neither ignore Black contributions (as white scholars had done) nor consider them in isolation (as Black scholars had done). Instead, Brown wanted to recast the entire American story by focusing on prominent African Americans as well as anonymous ones from all backgrounds and show how they figured into the general sweep of the nation's history.

Perhaps the most important thing in his portfolio was an effort to collect testimonials of formerly enslaved people. This was a project with roots in the late twenties, when a few Black scholars sent their students into the field to locate and interview people who'd been born into slavery. A research assistant for one of these studies continued the work with FERA funding, the first time the federal government sponsored such an endeavor. Then, with the creation of the WPA, the FWP began gathering its own narratives.

These testimonials were historically invaluable but raised some tricky questions. The DC editors believed that they needed to balance accuracy with readability and style—thinking of a future publication, they insisted on faithful transcriptions that were also, ultimately, marketable. They distributed guidelines for constructing dialect—which words to spell phonetically, which to leave out. The narratives, then, are best understood as collaborations between the informants and the federal writers. Some are more like character sketches than testimonials. It was especially significant, too, that most of these federal writers were white, and that this affected the answers they received. (One white worker in the South accused his informants of telling false or overblown stories: "The general run of negro is only too glad of opportunity to record his grievances against the white race in black and white," he complained, while also criticizing sentimental whites who did the opposite.) Brown monitored this work carefully and argued for interviewers to adopt a simpler writing style, one that allowed them to capture idioms without slipping into racist caricature. It was a fine line: he knew the history of white plantation literature that put dialect speech in the mouths of Black characters in order to transmit white supremacist ideology. But he also wanted to capture the beauty and vitality of that speech: his poetry, like much of Hurston's prose, was marked by the deliberate and artful arrangement of it. He advised struggling FWP field workers to study the examples of creative writers who excelled at capturing speech respectfully but vividly: Erskine Caldwell of *Tobacco Road* fame, the Iowa novelist Ruth Suckow—and Zora Neale Hurston.

"AMBULATORY REPOSITORIES"

The Florida project was down to about sixty workers when Hurston joined. As they struggled to finish the guidebook, they were stymied by an abiding contradiction of the FWP—one that could never truly be resolved. The FWP's official mission was to sustain the jobless until they found private employment. At the same time, Alsberg and others wanted to create the finest books they could. But workers who found new jobs, fulfilling the official mission, were often the most adept writers and editors, and their departures set back progress on the guides and other publications. The FWP succeeded, in other words, by constantly draining its own labor pool. In Florida, a worker was preparing a good portion of the tours when he left for a private job—but he never turned in the material. A field representative from DC had to drive more than 1,200 miles of tours all over again.

The purloined tours weren't the only setback: the DC editors thought the Florida copy was weak, and they combed through it for exaggerations and outdated information and outright errors. The prose often needed punching up or smoothing down. "The Citrus essay is vastly overwritten" was a typical comment.

Hurston's work was being sprinkled into the guidebook, but she wasn't involved with its actual preparation. Instead, she focused on the Negro Unit's main task, "The Florida Negro." The unit had been gathering material from across the state, interviewing the lofty and the lowly, scribbling down notes in barbershops and churches, at funerals and gambling games. Jim Crow relegated the unit's workers to libraries at three of the state's Black colleges, which weren't as expansive as the whites-only libraries. So they relied heavily on interviews. Hurston, the de facto editor, was supposed to add new chapters to the manuscript and flesh out a few others, mostly having to do with folklore. She knew that Florida, with its vestiges of the frontier and confluence of many cultures, was an especially rich treasury of folk material. "There is still an opportunity to observe the wombs of folk culture still heavy with life," she wrote in a report. "The drums throb: Africa by way of Cuba; Africa by way of the British West Indies; Africa by way of Haiti and Martinique; Africa by way of Central and South America. Old Spain speaks through many interpreters. Old England speaks through black, white, and intermediate lips. Florida, the inner melting pot of the great melting pot America."

By the time she joined the project, Hurston had been gathering and studying folklore for over a decade. It was her vocation and she excelled at it. But her career was a multilayered thing, folding together different approaches and sensibilities that were all simultaneously present in the Americana turn of the twenties and thirties. There was her work for "Godmother" Charlotte Mason Osgood, the wealthy white patron who made Hurston her contracted agent and, through her, hunted for folk material as if it were some exotic treasure to be scooped up and shipped back to New York. Osgood's approach epitomized the sensibility of the Americana collectors who emerged in the late nineteenth century and saw themselves as snatching objects away from the encroaching obscuration of the past—whether it was a Brewster chair, an antique plow, or a children's rhyme they sought to preserve and admire. But in other instances, Hurston's work belonged to a different trend, the social-scientific mode of treating folk material as the basis for serious anthropological study. Hurston's inclusion in Franz Boas's Columbia circle, her advanced academic training, and her membership in professional societies put her at the center of this developing field. And yet her methods and interests didn't neatly align with those of the professional scholars, either—that world held too little art and too little imagination for her. Hurston's deepest affinities lay with the creative writers who luxuriated in folk material while putting it to their own poetic uses: Carl Sandburg and Stephen Vincent Benét, say, or her sometime friend and collaborator Langston Hughes. (Vardis Fisher, whose first novel, *Toilers of the Hills*, was saturated with folk beliefs and expressions, was influenced by this current as well.) Hurston's idiosyncratic career as a folklorist gave her experience in all of these areas, which meant she was sitting on a three-way fault line: between the old-fashioned antiquarians, the

Harry Hopkins, head of the WPA, speaking before the Senate Unemployment and Relief Committee in 1938 to discuss the need for
a permanent anti-poverty program (Library of Congress, Prints and Photographs Division, photograph by Harris & Ewing, LC-DIG-hec-24402)

Henry G. Alsberg, director of the
Federal Writers' Project from 1935
to 1939 (Library of Congress, Prints and
Photographs Division, LC-DIG-ds-07663)

ABOVE: Alsberg and Katharine Kellock, the FWP's national tours editor and its highest-ranking woman, working in the Ouray Building, the FWP's third home in Washington, DC (Library of Congress, Prints and Photographs Division, LC-DIG-ds-07666)

RIGHT: Federal writers at work in the McLean mansion, the FWP's second home in Washington, DC (Record Group 69-N, National Archives at College Park)

Relief Blues, a painting by the federal artist O. Louis Guglielmi, depicting a social worker interviewing a family before they can qualify for relief (Circa 1938, tempera on fiberboard, Smithsonian American Art Museum, Transfer from General Services Administration, 1971.447.34)

Vardis Fisher, right, standing in front of Idaho's Caxton Printers with its publisher, J. H. Gipson (Special Collections and Archives, Boise State University Library)

Fisher visiting Caxton Printers in 1939, around the time he resigned as director of the Idaho project (Special Collections and Archives, Boise State University Library)

Publicity portrait of Nelson Algren in 1942, around the time he left the Illinois project and published his second novel, *Never Come Morning* (Photograph by Reuben Segel, Chicago, Library of Congress, Prints and Photographs Division, NYWT&S Collection, LC-USZ62-112303)

ABOVE LEFT: Zora Neale Hurston examining a copy of *American Stuff* at the New York Times Book Fair in fall 1937, shortly after she published *Their Eyes Were Watching God* and several months before she would join the Florida project (Zora Neale Hurston Papers, Special and Area Studies Collections, George A. Smathers Libraries, University of Florida, Gainesville, Florida)

ABOVE RIGHT: Hurston resting on the porch of a turpentiner's cabin in Cross City, Florida, during an FWP expedition in 1939 (Photograph by Robert Cook, Zora Neale Hurston Papers, Special and Area Studies Collections, George A. Smathers Libraries, University of Florida, Gainesville, Florida)

Richard Wright, photographed by Carl Van Vechten in June 1939, shortly after winning a Guggenheim Fellowship, leaving the FWP, and finishing a draft of *Native Son* (Library of Congress, Prints and Photographs Division, Carl Van Vechten Collection, LC-USZ62-42502)

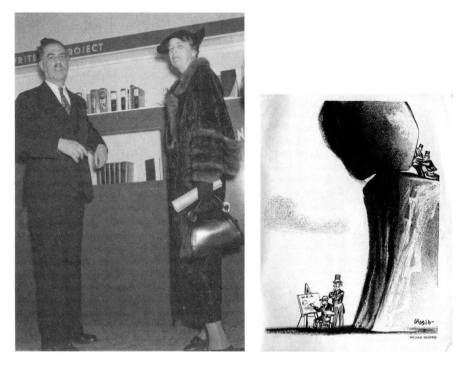

ABOVE LEFT: Alsberg and First Lady Eleanor Roosevelt, a staunch supporter of the WPA arts projects (Record Group 69-N, National Archives at College Park)

ABOVE RIGHT: Cartoon by William Gropper of the Treasury Section of Fine Arts, protesting cuts to the WPA, from the pamphlet *12 Cartoons Defending WPA*, published by the American Artists' Congress, likely in 1939 (Courtesy of the Wolfsonian Museum, Florida International University)

Martin Dies, Jr., representative from Texas, in November 1938, before a meeting of his committee to investigate subversive activities (Library of Congress, Prints and Photographs Division, photograph by Harris & Ewing, LC-DIG-hec-25320)

Alsberg defending the FWP before the Dies Committee in December
1938 (Library of Congress, Prints and Photographs Division, photograph by Harris
& Ewing, LC-DIG-hec-25538)

ABOVE LEFT: Poster advertising the FWP book *Who's Who in the Zoo*, created by the Federal Art Project in New York City (Library of Congress, Prints and Photographs Division, LC-USZC2-958)

ABOVE CENTER: Advertisement for another FWP book, *Birds of the World* (Library of Congress, Prints and Photographs Division, LC-USZC2-965)

ABOVE RIGHT: *Gathering of Nuggets*, frontispiece of the FWP's 1939 book *Idaho Lore*, depicting federal writers at work; a linoleum block print by the federal artist Adrian Troy

CLOCKWISE FROM TOP LEFT: *Illinois: A Descriptive and Historical Guide* (1939), jacket illustrations by the Federal Art Project in Chicago; *Nebraska: A Guide to the Cornhusker State* (1939), jacket illustration from a wood engraving by Joseph Di Gemma; *New York: A Guide to the Empire State* (1940), jacket photograph of the American Falls in Niagara by E. M. Newman; *The Ohio Guide* (1940), jacket photograph of a worker in the B. F. Goodrich tire factory (Photographs of covers by Addie Borchert)

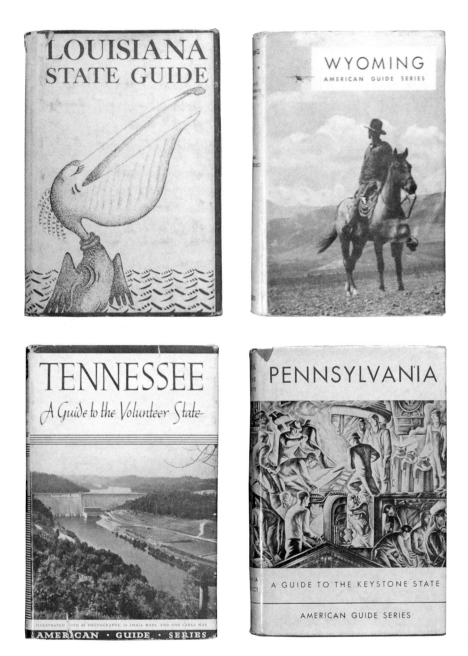

CLOCKWISE FROM TOP LEFT: *Louisiana: A Guide to the State* (1941), jacket illustration by Caroline Durieux, state director of the Federal Art Project in Louisiana; *Wyoming: A Guide to Its History, Highways, and People* (1941), jacket photograph by the rancher and photographer Charles J. Belden; *Tennessee: A Guide to the Volunteer State* (1939), jacket photograph of the Tennessee Valley Authority's Norris Dam; *Pennsylvania: A Guide to the Keystone State* (1940), jacket illustration from a mural by Howard Cook, installed in the Pittsburgh post office under the auspices of the Treasury Section (Photographs of covers by Addie Borchert)

increasingly influential social scientists, and the folksy fringe of modernist writing.

The FWP was in the same uneasy position, and no one embodied that tension better than John Lomax. He was the project's first national folklore editor, just as Katharine Kellock oversaw the tours and Sterling Brown oversaw Negro Affairs. *Lore* was too narrow a label, though: everything in the realm of vernacular culture fell under Lomax's purview. He was essentially a special consultant who evaluated incoming material from the states and helped sketch out the project's strategy for gathering, and eventually making use of, such material. Lomax wrote the folklore supplement to the American Guide Manual and directed field workers to search for lore and customs that could be pinned down to a specific place: local witches and hauntings, cures and conjurations, omens and intelligent animals. His approach was vigorously populist in spirit, but it also assumed that vernacular culture was a kind of appealing relic left over from a more primitive time. "Obviously, leading citizens of towns are not always the best sources for lore," the manual said. "Rather an old cook, washerwoman, gardener or other retainer of some long-established family should be contacted. Oldest residents, close to the soil, who, because circumstances have cut them off from education and progressive enlightenment, are repositories for local lore, legend and superstition, would be ideal sources for the field worker."

As a folklorist, Lomax resembled the eighteenth-century gentlemen collectors who scoured the Scottish Highlands for ballads more than the early twentieth-century scholars who were developing an academic discipline. His approach had the same antiquarian thrust as that of Charlotte Osgood Mason, Hurston's former patron and Lomax's generational contemporary. He was born in Mississippi two and a half years after Appomattox and raised in Texas among cowboys and cattle drives. He did some teaching and studied part-time at Harvard, but he worked mostly in college administration and as a bond salesman. In 1910, he published *Cowboy Songs and Other Frontier Ballads* and helped legitimize the collection of original American songs and lore. Teddy Roosevelt provided an introduction by way of a scribbled letter reproduced in the front matter. By the time of the FWP, Lomax was a popular speaker who sang and whooped at his audiences. In 1934, he and his son Alan published *American Ballads and Folk Songs*, a collection that, along with Carl Sandburg's *American Songbag* from 1927, was an emblem of the rising fascination with such material. Appointing Lomax made sense. He already worked under the auspices of the Archive of American Folk Song at the Library of Congress, where he was an honorary consultant. And he possessed tremendous expertise: for instance, while reviewing a manuscript from Indiana, Lomax spotted a tale that he knew hadn't originated in the Hoosier state but among the German folk stories about Baron Munchausen. A year into the project, he gleefully reported to Alsberg that he had material from every state, and that twenty-eight of them had sent substantial copy on folklore and folkways. He was optimistic about their progress.

But, over time, it was Lomax who became the obstacle. He'd always been out of step with his more cosmopolitan and liberal FWP colleagues—his relic-hunting style carried a strong whiff of paternalism, and he didn't seem interested in observing or interpreting the living, changing vernacular culture of the present moment. Sterling Brown argued with him about the blues and Bessie Smith and considered him "an unreconstructed rebel." Lomax, meanwhile, accused Brown of projecting his ideas onto the "authentic" Black folk.

Hurston seemed to have a better opinion of Lomax—at least, so she told him when they corresponded. She may have been simply, and understandably, buttering up a leading figure in her field. But an incident in the summer of 1935, just as the FWP was being created, suggested that Hurston and Lomax, as folklorists, shared a stronger sympathy. That summer, she was recruited for a collecting trip through the South by Mary Barnicle, an NYU professor, and John's son, Alan, who were collecting on behalf of the Library of Congress. (Alan was still a college student and a few years away from recording such luminaries as Woody Guthrie and Jelly Roll Morton in sessions for the library.) Hurston, in a letter to his father, called the twenty-year-old Alan "little Boss" Lomax, and she seemed pleased by their collaboration. Alan, for his part, was in awe of Hurston. "I was entranced and dazzled and almost worshipful," he wrote later. She was a serious ethnographer and a vibrant raconteur and a powerful literary stylist who owned the contradictions between her constituent parts—a synthesis that Alan found greatly appealing. But tensions between Hurston and Barnicle undermined the trip and then came to a head when Barnicle, who was white, insisted on photographing a Black child eating a watermelon. Hurston was enraged and quit. She later wrote to John Lomax and described the wreckage of the trip: according to Hurston, Barnicle was a fraud attempting to trade on the Lomax name by turning Alan against his father, with the help of other "Reds"; Hurston, meanwhile, was obliged to set him straight. Within the fraught world of thirties folk collecting, it seemed, Hurston was more comfortable aligning with a paternalistic white southerner like John Lomax than any Yankee communists.

By the time Hurston joined the FWP, though, John Lomax was gone: felled by the academic folklorists from whom he'd always been estranged. At a 1937 conference, the American Folklore Society refused to endorse the FWP unless its folklore efforts came under expert supervision—that is, by someone other than Lomax. The next year, Alsberg replaced Lomax with Benjamin A. Botkin, and the society offered its endorsement.

Botkin belonged to a scholarly new guard of folklorists that was supplanting old-fashioned collectors like Lomax. He was born in Boston to Jewish Lithuanian immigrants and educated at Harvard and Columbia; he quit the east coast for the plains, where he finished his PhD at the University of Nebraska and then taught at the University of Oklahoma. For four years he edited *Folk-Say: A Regional Miscellany*, a key vector for the heightened interest in folk material that characterized the Americana turn, a complement to the Illinois project director John T. Frederick's journal *The Midland*. (*Folk-Say* also published many poems by Sterling Brown.) Botkin was omnivorous: he believed that folkways emerged from diverse ethnic and geographic contexts, from rural and urban settings, in forms that could be antique or strikingly new. It was Botkin who called the project's attention to industrial testimonials and folklore, an idea that put Nelson Algren's and Jack Conroy's talents to such good use. His abiding vision was of a pervasive grassroots movement, the folk itself learning to present and celebrate its own folk culture. In lines that could have been a rebuke to John Lomax, Botkin wrote: "The folk movement must come from the below upward rather than of above downward. Otherwise it may be dismissed as a patronizing gesture, a nostalgic wish, an elegiac complaint, a sporadic and abortive revival—on the part of paternalistic aristocrats going slumming, dilettantish provincials going native, defeated sectionalists going back to the soil, and anybody and everybody who cares to go collecting." The FWP and its legions of federal writers offered the perfect machinery to realize Botkin's democratic and participatory vision. Although not as colorful as Lomax, the beefy Texan, Botkin was committed to his ideas. Jerre Mangione, the national coordinating editor, once took Botkin out to a belly dancer show. Amid the gyrations, Mangione noticed the folklorist hunched over in his seat, eagerly scribbling in his notebook—alive to all the possibilities of living lore.

Botkin joined the FWP shortly after Hurston, and their catholic approaches were perfectly matched. Hurston's contributions mixed fantastical stories with children's games, workplace sketches, local history, and lists of piquant sayings. She wrote about Big John de Conquer and John Henry, but also John Hamilton, a citrus picker who described the rhythms of work in the groves and the jargon that only pickers knew. She wrote the sketch of Eatonville and its mighty, supernatural alligator. (Her original draft, seven paragraphs on that shapeshifting gator, was a far stranger account.) She wrote a brief history of Goldsborough, the inverted Eatonville—a Black-incorporated town that was deemed an obstacle to the expansion of white Sanford and then forcibly absorbed by it.

"Folklore is the boiled-down juice of human living," she wrote in an essay for "The Florida Negro." It was at once a treatise on the nature of folklore and a treasury of Florida songs and stories, the kind of stylized hybrid writing that only Hurston could offer the project. By now, decades removed from the lying sessions on Joe Clark's store porch, she was possessed of a hard-earned expertise, tempered by uncountable hours of fieldwork. She could see how a tale—a mere amusement to her as a child—belonged to a vibrant, intricate folk culture, one that was shaped spontaneously and collectively by people who were largely powerless. Take Big John de Conquer, whose stories had persisted since the days of slavery. "He is the story that all weak people create to compensate for their weakness," she wrote. "He is a projection of the poor and humble into the realms of the mighty."

Because Hurston was detached from the project office, she may not have realized that a new fault line—in addition to the color line—had opened up. The Florida project was split between those who wanted to promote the state and those who wanted to apply searching, honest criticism. The question came up in every FWP office and it got to the heart of the project's mission.

Were the American Guides just books for tourists, or was the FWP assembling a social portrait of the nation? In Florida, the conflict was especially acute because tourism was an essential industry—and key to any economic recovery.

Among the divided federal writers, there was the "palm trees and bathing beauties" faction (as one of their opponents characterized it), led, not surprisingly, by Carita Corse, whose sympathy for the Chamber of Commerce line Alsberg had detected early on. Corse was backed by her office assistant and the project's two chief editors, Max Hunter and Roland Phillips. (Hunter was a seasoned journalist and editor; Phillips had, for twenty-five years, made a living writing fiction for pulp magazines. Together, they constituted the St. Petersburg district office before moving into the main one in Jacksonville.) The opposing faction included Stetson Kennedy, the young worker who prodded Hurston with letters, and an assistant editor, Robert Cornwall. They wanted to lay bare the dark side of Florida: Jim Crow, Klan violence, exploited labor. Although Kennedy grew up in a middle-class family and even had an uncle in the Klan, he grew to detest the racial oppression he saw around him. He dropped out of the University of Florida and took a WPA job raking seaweed that washed up onshore each night ("It was very much a job with a future," he later said.) Then he joined the Florida project and met Cornwall, an avid reader of *New Masses* and the *Daily Worker*, and the pair bonded over shared sensibilities. They fought a clandestine battle to smuggle "liberal dope" into the guidebook copy. Manuscripts bound for DC became sites of struggle as each side made surreptitious additions and deletions. Once, Cornwall was meeting with the rest of the editorial staff and going over essays for the guide. They came to a draft of the essay on Florida's contemporary scene, written by Stetson Kennedy. "Aren't we going to have anything in the contemporary scene except about niggers, sharecroppers, and the downtrodden?" grunted another editor.

The national staff was more in tune with Kennedy and Cornwall. Darel McConkey, a field supervisor, once called Corse out for downplaying the two fatal hurricanes of the twenties. According to the guidebook copy, the storms made national headlines and, at the same time, were a threat only to shrubbery and buildings of flimsy construction. "Newspapers do not give headlines to damaged shrubbery," McConkey wrote. He reminded her that, in a single cemetery, they'd found a monument erected over the grave of sixty-nine hurricane victims. "It is better to give a straight factual story about such events rather than attempt to cover them up," he said.

Still, McConkey himself put Hunter and Phillips in charge of all copy before it left the office. The point was to get the guidebook done, and the two editors were competent and reliable. That fall, they were summoned to DC to assist with the final editing. The FWP and the rest of Federal #1 had by then moved offices once more, from the McLean mansion to the more suitably bland Ouray Building on G and Eighth Streets. (When Hallie Flanagan of the Federal Theater Project arrived, her heart sank at the sight: "small dull offices with dull tan walls and dull brown woodwork and brown burlap screens chastely concealing corner hand-basins.") The FWP took up three floors, and the Florida editors needed a chart to find their way around. They were impressed by the frenzy of activity and by Katharine Kellock's usual scrutiny of the tours. Phillips even reported an encounter with the national director when he noticed "Uncle Henry wandering about the halls in a trance." They felt reasonably sure that their faction, Corse's faction, would win out, despite the DC staff's liberal sympathies. Hunter wrote to Corse, saying that he had successfully deflected attempts to add disagreeable material to their copy.

While Hunter and Phillips were in DC, the critical faction wrote an anonymous memo that attempted to analyze, "from a Marxian perspective," the various forces at work on the Florida project. Mostly, it was a rundown of characters in the office. The absent editors came in for particular scorn. Hunter was "a man of property" with ties to the Tampa political machine: "Could be a good field man if he worked more and drank less." Phillips was anti–New Deal: "Hard worker, but his mind is chained to the pulp stories he once wrote." It praised a few workers (including, not surprisingly, Kennedy and Cornwall) and a "lady handyman" named Bebe Lang: "Proletarian wit, often cruel, distrusts those slick-talking writers, narrow-minded, good with a cross-cut saw." The memo's author, or authors, could be cruel as well. Of one editor: "wants people with new ideas to leave him alone." A typist was simply "fat, crippled, gossipy, reactionary, servile."

The memo didn't mention Hurston, who was rarely seen in the office.

But its longest passage was a scathing, if oddly respectful, portrait of Carita Corse:

> She is opinionated, superficial, clever, a typical southern conservative in matters political, social, economic (despite her ability to pose as a liberal when meeting a superior in office or influence). Greatest enthusiasms: history of Florida, thwarting progressive tendencies on the project, the folklore of Negroes (servile ones only), ridiculing the Washington staff, being charitable to unfortunates, taking command of a situation, being sweet, and working fast so there will be time enough for new enthusiasms.

With the guide nearing completion, the DC editors could not understand why the folklore material was so "skimpy and patchy" when the Florida field notes were so abundantly rich. They especially wanted more Black folk songs, tales, and descriptions of juke joints. Whether they were pointing to Hurston's work is impossible to say; clearly, though, the copy needed more of her touch. Eventually, they sent for Hurston herself, and she arrived in DC to work alongside the editors, although she was still denied their rank.

In Washington, Hurston was pulled into an argument that activated all the major schisms of her time on the project. The details are murky, and the only account came from Stetson Kennedy, who, at that time and later, admired Hurston but was skeptical of her politics. According to Kennedy, Hurston and Sterling Brown clashed over the guide's description of the 1920 massacre in Ocoee, northwest of Orlando, where more than thirty Black residents—possibly twice as many—were murdered by a rampaging white mob on election day. Brown thought the guide's scant treatment needed to be replaced with a fuller account, something closer to the devastating contemporaneous report written by Walter White of the NAACP. In this, he was backed by a prominent outside consultant: W. E. B. Du Bois.

Hurston had known Du Bois for more than a decade, but they were not close and their relationship was somewhat vexed. Hurston insisted that White's reporting was exaggerated, and she even claimed to be an eyewitness—Ocoee, after all, was not so far from Eatonville. Ultimately, Hurston won. Katharine Kellock told Hurston to set up a desk in her office and submit all the material directly to her, bypassing Brown and Du Bois. Back in Florida, Corse was thrilled. When Hurston returned to the state, she lambasted the DC staff from Alsberg to the janitor and said she had been ready to fight with knives and razors out to keep misinformation from getting into the guide. She and Corse agreed that there were too many biased writers out there who were simply bent on discrediting the South.

This wasn't just an instance of Hurston currying favor with her boss in order to protect her job. She had well-formed opinions about how the South ought to be depicted, and few things bothered her as much as those who, from her perspective, used Black suffering for propagandistic purposes. Such insincerity, as she saw it, was a major factor in her estrangement from the left; she believed that radicals, Black and white, who heaped aspersions on the South were more interested in recruiting for the Communist Party than improving any actual lives. "Being poor myself I am heartily in favor of poor people getting hold of money but I fail to see the difference between an under-paid cotton picker and an under paid factory hand," she wrote in a letter a few years earlier. "So why stress Alabama? The underdog catches heck everywhere."

But the matter of Ocoee wasn't really settled. Eventually, Corse sent Hurston to investigate for herself. (Hurston, it turned out, had not been an eyewitness—she was at Howard University during the massacre.) While interviewing some of the townspeople, Hurston was confronted by the full scope of the violence that had unfolded there. Brown and Du Bois, it seemed, had been right. She wrote a new account, beginning with Ocoee's Black residents turning out to the polls, and ending in a storm of fire and bullets, along with the lynching of a man, July Perry, who had resisted the mob. It was harrowing in its matter-of-factness. Kennedy, however, was still disappointed: Hurston had described the massacre as a spontaneous eruption confined to Ocoee, while he believed it had been an organized Klan operation that spread into neighboring towns. His objections were reflected in what ultimately appeared in the guide: a long paragraph condensing and adjusting Hurston's narrative. And yet, for all the arresting power of that passage, it was saddled with a jarring opening sentence that conveyed the "white" version of events—"one of several conflicting stories."

At least, this is Kennedy's explication of the circumstances behind Hurston's Ocoee essay. He claimed to have heard her speaking to Corse when she returned to Florida, and he took contemporaneous notes on the exchange. His story would explain a letter Hurston sent to Corse after her visit to DC. "You might have been a little proud of your pet darkey," she wrote. "Yes, I know that I belong to you and that Sterling Brown belongs to Allsberg. I laugh at the little phenagling he does to give Sterling the edge over me. BUT, he cannot make him no new head with inside trimmings and thats where he falls down. You ought to see Sterling exhibiting his jealousy as I top him time after time." Her language was striking, but not out of character. Hurston was a keen strategist of racial deference, especially when her work depended on it, and she'd taken a similar approach in letters to Charlotte Osgood Mason and other white benefactors. She and Corse were growing closer, too, although how much of their friendship was based on calculated flattery or on mutual affection isn't clear. The director was kind and overlooked Hurston's frequent absences; she was relatively liberal on racial matters and she always supported the Negro Unit—that is, within the parameters of a segregated society. For Hurston, who distrusted radicals of any race, that may have been enough. As with John Lomax, she knew where she stood with a conventional white southerner like Carita Corse.

And yet Hurston's rivalry with Brown was real. Even though she made him out to be the jealous one, it's difficult to imagine Hurston, who was not even an official editor of a single unit of a state project, being unenvious of Brown, a national editor of the top rank. More significantly, they shared a fundamental disagreement over Black literature and "the race problem." Hurston's long-simmering ideas put her at odds with Brown and W. E. B. Du Bois and many others. She'd never forgotten Brown's criticism of *Mules and Men* and, more recently, she was put off by his lukewarm review of *Their Eyes Were Watching God.* ("Living in an all-colored town, these people escape the worst pressures of class and caste," he wrote. "There is little harshness, there is enough money and work to go around"—although he did applaud the "bitterness, sometimes oblique, in the enforced folk manner, and sometimes forthright," that occasionally seeped through.) Her resentment bubbled up in the essay "Art and Such," which she wrote for "The Florida Negro." She was supposed to cover Black contributions to the arts in Florida. Instead, she wrote an attack on those she deemed "Race Champions" and their pernicious effect on creative expression. Such people, Hurston believed, chased racial grievances with a single-mindedness that was outmoded, self-serving, intellectually lazy, and artistically bankrupt. "To him," the Race Champion, "no Negro exists as an individual—he exists only as another tragic unit of the Race," she wrote. "This in spite of the obvious fact that Negroes love and hate and fight and play and strive and travel and have a thousand and one interests in life like other humans. When his baby cuts a new tooth he brags as shamelessly as anyone else without once weeping over the prospect of some Klansman knocking it out when and if the child ever gets grown." A Race Champion had one long, loud note—the suffering inflicted on African Americans in the past and in the present—and Hurston feared that note would drown out the rich, complex music of Black life in America. Eatonville, after all, got along just fine without white people. Why couldn't her writing do the same? Why be held hostage to a confrontation with white supremacy instead of striving to approach the universal through the particular—the foundation of all great art?

She probably wrote this essay as a missive to Brown, though he likely never saw it. Brown, for his part, never stopped admiring Hurston even while he doubted her literary politics. When he was hired to oversee Negro Affairs, he drew up a list of people they ought to consult in each state—and there, in Florida, was Zora Neale Hurston.

By early 1939, Hurston was restless and thinking of leaving the FWP. She'd been stealing moments, or sometimes days and weeks, to write a new novel, *Moses, Man of the Mountain*. Her writing never waited—not for graduate studies, not for romantic relationships, not for the FWP. (The WPA did bring her one unexpected development that year: she met a man, Albert Price, who worked for a WPA education project, and married him. Price was in his early twenties—not quite half Hurston's age—and their brief marriage was doomed from the start.) When she turned her attention to the FWP, she found that prospects for "The Florida Negro" weren't good. Hurston, acting as a de facto editor, contacted at least two publishers about the manuscript. Both of them passed.

Florida: A Guide to the Southernmost State appeared that year, bound in a vibrant teal cloth case beneath its dust jacket. Even if the FWP hadn't fully recognized Hurston's value as a worker, the guide does celebrate her, clearly and frequently, as a writer. Along with Hurston's long, signed ramble through Eatonville, there's a lengthy extract from *Their Eyes Were Watching God* describing migrant workers in Pahokee, and, in the literature essay, a solid paragraph devoted to her books. It's hard to miss the implication—no other writers but James Weldon Johnson, Marjorie Kinnan Rawlings (whose novel *The Yearling* won the Pulitzer Prize that year), and Ernest Hemingway were granted as much space on the page.

With the guide behind them, the FWP drew Hurston in with new responsibilities. First, Corse recruited her to put on a dance show in Orlando, a way of publicizing the arts projects. Hurston found young dancers and boarded them with neighbors in Eatonville while she taught them the "Fire Dance," a springtime ritual with African roots that she'd first witnessed in the Bahamas and had used in her musical showcase *The Great Day*. The show was performed twice and Corse was pleased—not least by Hurston's decision to hire younger dancers, whose movements were suggestive, but only slightly. "In older people," Corse said, "they would have been quite shocking."

Next, the project finally gained some equipment that Hurston had requested from the very start: a recording machine. She'd used one during her fieldwork with Alan Lomax (possibly the same machine, loaned from the Library of Congress) and she knew its value. It was extremely difficult, for instance, to transcribe a song in one take, and if you asked a singer to repeat the song, the words often changed. But federal writers didn't have access to such technology: all the life histories and industrial lore and slavery narratives they collected were scribbled down by hand.

Now, in Florida, they did. The recording machine came by way of the WPA's Joint Committee on Folk Art, a kind of Federal #1 umbrella group organized by Benjamin Botkin. The machine, which recorded directly onto acetate disks, was carried in an old army ambulance that had been refurbished by WPA workers; it was escorted by Herbert Halpert, a folklorist sent by the Joint Committee on a fourteen-week expedition through the South. (By the trip's end, he'd record 419 disks and mail them back to DC.) The Florida project made Hurston the advance scout who traveled ahead of her white colleagues, better to gain the trust of informants and avoid the appearance of an integrated group. On one trip, she entered a turpentine camp near Cross City in northwest Florida. Workers, most of them Black, toiled among the scarred and weeping pine trees in harsh conditions. (The camps were usually closed to outsiders.) Hurston spoke to foremen who seemed to enjoy their jobs, although they'd known nothing else. But she also heard rumors of workers who were killed and buried in the woods or dumped in the Gulf of Mexico; she heard of white overseers who raped Black women in the camps; she heard of beatings and forced marriages and peons who would never escape the debt they owed to the company. Her white colleagues followed soon after and recorded what material they could. Stetson Kennedy was unnerved by the notes Hurston sent back and, when he and a project photographer, Robert Cook, arrived, he was surprised to find that she was still there—sitting on the porch of a turpentiner's shack and smoking a cigarette. Cook pointed his camera and took a candid shot, to Hurston's annoyance. In the photo, her usually vivacious demeanor was suspended, just for a second. In its place was a look of weariness and contempt.

Kennedy and Cook hung around for a few more days, clandestinely interviewing the workers. Finally they packed up and bade farewell to the white overseer. "Who was that colored gal who came here before yall did?" he asked. They told him. "She was pretty smart for a colored gal," he said. "Of course, I figure she's about three-fifths white!" They left without saying anything.

The Florida project workers didn't always lug the recording machine so far afield. Over the course of several days, they recorded folk songs at the Clara White Mission, where the Negro Unit was housed. Hurston chatted with the singers and got them ready. Kennedy wanted to record a bit of sound and play it back to show the people what it was like. He did, and Eartha White, who ran the mission, interrupted him. She insisted that they begin with a prayer: "Dear Lord," she said, "this is Eartha White talking to you again. We just want to thank you for giving mankind the intelligence to make such a marvelous machine, and for giving us a President like Franklin D. Roosevelt, who cares about preserving the songs people sing." And so they sang.

Kennedy was becoming a seasoned collector. When he was in the field, he sought out the people he called "ambulatory repositories"—walking, talking storehouses of oral tradition. He noticed that just about every community had such a person. And then it dawned on him—so did the Florida project. Their ambulatory repository was named Zora Neale Hurston.

She sang more than a dozen songs that day. They were songs she'd picked

up from railroad work crews, gamblers, children; songs she'd heard in lumber camps, juke joints, the Bahamas. Some songs she never learned anywhere
in particular but heard everywhere—she'd known them all her life.

She introduced herself: Zora Neale Hurston, born in Eatonville, age
thirty-five. (She was born in Alabama but, as an artist and thinker, her true
origin lay in Eatonville; she was really forty-eight, but good for her.) Her interviewer was Herbert Halpert, the young white folklorist attached to the WPA
Joint Committee on Folk Art, who'd come along with the recording machine.
As Hurston sang and explained each song—where she learned it, the social
and economic context—Halpert peppered her with questions. He was being
thorough, but it was also as if he couldn't quite reconcile Hurston's two roles,
as both an informant and his peer (Columbia educated, she pointed out).

But that was the point. In certain ways, the FWP failed Hurston. It kept
her alive but squandered her talents and demeaned her with a low rank. (Her
contributions to "The Florida Negro" were eventually discarded by the
white editors, including Corse and Kennedy, and then the manuscript was
shelved.) And yet, sitting in front of the recorder, Hurston collapsed the distance between the federal writer and the source, the method and the text, and
embodied one of the FWP's most appealing and democratic visions. Halpert
asked how Hurston learned her songs, and she said:

> I learn. I just get in the crowd with the people if they are singing and I
> listen as best I can and then I start to join in with a phrase or two and
> then finally I get so I can sing a verse and then I keep on till I learn all the
> sounds and all the verses and then I sing them back to the people, until
> they tell me that I can sing them just like them. And then I take part and
> try it out on different people, who already know the song, until they are
> quite satisfied that I know it. Then I carry it in my memory.

"Well," he asked, "how about those that you have in your book and publish in the journals?"

"Well, that is the same way I got them. I learned the song myself and then
I can take it with me wherever I go."

RICHARD WRIGHT, NEW YORK CITY

"A TEN-TON TRUCK RUN WILD"

New York City was the WPA's forty-ninth state. Its five boroughs contained so many people on relief that the city was treated as its own administrative unit. The Federal Writers' Project followed suit: NYC had its own project, housed in Manhattan and independent from the state project, which was relegated to the backwater (relatively speaking) of Albany. Because it was situated in the literary capital of the United States, because it could harness the city's unsurpassed writerly firepower, because it would attract the attention of the city's influential news media, the NYC project was poised to become the FWP's finest, most important outpost.

It became, instead, the most conspicuously dysfunctional. For instance: over the course of its life, the NYC project would have six directors total, plus two acting. It soon became more infamous for generating dramatic headlines than admired for producing high-quality publications. Turmoil on the project would make the "Red Baedeker" episode and the backlash to the Massachusetts guide seem like polite quibbles. Even when the NYC project began to issue diverse and well-regarded books, including an acclaimed two-volume guide to the city, its instability threatened to bring down the entire FWP. It was both crown jewel and albatross.

An NYC project, considered in the abstract, inspired optimism for good reason. By the thirties, New York had long completed its gradual eclipse of Boston, and of Philadelphia before that, as the nation's literary capital. Manhattan was dense with publishing houses, weeklies and monthlies, and literary agents; its newspapers transmitted their influence through widely read book supplements and syndicated columnists. Some of America's most outstanding writers, from Washington Irving on down, had made the city their home and its people and environs their subject. Writers who lived elsewhere passed through in a constant stream. In the twenties, the self-exiled writers who set sail for Europe—the ones Malcolm Cowley described in *Exile's Return*—mostly embarked from New York and Hoboken; when they returned, it was to the city or the surrounding countryside. It was no accident that the American Writers' Congress assembled in New York, or that the League of American Writers made its base there. New York was, simply, the nation's largest and most important "Market Place for Words," as the New York City guide would title its literature essay. ("Whether or not it may accurately be termed the country's 'literary capital' is a more or less academic question . . . New York does not seem to have given the question a great deal of thought, but busily went on with its publishing, editing, printing, book reviewing, its occasional making and unmaking of reputations; with not a little writing, though by no means all the writing in the country, being done in the shadow of its skyscrapers.")

New York's literary density meant that once the Depression hit the five boroughs, there were more jobless writers and editors than the FWP could possibly employ—something the professional organizations and guilds, also headquartered in Manhattan, never tired of pointing out. The project had an abundant and diverse labor pool on which to draw: creative writers who came of age among Greenwich Village bohemians or in Harlem's New Negro movement, reporters and editors discarded from emptying newsrooms, scholars cut loose from universities and museums, refugees from ad agencies and public relations firms. Anzia Yezierska, an impoverished author who'd known fame and security in the twenties, who'd gone from lunching at the Algonquin to the relief rolls, described the motley bunch of New Yorkers who gravitated toward the project: "There was a hectic camaraderie among us, although we were as ill-assorted as a crowd on a subway express—spinster poetesses, pulp specialists, youngsters with school-magazine experience, veteran newspaper men, art-for-art's-sake literati, and the clerks and typists who worked with us—people of all ages, all nationalities, all degrees of education, tossed together in a strange fellowship of necessity."

Such diversity of talent and experience heightened the project's potential. It didn't hurt that NYC's federal writers also had access to the finest libraries and museums, or that the city was teeming with specialists and experts. Here's an example of both: in Jacksonville, Carita Corse was struggling to assemble a bibliography on Florida subjects, so she wrote to the NYC project for help, and they sent four workers into Manhattan's ample libraries to augment her research. A few months later, Corse wrote again. Did they have anyone who could read archaic Middle Spanish? Indeed, the NYC project had *two* such people and put them on the job, researching old Florida missions. The project even had enough investigative capability to launch an operation called "The Boondoggle and the Fact," which debunked snarky attacks on the WPA that appeared in New York newspapers (such as "Today's Boondoggle," a series in the *New York Sun*). Project supervisors knew they had a surplus of experienced writers, situated within a superior cultural infrastructure, and this—combined with the usual cheeky chauvinism of New Yorkers—gave them a basis for confidence. "We are here to write the world's best guide book," one editor announced, "and probably will."

It wasn't that simple. The national coordinating editor Jerre Mangione, looking back at the record of the NYC project, called it "a vast psychodrama." "Although my reaction is based upon hasty observation," reported a field supervisor on an early visit to Manhattan, "I am inclined to believe that they have developed entirely too big a machine for the task before them." The bigness of the project, a source of strength, also made it unwieldy and combustible. But size alone didn't turn the project into a "psychodrama." That privilege belongs to human beings, and the NYC office was populated by a ripe selection of them. Communist Party members and fellow travelers, Trotskyists and anarchists, devout New Dealers, the aggressively apolitical, and a small band of reactionaries and assorted nutcases jostled against one another in the office's confines. The Communist Party had an official shop unit on the NYC project, just as it aspired to have in factories and mines and warehouses everywhere. (This was the basic building block of the party, a group of three or more members in a single workplace. Shop units were · responsible for recruitment, distributing the *Daily Worker*, and, when the time came, seizing crucial means of production.) For a while, the FWP shop unit had its own newsletter, *Red Pen*, just as the theater project had *Red Spotlight*, and the art project, *Red Paint*. And even though no groups were immune from squabbling, the conflict was especially intense, and sometimes violent, between Communist Party members and their fraternal enemies, the Trotskyists. What had begun as a power struggle in the Soviet leadership— Stalin and his allies expelled Trotsky from the Comintern in 1929—played out as a kind of gang warfare among radicals in the United States, with both sides believing that the fate of the workers' revolution was at stake. The NYC project wasn't insulated from their dispute.

Political feuding wasn't the only problem. Many federal writers weren't used to being corralled into such an operation, especially one that was both stiffly bureaucratized and maddeningly in flux. Others had been damaged by the Depression and by the usual hazards of life. "Our workers were not like the neat-looking office workers who sat at the hundreds of desks surrounding them," wrote an administrator, when the project initially shared space on a wide-open floor with other WPA units. "They lounged in and out, sprawled and traded wise-cracks, wore their hats and h'isted their feet as journeyman reporters do. They were all from the home relief rolls and it took weeks for some of them to get the habit of clean shirts and pressed trousers. They ran the gamut of mental states, the scared and the stolid, the humble and proud, reserved and excitable, with a scattering of plain drunks."

This mélange of surly reporters, pickled novelists, and incurable weirdos occasionally, and predictably, became explosive. Take the case of Norman Macleod, the poet. Alsberg one day received an aggrieved letter from the project's first director, Walter K. Van Olinda, explaining why he'd just fired Macleod. Van Olinda was meeting with a union delegation when Macleod burst into the room—drunk, "again"—and raised such hell that the delegates, whom Macleod was there to support, kicked him out. "He then went to his own desk," Van Olinda continued, "and removed all Guide Book papers and tore them to pieces." So ended Macleod's career on the NYC project.

When the first federal writers reported for work on October 28, 1935, they had one desk and a swivel chair and that was it. Supervisors sent them out into the streets to compose word sketches, just to give them something to do. They brought pencils and paper of their own; most had already hocked their typewriters. When the office eventually placed an order for pencils with DC, they received 144 gross—that is, 144 x 144 pencils. The supervisors decided that keeping them would be easier than navigating the red tape to send them back. "We were lousy with pencils," one said. The entire bureaucratic apparatus was so confounding that it distracted them from the work of training writers and producing copy. "We could never find the right tree in the forest to shake for the nuts," said another supervisor. "It was necessary to memorize a glossary of new terms: workschedule, write-in, man-months, reclassification and re-rating (which meant promotion or the reverse). And forms, forms, forms, in sextuplicate, on white, salmon, blue, pink, yellow and green paper!"

Puzzles of the bureaucracy provided much fodder for the layers of unions that represented federal writers. The office had been operating for a little more than two weeks when Alsberg was hit with a petition from workers protesting a meaningless discrepancy in WPA wage classifications. (Their grievance was understandable: "newspapermen" were apparently being paid $9.90 less per month than "journalists.") On a visit from DC, the associate director George Cronyn met, in twenty-four hours, delegations from the Writers' Union, the Authors' League of America, the Newspaper Guild of New York, the League of American Writers, the Writers' Union again, the Yiddish Pen, and the Yiddish Writers' Union. One supervisor, exaggerating only slightly (perhaps), recalled spending 90 percent of his time dealing with complaints lodged by thirty-some unions and splinters of unions. "They picketed in our laps and in our hair and underfoot," said an editor about the Writers' Union.

The Workers' Alliance was among the most important of these labor groups. It was launched by the Socialist Party, the Communist Party, and followers of the pacifist pro-labor pastor A. J. Muste, when all three outfits decided to combine their efforts to organize the unemployed. Soon enough, the Communist Party became the driving force behind the Workers' Alliance. But instead of being a mass vehicle for the jobless in general, it essentially became a trade union for WPA workers, who dominated its ranks. WPA

administrators found the Alliance a vexing partner: it pursued grievances
and staged constant demonstrations and drew unwanted publicity because of
its radical tinge. But it was also the WPA's most passionate advocate. Officials
knew this and even Roosevelt allegedly welcomed the Alliance's support.

Day-to-day relations between unions such as the Workers' Alliance and
the FWP were often tense. If a worker was fired, a picket would usually appear outside the project office. Jimmy McGraw, a supervisor in NYC, once
heard coming through his office window, "Tom Girdler and Jimmy McGraw
must go!" (Girdler was the chair of Republic Steel, and especially despised
by the left.) McGraw was amused to find himself compared with a powerful steel magnate when, at that time, he could barely afford a pair of socks.
In general, though, the pickets amounted to a sustained pressure campaign.
WPA workers lived in fear of pink slips: the agency that employed them was
constrained by a yearly appropriation from Congress and, to some degree,
responsive to seasonal fluctuations in employment and the rise and fall of
the labor market. Its rolls were always changing, so workers protested outside WPA offices, demanding an end to cutbacks and an expansion of hiring
quotas. As one of the union locals explained in its newsletter, "The banners
they carry, demanding jobs for writers, may tend to aid in the development of
forearm muscles, but that isn't their prime purpose. Those people are there
because you who are employed stand in constant danger of becoming unemployed, and because competent writers are undergoing that subtle form of
starvation known as Home Relief." In this sense, the pickets were there to defend the WPA against those who would undermine it, including the officials
who were complicit in curtailing its scope.

The sheer amount of commotion outside the office was one reason that
the project moved several times. Harry Hopkins once even intervened and
suggested that they relocate to a less visible part of town. They started out at
111 Eighth Avenue ("one eleven," they called it) in the massive Port Authority
building, along with other WPA units housed on two vast, open floors and sec-
tioned off by railings. Soon they had their own quarters on East Thirty-second
Street, and then they bounced around to Varick Street and East Thirty-ninth
Street and East Forty-second Street. After Hopkins intervened, they slunk
down to the corner of Hudson and King in an out-of-the-way neighborhood.

The project's unruly tendencies might have been tempered by a strong director. The Chicago office, for instance, was nearly as big and had its share of radicals, but also the steady hand of John T. Frederick. In NYC, the directorship instead passed from one person to another, each knocked aside by circumstances that were tragic, farcical, or both.

First was Walter K. Van Olinda (the scourge of Norman Macleod), an encyclopedia editor who got the project up and running. But soon Alsberg decided that Van Olinda hadn't imposed sufficient order on the office, so he removed him and resituated him in Washington as an editor. Next, Alsberg hired Orrick Johns, a poet and journalist who'd been running the parallel and short-lived Reporters' Project in NYC—an informational operation that covered WPA undertakings in general. Alsberg thought highly of Johns and hoped that he would raise the project's morale. Johns believed that his radical politics would allow him to have a less adversarial relationship with certain factions of the workers, and he was probably right. (It was Johns, an editor of *New Masses*, who vouched for Nelson Algren when he was trying and failing to join the Illinois project.)

Before Johns could do much of anything, though, the project was consumed by a bizarre and potentially damaging episode instigated by a tiny group of right-wing federal writers. At the center was Samuel Duff McCoy, the project's assistant director, a multitalented author who'd won a Pulitzer Prize for investigative reporting and helped negotiate the delivery of American relief to Irish civilians during their war for independence from the United Kingdom. McCoy, despite his pedigree, shared in Van Olinda's failure to successfully administer the office; worse, he constantly clashed with the project's radical workers and chose to align himself with a right-wing faction who'd formed an anti-union, anti-left outfit called the Federal Writers' Association. When Johns took over the project (leaving McCoy noticeably passed over), the association reared up in opposition. Its main organizer, William O. Lucas, sent Alsberg a scathing letter that attacked "the unfit, the unruly and the shiftless" who he claimed made up half the project workers. "Stalinists, Trotzkyists, and all other sorts of ists, debated it out during business hours, to the utter disgust of every serious-minded member of the organization," he wrote. Lucas wasn't wrong that the office was an arena for political jousting. But his agenda was clear. He referred to his colleagues as a "human cesspool" and "an aggregation of habitual drunks, loafers, misfits and political agitators, who flout the very idea of honest work" and "one of the meanest, filthiest rackets that ever existed." He closed with a threat: unless Alsberg backed their association publicly and unequivocally, he would face "a national scandal unequaled since the days of Teapot Dome."

While Alsberg and others contemplated their response, the NYC office erupted. McCoy arrived at a staff meeting flanked by uniformed cops. He refused to give any explanation, so Johns fired him. (Project workers whispered that it was a botched frame-up job: McCoy or an ally had planted a gun and communist pamphlets in Johns's desk, but Johns found them before the police could.) The confrontation set off frantic discussions among WPA officials, including Harry Hopkins's aide Jacob Baker, who was still in his position at that time. They decided that Lucas was basically a fascist and that McCoy was losing his mind. "Is there any way you could kidnap McCoy and put him in a sanitarium until he gets to feeling better?" Baker asked an official in New York. When McCoy tried to blackmail the WPA into firing Alsberg—he threatened to go to the papers and claim that the project was overrun by communists—Baker refused to budge. At first, the press framed the blowup as an isolated conflict between fascists and communists on the project—an assessment that, remarkably, seemed to satisfy WPA officials. But then McCoy went to the papers and made himself out to be an anti-communist martyr, handing more ammunition to the WPA's enemies. "M'Coy Says Fight on Reds Cost Job," announced *The New York Times*. "Federal Officials Silent."

The story eventually died down, but, as with all charges of subversive influence on the FWP—from the "Red Baedeker" to the Massachusetts guide—it never really disappeared. Alsberg assured Baker that Lucas's mutiny was hollow: reports from the NYC project suggested that his association had the backing of only five people. Ninety percent of the staff signed a resolution denouncing both his and McCoy's actions. "Everybody hated them," recalled a supervisor, who remembered the faction as "a rather pathetic little group of extreme right wing lads." Lucas, meanwhile, embraced his role as a reliably outraged internal critic of the FWP whenever the press needed one. Project workers took notice: *Federal Writer*, a union newsletter, printed a parody telegram ostensibly dropped by Lucas from a zeppelin onto the project office's roof, offering salacious information about the project for cheap.

Such was the reigning attitude inside the office, where Orrick Johns might have been a stabilizing force, as he'd predicted. He was firmly on the left—a Communist Party member, in fact, who'd joined during the early years of the Depression and spent time working as an organizer. His high position in the FWP epitomized the about-face that the new Popular Front had demanded of party members and fellow travelers. As recently as 1934, when the party still held a hostile view of the New Deal, Johns reported on a John Reed Club conference for *New Masses* and took a dig at "Roosevelt-fostered national-chauvinist art." (Presumably, he meant the artists working for the PWAP and other pre-WPA efforts.) Now, buoyed by the new Popular Front sensibility, he was keen to begin fostering some of that art himself, in its literary form, as director of the NYC project.

Bundled up with Johns's politics were some bad habits. He could be volatile and combative, especially when he drank, which was often. "Orrick was a man of terrific emotional intensity," recalled an editor. "A real Captain Ahab, he was." Johns shared more than a volcanic temperament with Ahab: he also had a false leg. He'd lost the leg after being run over by a trolley when he was a boy of seven in Missouri. But not even a wooden leg could slow him down. "Every payday he would go to the nearby bar and take off his peg and lay it up on the bar so he could engage in a fight," said Jacob Baker, who thought Johns was a very good writer and a decent guy. "We couldn't persuade him not to, and he got a little publicity out of it."

Still, Johns managed to get the office on track. They divided the workers into various subprojects—the guidebook, mainly, along with a city encyclopedia and a bibliography, surveys of racial groups, a book about zoos. They secured cooperation across the board from state and municipal offices and universities. At least thirty-five workers found private employment—one as a war correspondent in Spain, another the beneficiary of a Guggenheim, still more with publishing houses and newspaper staffs. Johns, like the Massachusetts director Ray Billington, noticed a change in the workers, not only in their attitudes but in their nutrition and how they dressed. "If one could have taken a photograph of the Project personnel at the beginning of the Writers'

Projects and another at the present time," he wrote to DC, "we feel the difference in physical appearance, let alone the mental condition, would have been startling, to say the least. There is humour on the Project now, where before there was only fright and worry."

But there were problems, too. The project's copy often fell short of expectations. George Cronyn's dismayed reaction to an early pamphlet was typical: "It is afflicted with the cheapest sort of ballyhoo, beginning with the opening paragraph." Johns was stung and complained to Alsberg. Worse was the matter of his drinking, which wasn't limited to brawling on one leg in a tavern down the street. Alsberg once got an anxious call from William Nunn, the WPA administrator who oversaw Federal #1 in New York City. "Henry, I don't know what is to be done with him," Nunn said. "You know he is a heavy drinker. He is 'tight' a great deal. And then he makes perfectly ridiculous statements." Alsberg *did* know. Johns sometimes took a minor problem—over an official car or a mimeograph machine—and turned it into a spectacular argument. They also knew about his habit of tying one on and complaining to other people inside and outside Federal #1. Nunn had heard it himself: "Once, when he was tight he said: well if they don't like what I'm doing then I can quit."

"If he says that again, we may take him at his word," Alsberg replied.

Fate intervened before they reached a decision. By Johns's account, he'd been harassed for weeks by a beefy redheaded sailor who wanted a job on the project. One night, he went to an FWP party and found that everyone had already left—except the sailor, who was waiting for him. "You wouldn't give me a job," the man said. "Well, I'll give you one." He beat Johns senseless, and then poured liquor all over Johns's wooden leg and set it on fire. Other accounts say that Johns was in fact sleeping with the sailor's girlfriend, and that he was with her when the trap was sprung. Either way, he was hospitalized for weeks—the *Times* reported that he suffered lacerations on his face and nose and burns on his arms, lost two teeth, and possibly had his ribs broken. Once he recovered, Alsberg considered transferring him to California, but the director there, James Hopper, said that the WPA state administration was hesitant: they had "exaggerated ideas of Mr. Johns' red activities, his reputation as a stormy petrel, and his tendency, under certain physiological stimuli, to make rather disastrous scenes." ("Please note that I have used the word 'exaggerated,'" Hopper added judiciously.)

It didn't matter. Johns resigned under pressure, after less than a year as director. He angrily announced that his resignation was a protest against cuts to the FWP made after Roosevelt was safely elected to a second term. "The project is being made a football," he told Alsberg. "It was blown up every month before November, and immediately after November it is deflated."

And so the project moved on to another director and another period of turmoil. Next was Travis Hoke, Johns's assistant, a writer of light verse and humor pieces for *The New Yorker*, *The Saturday Evening Post*, and elsewhere. Alsberg thought Hoke was "a swell chap and a fine writer" and knew that he'd handled much of the work when Johns was deteriorating. But the project consumed him, too. Hoke already suffered from anxiety—as a WPA official put it, "his nerves were plainly in bad condition, and he was obsessed by fear of labor delegations on his project." To make matters worse, the official said, Hoke stayed up late to write and "the loss of sleep made his nerves shakier than ever, and to steady them, he resorted to drinking in the morning." As Hoke unraveled, he asked friends to stay with him at the Chelsea Hotel, where he lived, to make sure he didn't jump out the window. One night, he nearly did, and he was voluntarily hospitalized. It was a sad turn of events—Hoke loved the project—but the pressure was too great.

Rather than hiring yet another director, Alsberg tried something new. A trio of editors took over the office and introduced a measure of stability. One of them, a lanky poet and novelist in his early thirties named Vincent McHugh, was the essential figure: he was precisely the type of organized and empathetic person the project needed. When it was decided to split the NYC guide into two volumes—a book of essays, *New York Panorama*, and the guidebook proper—McHugh restructured the office around that plan. He also wrote most of the opening essay for *New York Panorama* and set the tone: "All the rays of force alive in the modern world move inward upon the city, and the burning glass of its attraction concentrates them in the flame that is New York." The essay seemed to recognize that the great city deserved a better portraitist, and a project on sounder footing.

As if on cue, progress on the guides was matched by an upsurge of labor strife. There had been strikes on the NYC project before. Once, when Orrick Johns was still in charge, unemployed members of the Writers' Union staged a sit-in hunger strike and occupied the office for twenty-six hours, demanding spots on the project. (Johns, sympathetic to the cause, accommodated them.) Two months later, cutbacks across all of Federal #1 triggered more strikes and two hundred FWP workers barricaded themselves inside the office. (They didn't go as far as workers on the NYC art project, who took over their office, cut the phone lines, kidnapped the director, and encircled the police, which set off a police riot and left thirteen strikers and four cops hospitalized.) In the aftermath, a union leader sent FDR a holiday telegram: "A MERRY CHRISTMAS FROM DISMISSED FEDERAL WRITERS PROJECT WORKERS WHO NOW FACE A WINTER OF DESTITUTION AS A RESULT OF YOUR FAILURE TO KEEP YOUR PROMISE."

In the summer of 1937, Congress again voted to slash the WPA appropriation. Roosevelt acquiesced. He'd always possessed two warring instincts, one a desire for bold action and the other a conservative discomfort with deficit spending. Now, he was slipping toward the latter. The economy seemed to be improving, while anti–New Deal forces in Congress were gaining strength, so Roosevelt followed the advice of his budget-balancing advisors, against Harry Hopkins and others to their left. He instructed Hopkins to request a new relief appropriation of $1.5 billion, far less than the $4.8 billion of the original 1935 bill that created the WPA. He made cuts to the PWA as well. These measures, combined with other steps—such as the new Social Security payroll taxes that were removing money from circulation—had the predictable result of spiking the economic recovery. The downturn was the worst since the Depression began. Soon, the administration's critics dubbed it the "Roosevelt Recession." Roosevelt, by cutting spending and attempting to meet his enemies in the middle, ended up handing them a political gift anyway.

This was the biggest cut yet to the WPA, and it meant that a staggering 25 percent of WPA workers would lose their jobs. Around 11,000 would be kicked off Federal #1, with 2,800 of them in New York City alone. But federal writers, and the unions that represented them, did not intend to go quietly. The mood of labor, nationwide, was pugnacious. It had been since the lauded "Section 7a" of the 1933 National Industrial Recovery Act, which, for the first time, protected collective bargaining. (After the Supreme Court quashed the NIRA, that right was renewed by the 1935 Wagner Act.) The next few years saw the explosive growth of the CIO, prominent victories for the labor movement, and constant skirmishes with bosses. The year of the Roosevelt Recession and the WPA cutbacks, 1937, began with autoworkers launching sit-down strikes and seizing multiple General Motors plants in Flint, Michigan. They won recognition for the United Auto Workers, and soon after, steelworkers won a similarly grand victory. But successes such as these were accompanied by failures and eruptions of violence, including two that spring: first, organizers were beaten outside Ford's massive River Rouge plant in Dearborn, and then, on Memorial Day, the police killed ten strikers and supporters and wounded thirty others outside the Republic Steel plant in Chicago.

The WPA dismissals began in the aftermath of these incidents. But the workers were ready. Federal writers carried out their own sit-down strike and occupied their office for four days. A group of six hundred workers from all the arts projects stormed the office of Harold Stein, the current WPA official in charge of Federal #1 in New York, and held him hostage. (From London, George Bernard Shaw sent the strikers an unambiguous message: "Of course, the first thing they curtail is American culture. Congress needs drastic lynching. Those who vote for barbarism should perish by it.") The strike unraveled when Stein agreed to meet their demands, to the extent he could—which turned out to be not much at all. The unions could target WPA administrators all they liked, but the blame, as G. B. Shaw recognized, lay with Congress.

Between the strikes and the constant turnover and the office drama and the wasted potential, Harry Hopkins decided to formally evaluate the NYC project. He brought in an outside firm to study the office and its 525 workers. The investigator, Robert W. Bruere, was sympathetic to the project and said so in his report, but he didn't hold back. "Almost from the start," he wrote, "the Guide Book has careened down through the total project enterprise like a ten-ton truck run wild." He blamed the parade of faulty directors who, one after another, were unable to stabilize the office. But he also blamed DC for its imprecise orders and constant reshuffling of the guidebook outline (which confused and demoralized the project workers), and, most of all, for its poor choices of directors in the first place. "An unfortunate atmosphere of planlessness still hangs over the entire project," Bruere wrote, "an atmosphere of insecurity, caprice and incompetent management," despite the efforts of some supervisors and editors to correct it. Still, he was mightily impressed by what the project had managed to accomplish under the circumstances, and even applauded the workers for striking to defend their jobs—and their self-respect—against congressional cutbacks.

And, in fact, the NYC project could point to some accomplishments. It published one city almanac and had another in the works; a few national, thematic publications, such as *Who's Who in the Zoo*, came out of the Manhattan office; *Italians of New York* was imminent; and around two dozen other books were in various stages of completion. The New York City guide was coming into shape, too—it was already under contract with Random House. NYC's federal writers could take heart from the overwhelmingly positive reception they found at the New York Times Book Fair in Rockefeller Center, where the NYC project set up a display. Complaints mainly came from people who wanted to buy FWP books but had trouble finding them. Not a few passersby took the opportunity to express their support for the Massachusetts guide, which had recently passed through its firestorm of criticism. At one point, Zora Neale Hurston, wandering through the fair with her friend Fannie Hurst, paused in front of the booth and examined some of the books. She'd just returned from her Guggenheim research in the Caribbean and was on her way back to Florida, where, eventually, she'd join the project herself. For now, she posed for a photo.

"THESE ARE YOUR COMRADES"

In late May 1937—as the NYC project was careening into its most unruly summer—Richard Wright quit the Illinois project, left Chicago, and set out for Manhattan. He was twenty-eight years old and already an FWP veteran. In Chicago, he'd been promoted from field worker to supervisor, the first Black federal writer to hold that position in the state. But he was chafing against the confines of his life in the city. Unlike his friend and comrade Nelson Algren, whose writing was becoming deeply imprinted with the social textures of Chicago, Wright thought that relocating would better serve his work: the poems, stories, and two inchoate novels that absorbed his off-time hours. He wanted a new setting—and he wanted New York. His transfer to the NYC project hadn't yet been approved, but still, he was hopeful that things would fall into place. The FWP, he believed, would be his bridge.

It wasn't his first big geographic leap. In 1927, when he was nineteen, he'd escaped from the Jim Crow regime—Mississippi, mostly, by way of Memphis—and took a train bound for Chicago. When he arrived there, he'd felt disoriented in the soot-stained city with its factories and stockyards and tenements and streets full of icy wind. The intricate system of rules that he'd lived by in the South—and that others had died by—was scrambled in the North, not erased but revised into a more subtle and confounding form. He knew he was freer but the *extent* of it was murky and kept him guessing. As a writer, he wanted to confront the North's dangers and contradictions; at the same time, he would draw on the terrors and lessons of his formative years to create an unsparing portrait of the South. His scope had to be national, and he had to dig deeper, past particular events—the lynchings and beatings, the poison words and loaded glances—toward the underlying emotional experience of living in a white supremacist society. "I sensed that Negro life was a sprawling land of unconscious suffering," he wrote, "and there were but few Negroes who knew the meaning of their lives, who could tell their story." The poems and fiction that Wright was struggling to compose would be guides to that land, attempts to make the suffering conscious.

New York, literary capital of the nation, struck him as the place to do it. The qualities that made the NYC project seem so promising—Manhattan's density of writers, agents, publishing houses, magazines, and newspapers—drew Wright there, too. His timing seemed perfect: he arrived just before the opening session of the second American Writers' Congress.

He'd been a delegate to the first, back in 1935, when Algren was mid-meltdown and Jack Conroy was feted as an echt proletarian author. It was a deeply ambivalent experience for Wright: he was invigorated by the gathering but put off by racist treatment he encountered while searching for a place to stay. And he was bitter over the demise of the John Reed Club—by that point dissolved within the new Popular Front strategy, which required alliances with prominent writers, not the cultivation of unknowns like Wright.

The club had given him a vocabulary and a forum, as it had to Algren, whom Wright met there. The two of them forged a friendship as they sat beneath murals of workers and discussed revolution and literature and pored over issues of *Left Front*, the chapter organ. (Algren was so impressed by Wright that he saved a place for him in *Somebody in Boots*, as the character Dill Doak, a sharp Black radical who didn't drink, hated the South, and thought the United States ought to go the way of Russia.) When Wright learned that the club was being disbanded in the run-up to the first congress, making way for the League of American Writers, he was devastated.*

Now, listening to speeches at the second congress two years later, Wright discovered that the tone of the gathering had modulated. The civil war in Spain and the rising fascist threat loomed over the proceedings, and the Popular Front strategy of courting well-known authors was even more apparent. The opening session at Carnegie Hall brought together Ernest Hemingway, Archibald MacLeish, and Donald Ogden Stewart, with greetings shipped in from Albert Einstein, Thomas Mann, and writers fighting with the International Brigades in Spain. (Martha Gellhorn, a rare woman speaker, addressed a later session, as did Benjamin Botkin, soon to become the new FWP folklore editor, as did Kenneth Burke, apparently undeterred by the controversy he had stirred up last time.) Wright was no doubt pleased to hear Eugene Holmes, Sterling Brown's assistant in charge of Negro Affairs, praise his poetry and rank him alongside Brown and Langston Hughes, as he'd done during the first congress.

On the last day of the congress, Wright chaired the second half of the final session. He announced that they would be hearing from an outside speaker, not a delegate, "a man who has been associated with one of the most interesting experiments in the history of America." Up stood Henry Alsberg. Old Communist Party partisans knew that Alsberg had broken with the pro-Soviet left many years before; Alsberg's philosophical anarchism may have mellowed but he never really changed his views. By 1937, though, their positions had converged in the broad embrace of the Popular Front. Alsberg

---

* Not everyone felt that way. Jerre Mangione, the future FWP national coordinating editor, was glad to see the club's demise. He thought it had become "grossly sectarian" and he was sick of the "constant hair-splitting dialectical jousting." A big, broad Popular Front organization seemed like the better approach—although he did worry about being well-established enough to join, a predicament validating Wright's opinion that the party was undermining aspiring writers.

spoke off the cuff, beginning with a rundown of the FWP's goals and accomplishments—it was on track to publish 5 million words and more than
sixty books by the close of summer—while he slipped in some editorializing.
("People who review books merely to get the review copies are scabs and
people who review books for practically no pay at all, to my mind, are also
scabs," said the veteran freelancer. The room applauded.) Then he hit on a
concept that the FWP usually circled around, even though it was an important one. "We must get over the idea that every writer must be an artist of the
first class, and that the artist of the second or third class has no function," he
said. "I think we have invested art with this sort of sacrosanct, ivory-tower
atmosphere too much. The craftsmen who worked on the cathedrals were
anonymous." And so, he implied, were the writers busily constructing the
American Guides. By making room for those second- and third-rate writers,
the FWP was pushing against romantic ideas about art and insisting, instead,
that cultural work was a form of labor. This idea wasn't going to win over critics who jeered the FWP for hiring capable but undistinguished writers—and
yet it was essential to the project's mission.

Alsberg, being Alsberg, threw in some gripes. The WPA made it too
difficult for federal writers who found private employment to return if those
jobs fizzled out, and there were too many barriers to promoting their creative
work. But he directed his sharpest words toward the audience. A "terrible
gap" had developed between the FWP and organized groups like the league,
which offered little but criticism regarding the project's failure to hire enough
unemployed writers, even if those writers weren't on relief. "I wonder how
many people in this room, for instance, have expressed any opinion to Mr.
Hopkins about how they feel on the curtailment or increase of the Writers'
Project," he said. "I venture to say very few of you. There are a lot of people
here from the Writers' Project, who have, of course, expressed an opinion.
But I do not think that most of you know what we are doing, and I feel most of
the time that nobody cares. And yet these are your comrades."

Alsberg couldn't help letting a note of self-pity slip into his remarks. But he
wasn't there to complain; he was there, really, to issue a warning. He was telling
them, in so many words: This is your project. Defend it.

"MASTERPIECES A CRUDE COMMERCIAL
WORLD HAD SCORNED"

Wright left the congress and spent the summer, and then the autumn, in FWP limbo. It was his mistake to move immediately and run afoul of the residency requirement. But his case hadn't gone unnoticed. The editorial director in Chicago wrote to DC on his behalf; Donald Thompson, NYC's director of the moment, was ready to welcome Wright to the project. Both Alsberg and Sterling Brown tried to help—Alsberg thought of bringing Wright onto the DC staff but there were no openings; Brown, who was familiar with Wright's work in Illinois, gave him a fulsome recommendation. Even Ellen Woodward, one step below Harry Hopkins in the WPA apparatus, offered her endorsement. And yet the NYC WPA refused to make an exception.

Wright marked time by writing for the *Daily Worker*. His job as the Harlem correspondent helped introduce him to a community that he'd only glimpsed before. In Wright's dispatches, Harlem, cast in the pall of the Depression, was almost unrecognizable as the place that had inspired rhapsodies from Zora Neale Hurston and her companions a decade earlier. "This isn't fiction; these are not scenes from the novels of Charles Dickens," he wrote. "The sidewalks of Harlem are real and hard; and black people on those sidewalks are truly starving." He wrote forty articles and many more unsigned dispatches, often filing several a day. They constituted a litany of violence, discrimination, and poverty, along with the occasional nod toward beneficial, if limited, New Deal interventions: the PWA's Harlem River Houses, the WPA's Harlem Community Art Center, classes for adults and children by the Federal Art Project, the Negro Unit of the Harlem Federal Theater Project.

Wright's relationship with the Communist Party was strained. He had become a member back in Chicago, after being elected to a leadership position in the John Reed Club. But he never clicked with the other Black Communists: the rank and file saw him as bourgeois; the leaders saw him as unreliable. They suspected that he was more committed to his writing than to the party, and they were right. Eventually, Wright began avoiding meetings altogether, until a Black party leader asked him to join an organizing campaign that addressed the high cost of living. Wright balked and explained that he needed to finish his novel. It was no use. "I gritted my teeth as the daily value of pork chops was tabulated, longing to be at home with my writing," he recalled. "I felt that pork chops were a fundamental item in life, but I preferred that someone else chart their rise and fall in price." Now, in Harlem, stationed at the *Daily Worker*, at least he was serving the party with his typewriter.

Still, he felt like a hack. He hadn't moved to New York to churn out newspaper copy—even if the *Daily Worker* took an admirably strong stand on race issues. So he pushed forward with his own writing on the side. He had two novels in manuscript, "Lawd Today!" and "Tarbaby's Dawn," which publishers were busy rejecting. He had a collection of short stories sitting inert. And he was developing his ideas about literary expression, most significantly in an essay, "Blueprint for Negro Writing," that advocated fusing the autonomy of craft with a strong sense of political purpose. During these months in New York, waiting for his FWP transfer, he was working through some thorny oppositions: between radical thought and the limitations of the Communist Party, between political commitment and clumsy propaganda, between Black nationalism and Marxist universalism. He sought, in other words, to define the kind of writer he was.

He also sought to define the kind of writer he *wasn't*. In October, he reviewed two novels in *New Masses*, both by Black authors. *These Low Grounds*, by Waters Edward Turpin, he judged a respectable failure, short on intensity and artistic facility. But *Their Eyes Were Watching God*, by Zora Neale Hurston, was not even that. He was scathing. "Hurston seems to have no desire whatever to move in the direction of serious fiction," he wrote. He admitted that she was a talented writer but disparaged the "facile sensuality" of her "highly charged" prose. "Miss Hurston *voluntarily* continues in her novel the tradition which was *forced* upon the Negro in the theater, that is, the minstrel technique that makes the 'white folks' laugh. Her characters eat and laugh and cry and work and kill; they swing like a pendulum eternally in that safe and narrow orbit in which America likes to see the Negro live: between laughter and tears." For Wright, *Their Eyes Were Watching God* was all aesthetic surface, a book that was easily digested by white readers who were willing to pity "the Negro" without confronting the horror of white supremacy.

His disdain for the book emerged, in part, from his and Hurston's sharply conflicting attitudes toward the South. Wright couldn't look back at his youth there in the way that Hurston fondly recalled Eatonville; he didn't share her eagerness to celebrate Black culture at a distance from its oppressive backdrop. The South, in his telling, was grotesque and dangerous, and his task as a writer was to illuminate its dangers. If Hurston's literary mode was essentially anthropological, Wright's was essentially gothic; if her aim was to bestow a poetic dignity, his was to reveal—and sometimes sensationalize—social decay. This was Wright's overriding concern as a writer. He wasn't willing or able to see that Hurston's portrayal of the intimate experiences of a complex, self-motivated Black woman was itself a subversive decision (a blind spot that had something to do, perhaps, with his own ambivalent feelings toward the dominant female relatives who loomed over his early life). Nor was he willing or able to see that her celebration of a rich Black community was also the statement of a political idea, and not one necessarily opposed to the Marxist commitments that fueled his own writing. Instead, he saw only that Hurston had failed the challenge he'd laid out in "Blueprint for Negro Writing," and so deserved to be pilloried.

Wright, like Hurston, was attempting to work out a tangle of problems related to fiction writing, self-expression, and social obligation by attacking them on the page, in his private work. The FWP, up to that point, sustained this kind of inquiry only indirectly: federal writers could feel secure knowing that the rent was paid and the icebox filled while they tackled fiction and poetry in their off-hours. But, slowly, this stance was changing—most consequentially in the unruly Manhattan headquarters of the NYC project. Wright, still hoping for his transfer there, likely had no idea that Alsberg had quietly put machinery in place to support a handful of creative writers. But, while he waited, he was poised to benefit from another special, creative undertaking that was stirring within the FWP.

Even before the launch of the FWP, it was a question: did work relief for writers mean subsidizing novels and poems? Many believed so. "As the Works Progress Administration took shape," Katharine Kellock remembered, "friends of the arts, especially in the influential metropolitan areas, began to dream dreams and see visions." The arts projects of Federal #1, they believed, could become the patron of last resort. "Almost every worth-while artist could qualify for work relief, they assured one another, and soon the federal government would be fathering and producing the masterpieces—dramas, pictures, novels, operas, epic poems—a crude commercial world had scorned." This idea quickly evaporated, at least for the FWP, where the American Guides required a full commitment from all its workers. But Henry Alsberg spoke openly about wanting to support more creative work, even though that kind of initiative fell outside the project's mandate. It was a major part of his speech at the second American Writers' Congress, where Wright introduced him. He knew that the FWP fostered creative writing simply by giving workers ample free time—the rank and file usually clocked thirty hours a week. But Alsberg believed they could do more to bring imaginative writing into the FWP's mission. Field representatives sent word to DC that project workers were eager for an official creative outlet. Advocacy groups outside the FWP felt the same; the executive secretary of the Writers Union NYC local once wrote to Alsberg, "We know that you agree that it is disgraceful to have creative writers waste their talents by reporting on Bronx sewers and Brooklyn bathhouses." (Alsberg resisted the snobbish idea that writing about sewers and bathhouses wasn't a legitimate application of creativity—in fact, it was this very aspect of the FWP's work, the spirited chronicling of the mundane and the local, the infrastructure of everyday life, that made the project so vital.)

Alsberg's plan was to complement the American Guides and other documentary studies with a federal magazine of creative writing, but, for various reasons, he could never pull a freestanding publication together. Instead, small groups of federal writers around the country launched their own magazines, usually one-offs, that they compiled and printed on their own time. In San Francisco, the poet Kenneth Rexroth and other workers published *Material Gathered*; it was something of a trial balloon and a call for others to follow their lead. Then they published another, *The Coast*, and soon there were more: *Shucks* in Nebraska, *Over the Turquoise Trail* in New Mexico, the unimaginatively titled *6 x 9* in New Jersey. Established publications began showcasing the work of federal writers, too: there were special editions of *Poetry*, *New Masses* (which included Wright's story "Bright and Morning Star"), *The New Republic*, and *Frontier and Midland*.

Amazingly, there was even talk of absorbing Jack Conroy's old proletarian magazine, *The Anvil*, as an FWP offshoot. Jack Balch and two other former *Anvil* editors wrote to Alsberg, boasting of the magazine's impact as a venue for short fiction and an important regional nexus outside of the New York literary bubble. Conroy, they insisted, was willing to turn over rights to the name and the mailing list, as long as he could serve as editor-in-chief with full independence. They wanted an "Anvil project," essentially, to exist at the federal level, free of entanglements with state WPA administrations. The project would be answerable only to Alsberg—a clear appeal to his sympathy for marginalized literary radicals and his personal fondness for Conroy and Balch. Unsurprisingly, the proposal was dead on arrival, but Ellen Woodward at the WPA diplomatically replied that the uncertainty of their congressional appropriation after 1938 made the proposal impossible.

The FWP did finally publish one stand-alone volume of creative work: *American Stuff*, an anthology of stories, poems, and sketches by federal writers, ornamented with bits of material collected from the field. It offers a peek into the literary unconscious of the project, the predilections of style and preoccupations of form that moved in the minds of its workers—even though the selection is a little skewed. (Of fifty-one contributions, twenty-five came from New York and California.) The book is punctuated with documentary interludes—earthy humor and colorful sayings, spirituals from South Carolina and folk songs from Harlem and corridos from New Mexico, a Gullah testimonial, square dance calls from Arkansas, even extracts from the ship's log of a mutinied New Bedford whaler—all gathered by federal writers. The effect is that of the great American vernacular, like weeds in a sidewalk, pushing through the more assiduously crafted stories and poems. And it was a reminder that these pieces, or most of them, were deeply rooted in working-class experience. Alsberg said as much in his foreword. He described how the hundreds of manuscripts submitted for the volume shared an overwhelming focus on the down-and-out precincts of the country. "Apparently these young artists and writers are preoccupied with life as they have known it," he wrote, "with what they have seen and felt, with the tough sledding which constitutes American experience for millions of people today." The writing was "sometimes crude" and the technique "inexpert or diffuse," but the perspective was valuable and necessary. "This is the American scene to the life, very often as it appears from the roadside ditch, the poverty-stricken tenement or shack, the relief station."

Alsberg might have mentioned the segregated South, which was the vantage of the collection's most explosive and capable piece: an essay, "The Ethics of Living Jim Crow," by Richard Wright. It astounded the *American Stuff* editorial group when they dug it out from the submissions pile. The group was based in the New York City project and included Donald Thompson, then the acting director, and his assistant Jimmy McGraw; they met at night or on weekends, in the project office or a smoky hotel room, and sifted through hundreds of manuscripts, arguing frequently and slowly becoming depressed by the sheer number of epic poems. Meetings broke up in a huff. When Wright's essay emerged from the stack, they could finally reach a consensus.

"The Ethics of Living Jim Crow" is a series of dispatches from a life behind enemy lines—Wright's life. It captures a sense of the daily outrages and humiliations that Wright either suffered or witnessed, first as a child and then as a young adult. A white boy hits him with a bottle during a play fight, and his mother lays the blame on him. Two white workers in an optical lens manufacturer threaten him for wanting to learn the trade, as the boss had promised. Two white shopkeepers beat a Black woman senseless over an unpaid bill and the police haul her away. Some white men give Wright a lift in their car and then smash a bottle in his face for not saying sir. The police nearly shoot him for making a delivery in a white neighborhood at night. And it continues, in prose that is sharp and controlled and full of compressed fury. Wright describes overt acts of cruelty alongside the more nuanced expressions of white supremacy: the linguistic traps, the behavioral rules, the bad-and-worse options. In his telling, life under Jim Crow is a state of terror, but it is also, disturbingly, a kind of game.

The essay is true, but not exactly straight autobiography. It is more of a conversion narrative: it charts Wright's progress as his eyes are opened to the invisible power that governs his world, as his surroundings become symbolic of a larger meaning. There's a great deal left out. Wright doesn't discuss his family or the circumstances of his upbringing, though there's a hint in his mother's words when she admonishes him for play-fighting with white boys: "'How come yuh didn't hide?' she asked me. 'How come yuh awways fightin'?'" He was raised to be obedient, to work hard, to hide in the safety of his prescribed place. His parents were sharecroppers and he was born on a plantation east of Natchez, in 1908. They had ample opportunities to test this philosophy as, for the next twelve years, they lived in a swirl of movement, up and down and around a swath of land that ran about three hundred miles along the Mississippi River valley. They lived in Natchez, abutting the Mississippi, then went upriver by paddle-wheel boat to Memphis. (His father left them then, and Wright and his younger brother spent a harrowing spell in an orphanage.) His mother, Ella, came from an educated family—she'd been a schoolteacher before she married Richard's father—and to this family, the Wilsons, she retreated for support. Now Wright moved in various arrangements with his Wilson kin: first to Jackson, Mississippi; then to Elaine and West Helena in Arkansas; then back to Jackson; then West Helena again; back to Jackson; then Greenwood, Mississippi; Jackson again. Here was a relatively stable cluster of years before Wright eventually left for Memphis, a staging ground for northward migration, and his gateway to Chicago.

In the essay, Wright commiserates with friends and is warned about his behavior by "folks at home." He devotes only a handful of sentences to these moments. In reality, his entire experience of the segregated South was refracted through the prism of his family. They cared for him but the mood was tense, repressive, stifling. He lived with Wilson relatives, usually alongside his mother and brother, often in cramped quarters. His grandmother Margaret Bolden Wilson and various aunts shaped his life more than any male relatives, and when his mother suffered a stroke—and then another and another—his grandmother's influence grew. (When Zora Neale Hurston's mother died, the bonds that tethered her to Eatonville snapped and she went spinning out into the world; when Wright's mother nearly died but recovered, it pulled him into the close and claustrophobic embrace of his relatives.) Margaret Bolden was a strict Seventh-Day Adventist. In her home there were ample prayers and Bible readings and church services; no work on the Saturday Sabbath, no secular music or dancing, no pork, no gambling or smoking or drinking.

Grandmother Margaret stood out in another way. Most of her ancestors were European. "My grandmother was as nearly white as a Negro can get without being white," he wrote later, "which means that she was white." She passed for white and yet her grandchildren—Wright and his brother—were plainly Black. What did it mean, he wondered, that they were a family? She was an embodied lesson in the irrationality of race, and Wright, who rarely encountered whites during his early years, was left to sort through his confused feelings, trying to make sense of segregated train cars and derisive looks, the vague knowledge that, somewhere out there, were white people who wanted to hurt him.

"The Ethics of Living Jim Crow" doesn't mention Wright's grandmother. It doesn't mention the deep feeling of alienation that his family life engendered in him: because he was a Wright among Wilsons, his aunts said; because he was a religious puritan among Methodists and Baptists; because he was a boy among female relatives; because he was from a poor family with the outlook of the petite bourgeoisie. In some ways, all that was beside the point. The essay wasn't really about Wright, but about one version of "living Jim Crow" that was occurring across the South, for millions of African Americans, over and over. The incidents he describes are specific and detailed, but the narrator could have been anyone—anyone Black, that is, forced to navigate a white supremacist order. That was the idea.

Wright did leave one clue to his character in the essay. It's an episode that would become something like his intellectual origin story. He asks a co-worker, a white man, if he can borrow his library card:

> Surprisingly, he consented. I cannot help but think that he consented because he was a Roman Catholic and felt a vague sympathy for Negroes, being himself an object of hatred. Armed with a library card, I obtained books in the following manner: I would write a note to the librarian, saying: "Please let this nigger boy have the following books." I would then sign it with the white man's name.

Reading was the one thing that consistently brought Wright joy. As a child he would pick up the schoolbooks that other kids left on the sidewalk and peer at the confounding symbols. Soon his mother was helping him read the newspaper. When he lived with his grandmother, he spied a boarder reading novels, and she told him the story of Bluebeard, the serial wife-murderer. Wright later called it "the first experience in my life that had elicited from me a total emotional response." Eventually, he eased his way into all manner of pulp writing, westerns and detective stories, Zane Gray, Horatio Alger. (His grandmother burned the magazines when she found them and taught Wright a lesson: that fiction was inherently transgressive, a rebellious instrument.)

Around the time he was sixteen, he wrote a story called "The Voodoo of Hell's Half-Acre" and carried it over to a small, local Black newspaper; the editor published it in installments, much to the surprise of Wright's friends and the consternation of his family, who were shocked, beginning with the title. By the time of the library episode, he had discovered H. L. Mencken and was reading *The American Mercury* and other magazines like it; in fact, the note he passed to the librarian asked for two books by Mencken: *Prejudices* (a title that gave him pause, thinking of racial hate) and *A Book of Prefaces* (a title he couldn't fully pronounce). Wright devoured them, but not merely as an escapist indulgence. Instead, the essay implies—and proves—that Wright had found, in the accumulating influence of dime novels and Mencken, Dreiser and Russian literature, a means of combating the system that oppressed him.

Wright's essay was harrowing enough, even without mentioning two incidents that affected him deeply and permanently. When he was eight, his uncle Silas Hoskins, a successful saloonkeeper, was murdered by jealous whites. Someone brought the news in the middle of the night; Wright's family gathered their things and left town. His aunt Maggie couldn't even claim the body. His uncle's murder stripped the world bare and revealed what lurked beneath its mundane surface. Wright later called it "my first baptism of racial emotion." A less violent but equally significant revelation came when Wright graduated from middle school. He was the class valedictorian. When the principal tried to give Wright a prewritten speech—knowing that visiting whites would be in the audience—Wright balked. He refused to replace his speech or alter it. In the principal's behavior, and in the reactions of his family and many other students, he saw the face of Jim Crow, and the deference and bargaining it demanded. He was hurt and shocked. He gave his own speech and walked out of the ceremony. He took a stand but, in a sense, it didn't matter. Most of the other students went on to the new Black high school but Wright dropped out because he needed to work. That ended the only period of formal study he would know.

The essay says nothing, either, about Wright's radicalization, about the Communist Party and the John Reed Club, about his ideas regarding artistic creation, revolution, and Black nationalism that he was working out in essays such as "Blueprint for Negro Writing." There's only the closing sentence, a succinct analysis of how the southern racial order rested on a foundation of repression—and yet was threatened by the latent revolutionary power of the Black masses. Or, as a friend of his puts it: "Lawd, man! Ef it wuzn't fer them polices 'n' them ol' lynch-mobs, there wouldn't be nothin' but uproar down here!"

When *American Stuff* appeared, "The Ethics of Living Jim Crow" was sandwiched between an inscrutable poem by Kenneth Rexroth and a few pages of folksy humor collected in the mountains of Appalachia. ("The visitor is apt to be told by a native, quite earnestly, that the corn is sown by standing on one hillside with a gun and firing it into the opposite hillside.") Reviewers noticed the essay's power. In *The New York Times*, Eda Lou Walton wrote that Wright's piece "hit me squarely between the eyes"; Stephen Vincent Benét, in the *New York Herald Tribune*, called it "bitter, factual, and quite unforgettable." Jack Conroy turned in a mixed review of the book for *New Masses*—he was bitter over the FWP's failure to support creative writing more vigorously—but wrote that Wright's essay "easily surpasses others of its genre."

American Stuff gave Wright's career a boost. Then, in December, came another. *Story* magazine was running a contest for federal writers; the prize was $500 and a book deal with Harper and Brothers. Alsberg, still struggling to expand outlets for creative writing after *American Stuff*, thought the contest was "an excellent thing." There were six hundred entries, including Wright's *Uncle Tom's Children*, a collection of four long stories he'd written in Chicago. It won. (Second place went to his comrade and fellow federal writer Meridel Le Sueur, for her novella *The Horse*.) That very same day, Wright learned that his transfer to the NYC project was finally approved. He quit the *Daily Worker*. He told them he was taking a leave, but he never intended to return.

"MORE FISHY THAN THE FISH ITSELF"

Wright's initial stint with the FWP, back in Chicago, was his first writing job. Before that, he'd been a porter in a deli and a dishwasher in a café and a mail sorter in the post office—that was his best gig. Work in the vast and bustling sorting room meant reaching "Sixty-Third and Stoney Island," as his peers put it: the crossroads at the northernmost boundary of Chicago's Black Belt, the highest point before crossing into the white world. But the work was grueling. He described it in a draft of a novel: "A wave of dust struck their eyes and nostrils as they waded through an ocean of gloom and letterracks. A penetrating drone hovered persistently, filling their bodies with a faint, nervous tremor." The clerks stood at enormous sorting tables or flung letters into pigeonholes labeled with the names of the states while shifting their weight from foot to foot and tasting their saliva turn black with dust. In the din of conveyor belts and tumbling packages Wright bonded with his fellow workers, including the future federal writer Abe Aaron—the one who would collect testimonials from post office workers for the Illinois project. It was Aaron who introduced Wright to the John Reed Club and the Communist Party; Jack Conroy called these young aspiring writers "the Chicago Post Office school." There were other jobs: he tried Chicago-style electioneering (the crooked kind) and pushed burial insurance on the ghetto poor. Both shamed him. Finally, he went on county relief, though the idea of it shamed him, too. The relief office put him to work sweeping streets and digging ditches. Then it placed him in a hospital where he scrubbed floors and tended to animals used in medical experiments. Eventually it made him a supervisor at a boys' club on the South Side.

When Wright joined the Illinois project in 1935, it gave him occasion to explore that "sprawling land of unconscious suffering" he was determined to survey and expose through his writing. He submitted a report titled "Ethnographical Aspects of Chicago's Black Belt," and it began: "Since the year of 1860 there has been a steady influx of Negroes from southern to northern states." Wright, of course, was part of that influx. He didn't flinch from describing it in all its aspects. "A form of organized resistance to the moving of Negroes into new neighborhoods was the bombing of their homes and the homes of real estate men, white and Negro, who were known or supposed to have sold local property to them," he wrote. Wright counted fifty-eight bombings between 1917 and 1921 alone—not to mention the arsons, stonings, and other clashes. And yet: "The repeated attacks made the Negroes firm in their stand." The rest of the report charts the Chicago territory where he'd lived for seven years, where he'd reached adulthood, struggled to become a writer, attained political consciousness. It was, in part, a hidden memoir. "Another sphere in which Negroes have had a great deal of difficulty in making adjustments is the realm of daily personal contacts"—and who knew better than Wright? He spent his first years in Chicago in a constant state of anxiety, fretting over the rules of racial association that both upended and complicated the ones he'd known in the South. (Could he sit next to this white man on the streetcar? Could he squeeze past this white waitress in the café where he worked?) The report ends by answering questions it doesn't openly pose: with a litany of racial conflicts, culminating in the deadly riot of 1919, and ending with a sentence, a dose of simmering irony, that contains yet another essay: "The decline of migration has tempered the anxiety of the whites." White field workers weren't likely to confront such unsettling, and potentially traumatic, material, just by surveying their own communities. For whites, fieldwork was usually diverting, bland, or somewhere in between. For their Black colleagues, it could be like touching a wound.

"Ethnological Aspects of Chicago's Black Belt" emerged from library research. Other assignments put Wright into the streets, where he was already a sensitive observer: noting the slang and opinions of his neighbors, the reckless defiance of street-corner communists, the mournful fantasies of the Garveyites. His family was out there: he lived, in various combinations and apartments, with his mother, brother, grandmother, and different aunts, all migrants like him. He had friends there, too, many of whom he'd known as kids in the South. His task now was to survey that world, *his* world, as an agent of the FWP's participatory self-portrait of the nation.

He wrote, for instance, about amusements in the Black Belt, and explored his own neighborhood ("almost solidly lumpenproletariat" in one section, he reported). Wright, with a mind full of Dreiser and Dostoevsky, wandered around and peered into the reeking dark taverns, the eateries and pool halls, the movie theaters and nightclubs.

Most of the beer taverns are dark, dank places where the neighborhood drunks hang out night and day . . . Naturally, some of the places are understood to be for white and others for Negro . . . Louis Armstrong used to play here to huge crowds . . . Usually a bowl of soup, crackers and shrimps, or a hot-dog, or an egg is given with a purchase of beer . . . It is here that the neighborhood wiseacres congregate to dispute the merits of political and religious isms . . . The place is Italian owned, and caters, it is rumored, to 'gangster trade' . . . In front, covering the entire façade, is a gigantic electric sign, shedding a red haze for blocks around . . . The talent of the entertainers is nil . . . If the taverns are dingy, the restaurants are dingier . . .

For a time, Wright kept up this fieldwork. But then, like Zora Neale Hurston, he took a detour into the Federal Theater Project. It did not end well. He was transferred there as a publicist but, inspired by John Houseman and Orson Welles's Vodou *Macbeth*, which he saw in Harlem, he convinced Chicago's own Negro Unit to stage Paul Green's *Hymn to the Rising Sun*, a harsh one-act play about a southern chain gang. Wright wanted Charles DeSheim, a white radical, to direct it. But where Wright saw uncompromising realism, the Black actors saw a play that was bleak and unflattering, written by a white man and directed by another. (Wright would dismiss them as uncultured vaudevillians, too afraid of public opinion and too childlike in their attitudes to take on such a demanding production.) They rebelled—by Wright's telling, they harassed him, and a group of men pulled their knives and said, "You get the hell off this job before we cut your belly button out!" He switched to another theater unit before transferring back to the FWP in July.

Eventually he was promoted to supervisor and was editing essays for the Illinois guide. And yet he wanted something bigger. He outlined a book about the Black experience in America, focusing on the previous two decades and drawing on the files of the Associated Negro Press. Sterling Brown was impressed by Wright's plan but realized that it overlapped with his own projected book, "The Portrait of the Negro as American." Reading over the Illinois project's Black material, he thought that Wright did a good job, though he was put off by Wright's habit of mixing leaden phraseology (a habit he'd picked up in Marxist circles) with a more casual tone. (Brown could be harsh when he thought the material fell short; of one piece he simply wrote, "spoiled by the author's faults of style.") Still, he wanted Wright to help with the book in some capacity.

Soon after, Wright decided he'd outgrown Chicago. It wasn't an easy decision. Leaving would mean giving up his job on the Illinois project, of course. But it also meant withdrawing from another supportive network, the South Side Writers' Group. This was an informal bunch of writers, all of them Black, whom Wright had helped to assemble after a Chicago meeting of the National Negro Congress. They shared and discussed their work while commiserating over the challenges of writing in a white world. Frank Marshall Davis, a working journalist (and Nelson Algren's neighbor in Rat Alley), brought poems; Theodore Ward brought portions of *Big White Fog*, a play that would eventually be staged by the Federal Theater Project. Arna Bontemps, who'd known similar camaraderie in Harlem during the twenties and had already published several books, dropped by. About twenty of them met every other Sunday. Wright assumed a kind of leadership role but he was just as eager for feedback, or maybe just affirmation, as the rest.

He'd formed a close and consequential friendship with one of the group's members in particular: Margaret Walker. She, too, became a federal writer, and they bonded during their off-hours on the Illinois project. Like Wright, Walker had arrived in Chicago from the South but under sharply different circumstances. She was raised in New Orleans by strict but supportive parents; her father, a Jamaican immigrant, was a minister and her mother, a music teacher. She took to writing early, finished high school at sixteen, studied at New Orleans University (where both her parents taught), and eventually enrolled at Northwestern University. A passing exchange with Langston Hughes put her in touch with Wright and the South Side Writers' Group, and when she arrived at the first meeting, she found Wright discoursing on the state of Black literature and cursing mightily. "I drew back in Sunday-school horror, totally shocked by his strong speech," she recalled, "but I steeled myself to hear him out." They became literary confidants, talking novels and ideas and comparing rough drafts. Walker was sheltered and a little naïve; Wright was neither. But their friendship was nurtured by the writers' group and the FWP, to which Walker gained admission with a lie—she was twenty but said she was twenty-one, the minimum age.

She was likely the youngest worker on the Illinois project. Whenever she visited the office—only twice a week, because she was a field worker and did her writing at home—she made a point of stopping to chat with Wright. Sometimes she'd find him during a quiet moment, struggling with his own work, stabbing at the typewriter with two or three fingers, the way he'd taught himself to type—someone who'd clearly never benefited from her depth of education.

   She formed other friendships on the project. She was fond of Arna Bontemps and Willard Motley and Frank Yerby and Fenton Johnson. (She didn't know Saul Bellow, who'd been two years behind her at Northwestern and had the same creative writing teacher.) She thought Jack Conroy was wonderful, a habitual storyteller and an advocate for younger writers on the project. And she liked Nelson Algren, though she was leery of his gambling habit. Compared with the world outside—the miseries of the Depression, the racial strife of Chicago—the FWP struck Walker as an oasis of warmth and camaraderie, where creative people, Black and white, had a place to mingle and talk, to inspire and challenge one another. Through Wright, she socialized with white radicals, many of them Jewish, attending parties where people read poetry and argued about the labor movement. ("The food was always the same," she recalled, "cold cuts—salami, bologna, sometimes lox or smoked salmon—and pickles, rye bread and pumpernickel, beer and pretzels.") It was, in every sense, a feast. And it nurtured her own work. When she joined the project, she was no dilettante: she had a notebook stuffed with three hundred poems that she'd written as a student. But her style began to change as she abandoned the sentimental verse she wrote in college for more realistic and political subject matter.

   This new attitude seeped into her FWP assignments, too, noticeably in her text for a tour of the Chicago Art Institute's Expressionist collection. (This was a point of cooperation between the institute and the FWP, just as were Studs Terkel's radio scripts.) Her observations were playful and a little glib. On Van Gogh: "Here in the fish picture he paints the fish more fishy than the fish itself." On Gauguin: "His Landscape is tropical and flat and Gauguin." On Matisse: "As long as the Matisse colors were there and the Matisse name is signed to the picture, why should he finish it?" On Picasso: "Of course he used blue." But she closed the tour with a pronouncement that, whatever its merit as art criticism, captured the spirit of the moment, the fusion of radicalism and Americana, the new enthusiasm and confidence that the FWP fostered, especially in its Black workers: "These Expressionists all belong to the School of Rugged Individualists, to the Ideal of the Businessman. But today the Individualist is giving place to the Socialist. Values are no longer Individual but Social. This has been true in America since 1929 and today the Artist who is greatest paints the American scene."

Wright was a tremendous influence on Walker, passing her books such as *Ten Days That Shook the World*, John Reed's report from the Russian Revolution, and expounding on radical ideas. But so was Nelson Algren: he encouraged both her writing and her activism. It was Algren who signed her up for the American Writers' League. (Many of the FWP's prominent Black writers also joined.) It was Algren who co-edited *The New Anvil*, which published Walker's first short story. And it was Algren who gave her perhaps the most significant advice she would ever receive, even if, in the moment, it didn't seem that way. She was having trouble with a poem, "For My People," and couldn't decide how to end it. Algren suggested that she write whatever it was that she wanted for her people, so she added the stirring lines: "Let the martial songs be written, / let the dirges disappear. Let a race of men now rise / and take control!" This poem became the title piece in her first collection, which won the Yale Younger Poets Award—making her the first Black woman to do so—and launched her career. Stephen Vincent Benét chose her for the prize and contributed a foreword to her collection, but it was the FWP that provided an essential staging ground, a convergence of advice, encouragement, and exposure to new styles and ideas. In every way, the project was crucial, not coincidental, to her development as a writer.

While they worked together on the Illinois project, Walker developed a strong emotional attachment to Wright. One Friday afternoon, they collected their WPA paychecks, and Wright said he'd be leaving for New York that night. He also revealed that, after years of working on and off at the post office, he'd finally qualified for a permanent job there, one that was well-paying and secure. But it felt like a step back from his writing career, so he tore up the offer. WPA officials may have been dismayed to learn that someone on work relief was giving up a chance for private employment—which was, after all, the ostensible point of the WPA. But Wright understood that the FWP offered him a rare opportunity, an entryway into cultural work that would have been vastly more difficult to break into on his own. He'd hold out for a transfer to the NYC project. Walker understood and gave him her blessing. But she was sad to see him go.

"EVEN IF THAT LIGHT BURNS RED"

Just after the New Year, 1938, Richard Wright walked into the NYC project office on East Forty-second Street. At that moment, more than 200,000 people were on some kind of federal work relief—in New York state alone. Wright's arrival coincided with the appointment of yet another director: Harry Shaw, a young but well-regarded instructor at New York University with experience in both magazines and book publishing. He'd been selected from forty or fifty candidates to replace the ad hoc trio that had been running the project all summer and fall.

Work on the two volumes of the New York City guide was well under way. Wright found himself going over the Harlem material for the guide as well as "The Negro in New York," a counterpart to the studies of African American life being assembled by Zora Neale Hurston in Florida, and Jack Conroy and Arna Bontemps in Illinois. During a radio interview that spring—PR for the project and its prizewinning new worker—he explained the task as he saw it. "The fact remains that the average American's conception of Negro culture and life as it exists in New York is probably derived from not very accurate novels, or Hollywood representations of the urban Negro as a man who is either shabby and comical or one who is an exceedingly prosperous conductor of a popular swing orchestra," he said. The FWP, instead, was going to show "Harlem without makeup," a true picture of the struggle for dignity by African Americans in the nation's largest city.

In practice, this meant Wright worked on two pieces: a portrait of Harlem for *New York Panorama*, the guide's first volume, which was devoted to essays; and a shorter introductory passage for the Harlem section of the second volume, a guidebook proper. The *Panorama* essay was begun by another federal writer, Claude McKay, but Wright reworked the material and, in the end, Alsberg preferred his.

McKay was almost two decades older than Wright and his literary reputation was well established. He'd left a comfortable peasant family in Jamaica to study agronomy in the United States; instead, he ended up in New York, where he became a revolutionary socialist and inhabited the same world of radicals and bohemians as Henry Alsberg. His 1922 collection *Harlem*

Shadows established him as an important poet of the Harlem Renaissance. "If We Must Die," his defiant response to the white violence that spilled over the land in 1919, became something of a signature poem. He spent most of the twenties overseas—including a consequential trip to the USSR, where he attended the fourth congress of the Comintern and met Trotsky and other Bolsheviks. His first novel, *Home to Harlem*, was a raunchy tour of the Harlem underworld that became a surprise bestseller but infuriated many Black critics. (W. E. B. Du Bois said it made him want to take a bath.) His next novel, *Banjo*, did well, too, and he lived off the royalties. But a story collection, *Gingertown*, and the novel *Banana Bottom*, published in the first years of the Depression, sold poorly. McKay had to borrow money to return to the United States, and when he did, he took a place in a city-run relief camp upstate, then found his way to the FWP.

He might have been a mentor to Wright—he was steeped in the literature of socialist revolution and Black militancy, and his poems (especially his sloganeering early ones) were clear precursors to Wright's own. But they didn't get along. McKay, like his friend Max Eastman, was by now intensely critical of the Communist Party and the Soviet Union while Wright was still vocal in his support. McKay also thought Wright was rude. The younger writer, meanwhile, saw McKay as a relic of an older, inferior movement—he very well might have been thinking of McKay when he dispatched the work of the Harlem Renaissance writers in "Blueprint for Negro Writing."

Wright's portrait of Harlem for *New York Panorama* isn't as dire as the one that emerges from his articles for the *Daily Worker*. But it doesn't overlook the "handicaps and penalties" imposed on its residents by the racial order, from the repression of slave insurrections to the inflated rents, inferior schools, and discriminatory practices of the current day. And yet the texture of the prose is dry, and it too much resembles a conventional encyclopedia essay, especially when it shifts from Harlem's history to inventorial passages on economic, political, and cultural life. Wright's introductory essay for the Harlem section of the *New York City Guide*, though half as long, is imbued with more of the "verve and frankness" that Alsberg demanded of the guides.

As Wright settled into the work, his reputation grew. *Story* magazine officially announced that he'd won its contest and his book *Uncle Tom's Children* appeared shortly thereafter. The response was excellent. A review in *The*

New York Times compared him to Hemingway in the very first sentence (although it ended on a condescending note by suggesting that Wright's success meant things weren't as bad as he claimed). The *New York Post* ran a profile with the remarkable lede: "Whatever else Communism in America may have to answer for, you may chalk up to its credit the development of one superb writer." Eleanor Roosevelt plugged the "beautifully written" book in her syndicated column "My Day"; in a letter to Wright's publisher, she said the book was "so vivid that I had a most unhappy time reading it." She'd paid him the ultimate compliment.

One reviewer who had a most unhappy reaction, and truly meant it, was Zora Neale Hurston. In *The Saturday Review*, she seized Wright's attack on *Their Eyes Were Watching God* and turned it around on him: she praised the craft in his writing but dismissed his subject matter and unsubtly implied that he'd done a disservice to the race. "This is a book about hatreds," she wrote, one that confined itself to the grim and spectacular and was too obsessed with violent wish fulfillment to successfully address the "broader and more fundamental phases of Negro life." She took a dig at the Communist Party and its monolithic attitude toward the South, accusing Wright of having nothing to offer in his work but the party line: "state responsibility for everything and individual responsibility for nothing, not even feeding one's self. And march!" That the book might actually complement her own writing, Hurston did not allow, just as Wright didn't when he dismissed her novel. They'd staked out positions on opposite edges of a widening rift.

Wright signed a copy of *Uncle Tom's Children* and sent it to Alsberg, who found it "very moving." He asked Wright for another signed copy, which he passed along to Harry Hopkins with a note. "I consider Richard Wright the most talented Negro creative writer in the country," he wrote, "and I think we can be proud to have had him on the Project." (He added: "He is like most of the young writers, very far on the left, but then, most young writers of today are left wing.") Alsberg was complimenting himself a bit—the FWP was making Wright's career and Alsberg personally went to a lot of trouble to get him on the NYC project. But his admiration was genuine.

As he'd done in Chicago, Wright found himself working alongside a collection of writers from various backgrounds, possessing different degrees of prominence and talent—the "strange fellowship of necessity" that one of them, Anzia Yezierska, would call it. Some, like him, were on their way up, or hoped to be; some were left holding the shards of their careers and wondering, before they found the project, how they'd pay for food.

Wright already knew Dorothy West, another federal writer—in fact, one of the reasons he'd moved to New York was to join her in launching the magazine *New Challenge*, a reboot of her earlier publication that had appeared in six issues from 1934 to 1937, a sort of last gasp of the Harlem Renaissance. (Wright wanted *New Challenge* to resemble a Black *New Masses*, but West disagreed and killed it after one issue; from Chicago, Abe Aaron offered his assessment: "It stinks, Dick, stinks bad.") On the NYC project, West was a field worker, and she imbued her reports with a literary touch that prefigured her 1948 novel, *The Living Is Easy*, a chronicle of Boston's Black upper class.

Working there, too, at one point, was Edward Dahlberg, whose novels (including *Bottom Dogs*, a clear precursor to Algren's *Somebody in Boots*) earned him great respect from Alsberg—even if the current NYC director thought Dahlberg was "definitely psychopathic." There were the editors of *Partisan Review*, Philip Rahv and William Phillips (the latter of whom earned a reputation as "a quiet but determined non-producer" and was dismissed). There were a few who were known mostly, then, for their poetry: Kenneth Fearing and May Swenson, Kenneth Patchen and Charlotte Wilder (sister of Thornton), and others whose names and verse have fallen from view with the passing years.

Harry Roskolenko, another poet, was one of the project's fiercest Trotskyists. This was a label that Communist Party members tended to fling at anyone on the left who opposed them, but Roskolenko was the genuine article. He'd joined Trotsky's small core of followers in the United States early and was among those who tried boring from within the Communist Party—until he was found out, beaten up badly, and expelled. He even corresponded with the man himself on art and politics. When Diego Rivera painted his controversial mural *Man at the Crossroads* in Rockefeller Center (which portrayed a confrontation between socialist progress and capitalist decay, complete with a surreptitious portrait of Lenin—and which the Rockefellers quickly destroyed), Roskolenko posed as a worker in overalls. In exchange, Rivera painted Roskolenko's portrait and gave him a wineskin with some tequila in it and a foul-smelling serape that, Rivera claimed, had belonged to Pancho Villa.

Roskolenko wasn't afraid of confrontation. At the second American Writers' Congress, just before Wright introduced Henry Alsberg, Roskolenko asked a speaker this loaded question: why was Trotsky's *Literature and Revolution* suppressed in the Soviet Union? (He didn't join the small group that included Dwight Macdonald, Mary McCarthy, and the *Partisan Review* editors who disrupted an earlier session in the name of Trotsky.) Roskolenko subsequently became a favorite target of *Red Pen*, the newsletter of the Communist Party's FWP unit in New York. One article identified him and Lionel Abel, the future playwright and critic, as "ugly specimens of Trotskyite intellectuals" whose "loud-mouthed hooliganism" included shouting at a union representative: "We're not paying dues to you bastards anymore!" Another attacked his contribution to *American Stuff*, a poem that *Red Pen*'s anonymous authors considered insulting to Marx.

In other words, he was someone whom Richard Wright, fresh from a desk at the *Daily Worker*, was supposed to hate. But Wright got along with most everyone, even reputed enemies of the Communist Party. For Roskolenko, the feeling was mutual. When Roskolenko's *American Stuff* poem was causing people to sneer "Marx-hater!" and spit on the ground in front of him, Wright promised that he wouldn't call for Roskolenko to be shipped off to Siberia. When Roskolenko was shoved into the street by a random drunk, Wright was the person who helped him up and bought him a round.

As for his project work, Roskolenko thought of it as another in a long list of unusual jobs. He'd escaped the immigrant ghettoes of the Lower East Side—where a truck tore off his mother's arm as she lay beneath it, gathering blocks of ice that had fallen into the street; where another truck ran down his sister as she crossed Lafayette Street—to sail as a crew member on freight ships. He later became an elevator operator, a clerk, a hobo, a thief, and finally a controller of a drawbridge over the Harlem River. Now he found himself in the New York Public Library on Forty-second Street, researching the city's maritime history and skiing on the East Coast. It could have been worse. He knew of another poet on the project who was indexing street names in the Bronx and said that, if he was forced to cover one more street, he'd kill himself. According to Roskolenko, this man had written only one poem: "an ode to a goat in the Bronx zoo."

Roskolenko shared a social origin with the project's only true literary celebrity (of the moment, anyway). Anzia Yezierska was a full generation older but she came of age in those same tenements. She built her career in the twenties with stories and novels about Jewish immigrant women much like herself, whose lives began in the shtetls of Eastern Europe and who were transported to the Lowest East Side, who worked in laundries and sweatshops and sweltering kitchens, who strained against their patriarchal families. The Triangle Shirtwaist dead were her peers and contemporaries—although by the time of the fire, in 1911, she was approaching the middle class, by way of Columbia Teachers College and marriage. She began writing stories about women who were poor and overworked, and she took pains to reproduce their lively ghetto idiom even as she struggled to write fluidly in her second language, English. She hated being a dependent wife and the stories were her escape; when magazines started buying them, she left her husband.

Her stories were a hit. *Good Housekeeping* ran a personal narrative, "The Immigrant Speaks," introducing her authorial persona, and Houghton Mifflin published a story collection, *Hungry Hearts*, solidifying it. Yezierska had a hand in the mythmaking—according to one tale, recycled by publicists, she celebrated the book's publication with a party at the Waldorf-Astoria, where, only two years earlier, she'd gone begging for a job. Next was a movie deal with Samuel Goldwyn—worth a staggering $10,000, compared to the $200 advance for her book—and then novels, another movie, and a steady demand for her stories. Goldwyn's publicist dubbed her "the sweatshop Cinderella." Her books were raw and revealing and pulpy and melodramatic, enlivened by the cadences of ghetto speech, charged with the authority of her life story.

Success made her feel guilty. What was the difference, she wondered, between a boss who exploited the workers and someone who got rich writing about them? She kept swanky addresses but lived austerely and maintained some distance from the ostentatious Jazz Age literati. She was consumed by her work. And yet, after a decade of achievement, she couldn't transcend the mode that made her famous. The first novel she published after 1929 was a flop. Her investments had been obliterated by the stock market crash. Her royalty checks disappeared. Magazines stopped buying her stories. Her lifelong frugality—she always borrowed or stole books from friends and fished newspapers out of trash cans—was not enough to stave off ruin. She rented a furnished room on Riverside Drive and then shared an apartment with her daughter on Twelfth Street. The poverty she had escaped through fiction rose up to claim her once again. After she went on relief and joined the NYC project, she thought of Samuel Goldwyn, who demanded one-sentence summaries of movie plots. Hers would be: "From an author in Hollywood to a pauper on W.P.A."

And yet, like Nelson Algren and so many others, she was struck by how the project transformed her fellow workers. "Their waiting was no longer the hopeless stupor of applicants for mass relief; they were employees of the government. They had risen from the scrap heap of the unemployed, from the loneliness of the unwanted, dreaming of regeneration, together. The new job look lighted the most ravaged faces." Their first payday became a revel. "Men who hadn't had a job in years fondled five- and ten-dollar bills with the tenderness of farmers rejoicing over new crops of grain." She compared herself to "a bit of withered moss that has been suddenly put into water, growing green again."

When Yezierska met Richard Wright, she saw confidence, defiance, talent, and good looks—he had "the calm smile of a young Buddha." ("Your face is young, but you have an old head on your shoulders," Yezierska says to him in her fictionalized memoir.) She probably saw some of herself in his ambition and commitment and even his politics—she'd never lost the socialist sympathies that pervaded life in the Lower East Side tenements. She remembered him as a firm supporter of the FWP, although he held no illusions about it. He didn't agree with leftists who saw the project as a form of capitalist bribery, but he also didn't see it as the fruit of government beneficence—it was simply what they deserved, especially Black artists who'd been persistently overlooked. It was a kind of justice.

In her memoir, Yezierska describes another character: an elderly man who carries a briefcase stuffed with the manuscript pages of his Spinoza biography and complains that the project is hackwork, that it is destroying his capabilities as a writer, that he must be free to complete his masterpiece. Finally, he rails against the other workers, pukes up blood, and dies. Yezierska inherits his briefcase and finds that the pages are covered with gibberish. The character is no doubt inspired by Joe Gould, the peerless eccentric who spent several years on the NYC project. He lurked on the fringes of office life, mostly sniping at communists and behaving oddly. His project work, if he did it at all, may have become hopelessly entangled with his own fetishized manuscript, the mammoth oral history of the world he claimed to be writing, even though he said that these were separate endeavors. "My own book is too good, of course, to be subsidized by a mere government," he told the *New York Herald Tribune*.

Unlike Yezierska's character, Gould didn't drop dead in the office. He was fired from it. In the aftermath, E. E. Cummings and Malcolm Cowley both wrote to Alsberg in protest, but to no avail. The NYC project was facing a reduced quota and workers far more productive than Gould were being laid off. "I know Gould is an 'Institution,'" Alsberg told Cummings, "but couldn't do anything to save him." Gould, meanwhile, suggested that he was willing to stir up trouble; he could tell the press that he'd been fired because of a satirical poem he wrote about the general secretary of the Communist Party, which appeared in *The New Republic*: "From Russia, Earl Browder / Is getting divorscht / He likes clam chowder / Better than borscht." He pressed Alsberg for an explanation and got the standard reply about cutbacks. Gould took this as permission to say to anyone who asked if the poem led to his dismissal, "Mr. Alsberg refuses to deny it."

While Alsberg dealt with headaches like Gould, he also had assets in the NYC project. John Cheever was one of them. Cheever first wrote to Alsberg in the fall of 1935, when he was twenty-three and looking for a job. (He did so at the recommendation of Saxe Commins, a book editor who also happened to be Emma Goldman's nephew. Alsberg lived with Commins and his wife, Dorothy, in Paris for several months in the late twenties and they remained close friends.) Cheever by then had published a few stories, including two he'd sold to *The New Yorker*—the first two vertebrae in the spine of his writing career. He admitted he didn't know anything about the FWP ("the FERA writers' projects," he called it) but he tried to make himself sound qualified. "It is hard to say, but I can say sincerely, that I can handle my own language with clarity and ease and meaning," he wrote. "And if you could give me some information about the projects, I would be grateful." At the time, he was staying in the apartment of Walker Evans, while the photographer was documenting the Depression-ravaged South for Katharine Kellock's former outfit, the Resettlement Administration. (Cheever's last apartment had been so grimy and sad that Evans took out his camera and photographed it.) He needed the work: he was writing synopses of novels for MGM and stretching out a $400 advance for a novel of his own. But he couldn't fulfill the residency requirement to get on relief, so he couldn't get on the project. Not long after he wrote to Alsberg, his apartment suddenly went dark—Evans hadn't paid the electricity bill, and Cheever was left writing by candlelight.

It took two and a half years for him to actually join the project, in May 1938, four months after Wright did. (In between, he spent a lot of time at Yaddo and had his novel rejected and sold a bad story to *Collier's* for a good price.) But rather than ending up in New York City, Cheever found a job in DC as an editor on the national staff. He hated it. Unlike the radicals and New Dealers who celebrated the concept of work relief for writers, Cheever, like Zora Neale Hurston, was uneasy about the whole operation and slightly embarrassed to be part of it. He was bored with the work but also frustrated that it impinged on his own writing (although he still found time to carouse in DC). He wasn't impressed with his boardinghouse, either. "There is also an old lady who sits at the head of the table and says all W.P.A. workers are lazy and good-for-nothing and she's finding it harder and harder to get me to pass her the lima beans," he wrote in a letter. Six months into the job, he tried to quit, but Alsberg convinced him to accept a traveling assignment instead.

So Cheever decamped to Manhattan, checked into the Chelsea Hotel, and attached himself to the New York City project. He helped with final preparations for the second volume of the guide and ended up contributing some prose to the opening essay on Manhattan. He still wasn't won over by the mission and described his work as "twisting into order the sentences written by some incredibly lazy bastards." (Not all of whom were in New York: Alsberg sent Cheever other assignments, too. On one occasion, it was the manuscript of a guide to Macon and the Ocmulgee National Monument in Georgia; another time, it was the Pittsburgh guide and some Pennsylvania educational pamphlets.) Before the guide was finished, Cheever again tried to resign. And once more, Alsberg convinced him to stay, at least through the end of the month. At some point Cheever took a leave without pay and disappeared to Yaddo. "The novel I've been fooling around with seems to be coming along," he finally wrote to Alsberg, "and since it may be a matter of years, I feel that I'd better resign from the project." (It turned out to be eighteen years before Cheever's first novel, *The Wapshot Chronicle*, was

published.) Alsberg's reply began, "My dear John," a rare informal salutation that, in his official correspondence, he saved for those he felt affectionate
toward. He accepted Cheever's resignation sadly. But the FWP had served
its purpose and carried another vulnerable writer—an especially fine one—
through an uncertain period. That writer's ambivalence toward the project
was, ultimately, beside the point.

It isn't likely that Richard Wright saw much of Cheever, in the sense of
working alongside him. Of all the federal writers in New York, he was closest
with Ralph Ellison, who joined in the spring of 1938, just after *Uncle Tom's
Children* appeared. Wright met Ellison only after he arrived in New York
from Chicago—Langston Hughes put them in touch, and together they attended the second American Writers' Congress. Ellison, six years younger,
was becoming rapidly attracted to radical ideas, just as Wright had been in
Chicago around the time he met Nelson Algren. But Ellison was only just
beginning to think seriously about writing.

Ellison's path to the FWP was unusual. He grew up in Oklahoma; his
name, "Ralph Waldo," was a gift from his father, who died when he was three
and had wanted him to become a poet like Emerson. He was a steady reader,
just like Wright, but he gravitated toward music—he played trumpet in the
high school band, took formal lessons, and ended up on a scholarship to Tus-
kegee. When his scholarship money ran out, he left for New York, thinking that his time there would be a hiatus and that he would study art. But
the hiatus became permanent and Ellison, urged on by Wright, gradually
replaced his art lessons with experiments in writing. He hung around the
Daily Worker office in Harlem when Wright was the correspondent, sometimes even sleeping there, and he paid close attention to whatever Wright was
typing. Finally, Wright encouraged him to try a book review, and then a short
story. Eventually, he followed Wright onto the NYC project, which formal-
ized his apprenticeship as a writer. His admiration for New Deal work relief
preceded his job. During the unruly strikes against cutbacks the previous
summer, he wrote to his mother: "These rich bastards here are trying to take
the W.P.A. away from us. They would deny a poor man the right to live in this
country for which we have fought and died."

As a federal writer, Ellison spent much of his time in the New York Public Library and the Schomburg Collection, researching for the Negro Unit,

which consisted of about thirty people under the direction of the journalist Roi Ottley. They gathered material for use in all project publications but especially "The Negro in New York." (Like "The Florida Negro," this would never be published during the life of the project, but a version did appear in 1967, with a preface by James Baldwin, who wrote: "It proves that anyone who contends that the Northern racial attitudes have not always been, essentially, indistinguishable from those of the South is either lying or is deluded.") Ellison's research could be tedious, but he recognized that it was beneficial, too, and it put him in contact with some fascinating history that he'd never before encountered—a story, he realized, beneath the official story of white America. He was assigned write-ups on the slave insurrection of 1741, the draft riots of 1863, the origins of "miscegenation of the Whites and Blacks," the history of Black printers and presses, along with lighter subjects, such as "Swimming as an Amusement for Negroes."

Eventually, he emerged from the library and was sent into the streets to collect living lore—he didn't know it, but he was working in parallel to Nelson Algren and Jack Conroy, who were doing likewise in Chicago. With his new assignment, Ellison might have encountered Herbert Halpert, the WPA folklorist who'd recorded Zora Neale Hurston in Florida. Halpert spent several months working for the NYC project, recording street rhymes and children's songs with the same refurbished army ambulance he'd parked in front of Hurston at the Clara White Mission. Ellison, however, was working with pen and paper, taking down impressions of city life by hand. He was uncovering material—images, feelings, phrases—that he stored away and would someday dig out again for his own work. On one summer day, he stood at the corner of 135th Street and Lenox Avenue, speaking with a passerby named Leo Gurley, who was telling him about a man known only as "Sweet-the-Monkey," from Florence, South Carolina. "He was bad alright," Gurley said. "He was one sucker who didn't give a dam bout the crackers." (The words, as written, were Ellison's; he was training himself to take down the sound of someone's speech without mangling it into misspelled dialect.) Gurley explained that Sweet-the-Monkey made all kinds of trouble for the white people in Florence, which was an especially hard town, and yet they couldn't do anything about it. Then the anecdote revealed its true nature: "It was this way: Sweet could make hisself invisible," Gurley said. "You don't believe it? Well here's how he done it." This wasn't idle gossip but exactly the sort of folktale, carried up from the South to Harlem, that Zora Neale Hurston had dedicated her career to documenting and celebrating. And as Gurley told his story of the invisible man, the details sank into Ellison's mind, where they would sit for a quite a while, and percolate.

Wright, meanwhile, was eager to dedicate himself more fully to writing fiction. At first, he was forced to continue the same routine he'd known in Chicago, on the Illinois project: handling assignments by day and turning to his own work at night. But the success of *Uncle Tom's Children* meant that he was now a candidate for the NYC project's special feature—the secret, or maybe not so secret, creative writing unit.

When Travis Hoke succeeded Orrick Johns as director, he was surprised to learn that a handful of project workers were doing their own self-selected creative assignments at home. The unit was somewhat clandestine, although "unit" perhaps oversold the group's cohesion—these were individual writers who reported to the office once a week and otherwise controlled their own work. Alsberg had set it up himself in the fall of 1936 and made most of the arrangements with Johns verbally. Hoke, who'd been Johns's assistant director, couldn't even find a list of the people involved. The whole thing was kept quiet because it didn't exactly fit the FWP's explicit mandate, and the idea of supporting creative writing with tax dollars might have raised uncomfortable questions. But Alsberg thought it was essential. Initially, Johns gathered submissions and found out who was interested—which, it turned out, was quite a lot of people. "This is good, and it is also not so good," he wrote to Alsberg. "I am afraid we are going to be on the spot." But Alsberg kept the group small and selected its members himself. Johns set it up as a special assignment, reporting directly to him. By the time Robert W. Bruere, the investigator dispatched by Harry Hopkins, arrived to observe the project in the summer of 1937, he found ten people on the clandestine creative writing unit—free to pursue their own work with minimal oversight, for the same government paycheck. Bruere believed this was a good thing and that such writers needed encouragement. Wright, at that moment, was languishing in the city, hoping for a transfer to the NYC project and writing for the *Daily Worker*. But Bruere's words anticipated the place he'd find on the creative unit. "I feel that everyone on the Project capable of artistic expression should be encouraged to follow his own inner light and leading," he wrote, "even if that light burns red." Wright would bear this statement out.

For certain writers, the unit was a boon. Claude McKay, one of the first selected, used the time to bundle the events and people and locales of his peripatetic life into an autobiography, *A Long Way from Home*. Willard Maas and Sol Funaroff worked on poetry collections. So did Harry Roskolenko, who finished his first collection, *Sequence of Violence*; when it was published, it carried an effusive foreword by Lewis Mumford, who called Roskolenko "the very voice of the modern city: the inevitable commentator on 'those bandaged years.'" Roskolenko couldn't quite believe it. "Suddenly I was a poet with a book, proclaiming my version of Hell and being paid for it by the United States Government." Henry Alsberg followed his usual procedure and sent copies to Eleanor Roosevelt, Harry Hopkins, and other officials.

Other writers didn't live up to Alsberg's expectations. The poet Harry Kemp got on the unit by sending Alsberg a pleading letter and an original poem, and adding, "Believe me, this is written without a single drink!" But he didn't accomplish much. A lesser-known writer named Emmett Gowen was supposed to turn in one piece a month, but two and a half months went by before he finally produced a short poem. An editor deemed it "an insult to the intelligence of any adult," and he was kicked off the unit. Maxwell Bodenheim initially seemed like an excellent candidate—he'd been a prominent member of the Greenwich Village set in the twenties and had many poetry collections and novels to his name. (After the Depression, he became an outspoken communist; often, it was Bodenheim who took up the constant picket outside the FWP office, alone.) He was also a stupendous drinker. He once gave a poetry reading at the Chicago John Reed Club, when Wright was a member. Wright, and possibly Nelson Algren, watched as Bodenheim read his poems, written on ripped-up paper bags, and then disappeared to the bathroom to sneak a drink from a flask, then returned and read some more, then disappeared again, until he drank himself into a stupor. And yet, when Bodenheim first joined the project, his initial work was good. It was the creative unit that became his undoing. Without the structure and responsibilities of his regular project job, he'd arrive for his weekly check-in already drunk, and then reroute himself to a bar across the street until other project workers dragged him into the office.

Wright, ambitious and disciplined, was perfectly matched to the unit's purpose. He was living in Brooklyn with a couple he'd known in Chicago, Jane and Herb Newton. (They were communists; she was white and he was Black.) He wrote furiously, knowing that he needed to finish a novel while *Uncle Tom's Children* was in the public eye. Sometimes he'd get up in the morning and go write in Fort Greene Park, filling page after page in yellow legal pads, attempting to form a statement on art and politics while he still had a platform to deliver it.

As he worked, he called on another federal writer for help: Margaret Walker, back in Chicago. Wright wrote to her from New York, asking if she would handle some research for his new novel, and she immediately agreed. That year, a young Black man named Robert Nixon killed a white woman during a home break-in. His guilt wasn't really in doubt, but the case brought out the worst racist impulses of the Chicago press. At Wright's request, Walker carefully followed the story in Chicago newspapers, clipped the articles, and mailed them to him in Brooklyn. ("When I went into news offices or bought papers on the stands," she said, "I heard jeers and ugly insults about all black people.") Wright would lay the clippings out on the floor and read them over and over, letting them catalyze his own creative process, interacting with the private emotional truths and remembered concrete details of his life in the Jim Crow South and the tenements of Chicago. But there was a public dimension to how he tackled the novel as well: he and Jane Newton discussed the smallest details of plot and character; many of his friends read drafts or heard Wright read passages aloud. Ralph Ellison watched it come together as a work in progress. Instead of locking himself away to spontaneously generate a masterpiece, Wright took up a method that resembled the cooperative, open style of the FWP—and it was the FWP's support that allowed him to do it at all. He finished a first draft, and then a more polished second draft, while he was on the project payroll.

Finally, the NYC project completed its guide to the city—or *guides*. They'd initially planned to split it into three volumes: essays, a guide to Manhattan, and a guide to the rest of the boroughs. But the publisher, Random House, insisted on a single volume for the guide material—its executives doubted that shearing off the outer boroughs into a stand-alone volume was a prudent idea. They were also growing weary of the NYC project's inner turmoil and frequent delays. Bennett Cerf, president of Random House, was icily clear: "Only my deep interest in the whole project keeps me from saying in this letter just what I think of the way the work in the New York office has been conducted to date."

Alsberg, a born New Yorker, scrutinized the copy and made his own adjustments. Once, he wrote to the director to say that he'd been driving around uptown with some friends, and they passed the gas station on Lexington Avenue where the kidnapper of the Lindbergh baby had been caught—could they add this to a tour?

New York Panorama, the book of essays, appeared in September 1938, and the NYC guide followed that June. "It is hard to believe that in any one volume the color, squalor and vitality of the great city could have been better expressed," said the *Times* of *Panorama*; it was the "most original and admirable volume to date" of the American Guides, according to *The New Yorker*. When the NYC guide appeared, the *Times* called it "useful, broadly informative and amazing," and said it was "the best possible justification of that imperiled organization," the FWP. A mollified Bennett Cerf wrote on behalf of Random House's directors to say that they considered it "one of the finest books that has ever been published under the Random House imprint." (An unexpectedly harsh response arrived from the literary editor of *The Nation*, Margaret Marshall, who was incensed by a passage in *Panorama* unfavorably comparing her department to Malcom Cowley's at *The New Republic*—a reflection, she suspected, of the Communist Party line. It was an especially galling situation because she happened to be a member of the Guilds' Committee that sponsored the book—or *was* a member, since she resigned in a huff.) Wright's Harlem pieces appeared in both books, although his name appeared only in the *Guide*, tucked within a list of editorial staff in the front matter (below "editorial assistant" John Cheever), an unusual credit in the typically anonymous American Guides.

Meanwhile, the directorial churn continued. After *Panorama* appeared, Harry Shaw, who'd taken over just as Wright joined the project, resigned to focus on his teaching responsibilities and an overdue book for his publisher. In his place was appointed Harold Strauss, a young editor at Covici Friede, who lasted for about six months before he, too, stepped down, unable to devote enough time to the project.

By then, Wright was on his way out. That summer, with a draft of his new novel far along, he'd applied for a Guggenheim Fellowship, and asked Alsberg if he'd write a recommendation. "Several of the project boys are submitting applications and I thought I may as well too," he told Alsberg. (He also asked Eleanor Roosevelt, among others.) Alsberg agreed, and in March, Wright learned that he had actually won the fellowship. He wrote to Alsberg with the news and thanked him for the support. "I hope that I can justify in terms of creative work the kind faith you have placed in me," he said.

It was a good month for Wright's reputation. The WPA cranked out a press release announcing both the Guggenheim and the previous year's *Story* prize, and it placed Wright alongside other FWP recipients, past and present: Sterling Brown, Jack Conroy, Kenneth Fearing, Kenneth Patchen, and Joseph Berger, the sole author of a popular and colorful book of local lore issued by the Massachusetts project, *Cape Cod Pilot.* A few weeks earlier, there'd been another press release promoting the FWP's planned publications on African American subjects, from state books such as "The Florida Negro" to Sterling Brown's sweeping national history to compendiums of slavery narratives and folklore. It boasted that three of "the country's best known writers" were also federal writers: Claude McKay, Zora Neale Hurston, and Richard Wright. The range of literary ideas and styles represented by this particular trio—and marshaled by the FWP—was striking, even if only close observers knew that they shared a fair amount of spleen between them.

Wright was only one of many young federal writers who would go on to great things. But his success story—and the FWP's clear instrumentality in propelling it—had no real rival. His editor at Harper and Brothers, Edward Aswell, put it succinctly when he wrote to Harry Shaw, the NYC project director: when Wright took his place in American letters, it would be "a feather in the cap of WPA." Aswell even suggested that they give the FWP credit on the jacket of Wright's next book, the one he was busy composing while he was on the creative unit. That book, *Native Son*, would be among the most significant American novels of the twentieth century—a book that detonated against the literary landscape as few novels ever do. "It seems to me a fine thing that the Federal Government, through WPA, is making it possible for a man of Mr. Wright's caliber to continue his creative work," Aswell said. There was no need to spell out the alternative.

But even as Wright became a case study in how the FWP benefited the world of American letters, a shadow was falling over the project. All the political scuffling and the strikes and the administrative breakdowns had pushed it right into the sights of its staunchest adversaries, the critics who dwelled on sensational headlines while dismissing the project's indisputable accomplishments. Reed Harris, Alsberg's loyal assistant who'd followed him from the FERA, understood this—he understood so well that he quit the project altogether. He sensed that the FWP was heading toward a conflict that it could not win, and he wanted out. Alsberg was dismayed. But it was impossible to ignore the looming threat. Around the same time, Wright and his colleagues on the NYC project were startled by the appearance of a special bulletin, issued by the WPA. It said:

> All workers on Federal Project No. 1 for New York City, are hereby requested to cooperate to the fullest extent with the Dies Committee of the U.S. House of Representatives, which has been appointed to investigate "Un-American and subversive activities."

If you are subpoenaed, it went on, you must make arrangements with your supervisor to face the committee—promptly.

HENRY ALSBERG AND MARTIN DIES, JR., WASHINGTON, DC

"FOR OR AGAINST OUR COUNTRY"

Looking back, Representative Martin Dies, Jr., Democrat of Texas, seemed bound to collide with the Federal Writers' Project. But it wouldn't always have appeared that way. Dies entered Congress in 1931, midway through the Hoover administration. His constituents in East Texas—along with the rest of the country—were tumbling into the nadir of the Depression. Dies believed in aggressive remedies and he urged Hoover to take emergency measures that anticipated elements of the New Deal. (He wanted expanded public works, a one-year moratorium on foreclosures, and new business regulations: nothing that required massive deficit spending or would lay the foundation for a welfare state.) Hoover disappointed him. So when Franklin Roosevelt launched his campaign, Dies was all in. Roosevelt's vague and sometimes contradictory message made it easy for Dies to pick out what he wanted to hear—the "economy" approach of bold policy measures combined with spending cuts and a balanced budget. He stumped for the New York governor across the West. "When Roosevelt was elected," Dies wrote later, "he had no more enthusiastic and sincere advocate than myself."

Dies was thirty-one and during those early Roosevelt years he wore his enthusiasm openly. He was a southern populist who looked the part: his blond hair slicked back like a revivalist preacher's, his round face ornamented by a black cigar. (It was the face of a good old boy possessed of a sly intelligence.) He gave vigorous speeches that made his preacher hair flop onto his forehead until he swept it up again with one hand. He put his feet up on desks and smoked eight cigars a day and chewed gum in between. His voice was loud and strong and he stood six-foot-three. He enjoyed an informal acquaintance with Roosevelt (he said so, anyway), but belonged to the bloc of conservative Democrats that included Vice President John Nance Garner, a fellow Texan and Dies's patron. He was hostile to concentrated wealth and warned of a growing financial and industrial oligarchy that was undermining American democracy. At the same time, he despised the socialist left and anything that smacked of collectivism. Dies was for the little man, the littler the better, and thought that taxes were a good way to redistribute the wealth, as long as those little men were small landholders and small business owners. This position—hardly unique to Dies—allowed him to cheer for the New Deal while eventually becoming its foe.

Something else made his clash with the FWP inevitable. It was in there his first bill, which he introduced on his second day in the House of Representatives. He proposed halting all immigration to the United States for five years. His father, Martin Dies, Sr., who'd represented the same East Texas district for a decade, would have approved. From that very same seat, the elder Dies railed against unrestricted immigration and foreign entanglements as he launched attacks on illiterate foreigners and socialist radicals (and women with the ballot and conservationists, too). His attitude didn't belong to a fringe; a sizable chunk of the white electorate felt the same way. (In 1924, congressional nativists passed legislation that drastically reduced the number of immigrants allowed into the United States, barred those from Asia altogether, and imposed a racist quota system on the rest.) The younger Dies kept his father's commitments, but his immigration bill went nowhere. The next year, Dies introduced legislation that would deport and exclude all alien communists. That meant, in practice, most of them: at the time, a majority of Communist Party members were foreign-born; it wasn't until 1936 that the native-born made up 50 percent of the party. There were other bills proposing similar measures but the House actually passed Dies's version, before it died in the Senate. These two bills, anti-immigrant and anti-left, formed an overture to his legislative career.

In the spring of 1935—days after Congress passed the relief act creating the WPA—Dies wrote a pungent summation of his views for *The Saturday Evening Post*. It was the old story. He split American history into two phases. There was the racial homogeneity that prevailed from Bunker Hill to Appomattox, and then there was "the great alien invasion of the United States," the influx of migrants from southern and eastern Europe, and from Asia and Mexico, a demographic augmentation spurred on by the "industrial greed" of bosses who wanted cheap labor. "Today, as a result of this policy, we have more than 40,000,000 people of foreign stock in our midst," Dies wrote, as if the wickedness of this situation was self-evident. He couched his argument in terms of unemployment—that kicking out foreigners would open up scarce jobs for deserving Americans—but the racial ugliness of his position was unmistakable. Dies closed with an attack on undocumented immigrants, of which he claimed there were 3.5 million in the country. "Among this number are hundreds of gangsters, murderers and thieves"—rhetoric that would echo in the words of nativist politicians for generations—"who are unfit to live in this country and, God knows, unfit to die in any country," he wrote. "Driven out of Europe, they have taken advantage of our maudlin sentimentality and plagued us long enough. Relentless war without quarter and without cessation must be waged upon them until the last one is driven from our shores. There is no middle ground or compromise. Either we are for or against our country."

Our country. That phrase contained the irreconcilable difference between Dies and the FWP. Dies held no special animus toward the federal arts projects, no more, at least, than other conservative Democrats. But "our country" meant one thing to Dies and his co-ideologues, and something else entirely to the architects of the FWP. Dies's America was an abstraction, inspired by a Christian God and realized by white British colonists and inherited by select descendants. It was the rhetoric of exceptionalism overlaid on blood and soil—the essence of American nativism. Dies spoke for many in the thirties who were driven by the stresses of the Depression into ideas at once comforting and ugly. But his voice was as old as the Republic.

The attitudes and assumptions that drove him were pervasive and well established, and yet they were inimical to the portrait of America, and the loose definition of American identity, that the FWP was busy assembling: in the crowded and inclusive guidebooks, the life histories, the slavery narratives, the ethnic studies. That American scene was treated mournfully and playfully as often as it was celebrated; it was unapologetically diverse, permanently changing, shaped by economic struggles, tinged with class conflict, and welcoming of immigrants. It implied a vision of nationhood, and a subtle idea of patriotism, that was firmly grounded in the details of American life—a sensibility that arose from an engagement with specific places, communities, incidents, stories, roads, and rituals. The idea of holding a mirror up to America was a little trite and yet it implied a sophisticated and important argument: that the country was whatever appeared in the reflection, an aggregate of particulars, a multitudinous assembly that could not be reduced to, or erased by, some abstract nationalism. "Our country," they might have said, was whatever federal writers found out there—including the federal writers themselves, and the process by which they found it.

Dies's break with the Roosevelt administration took time. At first he was merely put off by the weird forces assembling in Washington to launch the New Deal. "Free silverites, single taxers, Socialists, Technocrats, Townsendites, all were there in profusion," he wrote. "Name your fantasy, and you could find it. They were excited, happy, eager zealots, about to remake the world." (People, in other words, like Henry Alsberg, whose residual anarcho-bohemianism clung to him all the way from Greenwich Village.) But the real outrage, the Roosevelt administration's original sin, was its recognition of the Soviet Union. Dies grimaced as he imagined parties at the Soviet embassy, the college professors and smug radicals—and worse, government officials—gulping down free champagne and Bolshevik caviar. He complained to Democratic leaders. They ignored him. For Dies, recognition not only gave legitimacy to the Soviet state but emboldened communists on American shores. "Marxists of every hue from deepest red to palest pink gathered along the Potomac early in the New Deal, and soon began to flourish," he wrote. This diverse band—"of all shades from sincere idealists to rabid crack-pots"—aimed to undermine the American system and abolish private property by constructing a sprawling bureaucratic state. (That was the story, anyway.)

Through the first Roosevelt administration and into the second, Dies hung on to the New Deal coalition, more or less, along with much of the Democratic Party's creaky right flank. But when Roosevelt's court-packing scheme was revealed and when the administration took a conciliatory approach to a wave of sit-down strikes—the ones that inspired strikers on the NYC project—Dies had enough. Radicalism, inside and outside the federal government, needed to be beaten back. And luckily for Dies there was a surge of support in Congress for just such an investigation—one that uncovered, as the new committee's founding resolution put it, "the extent, character, and objects of un-American propaganda activities in the United States," whether those activities were directed from overseas (from Fascist Italy, Nazi Germany, and Soviet Russia) or carried out by domestic groups. "Un-American," in this case, quite narrowly meant propaganda that "attacks the principle of the form of government as guaranteed by our Constitution." But when it came to "un-Americanism," the East Texas Democrat kept an open mind.

Dies's committee wasn't the first to investigate subversive political behavior. In 1919, the Senate launched investigations into Bolshevism when its members were spooked by a pro-Soviet meeting at a local DC theater. The committee mostly gathered information about the communist project and the upheaval in Russia; among its witnesses were the radical journalists John Reed and Louise Bryant. But critics saw the chilling effect of such investigations. Meyer London, a representative from New York and member of the Socialist Party, issued a charged warning: "The worst of it is that every movement, every new idea, every new suggestion, every new thought that is advanced is immediately denounced as Bolshevism," he said. "It is not necessary to argue any more with a man who advances a new idea; it is enough to say 'That is Bolshevism.'"

The twenties saw sporadic hearings and more calls for investigations. Then activity shifted from the Senate to the House with a new committee led by Representative Hamilton Fish, a Republican from the Hudson Valley. (Previous Hamilton Fishes, his father and grandfather, had served in Congress and as secretary of state, respectively.) The Fish Committee heard testimony through the second half of 1930, mostly from anti-communist witnesses on the operations and scope of the party. The hearings reached a crescendo when a few Communist Party members, including the general secretary, William Z. Foster, testified. Edmund Wilson, sympathetic to the party, observed the proceedings and marveled at the ignorance of the committee. "They do not seem to know even so much about Russia as one would suppose any ordinary newspaper-reader could hardly have helped picking up," he wrote. The committee's report contained thirteen recommendations of dubious legality and practicality (such as deporting alien radicals to the Soviet Union, which the United States didn't even recognize). Its aim, plainly, was the open repression of the Communist Party. One of these thirteen recommendations was the impetus for Dies's bill to deport and exclude all alien communists, which passed in the House but went no further. Fiorello La Guardia, then a Representative from New York and a critic of the committee, exclaimed that Fish and Dies and their cohorts would next propose a bill for burning witches.

The Fish Committee begat the McCormack Committee, which operated in the summer and fall of 1934. The true architect of the committee, chaired by John McCormack of Massachusetts, was Samuel Dickstein, who represented a district on Manhattan's Lower East Side. (He won the seat, coincidentally, by defeating the socialist Meyer London.) Many of Dickstein's constituents were, like him, Jewish immigrants from Eastern Europe alarmed by pro-Nazi activity in the United States. While the new committee did take up the question of communist subversion, mostly by reiterating findings of the Fish Committee, it spent more energy investigating Nazi sympathizers and native fascists such as William Dudley Pelley's Silver Shirts. Hearings were usually closed to the public, but Dickstein knew how to make headlines. After investigating a pro-Nazi children's camp in New Jersey, he told reporters, "I would not keep a dog there. The camp is full of poison ivy, and there are unsanitary conditions. They goose-step all day." The committee's final hearings, held in New York, were interrupted by hundreds of Nazi sympathizers saluting furiously and chanting "Down with Dickstein!"

Dies, meanwhile, was watching. He paid attention when Dickstein, unsatisfied with the results of the McCormack Committee, proposed something far broader: a congressional investigative body that would examine all manner of subversive activity of an "un-American" nature. This was a step beyond uncovering the foreign propaganda networks, Soviet or Nazi, that were ostensibly active inside the United States. Congress balked—even Hamilton Fish opposed the idea—and Dickstein, who'd become somewhat reckless with his accusations, was pushed aside by a mix of skepticism, anti-Semitism, and his own habitual grandstanding. His proposal was defeated—but not dead. Three months later, Dies introduced his resolution and was backed by some of the Democratic leadership, including Vice President Garner and the conservative southern bloc. (Dies later claimed that Roosevelt clandestinely supported the idea as well.) Dickstein approved of the resolution, lending it an anti-fascist imprimatur. But the chair would belong to Dies, and when the resolution passed, 191 to 41, the committee would bear his name.

Its members were appointed in June 1938—five Democrats, including Dies, and two Republicans, a mostly conservative bunch. They sent investigating agents into the field. Dies's statements leading up to the first public hearings in August were a model of probity. The hearings would not devolve into a "three-ring circus" or a bid for "cheap publicity"; there would be no "smearing" or "character assassination." They sought only the facts. His watchwords were fairness, impartiality, courtesy. Accused individuals and organizations would be allowed a defense and the committee would operate with no preconceived notions.

Dies may have reassured his critics for the moment. But soon his words became perverse. Even before formal hearings began, another committee member, J. Parnell Thomas, signaled the onslaught that was to come. Thomas was a first-term Republican, a stocky bond salesman and local politician from the suburbs of northern New Jersey—and enduringly hostile to the New Deal and all its works. He announced in July that he intended to investigate the Federal Theater Project and the Federal Writers' Project. Information gathered during informal hearings, he claimed, proved that both projects were lousy with communists. More, they were gears in a far-reaching New Deal propaganda machine that was itself a conspiracy against the American people. The FTP bore the brunt of his attack and the next day, its director, Hallie Flanagan, said she was willing to cooperate—but, she added, some of his charges were "obviously absurd."

Thomas—who made little distinction between the New Deal and *New Masses*—represented the committee at its most paranoid and partisan. But he was in sync with its basic impulse, the destructive urge concealed by Dies's sober, judicious statements. Soon, the nation would see the committee unbound. Henry Alsberg and the FWP had reason to be worried.

"ONE OF THE BEST BOLSHEVIKS
ON THE WRITERS' PROJECT"

The FWP was born in a cauldron of accusation. Conservatives attacked it as a frivolous boondoggle, the pencil-leaning counterpart to the WPA's shovel-leaners. The Republican Alf Landon, running for president in 1936, scoffed at the very notion of an administration that found time to create *guidebooks*. (The FWP's tart reply listed the various business and professional interests—transportation and hotel associations, chambers of commerce, thousands of experts and specialists—who believed that the guides, and the economic activity they might stimulate, were a splendid idea.) There was the "Red Baedeker" charge flung at Katharine Kellock. There was the Sacco-and-Vanzetti-fueled uproar in Massachusetts. There were regular attacks by the Republican National Committee. In the summer of 1937, Ralph M. Easley, an elderly reformer and head of the National Civic Federation, wrote an open letter to Roosevelt claiming that the FWP was dominated by communists and staffed by the undeserving—even as he managed to inflate the cost of the project and implied, wrongly, that it had no publications to show for its efforts. (It soon emerged that Easley was aided by none other than W. O. Lucas, leader of the right-wing faction in the New York City project. Lucas helped edit Easley's letters, but once he was exposed in the press, he resigned from the FWP—and took a publicity job with Easley's organization.) Alsberg demolished Easley's charges in his own statement, but the attack, and others like it, had a way of slowly poisoning public attitudes toward the project.

When the Dies Committee appeared, no one could say if it was another shell in the conservative barrage or a new kind of weapon entirely. "It was the fashion at that time," Hallie Flanagan recalled, "inside the W.P.A. and out, to laugh at the Dies Committee." But she was not so sure.

Formal hearings began on August 12, 1938. The first day's testimony covered the German American Bund and, briefly, the Silver Shirts. Over the next four months, the committee would turn its attention to fascist groups only sporadically. Its default target was the left. So brazen was its fixation that Samuel Dickstein, the committee's informal co-founder, turned against it, while *Social Justice*, magazine of the increasingly anti-Semitic Father Coughlin, named Dies "Man of the Week."

Most subsequent testimony was a frenzy of red-baiting, carried out by volunteer witnesses who hurled charges at the CIO and the ACLU, at the governors of Michigan and Minnesota, at the Department of Labor, at steelworkers in Akron and autoworkers in Flint, at the Hollywood film industry (a crusade carried on by later iterations of the committee), at the Indian Bureau, at the Farmer-Labor Party, at Harold Ickes and Frances Perkins and Harry Hopkins, at the National Labor Relations Board, and at the union leaders Harry Bridges and John L. Lewis. One witness, a right-wing magazine editor named Walter S. Steele, served up a real bonanza. He was chair of the American Coalition Committee on National Security (representing 114 "patriotic associations") and had appeared before the earlier Fish and McCormack committees. To the Dies Committee he offered a list of 640 organizations that were either infiltrated or controlled by communists, or in harmony with "communistic" goals—including Catholic peace groups, pretty much all pacifists, the Boy Scouts, and the Camp Fire Girls.

Through it all, Dies reiterated his warnings about fairness. He urged witnesses to avoid baseless smears. But he otherwise let the torrent roll forth while he leaned back and smoked cigars. J. Parnell Thomas, meanwhile, energetically tried to connect every aspect of the New Deal to an international communist conspiracy.

As the hearings unfolded, the Dies Committee began to resemble a right-wing, bizarro version of another highly visible committee, chaired by Robert M. La Follette, Jr., at that moment carrying out its work in the Senate. Beginning in 1936, the La Follette Committee on Civil Liberties investigated the repression of the labor movement, gathering information on strikebreaking, private police forces, espionage, munitions stockpiled by companies, and assorted acts of violence. (*The Labor Spy Racket*, a popular account of the committee's findings, was published by the socialist journalist and political economist Leo Huberman in 1937, while hearings were ongoing.) The two committees did not merely work in parallel; at points, Dies's witnesses lobbed charges against La Follette's committee, while the congressmen circled around the idea of investigating their Senate colleagues. And the distinction between them was not only political. La Follette's committee operated somewhat like a court. Accused parties were usually present in the audience and could immediately defend themselves by testifying or submitting a statement. Dies, despite his statements to the contrary, made few real efforts to hear both sides and presided over a much looser, freewheeling operation. The task of his committee, he insisted, was to put information before the public, not to maintain the evidentiary standards of a court. He even refused to vouch for the testimony of volunteer witnesses (subpoenaed witnesses were a different matter). When committee members and investigators spoke to the press as individuals, they were bound by virtually no rules or standards. On the first day of hearings, Dies warned, "It is easy to 'smear' someone's name or reputation by unsupported charges or an unjustified attack, but it is difficult to repair the damage that has been done." His own proceedings proved him right.

A cautious Roosevelt administration at first kept its distance from the committee. There was an early dispute over whether federal agencies, including the WPA, would assist the committee by assigning investigators and other staff, as had been the case with La Follette's committee. When the administration declined, citing different circumstances, Dies cried discrimination. Even when the committee attacked the cabinet secretaries Frances Perkins and Harold Ickes, along with Harry Hopkins, the administration sat by. But Dies crossed a line when he targeted Democratic (and Farmer-Labor Party) politicians in California, Minnesota, and Michigan just before the midterm elections—leaving no doubt that his own crusade now trumped his party loyalty. Roosevelt was especially outraged by attacks on Governor Frank Murphy of Michigan regarding his handling of the sit-down strikes. When Murphy subsequently lost re-election, Roosevelt broke his silence. In an unprecedented attack on an active congressional investigating committee, Roosevelt implied that Dies was a willing tool of "disgruntled Republican officeholders" and that the committee "permitted itself to be used in a flagrantly unfair, and un-American attempt to influence an election." Dies hit back forcefully and even claimed that the PWA had canceled two projects in his district in retaliation. (Roosevelt, speaking to the press, offered two syllables in reply: "Ho-hum.") Harold Ickes, whom Dies had placed on a list of "purveyors of class hatred" along with Frances Perkins and Joseph Stalin, began mocking Dies in public; in his diary, he called Dies an "ass," a "moron," and a "fascist," and wrote: "For his unmitigated gall, for his long-winded yammerings that seemingly go 'babbling' on forever, and for the strange power that he appears to have over Congress, I christen him 'Bubble Dancer' Dies who cavorts lumberingly on the Congressional stage with nothing but a toy balloon with which to hide his intellectual nudity."

Supporters of the FWP saw the investigation for what it was. Van Wyck Brooks, whose literary studies put him at the center of the Americana turn and made him a spiritual parent of the FWP, wrote to Alsberg with encouragement. "It is grand to see that the country in general is waking up to the work that you're doing," he wrote. "As one who has watched it from the beginning, I can't tell you how grateful I am to you. Every college in the country should give you a Ph.D. Of all the impossibly difficult jobs, this one has been carried out with a skill, taste and judgement that seem to me astounding. The reviewer was certainly right who said the other day that the American Guide Series will still be going strong when most of our current books are dead and forgotten." He stuck an asterisk onto that last sentence and, at the bottom of the letter, added, "*And when people have forgotten the rubbish about 'Red propaganda.'"

The committee's formal investigation into the arts projects began with the Federal Theater Project. Testimony dwelled on predictable subjects—Hallie Flanagan's communist sympathies, the subversive nature of the plays, the dominance of the left-wing Workers' Alliance union—but also veered into strange territory. (Declared a contemporary observer: "One of the weirdest collections of evidence ever permitted before the Committee was given at this stage.") A witness griped that an actor was on the payroll only because he had formidable sideburns. Another complained that her colleague, a Black man, asked her for a date, and when she reported this to a supervisor, the supervisor said it was the man's right. (Typical communist behavior, decided the committee members.) Perhaps most significantly, witnesses were allowed to ramble on about inefficiencies and faulty hiring practices that were far outside the committee's "anti-subversive" purview.

One month later, a subcommittee traveled to New York City and convened at the US courthouse in Foley Square, where hearings on the FWP began. The first witness was Edwin P. Banta. He was typical of a certain breed of federal writer: sixty-six years old, his career in newspapers (as a reporter and on the business end) and side career in real estate wrecked by the Depression. He'd been on relief since 1934 and the days of the CWA, the forerunner to the WPA. No one would mistake him for an aspiring poet or washed-up novelist. He was a white-collar worker in the winter of life with few prospects, facing poor health and looming cutbacks.

He was also a member of the Communist Party. He'd been recruited two and a half years earlier by another FWP worker. His party job was to secure advertisements for *Red Pen*, the broadside published by the CP shop unit inside the NYC project. He eventually also became a dues collector for the Workers' Alliance. He made no real contribution to the work of the FWP itself, and his supervisor recalled dismissing him from the project three times for "incompetence and crackpotism." He was one of those figures who shambled around all the bigger projects, reminders that the FWP was primarily a relief operation. In March 1938, other party members gave their late-blooming comrade a birthday gift: a copy of Earl Browder's *The People's Front*. It was inscribed: "Presented to Comrade Edwin Banta by the members of the Federal Writers' Unit No. 36S, Communist Party of the United States of America, in recognition of his devotion to and untiring efforts in behalf of our party and communism." Banta carried the book through the office, asking people to sign it, mentioning that it was his birthday. More than a hundred of them did—whether or not they noticed the inscription or even gave it a thought.

Now the book was evidence before the Dies Committee—along with Banta's Workers' Alliance dues records, telegrams and letters, and other documents he provided. He'd been a spy all along. The committee treated his copy of *The People's Front* as proof that more than a hundred members of the NYC project were dedicated communists. Most had simply signed their names; a few added benign messages, such as "To a swell fellow." But there were comradely greetings as well. "To one of the best Bolsheviks on the Writers' Project." "To one who has found in communism the fountain of youth." "Next the 'Order of Lenin.'" Some of the messages had a smirking quality ("No Bolshevik so fine—so true—so grand, etc. etc."), but the overall sentiment couldn't be denied. It didn't matter that the autographs proved only that a sizable portion of the staff were willing to sign the book of their elderly colleague on his birthday. It didn't matter that the political affiliations and beliefs of all WPA workers—including members of the Communist Party—were protected by law.

Banta's testimony was a protracted exercise in naming names. By his account, the whole operation was practically a Communist cell. But he was sloppy. At one moment, Ralph Ellison was a nonmember "O.K.'d by the Communist Party" and the next he was a "Negro Communist." (Banta always mentioned if an alleged communist was "colored.") Of all the project publications, Richard Wright's essay "The Ethics of Living Jim Crow," from *American Stuff*, received the most attention. "It is so vile that it is unfit for youth to read," Banta said—meaning the salty language, not the racist incidents depicted by Wright, "a Negro radical Communist." Near the end of his testimony, Banta seemed to become confused about where he was. Finally, the committee asked Banta about an announcement, printed in a German American Bund newspaper, saying that he would be addressing a Nazi meeting. Banta said it wasn't true; then he left and that was that. (In 1944, Banta was revealed to be a former member of the Bund and the KKK. After an author exposed his right-wing background, Banta tried to frame him on a rape charge but was caught. "It is our purpose to curtail your spiteful work," said the judge who sentenced Banta to jail, despite his poor health and old age.)

Next, the committee heard Ralph De Sola, an editor on the NYC project, whose road to the FWP was odd and poignant. He was a twenty-nine-year-old zoologist who, in the late twenties, traveled on expeditions to the Galápagos and Cuba collecting reptiles for the New York Zoological Society and the American Museum of Natural History. In 1933, he moved to Florida to pursue his dream: he and a partner opened a zoological garden. But he lost the zoo and its inhabitants to the Depression, so he returned to New York, where he joined the FWP. Like Banta, he also joined the Communist Party, but unlike Banta, he really meant it. De Sola was still reeling from the demise of his zoo and needed no convincing about the severity of the crisis. In New York, he became secretary of the shop unit comprising FWP workers. He was the one who recruited Banta. After a few years, frustrated by an ever-changing party line and suspicious of Soviet foreign interests, he became disillusioned with the party and quit.

Now he was a key witness for the Dies Committee and appeared twice during this first year's session. (It didn't matter that De Sola's public break with the party had made him a pariah and left him completely shut out of day-to-day activities.) He would become a fixture for such committees up until 1950, when even the FBI saw fit to discredit him for making baseless accusations against government workers. But for that moment, his beef was mostly with the party. He was less critical of the FWP and even warned the committee not to restrict the legal activities of radicals. De Sola believed that all Americans had the right to join any legal party—and, as he had done, to recognize that party's shortcomings, and leave. Then he torpedoed one of the committee's fixations—that subversive material was spewing out of the arts projects at taxpayer expense—when he insisted that FWP workers were under strict orders *not* to insert any such material into the guides. The rule seemed so clear and consistently enforced that, "as a loyal Communist," he was alarmed. But the committee had a way of gliding past any information that didn't fit the narrative. When they showed De Sola the signed book (which he, an ex–party member by then, had refused to sign), he counted the names at their request and agreed that it must mean those people were all communists.

That Communist Party members worked for the FWP was never in question. They did, as was their legal right. But Dies was operating under two flawed assumptions. The first was that all party members were elements of a disciplined, relentless cadre that took orders directly from Moscow. This was, perhaps, what some party leaders dreamed would come to pass. And yet the reality was far more underwhelming. Thousands of people passed in and out of "membership," especially in the early half of the thirties. Dropouts were so common and rosters so mismanaged that even the Comintern complained. Membership cards were lost; new recruits might pay dues once, twice, or not at all, and then disappear. "A good many people come in for one reason or another," said De Sola during his testimony, "and a good many people leave for one reason or another." For a party that asked a tremendous amount from its new members, and that involved considerable risk for those who stuck around, a high turnover was expected. It also meant the party wasn't the monolithic force that the committee imagined.

Dies's other flawed assumption was that Communist Party members were determined to monkey-wrench the FWP or turn it into a propaganda outlet. But that wasn't why they were on the project. Their primary purpose inside the FWP, as in any shop, was to recruit and influence their fellow workers. This was their intended audience: the federal writer at the next desk, and not necessarily buyers of guidebooks. It was true that they were utterly sectarian (though they were hardly alone in this), that they were quick to pull the trigger on strikes and demonstrations, that they were responsible for some unsavory local incidents. Take, for instance, a typical dustup in the NYC project. Vincent McHugh, the editor, assigned Philip Rahv an essay on the literature of New York. Outside the project, Rahv was an editor of *Partisan Review*, the former John Reed Club organ. But since the days when he'd helped orchestrate a takeover of Jack Conroy's *The Anvil*, he'd become a fierce critic of the party and turned *Partisan Review* toward that purpose as well. The party hated him back. Once Rahv finished his assigned essay, someone stole it from McHugh's office, and extracts from it turned up in a *Daily Worker* polemic against Rahv. McHugh ordered his assistant, a party member, to have the essay returned, and it quietly reappeared in his office. This type of low-level disruption was committed on a regular basis. But the idea that the Communist Party was somehow going to hijack the project was laughable. The Rahv episode, and others like it, was a headache, and it was a waste of time, but the project's work went on.

Vincent McHugh understood this, especially when he deployed his party-member assistant to pull some intra-office levers and get things done. "They used to say to me, you know you're working for us," he recalled. "And I'd say, we'll see who's working for who." He might have quoted John L. Lewis's remark about communist organizers in the CIO: "Who gets the bird, the hunter or the dog?" It was possible, in other words, to see party members as a resource for the project, a concentration of disciplined workers whose efforts could be harnessed toward the FWP's own ends. (The "bird," in this case, was a published guidebook.) Things didn't always develop that way, but sometimes they did. "The Communists were out to make this thing work, for reasons of their own," said an editor on the DC staff.

And if Dies and other critics found material in the guidebooks that resembled the party line, it was because the party had positioned itself as the left flank of the New Deal coalition. By the time of Dies's hearings, a broad swath of Americans had taken up a shared aesthetic and political sensibility that was, basically, social democratic, anti-fascist, and pluralist. This wasn't the result of CP infiltration but a spontaneous response to the crisis of the Depression, the rise of fascism, and the appeal of reforms implemented by the Roosevelt administration. The party, during the Popular Front era, merely chose to reflect that sensibility. So if the American Guides and other FWP publications carried a whiff of Popular Frontism, it was no wonder—run-of-the-mill liberals, trade unionists, African Americans, intellectuals, rank and file Democrats, progressive Republicans, and countless other Americans were thinking along similar lines. The FWP's leadership, though careful when it came to partisan politics, was never bashful about aligning with this loose and expansive movement, at least when it came to its values and its vision for the country.

And so, as expected, Dies circled closer to that leadership: Alsberg and the national staff. In executive session—closed to the public because of the sensitive nature of the testimonies—the committee brought in three FWP workers from the DC office.

Louise Lazell was essentially the FWP's censor. She'd been installed there by Ellen Woodward at the WPA after the calamitous backlash to the Massachusetts guide. Although she had no power to unilaterally delete copy, she delivered recommendations straight to Alsberg and other top editors. Her own background was in journalism and public relations and Democratic Party politics; she supported Roosevelt fiercely but was hostile toward anything to his left. For her, "subversion" could mean a simple statement of fact that stirred up the resentments of workers or African Americans. But she could offer only a few meager examples from the guides. There was a company in New Jersey that stockpiled reserves of tear gas, the implication being that it could, in the future, use the gas against striking workers. There was a passage, also from New Jersey, about Frank Hague's political machine and a "terrific tirade against Henry Ford" from Michigan. There was something about a criminal syndicalism law in Iowa, or maybe another state—she wasn't sure. She offered a few murky instances of Alsberg and others making overtly pro-labor edits, and claimed that Alsberg once canned a disparaging story about the IWW from a South Dakota publication, saying "What will the *New Masses* say if they get hold of it?"

And yet Lazell didn't need a pile of examples. She was willing to tell the committee what they wanted to hear. One line of questioning, carried out by Dies himself, revealed his intentions utterly.

"Would you go so far as to say that the tenor of the Guide from New Jersey has been class hatred and incendiary propaganda?" he asked. (Lazell had seen only the tours from the New Jersey guide and had hearsay knowledge of the rest.)

"Yes."

"And would you say that that propaganda would have the effect of starting up class hatreds?"

"I should think it would; at least they expect it to."

"Did that guide invariably condemn business and industry?"

"Yes."

"And picture them as pro-Fascist?"

"As being the enemy."

"As being the enemy of the masses of the people?"

"Yes."

"In other words, the material always took a partisan slant?"

"Yes."

"In favor of organized labor, we will say?"

"Yes."

"The C.I.O. particularly?"

"Well, not the C.I.O., but I should say more the radical element in the C.I.O."

"The radical element in the C.I.O. was championed in this guide?"

"Yes."

"While the business people and industrial classes were pictured as enemies of the mass of the people?"

"Yes, sir."

Dies called the tune and Lazell danced. But her position was notably unstable. She denied seeing any writing that was overtly revolutionary or that called for the overthrow of the government—passages that might be called truly "subversive," as opposed to being simply controversial. She also said that most copy contained little that was objectionable and that, on the whole, Alsberg and other editors accepted her recommendations. Alsberg, she told the committee, gave her no reason to suspect that he was a communist sympathizer, aside from his purported *New Masses* comment. And yet Lazell insisted, with no real evidence, that the FWP was becoming a dangerous propaganda machine, stuffed by Alsberg and his cronies with communists and other radicals.

"Would you say that the Federal Writers' Project is being used by a group of radicals to propagandize the States through the use of these guides?" asked Noah Mason, a conservative Republican from Illinois.

"I do; and that is just the beginning," Lazell said.

"And that unless we get rid of those who have the control of the policy in the Federal Writers' Project, that is exactly what will be accomplished by the issuing of these Guides?"

The crosshairs were gliding into place.

"Very soon."

Next was Florence Shreve, an FWP editor whose testimony echoed Lazell's. It was a hodgepodge of complaints and conjecture; even Dies at times seemed impatient with her. Unlike Lazell, Shreve was not an official censor, but an editor with purely technical responsibilities. She prepared texts for the printers and corrected proofs, looking for typos and basic errors of fact. But Shreve had a peculiar sense of what was and wasn't appropriate, and she constantly overstepped her authority in the office.

"What had you been taking out?" Dies asked. "Just characterize it."

"Oh, the struggle between capital and labor; that the Negro had been downtrodden; and always—there was a word they used; I can't think of it at the moment—"

"Underprivileged," said Lazell, who was still present.

"That is it—underprivileged; the underprivileged Negro."

Shreve objected to simple statements of fact in guidebook copy. She flagged, in the New Jersey guide, descriptions of a successful strike and of the fourteen workers who died building the George Washington Bridge. She flagged passages in the DC guide that said the 1919 race riots were inspired by the KKK. She didn't name Sterling Brown but alluded to his nefarious influence on the project. "There has always been an effort to build up subtly the oppression of the Negro everywhere, in all copy," she said. The Negro Affairs editors "often build up a case for the Negro where none is necessary." She told the committee how Alsberg reprimanded her for overstepping and, worse, going over the head of the supervising editor by complaining directly to him. Finally, Alsberg fired her, and she appeared before the Dies Committee with only a few days left on the job—a future disgruntled former employee.

Shreve was followed by Jeremiah Tax, a young proofreader who reported to her and mostly repeated her accusations. The enthusiastic witness offered to steal galleys from the FWP office in DC and bring them to Dies, even if it meant his job. Dies wisely put the brakes on his scheme.

After all, Dies could get the galleys himself. His investigation was running around the time that the Florida state editors Max Hunter and Roland Phillips were in DC, finishing their guidebook (and waiting, apparently, for Zora Neale Hurston to arrive in town). Hunter wrote to Carita Corse back in Jacksonville and said that the building was in an uproar over the hearings. "A handful of damn fool crackpot radicals are responsible for the whole mess," Hunter seethed. "Some of these fellows would like to turn this country into the land of the marching dead, only they don't know it. They will change their tunes if this project folds up on account of their swivel chair revolutions, and they have to get out and make a living." The next day, the office was locked down while agents of the Dies Committee confiscated galleys and took them from the building.

The WPA's counterattack began in early December. Alsberg and Hallie Flanagan were eager to make their case in front of the committee, but Ellen Woodward decided to spare them the hostile grilling. Woodward was the WPA's director of Women's and Professional Projects, so all white-collar work relief fell under her purview. (It was Woodward whose "southern womanhood" the racist Senator Bilbo sprang to defend after the integrated FWP party at Alsberg's home.) Administratively, she was the link between Harry Hopkins and Alsberg. She decided to take up the defense of the arts projects herself.

Woodward's strategy was to promote the respectability and success of the arts projects and deflect criticism from previous witnesses. Regarding radicals on the projects, she had a solid position: beginning in 1935 and repeating annually, Congress passed a relief act, and every one included language that prevented the government from discriminating against workers based on their political affiliation or membership in a labor organization, such as the Workers' Alliance. By allowing communists to work for Federal #1, Woodward argued, she was simply following the law.

Her testimony was a day-and-a-half-long struggle to read her prepared statement. It began under a veneer of cordiality that rapidly peeled away. She and the committee squabbled and veered from one subject to another. By now, the committee was obsessed with Richard Wright's "The Ethics of Living Jim Crow," which Starnes flung at Woodward like a rotten tomato. How could she defend such vulgarity being ushered into print, however obliquely, by the federal government? Starnes quoted lines in which Wright was called a "black bastard" and a "black son of a bitch," and he couldn't even utter the offending word here: "I'll rip yo' gut string loose with this f—kin' bar [so printed], ya black granny dodger!" ("Granny dodger" seems to have slipped by the committee.) Dies finally stopped him. "You have got enough of that," he interrupted. "That is the most filthy thing I have ever seen." No one—including Woodward, who agreed that it was "filthy and disgusting"— seemed distressed by the idea that Wright had actually experienced these racist attacks, or that he was now being pilloried for reporting the words of his attackers. Context was not on the committee's agenda.

At certain moments Woodward stood firm; at others, she lost her footing. Sometimes her counterattacks were a bit too sly. She read extracts from reviews of FWP publications, including a comment by Lewis Mumford: "These guide books are the finest contribution to American patriotism that has been made in our generation: let that be the answer to the weaklings who are afraid to admit that American justice may miscarry or that the slums of Boston may be somewhat this side of Utopia." The weaklings on the committee were not impressed by Mumford's challenge.

When the discussion turned to Edwin Banta, it left no one looking good. Woodward cast doubt on Banta's mental state and credibility. She explained that, following his testimony, Banta had sent William Randolph Hearst letters complaining that the Hearst newspapers hadn't given him adequate attention—and suggesting that they might be in on the communist conspiracy. (Hearst himself supplied these letters to the WPA.) Woodward also revealed that several years earlier Banta had been hospitalized for various physical ailments and diagnosed with a paranoid condition.

"And Mr. Harry Hopkins has been in the hospital, too, hasn't he?" Starnes interjected.

"Yes," said Woodward. "But it was for no mental difficulty."

"That might be a matter of opinion."

Woodward ignored the jibe and continued to question Banta's fitness to testify—and stepped into a trap. The committee members asked why the FWP had hired him if he was "mentally deranged," and how many other workers fit that description.

"Don't you think," Dies asked, referring to Richard Wright, "that the people who write this 'American Stuff' were somewhat mentally handicapped, anybody that would bring such filth in a publication of this kind?"

Woodward sidestepped and made the crucial point that the projects existed to help people in need, which meant, invariably, that they would sweep up people with diverse afflictions and in various states of crisis. "You must realize, Mr. Chairman and members of the committee, that we are dealing with thousands upon thousands of people who are pretty well licked by this depression."

The hearing went in circles until Woodward reached this passage in her prepared statement: "I must express my deep concern and disappointment over the very un-American way in which the committee has handled charges made against this project under my jurisdiction." At that word, *un-American*, the committee members seethed. But Woodward didn't relent: she accused them of favoring witnesses like Banta who were not credible and of making no serious effort to have people defend themselves and the projects; Dies insisted, as always, that the offer was open. Later, discussing the FTP, Woodward offered a series of positive reviews to prove that the plays were not crude propaganda. When Dies retorted that they weren't interested in whether the plays, and by extension the FWP publications, were any good, but only if they contained subversive material, Woodward sarcastically said, "You know, it seems to me the capitalistic press would certainly say so if we were doing that."

"What press did you say?" said Thomas.

"She said the capitalistic press," said Starnes.

"What do you mean by the capitalistic press?" Thomas again.

"That is a communistic term," Dies said.

Woodward feebly explained that she meant papers "where they have a lot of money," before she took the statement back in regret. But her point was valid: the committee was struggling to invent a reading of the FTP's plays and the American Guides that, with a few exceptions, simply did not exist among the public and the press.

The hearing dragged on to a second day, and the committee members continued to bristle over Woodward's charge that they were "un-American." Finally, she told them that she was done. She would give them what they wanted, and they wanted Alsberg and Flanagan.

Flanagan was the peppery defender the arts projects needed. She began with a flourish, declaring that, as director of a work relief agency, she was busy combating "un-American inactivity." (This caused some head scratching on the committee.) She was confident and eloquent, swatting away charges and standing up to Starnes's grilling about her Guggenheim book and a 1931 article she wrote about the proletarian-minded Workers Theater movement. Their purpose was to make her out to be, at the very least, a communist sympathizer. The result was to make the committee look foolish.

Starnes was relentless. When he zeroed in on a phrase from Flanagan's article—"a certain Marlowesque madness" in the Workers Theater—he set her up for one of the all-time great moments in congressional snark.

"You are quoting from this Marlowe," Starnes said. "Is he a Communist?"

"I am very sorry. I was quoting from Christopher Marlowe."

"Tell us who Marlowe is, so we can get the proper reference, because that is all that we want to do."

"Put in the record that he was the greatest dramatist in the period of Shakespeare, immediately preceding Shakespeare."

The room laughed, but Flanagan didn't. ("Eight thousand people might lose their jobs," she thought, "because a Congressional Committee had so pre-judged us that even the classics were 'communistic.'")

Starnes, trying to save face, said something about how communists went back to the Greek theater.

"Quite true," Flanagan said.

"And I believe Mr. Euripides was guilty of teaching class consciousness also, wasn't he?"

"I believe that was alleged against all of the Greek dramatists."

J. Parnell Thomas took up the questioning and, leaving Mr. Euripides aside, delved into administrative issues. Both Starnes and Dies stopped him because the matter was outside of their anti-subversive purview. In a revealing slip, Thomas protested, "We have touched everything in the world whether it has been un-American or not for 2 days now." ("Not by my wish," Flanagan said.) If Thomas was trying to temper his anti–New Deal animus, it nonetheless spilled out like a slippery fish from under his hat. Only Thomas could hear Flanagan describe the FTP—"national in scope and regional in emphasis and democratic in American attitude"—and actually splutter, "Democratic!"

He could not even pretend to be anything but his ultra-partisan self. Dies, meanwhile, tried to steer Flanagan into a confession that FTP plays were propagandistic, but she nimbly resisted—and even called him out for it. She held firm against their accusations until Dies announced a lunch recess. As they adjourned, Flanagan insisted that she be allowed to make a final statement when they reconvened.

They had lunch. Flanagan wasn't invited back to submit a statement. Instead, the committee called Henry Alsberg.

He approached the table, trailed by an aide pushing a library cart full of FWP publications. He set down an armload of documents and a pack of cigarettes. He'd watched as Ellen Woodward's testimony became a sloppy melee, and then as Hallie Flanagan parried the committee with poise and verve. He would try a different approach. From the start, Alsberg was conciliatory and easygoing, almost deferential. He spoke so softly at first that Dies told him to speak up. He retraced his unlikely path to the witness stand, from Columbia (class of the Naughty Naughtians) to his stint as a lawyer to journalistic adventures at home and abroad, and then to relief work overseas and the Provincetown Playhouse in downtown Manhattan. The committee, of course, wanted to hear about his connections with Russia. But Alsberg short-circuited their expectations when he described himself as a critic of the "tyrannical Russian situation." (Starnes, confused, asked if he meant the reign of the tsar.) Alsberg admitted that he'd spoken with old Bolsheviks, many of whom had since been purged by Stalin. Once, he was at an event in Moscow when his interpreter grabbed a passing politician and said, "Comrade Lenin, here is an American journalist." They spoke for about three minutes. The committee salivated over this type of thing—"WPA Writers' Chief Hobnobbed with Lenin" would be the headline—but whatever line of inquiry they pursued, Alsberg could establish himself as a Soviet critic. Yes, he'd spent time in Russia and chatted with the arch-Bolshevik—but he was jailed and expelled, and then attacked the Soviet Union in his writing, which shut him out of *The Nation* and *The New Republic* and lost him some friends. Yes, he'd attended the Amsterdam World Congress Against War in 1932—but he became disillusioned and refused to sign the resolutions when he saw that the congress was dominated by communists. Yes, he knew Emma Goldman—but they were casual acquaintances who bonded over their animus to the repressive

Soviet state. "We quarreled all the time, bitterly, because I did not believe in violent revolution—a quarrel that has been going on between Emma and me for years," he said.

All of this was true, sort of. Alsberg never explained that he criticized the Soviet Union from the left, and he glossed over his close friendship—and ideological alignment—with Emma Goldman. He denied ever writing for *New Masses* but did not mention the article he wrote for its predecessor, *The Masses*, in 1914. He was aiming for sympathy. He described himself in the language of his pro-Soviet critics, as "a poor liberal who has slipped." He even suggested that both he and his interrogators had more in common than they thought. "I hold no brief for the people who have attacked this committee," he said.

Alsberg succeeded in building a sense of trust. Dies even paused a few times to thank him. J. Parnell Thomas, scourge of Federal #1, barely spoke. But beneath Alsberg's frankness and politeness there was a strategy at work. He had a genius for compartmentalizing. He admitted to a few charges and blandly dismissed the rest. The NYC project, it was true, had been a mess. But that was an isolated case, a "rumpus" confined to a single office, and he had given it much personal attention, and the situation was well-near remedied. And yes, some controversial material might have slipped into the New Jersey galleys by mistake, but that guide was still a work in progress. And anyway, it was not as bad as they seemed to believe: "a little tart flavor all of the time," he said, "wise cracks about this town, and that town."

Alsberg was never evasive, never deflective. He gave the affirmative answers that Dies expected of him—"You agree those books should not be published for the purpose of presenting some idea along economic or social lines, do you not?" Alsberg, too, believed that government publications had no business promoting "class hatred." But, at times, he calmly nudged the conversation away from the issue of subversive activities. When Dies asked about "partisan" statements in copy from the states, Alsberg said, "We find statements of all kinds that are unwarranted, or overstatements—claims made that 'This is the biggest something or other that ever was'; that 'This is the most beautiful piece of scenery.' 'We have millions of Indian leaps,' and that sort of thing." (Jerre Mangione, watching from the sidelines, could not tell if Alsberg had bungled the question or if this was a bit of sly misdirection.)

When Dies said he didn't mean that kind of partisanship, Alsberg asked for specific charges and then addressed them. In this way he consistently lowered the temperature and blocked the committee's sweeping generalizations. The FWP would uphold fairness and objectivity, he insisted, and he asked for the committee to trust him.

Instead, the committee's line of questioning was obviously designed to expose Alsberg as a radical. Around 40 percent of his testimony concerned his background, before he ever landed in Washington. And when this approach backfired, the committee's questions became pointed and specific—they were looking for loose threads to pull. Even while they had the head of the FWP under oath, the committee made no effort to ask him questions that might explain the mission of the project. No one asked if the FWP had a guiding philosophy or if it had uncovered any lessons about the American scene during a period of tremendous uncertainty and change. No one paid any attention to the library cart by Alsberg's side, full of FWP books and pamphlets, created by people like Zora Neale Hurston and Nelson Algren and Vardis Fisher, whose talents would have been wasted by the Depression, or like Richard Wright, whose talent may have never been known at all.

And so the hearings ended. Alsberg and Flanagan provided the committee with briefs refuting the charges against their projects, but the briefs were not entered into the record. All they could do was wait for the final report. Alsberg was satisfied with his performance before the committee; to some liberals and radicals, he was overly cooperative, but others saw the underlying strategy. Even so, he suspected that there would be fallout. "I'll probably be shortly out of a job," he wrote to a friend.

The work continued. Alsberg's correspondence through the final weeks of 1938 reflected the gains the project had made. The magazine *Frontier and Midland* was giving an issue over to FWP writers. In Iowa, one of the volunteer consultants, Frank Lloyd Wright, wanted to buy an entire set of publications. Things were happening in New York: Richard Wright passed along a request from Harper and Brothers for the FWP to collaborate on a book about the Underground Railroad; John Cheever needed a travel extension to continue work on the NYC guide. In New Jersey, William Carlos Williams turned down an offer to assume the state directorship. Alsberg was disappointed and suggested that he might be able to pay Williams a visit and convince him otherwise.

And someone from the Federal Theater Project wrote to Alsberg about staging his adaptation of *The Dybbuk*, his hit from the downtown theater days. Wouldn't that be something? Assuming, of course, that the arts projects survived the year.

"GET THE WIND IN YOUR NOSE"

Then 1938 became 1939 and Harry Hopkins became the new secretary of commerce. The appointment was Roosevelt's idea, a way of positioning Hopkins as a potential successor and inheritor of the New Deal apparatus. (Roosevelt was not yet seeking a third term—not openly, anyway.) For Hopkins, a cabinet position meant prestige; Commerce in particular might help to soothe his inflamed relationship with business interests.

But a cabinet appointment would also mean walking away from the WPA and its achievements. As relief czar, he'd overseen the combination of millions of workers with billions of dollars. The results were impressive. In November 1938, the WPA reached its peak employment of more than 3.3 million people. It had already reshaped the American landscape by improving 119,000 miles of roads and building 43,000 miles of new ones—plus 10,000 miles of water and sewer lines, 19,000 bridges, 185,000 culverts, 105 airports, 12,000 public buildings, and 15,000 small dams, along with planting 10 million trees. Then there were the service projects—sewing operations, disaster relief, healthcare, education, the arts—that were harder to quantify. The work was ongoing. And while the WPA was susceptible to local politicking, outright graft was rare, and the national administrators were untouched by scandal.

Hopkins was proud of that record and yet he was prepared to leave it behind. His life, for one thing, had changed. Little more than a year earlier, his second wife, Barbara, succumbed to cancer. Then Hopkins himself underwent cancer surgery that left him with lingering ailments and only a portion of his stomach. His odds against remission were good, but not great. Nervy and gaunt, he accepted Roosevelt's plan. ("Don't kid me, boys," he said to reporters who asked about rumors of his appointment. "This is the Christmas season and I'm accepting anything.") On Christmas Eve, he was sworn in at the White House. Some in the press—and in the Senate—were baffled by the choice, but Hopkins survived a dodgy confirmation. He settled into his new office in the Commerce Building, imposing and spacious and clean, and turned his attention to the national economy—as well as the deepening crisis overseas. The cramped and shabby rooms of the relief agencies faded into memory, but from time to time, mixed in with his mail, he'd find a memento of those days: a package sent over from the WPA containing a new book produced by the Federal Writers' Project.

Henry Alsberg, meanwhile, took stock of the FWP and its 4,500 workers. By January 1939, their great collective undertaking had reached a point of maturity. Their networks stretched into every state and, at least for a time, every county. They were honing an editorial process that was comprehensive and vast: researching and interviewing and writing and editing, laying out pages and proofing galleys while drafting maps and collecting photos and driving tour routes. Alsberg estimated that FWP workers had covered 2 million miles of roadway—one third of all US roads, including the dirt ones. Their books both published and forthcoming constituted a body of national literature that no private publishing house would have been capable of producing on its own. They'd done more than create jobs for jobless writers— they'd created a new kind of public arena for cultural work, and a new kind of collective authorship.

And the books kept coming. In January alone, they published guides to Death Valley and Nauvoo, Illinois; plus *Skiing in the East: The Best Trails and How to Get There* and *An Almanack for Bostonians, 1939* with the decadent subtitle: "BEING A TRULY AMAZING AND EDIFYING COMPENDIUM of fact and fancy, designed primarily for the DELECTATION of those who live within the Shadow of the *Bulfinch* dome, but one which may be used with Profit and Pleasure by dwellers in the outer Darkness of Cambridge, Somerville, Chelsea, Newton, and even more OUTLANDISH PLACES, the whole compiled in a most Prim and Scholarly fashion by WORKERS OF THE FEDERAL WRITERS' PROJECT of the WORKS PROGRESS ADMINISTRATION IN MASSACHUSETTS and Embellished by the FEDERAL ART PROJECT IN MASSACHUSETTS." (The verve and zest that Alsberg wished to see in FWP publications sometimes found unusual expression.)

More books were gestating: state encyclopedias, following the lead of Vardis Fisher in Idaho; regional guides and a condensed, one-volume US guide; books about waterways and historical trails and significant highways; a series dedicated to the African American experience, kicked off by *The Negro in Virginia*; a volume drawing from the treasury of slavery narratives; social and ethnic studies; books on architecture and Native American tribal nations; life histories of workers and immigrants; pamphlets for classrooms. In all, they had 450 books in the pipeline.

The story of the California project was a good illustration of how the FWP had matured in just three years. One of the FWP's first major administrative crises was triggered in the Golden State, when the director, based in San Francisco, and the district supervisor for Los Angeles refused to devote all their energies to the California guidebook, as Alsberg had ordered. They'd been working on a smattering of projects that actually had begun under the FERA—studies of migrant workers, California authors, folklore, and the Bay Area labor movement—and refused to put them aside. Alsberg recognized that he needed to assert DC's authority, so, just as he would do later in Idaho with an obstinate Vardis Fisher, he sent George Cronyn as his enforcer. Cronyn suspended the project and fired both officials. (After a massive blowback, though, both were reinstated, with the director demoted to research editor.) California, effectively reset and reoriented toward the guide, became one of the FWP's more prolific and adept precincts. By 1939, they had published guides to the state, Death Valley, and San Diego, alongside a quirky almanac and other books, with guides to Los Angeles, San Francisco, Santa Barbara, and the Monterey Peninsula in the works. The project accomplished this despite a somewhat volatile radical contingent and hardly any well-known writers. (Few of the FWP's notable alumni worked in California. There was Kenneth Rexroth, the proto-Beat poet who enjoyed holding court in the office, but also wrote lyrical passages about California's landscape, and much else besides; there was Harry Partch, a hobo and musician, who joined the Southern California office after a stint proofreading for the Arizona project, and who'd later gain renown as an avant-garde composer and inventor of strange musical instruments; and there was Carl Foreman, the screenwriter who'd go on to write *High Noon* and be blacklisted by a later iteration of Martin Dies's House committee.)

In 1939, the first raft of American Guides—the heart of the FWP's corpus—was finding its way from bookstore shelves into homes and glove compartments. Another batch was about to be printed. Sales, overall, were strong—not overwhelming, but respectable. The numbers reflected an ongoing recovery in the publishing industry, which had been improving since 1935. (Between 1929 and 1933, the industry's Depression nadir, the total number of copies printed was halved.) By 1941, there would be 268,967 copies of the main American Guides in print, with nearly as many city and town guides. Combined with its other types of books, plus the myriad free pamphlets and booklets on local topics, the FWP would have more than 3.5 million items in circulation. In DC, folders grew thick with clippings of enthusiastic reviews. Most agreed that the FWP had surpassed expectations— that the guidebooks were better, more engrossing and more surprising, than they had a right to be. And as it became possible to look at the American Guides as a group, some unifying ideas revealed themselves.

Most obvious was the FWP's idea of Americanness—the thing that Dies found so vexing. It wasn't the exclusive property of whites from the old stock, and it wasn't an abstract notion, bestowed by divine favor. It was a composite, bluntly and unapologetically inclusive. Even when the FWP fell short in executing this vision—and it certainly did—the American Guides left no mistaking that America belonged to everyone who lived there, whether they were born on its soil or arrived yesterday, whether their ancestors sailed on the *Mayflower* or watched that ship from shore or were carried over the ocean in chains.

Less obvious was how the guides carried the ethos of the New Deal. Some skeptical reviewers were won over when they discovered that the guides weren't stuffed with propaganda for Roosevelt administration policies. But in a sense, they were wrong. As physical objects—like a sturdy bridge or a hillside planted with saplings—the guides were advertisements for the successful work relief program of which the FWP was a part. They also depicted the American scene as a partnership among government, capital, labor, and consumers, with the state playing an active role, rationally adjusting the balance of power and working toward a more stable and secure future. Subtly but persistently, the guides showed New Deal projects and policies at work on the American landscape: WPA and CCC crews everywhere making improvements, the TVA transforming the Tennessee Valley, AAA reforms matter-of-factly observed in the essays on agriculture, and so on. The guides didn't need to spout New Deal propaganda, as some witnesses before the Dies Committee (and its own J. Parnell Thomas) suggested they did—the FWP's allergy to boosterism precluded that. But their very tone, restrained and descriptive, did contain a political argument: that the New Deal was reshaping the nation, ubiquitously and undeniably, and that this process was not only acceptable but utterly normal.

The guides were expressive of the New Deal moment in another sense. The Roosevelt administration was, to an unprecedented extent, awash in information. Reports, opinions, and proposals flowed from various sources to Roosevelt and his key advisors, and circulated through the vastly expanded or newly created executive agencies. The president was ravenous for conversation and absorbed much information by talking and listening and more talking. Newspapers, stacks of memos, State Department cables, and letters from around the country flooded his office. He was keen on news from the field and once ordered Rex Tugwell, "Talk to people; get the wind in your nose." (The volume of Roosevelt's mail exceeded Herbert Hoover's by a factor of ten.) And the situation applied in reverse. Roosevelt aspired to be "a preaching president" like his cousin Theodore; he believed that information should flow back to the people, that political life needed an educational underpinning. The infamously bewildering NRA codes, he once said, were important because they got people thinking about the economy, not necessarily or even primarily because of what the codes actually did. He greatly increased the number of presidential press conferences, which had dwindled during previous Republican administrations, and, through his fireside chats, wielded the radio like no president before him, or perhaps ever. Less visible than the briefings and the broadcasts was the expanded federal bureaucracy and its lifeblood of memoranda and reports and announcements, all of it powered by official communication on an unmatched scale. The FWP was a variation on this theme: a nationwide mechanism for sucking up colossal amounts of information, processing it, packaging it, and sending it back to the public. That FDR inaugurated such a program made perfect sense.

The American Guides were deeply Rooseveltian in other ways, too—not deliberately, of course, but in that the books somehow *rhymed* with the man and his moment. This was a president who would invite visitors to draw a line across a map of the United States, after which he'd name every county through which it passed while commenting on the local politics. He had a geographical mindset and a habitual attraction to the concrete fact, the telling anecdote, the discrete image—and the more of them, the better. He was uncomfortable with abstractions but hungry for sights and scenes reported to him. (His most important reporter, of course, was Eleanor Roosevelt.) Rex Tugwell once recalled riding with him and being struck by how the president spoke like, well, a meandering guidebook: "He noted crops, woodlands, streams and livestock. To ride with him was to be deluged with talk, half-practical, half fanciful." One historian called Roosevelt's mind "a spacious, cluttered warehouse, a teeming curiosity shop continuously restocked with randomly acquired intellectual oddments"—which, as far as it goes, is not a bad description of the American Guides.

In public, Roosevelt defended the FWP, usually alongside the other arts projects. Privately, he read a little guide to New York's Dutchess County, his home territory, and was thoroughly delighted. The guidebook pleased him and so did the details, reported to him by Alsberg, of how it sustained the twelve federal writers who compiled it. One of them was Dillon Wallace, a long-ago bestselling author of outdoor adventures, now elderly and frail; another was a World War veteran with four children. Seven of the twelve workers had since found permanent jobs; another three were on track to do the same. Roosevelt concluded, typically: "I wish in some way we could have the story told to more people through the newspapers."

"A SPLENDID VEHICLE FOR THE DISSEMINATION OF CLASS HATREDS"

The Dies Committee Report appeared in early January. The bulk of its 124 pages covered the general operations and alleged influence of the Communist Party, while 27 pages contained a truncated survey of fascist activities in the United States. The committee threw in some grievances against the Roosevelt administration and the press, and a bit of self-congratulation, too. Nine pages dealt with the arts projects. The Federal Theater Project—so intensely scrutinized during the hearings—warranted only a paragraph. Everything else in those nine pages was an attack on the FWP. Reproduced there was a large chunk of Louise Lazell's testimony and most of Jeremiah Tax's. (She was the censor, he the young proofreader; both made sweeping claims about the FWP churning out communist propaganda, assertions based on scant, dubious examples of "subversive" guidebook copy.) Nowhere did the report quote Ellen Woodward or Henry Alsberg. Instead, in a perverse way, it used Alsberg's frank testimony to undermine his defense of the project. "Even Henry Alsberg admitted on the witness stand that he had had considerable trouble with Communist activities in the Writers Project," it reported. "He did not deny that a substantial number of the total employees were admitted Communists, and that they had been very active on the project, but Mr. Alsberg stated that he did everything within his power to stop these activities." His conciliatory strategy, seemingly so effective in the moment, allowed the committee simply to roll over him. Especially devious was the report's handling of the Edwin Banta episode. It assumed, as the committee did during the hearings, that everyone who signed his book was an "avowed Communist Party member" and then concluded: "It is therefore astonishing to find that one-third of the total number of writers employed by the Government in this project were admitted Communists." Read quickly, the report seemed to indict the entire FWP, not just the NYC project, which would have been a dubious claim anyway. (Dies hung on to this lie: a quarter century later, in his autobiographical *Martin Dies' Story*, he asserted that a third of all federal writers were communists, proven by signatory evidence.) But for the Dies Committee, the issue was settled. They even had an answer for why so many communists flocked to the FWP: the American Guides offered them "a splendid vehicle for the dissemination of class hatreds." And yet it was the committee—nakedly hostile to the left and to working-class politics, aggressive in its defense of business interests and the existing social order—that had truly earned the label.

The report closed with a single recommendation: continue the investigation. Dies and his cohorts saw a nation teeming with un-American activities and believed that they could not even recommend legislation to Congress—the committee's ostensible purpose—until they'd taken a deeper dive into the subversive muck. And, despite the critics, Dies had reason to think the committee would live on. Press coverage had been massive and mostly favorable. A December Gallup poll showed that 74 percent of respondents wanted the investigation to continue—68 percent of Democrats and 83 percent of Republicans. (One of those supporters was Evalyn Walsh McLean, the financially strained socialite whose DC mansion became the headquarters of the FWP.) When a vote to renew the committee came up in the House, it was not even close. Every single Republican who cast a vote did so in favor. So did most of the Democrats.

The committee, renewed for 1939, thus left the FWP behind like an injured animal in the rearview mirror. For those inclined to believe it, Alsberg was exposed as a hapless dupe of the communists. Some observers reached a more sinister conclusion. "So you are one of our lousy RED Crooks—a traitor to your country!! Why don't you go to Russia where your kind belong?" implored one letter. It was signed, "A Solider who hates the guts of men like you!" Alsberg, meanwhile, doubled down on his commitment to the project. He wrote to the state directors, urging them to push ahead with books that were close to publishable. The goal was to build up a critical mass of publications by the summer. They even began discussing a guidebook to Hawaii with the artist Rockwell Kent, who agreed to illustrate it—although he suggested that Alsberg join him on a trip to the islands in the fall and write the text himself. Alsberg was amenable and clearly deserved a vacation. But he wondered if the project would still exist by then.

Even without the Dies Committee, it was a perilous moment. The year 1939 was critical as the balance of power in Congress shifted between New Dealers and their opponents in both parties. Two years earlier, fueled by recession and diminishing patience for the New Deal's experimental policies, conservative Democrats organized as a counterweight to the administration (John Nance Garner, Roosevelt's estranged vice president and Dies's patron, helped lead the offensive). Roosevelt and his aides entered the 1938 primaries and attempted to beat them back, an effort that was labeled a "purge" of the party. It was a disaster. After the midterms, the conservative bloc was left standing and, even though Democrats still held majorities in the House and Senate, Republicans made gains in Congress and among governorships. By 1939, the New Dealers were on the defensive as never before. It was a trend

that only intensified into the forties, as Republicans and conservative Democrats gained power and the institutions of the New Deal were chipped away
at or discarded.

If Harry Hopkins had been at the head of the WPA, things might have
been different. He took attacks personally and fought with reporters right
up until the end of his tenure. (When a reporter asked about a WPA road-
work site that had seven workers, with four of them holding flags, Hopkins
snorted, "Are you just making a little speech? Fine." He said the story was
meaningless without context and didn't diminish the WPA's many accomplishments and that, for all they knew, maybe there should have been *eight*
workers holding flags.) In Hopkins's place, Roosevelt appointed Colonel
Francis C. Harrington from the Army Corps of Engineers. He'd been the
WPA's chief engineer and his appointment signaled a retrenchment: back to
the meat-and-potatoes WPA, of roads and sewer pipes and public buildings,
and away from the more experimental and ambitious vision that included
Federal #1.

Harrington ascended to his position just in time for phase two of the congressional assault on the FWP. This was a mopping-up exercise carried out
by a subcommittee of the House Appropriations Committee, chaired by the
Virginia Democrat Clifton Woodrum. If the Dies Committee intended to
discredit the FWP in the eyes of the public and of Congress, the Woodrum
Committee intended to extinguish it. They reheated charges of communist
domination and deployed the same cherry-picking and innuendo, especially
when it came to the NYC project. (The committee's investigators stooped to
planting communist literature in the NYC office and photographing it, but
the chief supervisor caught them in the act.) One witness, a demoted supervisor, accused Alsberg of instigating the sit-down strikes, asserted that Richard
Wright was an alien who'd been retained on the project while veterans were
being fired, and declared that *American Stuff*—although he'd never read it
and could not remember its title—was "reeking with communism." Ralph
De Sola, the ex-zoologist and ex–party member, again testified and was noticeably more bitter than he'd been the year before. He still worked on the
NYC project, overseeing a small department that put together its zoological
series, including the forthcoming book *Reptiles and Amphibians*. Since he'd

appeared before the Dies Committee, he said, other project workers began calling him and his team "the reptile corner."

Only Clarence Cannon, a Missouri Democrat, stood up for the project. (The Dies Committee's two skeptical Democrats, John Dempsey of New Mexico and Arthur Healey of Massachusetts, kept relatively low profiles.) Cannon reminded his colleagues that, constitutionally and as a matter of law, the WPA could not discriminate against anyone on work relief for their politics; he also made the obvious point that hostile witnesses who appeared before the committee were clearly biased. He was ignored.

Forty-four publishers, including most of the largest houses, signed an open letter supporting the FWP and testifying to the uniformly high quality of the guides. They repeated what many others had said along the way—that the FWP accomplished something no private operation could have, and by doing so, gave a sorely needed boost to the recovering publishing industry, while also aiding paper manufacturers, printers, and booksellers. It was a stupendous achievement, considering the circumstances, and no alleged failures of its administration could change that. The reading public and the body of national literature both would suffer, the publishers argued, if the FWP was dismantled.

In a way, it didn't matter. Throughout that spring of 1939—with Hopkins at the Department of Commerce, conservative reaction gaining strength, and Roosevelt increasingly focused on the situation overseas—the administration was making peace with the idea of a truncated WPA. Jerre Mangione got this impression firsthand when he was invited to an informal dinner at the White House. At the end of the night, Mangione found himself alone with Eleanor Roosevelt, and he brought up the fate of the FWP. Her tone of voice was all he needed to hear. "The affection with which she spoke of all the arts projects was reminiscent of the special kind of tenderness that people are likely to express for a dying friend," he wrote.

Great changes occurred that spring. First, as part of a restructuring of the executive branch, the WPA lost its independent status and was nestled within another federal agency. It also lost its name (but not its initials) and became the Work Projects Administration. This rearrangement didn't much affect day-to-day operations—Alsberg sent instructions that title pages now should read "Federal Works Agency, Work Projects Administration" under Harrington instead of Hopkins. But the Emergency Relief Act, which contained the appropriation for the WPA, changed everything. The act was the product of some wrangling among the House, the less-vengeful Senate, and the administration, which was anxious to renew the appropriation—otherwise, the entire WPA would evaporate. Roosevelt signed the bill reluctantly.

Congress abolished the FTP outright. The project had become something like a bargaining chip in negotiations between the House and Senate appropriations committees; the latter agreed to dispatch it so that the rest of the WPA might be preserved. "This singles out a special group of professional people for a denial of work in their profession," said an irritated Roosevelt. "It is discrimination of the worst type." One of the FTP's final performances, a production of *Pinocchio*, got a new ending: the boy turned back into a puppet, stage hands began striking the set, and Pinocchio was laid in a coffin with a sign: "Born December 23, 1938; Killed by Act of Congress, June 30, 1939."

The other arts projects remained but were fundamentally altered. A new rule required that all WPA projects needed to be funded at least 25 percent by a state or local sponsor and that no purely federal projects could continue. Practically, this meant the destruction of Federal #1 and the devolution of the various arts projects to state control—a loose confederacy of projects rather than a unified national one. (This achieved what Alf Landon, the Republican candidate who ran against Roosevelt in 1936, had proposed during the campaign.) The DC office would still exist but mostly to coordinate the volumes in the American Guides series that were not yet published. Congress also imposed cuts across the WPA and implemented a rule that fired every worker who'd been on the project for eighteen months, although it allowed them to be rehired after thirty days, if they were back on relief. That meant, in practice, laying off many of the best workers.

The FWP, diminished and fragmented, had survived. Its director did not. Harrington likely would have replaced Alsberg with or without the Woodrum Committee; after the hearings, his firing was certain. Alsberg was, again, a key target of the investigation. But this time, he made sure to clean out his office safe: he removed all personal papers and left behind only a pair of suspenders and a bottle of Bisodol, which he'd taken for indigestion. Unfortunately for

Alsberg, the committee's investigators uncovered something else: a letter he'd written to *The Nation* a decade earlier, protesting prison conditions and suggesting that prisoners organize for better treatment. Harrington was sitting before the committee when they whipped out this letter and read it aloud. The colonel listened and turned pale. After all the bad press triggered by the Dies Committee, and already suspicious of Alsberg's politics—and perhaps unsettled by rumors about Alsberg's sexuality—Harrington had reached his breaking point. He told Florence Kerr to fire Alsberg. "I'm not discussing it with you," he said. "You're to get rid of that man. I don't want to hear his name again."

Alsberg refused to resign immediately. He demanded to stay to help arrange the local sponsorships so that the project could live on and the remaining American Guides could be published. His obstinacy likely ensured that all the American Guides eventually appeared. When Harrington finally gave him the boot, more than a week had passed since the August 1 deadline to which Alsberg previously agreed.

By this time, Alsberg had his detractors within the FWP as well—there were hints of factionalism and impatience, exacerbated by Alsberg's decision to make Clair Laning, a field representative and his close friend, the new assistant director. But if Harrington thought that Alsberg would disappear quietly, he was wrong.

"The dismissal looks too much like a living sacrifice on the altar of Messrs. Dies and Woodrum and the red-baiting forces they represent," wrote *The Nation*.

"This project was one of the numerous worthy enterprises that were smeared with the Red label by the Dies and Woodrum committees, and Alsberg presumably is being made the scapegoat, however unjustly," wrote *The New Republic*.

"You have made a very real contribution which petty minis do not have the capacity to understand or appreciate," wrote Walter White of the NAACP.

A *Washington Post* review of four recent guidebooks, published in the wake of Alsberg's firing, became a sort of tribute to the deposed director.

Most touching was a letter from Dora Thea Hettwer, the secretary who had stuck by Alsberg through his entire tenure with the FWP. "You were the guiding star of our project," she wrote. "You inspired us to do our best, to do the almost impossible because you yourself showed us the way." The letter's salutation read "Dear Mr. Alsberg (Dear Henry)"—the first time she'd ever used his given name.

Now Henry Alsberg was gone, and the WPA Writers Program—the new name under the new regime—remained.

"UNPOPULARITY AND EXECRATION"

The destruction of the FWP and the ambivalent birth of the Writers' Program occurred at a tumultuous moment. By August 1939, the American left was still reeling from the defeat of the Spanish Republicans that spring. Then, on August 23, came the shock of the Nazi-Soviet Pact. "Dismay, dissension, and that private sense of guilt were spreading on the literary left," Malcolm Cowley wrote. "It was the time of resignations." Granville Hicks, perhaps the quintessential liberal intellectual who'd become radicalized by the Depression, quit the Communist Party. Cowley wrote a long, anguished letter to Edmund Wilson and admitted, "For the moment I want to get out of every God damned thing." In the New York City project, a veteran communist who'd been present at the 1919 German Spartacist Uprising (when Rosa Luxemburg and Karl Liebknecht were murdered), and who'd spent time organizing around the world, was found weeping in the office. For Nelson Algren, the pact only speeded up his break with the party, although he remained publicly supportive. And yet others endorsed the pact as a legitimate tactic toward preserving the only workers' state on the planet. One such supporter was Richard Wright, who called it "a great step toward peace" and said that if the pact stopped a global war between imperialist powers—including Britain and France, which "oppress more Negroes and colonial peoples than all the Empires of the world combined"—so much the better. A little more than a week after the pact, when Nazi Germany invaded Poland, it became clear that the arts projects—and the entire New Deal endeavor—needed to adapt to a world that was rapidly being consumed by war.

The new structure of the Writers' Program, which may have begun as an effort to dismantle the FWP, instead became a referendum on it. Only state projects that could find a sponsor and cover 25 percent of the costs, in accordance with the new rule imposed by Congress, were allowed to continue—and all but two of them did. Now WPA state administrators oversaw the projects in their states, an arrangement that most of them had desired from the start. Their influence, combined with the scrutiny of the local sponsors, meant that the projects took fewer risks and leaned a bit more toward boondoggling and boosterism. But there was still work to be done: the FWP left behind 128 books on press, 68 manuscripts ready for press, and more than 600 manuscripts in progress. The DC office, now sponsored by the Library of Congress (and its Librarian of Congress, the poet Archibald MacLeish), provided only technical and editorial guidance while overseeing the remaining national publications. Six editors were initially dispatched from the shrinking staff to work on the outstanding guides, but as their travel funds dwindled, they made less and less contact with the state offices, despite pleas for assistance. The project, hacked apart by Congress, was withering.

As the remaining DC staff adjusted to the new setup, they found themselves, again, in the old auditorium—the FWP's original home. There was no Alsberg gazing out over the bustle and the din, as he'd done in 1935. In his place was John D. Newsom, who watched his anemic staff arrange their desks in the echoing space. Newsom had been director of the Michigan project; he was a Cambridge-educated army veteran who'd become a journalist and the author of pulpy novels and stories about the French Foreign Legion (one of which was adapted as the 1937 film *Trouble in Morocco*). A fawning article in *Time* magazine portrayed him as an efficient, serious administrator whose task it was to "make WPA's writers write"—in other words, the anti-Alsberg. "Says he with an efficient snap in his voice: 'This is a production unit, and it's work that counts. I've never been for art for art's sake alone.'" (Alsberg, meanwhile, was cruelly described as the "tousle-headed, slow-spoken, walrus-mustached" former director who "seemed a little too pinko, talked a little too much about his indigestion, was a little too slow in getting production started on the Guide Books and other projects.") Newsom's approach was summed up in a telegram he sent to the states, ordering them to rush revisions of guidebook copy: "PERPETUATION OF FORMER PRACTICES CANNOT BE TOLERATED. ALL STATES VISITED CRITICAL OF DILATORY METHOD OF NATIONAL OFFICE. PERFECTION IS NOT OF THIS WORLD."

Along with the new structure, new director, and new (old) office, there came another consequential change. The WPA had previously protected the political affiliations of its workers—something the Dies and Woodrum committees refused to recognize. But no longer. The Relief Act of 1940, when it renewed the WPA for the fifth time, required workers to sign an affidavit attesting that they weren't communists or Nazis. Anyone who refused or was found to be lying was dismissed. Hundreds were suspended—including, from the NYC project, Maxwell Bodenheim—and more than four hundred across the WPA were eventually purged. At that moment, Congress was on the verge of passing the controversial Smith Act, which would eventually be wielded against radicals who allegedly advocated for the overthrow of the US government. Colonel Harrington imposed the affidavit requirement in anticipation of the new law. And yet far fewer people were ever successfully prosecuted under the Smith Act than were purged by the WPA in 1940.

One of the purged was Bip Hansen, a federal writer on the NYC project who contributed to the guidebooks. When he was questioned by a WPA investigator, he admitted that he'd joined the Communist Party—"the political organization which had fought hardest and most effectively against Fascism at home and abroad." But he'd been a member only for a year or two, and he resigned in 1938. He also admitted to signing Edwin Banta's infamous book and to having been arrested twice during strikes at the NYC project office. He told the investigating agent, bluntly, "I will not state anything pertaining to other members of the Communist Party because I feel that such information would make me a stoolpigeon and a rat." He allowed that, if he *had* been a member when he signed the affidavit, then, like antebellum abolitionists and drinkers during prohibition, driven by conscience to disregard unjust laws (his examples), he *might* have lied. The investigator decided that he did. Gone were the days when a federal writer in Chicago facing layoffs could write to Roosevelt: "The accusation has been made that some of us are radicals. Some of us are. I am a communist. And I am a communist because I am an American." That writer was full of pride for "the America that beat the living hell out of reaction and created a free democracy," he said, and in return he got a cordial form letter from a top WPA administrator—not an investigation and a pink slip.

Only two states didn't transition to the new Writers' Program: Idaho and North Dakota. The Idaho project disappeared when Vardis Fisher finally quit for good. It was a testament to his skill—or maybe the paucity of competent writers in Idaho—that the state WPA decided to shut down the project. Funding was low and the staff had dwindled severely. But a WPA official also admitted that there was no one talented enough to replace Fisher.

Zora Neale Hurston, like so many others, was subject to the new rule that laid off anyone who'd been on the project for longer than eighteen months. (The project rolls went from 3,366 in early August to 1,449 after the rule was imposed, although the numbers recovered by the new year, and there were around 4,000 working in March 1940.) She was cut loose, but she had other plans. Carita Corse continued to direct the project, now shifting its focus to pamphlets for classrooms and soldiers, and agricultural bulletins—such as *Tung Oil: An Essential Defense Industry* and the popular *Grow Your Own Vegetables*. By 1941, there were no Black workers on the project and "The Florida Negro" remained unpublished.

Algren was booted off the new Writers' Program because of the eighteen-month rule, too, but he soon rejoined. (His friend Richard Wright had already left the NYC project, in the wake of his Guggenheim award.) He had entered the last phase of his career as a federal writer, now with the Writers' Program of the WPA in Illinois, and found himself working on another national project: "America Eats," a sprawling culinary survey dreamed up by Katharine Kellock. (She had survived the 1939 restructuring and outlasted even Henry Alsberg.) As Kellock described it in an outline, the book would take up "American cookery and the part it has played in the national life, as exemplified in the group meals that preserve not only traditional dishes but also traditional attitudes and customs." It would be divided regionally, and each section would include an essay by the regional editor, descriptions of group meals, and then a few recipes and a bibliography of local cookbooks. Knowing perhaps that the subject invited gauzy treatment, Kellock insisted that "the tone should be light, but not tea shoppe, masculine rather than feminine. Generalizations should be avoided in favor of the concrete." Algren, whose own work was among the least "tea shoppe" of any federal writer's, was appointed Midwest editor. He drew on the rich store of material already compiled by project workers in Illinois and the eleven other states under his purview. He began preparing his introductory essay, a loose riff on the gastronomic history of the Midwest, replete with ballads and recipes. It leaned heavily on the "melting pot" trope—"These are the blue plate specials, the streamlined steaks, and the laborer's lunch pail, passed down an endless boardinghouse table from a brave in buckskin to a blue-turbaned voyageur, from a coonskin Yankee to a drawling steamboatman, from a Negro fish-vendor to an Irish section hand." As if to emphasize the point, the first three recipes were for apple pie, berenjenas rellenas, and blinis. The manuscript wasn't exactly a searching historical examination—"These are the foods of many nations, brought from many lands to nourish one land," was pretty much the gist—but it transmitted unambiguously the FWP's commitment to cultural pluralism. And anyway, it was a work in progress. Among the food-related odds and ends that Algren sifted through was a twenty-eight-line poem, "Nebraskans Eat the Weiners" by Hans Christensen, which began: "Nebraskans eat the weiners / And are they considered swell? / They are eaten by the millions / That is one way you can tell."

The Writers' Program, meanwhile, checked off the remaining American Guides. In early December, 1941, a field representative, Stella Hanau, visited the Oklahoma project, where twenty-five workers were putting the final touches on *Oklahoma: A Guide to the Sooner State*. It was the very last guidebook. Hanau wrote to DC with a positive report: the office was running excellently and could take on more work. By the time her report made it back to DC and was ready to circulate, Newsom had appended it with this comment: "Mrs. Hanau's recommendations were made before the Japanese attack on Sunday, December 7, and should, of course, be viewed in that light." Everything had changed.

The Oklahoma guide appeared in January 1942, and on May 1, the Writers' Program became the Writers Unit of the War Services Subdivision of the WPA. Newsom left to join the army.

By then, the DC staff had shrunk down to the size of the department Katharine Kellock once oversaw. She watched her colleagues either crumbling under stress or planning their entry into the war. She was often left alone in the old auditorium and was spooked by it. "Not a soul here but myself and it's so quiet that when I hear footsteps I jump up like an old maid imagining a man under her bed," she wrote in a diary. Part of the space was partitioned off for the WPA's old Safety Department, and occasionally she would hear the booms and thuds of people moving things. Finally she and a colleague wandered over and were startled to find a skull sitting on top of a packing box, staring back at them. The skull was likely left behind by a WPA archaeology project, but it was a fitting symbol.

Wartime made it difficult to complain about the rough conditions. "A rueful smile is apparently considered disloyal," she wrote in her diary. "On the other hand no-one even dares say, 'Luck of war'—that too might be misunderstood." The entire program was being subsumed by the war mobilization: gone were local guides and thematic studies and folklore, replaced by soldier's guides and air-raid-warden manuals and civil-defense bulletins— anything that would aid defenses, study the effects of the war, or build morale. A new edition of the DC guidebook was submitted to the Office of Censorship, where passages describing government buildings, particularly military installations around the capital, were stripped of certain details. "America Eats," Kellock's pet project, was abandoned once rationing began. "It seemed inadvisable for the government to promote a book on American feasting," she said. "A book on foods seemed frivolous." And yet, around the same time, Zora Neale Hurston's old fellow Boasian Margaret Mead landed in Washington to study American "food habits" for the National Research Council—an ostensibly more serious project that fit the demands of war mobilization in a way the FWP's more literary, ecumenical approach clearly did not.

Kellock knew that the project was at an end and she tried to accept it. Others found this difficult. One of her colleagues "simply could not get it through her head that the Writers' Project was really dead." Another "kept going through the motions, reacting at the sight of a letter or manuscript like one of those frogs who still go on performing even after the brain has been removed."

Finally, she and two other women were called into an administrator's office and given their two-week notice. Kellock was incensed to learn that she was being dismissed before the final stretch of the project, and especially before its last director, Merle Colby, was let go, too. (It was Colby who'd begun his long, strange journey to the directorship on a Boston relief line, clutching a fake note with a made-up Irish name, who bore the brunt of approbation during the uproar around the Massachusetts guide, and who was ultimately plucked up by Alsberg and resituated in the DC office.) "I remarked that I had a hell of a lot of seniority over Merle, also ten times as much administrative experience," she wrote to a friend. It was true—Kellock was as responsible as anyone for the shape of the project, second perhaps only to Alsberg, and, as tours editor, she had a hand in nearly all the major publications. But she was fired nevertheless. She pointed out that finding a new job in Washington was much harder for a woman than for a man—and especially for an older woman—but there was no arguing. She left the meeting and paused a moment to cry in the hall. Then she and her now-former colleagues marched off to the Powhattan Hotel for a drink.

The project was dead. Merle Colby and a few others attended to the remains: the letters and memos and reports (carbons and originals, typed and hand scrawled) that had once circulated from DC to the states and back again, the layers and layers of manuscripts, and, of course, the mountains of rough copy worked up by federal writers, word by word and line by line, as they moved over a bewildered and conflicted land. Some of this material was shipped off to the Library of Congress and the National Archives. Much of it, held by the states, would remain there, dispersed to the basements of libraries and historical societies and universities, pressed inside folders and boxed up in the dark and the quiet—for a while, anyway.

And then there was Henry Alsberg. He didn't take his departure from the FWP very well. When John Newsom assumed the directorship, he sent a brief message to the states introducing himself, praising Alsberg's "high standards of excellence," and saying that he hoped to "earn some measure of the friendship and affection" that they felt for their former leader. It was a generous sentiment, if a little bland. But to Alsberg, who got ahold of the message, it was an insult. He believed it implied that he'd resigned voluntarily—or worse, abandoned the project in a moment of crisis—and that he approved of the current direction, when neither was true. "I am not eager for expressions of appreciation," he wrote in an ornery letter to Florence Kerr. "And, in fact, there were none from anybody in the Administration, except from my own staff and from State and Regional Directors." All he wanted, he said, was for the truth to be known. He'd seen enough in his fifty-eight years not to expect anything greater. "If one is honest, upright and decent, that must be its own reward," he wrote to Dora Thea Hettwer, his former secretary, who was becoming a close friend and confidant. "In my life I have learned that a good fight is worth making; and that most good fights bring down on us unpopularity and execration. You have to get used to that." Her appreciation and understanding, he said, was worth more than any praise from Franklin Roosevelt.

Alsberg was angry but he was also relieved—he told a friend that leaving the FWP reminded him of leaving Russia. Over the next decade, he did the lecture circuit and wrote a few articles and even completed a novel, although it was never published. He mourned Emma Goldman, who died in Toronto in 1940—she'd spent the end of her life agitating on behalf of the Spanish Republic and imperiled anarchists everywhere, until she was silenced, finally and cruelly, by a stroke. When she died three months later, her body once more returned to the United States, and she was buried near the Haymarket Martyrs in Chicago. For Alsberg, it must have felt as though a chapter of his life had closed. And what seemed to lie ahead was deeply unsettling. He watched uneasily as Europe's "seething caldron of hates and prejudices," as he'd put it after another World War, began to overflow its brim. In the aftermath of Pearl Harbor, he reluctantly returned to DC, where he joined the Office of War Information as an editor. But his career there was brief, thanks again to Martin Dies, who attacked the office for hiring subversives. Alsberg, Dies announced on the House floor, had "crept back in the Government"—so Alsberg crept back out. He'd had enough.

In 1949, after writing a moderately successful book on the postwar order, *Let's Talk About the Peace*, Alsberg finally got the one-volume guide to America he'd envisioned when the FWP began. He was hired by Hastings House to assemble it—a huge, encompassing new American Baedeker, the definitive national guidebook that the FWP had seemed destined to create but, ultimately, never did. (The job turned into a permanent editorial position, which he held for most of the rest of his life.) *The American Guide* appeared in a hefty 1,348 pages, with only 86 of them devoted to essays and the rest taken up by tours, city profiles, and regional introductions. He had a team of ten editors, including Dora Thea Hettwer. She was one of several FWP alumni: Harold Rosenberg wrote the art essay and the poet Weldon Kees, who'd worked on the Nebraska project, wrote the literature essay.

When the guide appeared, a writer from *The New Yorker* visited Alsberg in his Hastings House office and found "a great Newfoundland of a man, staring moodily at a typewriter." Alsberg dutifully promoted the book and discussed his eventful life while he and the writer ate ice cream. The FWP, he said, had planned to create such a guide but "never got around to it." (That was an understatement.) Now, backed by a private commercial publisher, Alsberg had done it.

He must have been proud of the result—the book was a bestseller, after all. But perhaps it wasn't that simple. Anyone who knew Alsberg, or knew his history, would have picked up on a wistful note in the guide's bibliography, which directs readers to the "handsome volumes" of the Federal Writers' Project—the "foremost" of all the book series dedicated to exploring America. And, truthfully, it would have been hard to see this new guide as an improvement. There's a bit of the old FWP zest and verve, but not much. This one is far more utilitarian. The type is tight, crowded with ampersands and abbreviated words. It makes for choppy reading and repels the eye. It is dense but not rich, imposing but not intriguing. It's America forced between two heavy covers in a way that is meant to be authoritative and complete but, for exactly that reason, feels both limited and limiting. It feels like a burden.

The FWP took the better approach, even though it was partly by accident. Its portrait of America meandered across many books. It was spacious and messy and distinctly incomplete. It wasn't meant to end, not really, but that was the point. The FWP's work, taken together, less resembled an American Baedeker than Walt Whitman's *Leaves of Grass*—all nine editions of it, crafted and adjusted and recrafted, a ragged and sprawling thing that attempted to grasp and possess all of America and reached an end only because its creator did. A *process*, in other words, rather than a fixed statement. Or maybe it was a statement *about* process, about America being an open-ended series, an ongoing project, not a burden but an invitation—a standing one.

EPILOGUE

There was a moment in 1938 when the Federal Writers' Project, along with the rest of Federal #1, might have become permanent. It was a long shot but the project's defenders knew that federal support for the arts needed a firmer basis than the temporary and precarious WPA. As early as 1935, William I. Sirovich, a representative from New York City's East Village, held hearings to discuss the creation of a new cabinet-level federal agency: the Department of Science, Art, and Literature. Sirovich, a doctor by profession, was a forward-thinking and dedicated public servant whose self-dramatizing manner occasionally undermined his noble efforts. He was known for his flamboyant oratory, on the House floor and in personal conversation, and once said, "I regard Congress as the uterus and myself as the fertilizer preparing it for pioneer measures yet to be born." (He was a playwright, too, who maintained a long-standing feud with theater critics as a group and tried to launch a congressional investigation into their activities.)

By 1938, Sirovich had aligned himself with Representative John M. Coffee and Senator Claude Pepper, a duo whose own bill proposed the creation of a Bureau of Fine Arts. The Coffee-Pepper bill (so called, naturally) would convert Federal #1 into the foundation of the new and permanent bureau, housed within the Department of the Interior. Their proposal drew the usual adversaries, including those who thought the government ought to stay out of the culture business entirely. But opposition came from figures in the arts, too, who recoiled from the idea of creating a bureau out of secondhand material inherited from the WPA—that is, out of relief workers. This was an elitist position, and it didn't recognize the crucial role of the WPA in nurturing, and sometimes even discovering, artistic talent among the dispossessed and discouraged. And yet the Bureau of Fine Arts wasn't intended as a work relief program, but as a grand, democratic expression of the nation's highest creative forces (whatever that might look like). So perhaps its critics had a point.

Either way, it didn't matter. The bill went down in flames. On the House floor, it was openly ridiculed. "I would tender my resignation from this House today in order to take over the particular division that deals with dances and the allied arts," said Dewey Short, representative from Missouri, as he began prancing like a ballet dancer. His colleagues roared with laughter. Short popped up on his toes and threw out his arms as he mocked the very idea of "subsidized art." Sirovich was incensed and humiliated. (As Jerre Mangione put it, "H.J. Res. 671 was literally laughed out of existence.") Sirovich tried again in early 1939 but, in the aftermath of the Dies Committee, it was a hopeless gesture. That December, he died of a heart attack while he was at home, taking a bath. His fellow New York representative Samuel Dickstein—whose anti-Nazi fervor had led him to back the Dies Committee before he ultimately turned against it—concluded, "The work in Washington over the past few years has been enough to kill anyone."

The arts bill may have been defeated, but the question of federal support wasn't definitively settled. And yet the Second World War changed the subject entirely. During the mobilization, writers found themselves taking up a panoply of roles in research and intelligence and propaganda. (Others, such as Nelson Algren, were drafted as soldiers.) The Office of War Information was the closest thing to a successor to the FWP. It was a multimedia outfit oriented toward both the home front and overseas audiences and tasked with explaining, but more often selling, the war effort. It put journalists and historians and novelists into an uneasy partnership with radio and advertising executives; among its members were Robert Sherwood, Howard Fast,

Arthur Schlesinger, Jr., and Archibald MacLeish (who ran an early incarnation of the office). Ruth Benedict, Zora Neale Hurston's old anthropology professor, joined the OWI and was assigned a comprehensive study of Japan; the result was her influential and controversial book *The Chrysanthemum and the Sword*. Malcolm Cowley also joined, briefly, until he was chased out by Martin Dies—a fate he shared with Henry Alsberg. (The former FWP director appreciated his OWI paychecks while they lasted but thought the job was "hack work.") In 1943, Congress accused the OWI's domestic branch of liberal bias and—as if confirming that it was the true legatee of the FWP—abolished it, along with what was left of the WPA.

When the war ended, federal support for the arts was a dead issue. The postwar boom made the question of relief for writers and artists less urgent. Conservatives were enjoying power at a level they hadn't known since the twenties. The cultural temper had shifted, too, and the Popular Front aesthetic was rapidly fizzling out. Even by the end of the thirties, the stream of proletarian literature had turned to a trickle, although it didn't disappear entirely. (In 1943, the year the FWP was shut down, Woody Guthrie published his fine contribution to the genre, *Bound for Glory*.) The social documentary impulse that, to a great extent, drove the FWP's survey of the American scene was giving way to more subjective, inward-looking concerns. Writers who'd once been energized by the notion of a state-led project such as the FWP were settling into an anti-institutional mood—a celebration of total individual autonomy matched by a suspicion of organizational bigness. This was a sensibility that had certainly existed during the thirties and earlier, but was now congealing into a postwar consensus.

On the legislative front, the years from the end of the war until the mid-sixties saw little but a few failed arts bills in Congress and halting efforts by the State Department to initiate cultural exchanges with foreign countries. There was, however, a swell of government support for education: the 1944 GI Bill boosted millions of demobilized soldiers into colleges and universities, and the 1958 National Defense Education Act (passed by a jittery, post-*Sputnik* Congress) poured money directly into higher education for the first time. Since the Second World War, the federal government had awarded contracts to universities for specific research projects, but the new act provided a jolt of funding, mostly for the sciences and foreign languages. Thanks to this—along with some expansive billing practices on the part of the universities—tax dollars began coursing through the entire higher-education system, including humanities departments, and fueled an era of unprecedented growth. Writers who might once have worked for the FWP were now more likely to enjoy federal support, if they did at all, in this roundabout way: as academics. Others found succor in the funds that sloshed between government agencies, private foundations, and CIA front organizations, as certain little magazines and writing workshops enlisted—wittingly and unwittingly—in the Cold War. Such an atmosphere would have made the memory of a bona fide government cultural project such as the WPA's Federal #1—initiated, staffed, and run by the state—seem like a shocking aberration from a misguided time.

The federal government's hands-off stance appeared to change, quite suddenly, in 1965, when Congress passed the National Foundation on the Arts and Humanities Act, creating two grant-disbursing endowments. The National Endowment for the Arts would become the locus of federal support from that point on. Many years of frustrating advocacy had helped to prepare the moment; so had the Kennedy administration's conspicuous enthusiasm for the arts, which Lyndon Johnson, sworn into office two years earlier, sought to continue (or at least mimic). Crucial, too, was the psychic climate of the Cold War: support for the arts was an obvious way to enhance the nation's reputation and project sophistication on the world stage. When this legislation was proposed, funding for the creative arts was yoked to the humanities in order to gain support from potentially wary legislators. But perhaps such caution wasn't even necessary: the act creating the national endowments was the single most popular bill in the House that year.

The contrast between that moment and the doomed effort, twenty-seven years earlier, when the Coffee-Pepper bill sought to transform Federal #1 into a Bureau of Fine Arts, was striking. Claude Pepper, who participated in both votes, could appreciate this as much as anyone. The former Florida senator, now sixty-five, had returned to Washington as a representative from Miami. As he cast his vote on the House floor, he recalled the struggle over the WPA. "The difference now is that it is not so much a question of humanitarian relief for the destitute artist as it is a question of relief for our whole society, relief to meet fundamental needs of our people," he said. The National Foundation on the Arts and Humanities Act, as Pepper described it, was somehow grander and more essential than Federal #1 ever was, even if the latter admirably fit the purpose for which it was designed.

In a sense, this was true. The NEA would direct funds to all manner of artists and cultural organizations from a position that was far more secure and long-lasting than the WPA. It needn't get caught up in the politics of relief or job creation; it needn't worry about anything but carefully placed investments in the arts, including writing. It would operate like the patrons of old, and artists would compete against one another for its largesse. The NEA was not simply an alternative to the FWP model—it made an entirely different argument about the state and cultural work and what was possible at the point where they intersected.

Put another way: For those who desired a more robust commitment to arts funding on the part of the federal government, the NEA was a triumph. For those who believed the government ought to create jobs, directly, for cultural workers—that it ought to carry out collective cultural projects to enrich the nation's social infrastructure, just as bridges and hospitals enhanced its physical infrastructure—the NEA was a disappointment.

"TOUGH IT OUT, JACK, TOUGH IT OUT"

Following its demise, the FWP was more or less discarded as a template. But the American Guides were not forgotten in the years after the war. In 1962, John Steinbeck published *Travels with Charley*, his chronicle of a road trip he'd taken with "an old French gentleman poodle." The book was a languid echo of those thirties narratives that sought to rediscover America by traveling its roads and catching the voices of everyday people. It was fitting, then, that Steinbeck brought along some of the American Guides. He wished that he could have packed all of them, he wrote—he had every single one at home. After the book appeared, Dora Thea Hettwer—Henry Alsberg's former secretary who'd become, in the decades since the FWP, his close friend—wrote to ask if he'd seen it. Alsberg was eighty-one years old and living with his sister in Palo Alto. (It was "a college town with lawns and flower gardens along avenues lined with liveoaks and pepper-trees," says the California guide—a pleasant enough place to wind down.) "No, I haven't read der 'Steinbeck's' 'Charlie,' " he told her. "I hope 'Charlie' liked our Amer. G. series. And if he didn't he wouldn't know a Guide from a goulasch." (Then he added: "Personally, I prefer Goulasch, especially with a good Hungarian spetzle.") He lived in Palo Alto, there on the western edge of the United States—the former Europhile who'd completed an Americana turn of his own, by way of the FWP—until 1970, when he died, almost ninety years old.

Martin Dies continued his un-American crusade—that is, crusade against un-American activities—through several more terms in office. In 1944, he retired, motivated by ill health and a CIO political action committee's strenuous efforts to unseat him. On the first day of the very next congress, in 1945, the conservative Democrat John E. Rankin surprised his party's leadership with a proposal to make Dies's committee a standing one—the first such permanent, anti-subversive committee in US history. HUAC rolled on.

Eight years later, Dies returned to Washington, freshly elected as Texas's new representative at large. One night, he sat down to eat in Harvey's Restaurant, a favorite among the DC elite, when the junior senator from Wisconsin approached his table. Dies knew that Joseph McCarthy had been waging his own unsanctioned hunt for subversives in the press and was now poised to turn a senate subcommittee toward that effort. The senator wanted to know, before he began, if Dies had any advice for him.

HUAC's founder never again held a seat on his committee, even after the Democrats retook congress in 1955. Dies retired, for a second time, at the end of the decade, and died thirteen years later—convinced, more than ever, that his cause was righteous.

Zora Neale Hurston and Vardis Fisher were gone by then. The two of them aren't often discussed together, except as notable alumni of the FWP. They may have known of each other's work; it isn't likely that they met. But, as writers, they had much in common: both were intensely focused on the formative influence of their homeplaces, attuned to local speech and beliefs, sensitive to the underlying mythic potential in the worlds they observed. They shared a scholarly aptitude that infused their work—Hurston had her anthropological training with Franz Boas, and Fisher, his University of Chicago PhD. Toward the end of their careers, they drifted away from their native ground, at least in the novels they chose to pursue, and their work suffered for it. Hurston wrote *Seraph on the Suwanee*, about a family of "Florida Crackers," and then began a biography of King Herod, which consumed her final years but never found a publisher. The remainder of Fisher's life was dominated by an ill-advised series of ten didactic novels, *The Testament of Man*, that were something like chronological guidebooks to the universe, beginning with the dawn of consciousness and culminating in . . . Vardis Fisher. (He claimed to have read more than two thousand books while researching the series and later admitted that it had given him "a case of chronic mental indigestion.") You couldn't say that the FWP was the peak of either one's career, and certainly not in Hurston's case. But their experiences on the project coincided with the most accomplished phase of their professional lives.

There was something else: as the years went on, the prickly individualism they also shared propelled them rightward, complicating their participation in the New Deal's great literary experiment. Hurston's opinion of the FWP is lost to history but it's easy to guess how she felt. In 1942, she published an autobiography, *Dust Tracks on a Road*, that doesn't mention the FWP at all. During that time, she was occasionally in touch with Benjamin Botkin, the FWP's folklore editor, and saw many of her pieces collected in Botkin's *A Treasury of American Folklore* and *A Treasury of Southern Folkore*. But as she moved more decisively into Republican politics, she didn't hide her opinion of Franklin Roosevelt: "That dear, departed, crippled-up so-and-so was the Anti-Christ long spoken of," she wrote to a friend six months after Roosevelt's death. "I never dreamed that so much hate and negative forces could be unleashed on the world until I wintered and summered under his dictatorship." Hurston was mostly dismayed and disgusted by the war, which she regarded as a worldwide descent into bloodshed and hatred. But her antipathy toward "New Dealers" was as plain, if slightly less intense, than her scorn for the radical left and for Black writers who had slighted her. Fisher, meanwhile, did not take long to turn against the entire ethos of the New Deal. In 1943, the year the FWP was officially shut down, he put it succinctly: "In my philosophy it is still better to have free enterprise, with all its evils, and produce a Shakespeare or Darwin now and then, than to keep ten thousand morons from starving to death." Later in life, he'd blame—or credit—his experience as Idaho director for stripping him of any remaining socialist sympathies and even dismantling his faith in public service. He did not, apparently, need much of a push.

When Fisher died in 1968 after mixing too much alcohol and too many sleeping pills, his friends and family were left to argue over whether his death was accidental or intentional or a little of both. Hurston had died eight years earlier in a Florida county welfare home. Part of the ensuing Hurston myth was that she died penniless, solitary, and forgotten. She was indeed poor but she was not forgotten by her friends and family, who organized a large funeral. Her poverty was a fact she had kept from them. Like the time she went on relief and joined the FWP, it was a secret, a burden she would bear, as she felt was appropriate, alone.

Unlike Hurston and Fisher, who'd done much of their best work before the FWP, Nelson Algren and Richard Wright had the New Deal in the very DNA of their later accomplishments. The clearest example is Wright's *12 Million Black Voices*, which appeared two years after he left the project. The book, a collective portrait of African Americans with an emphasis on the Great Migration, combined text and photographs and belonged to the same documentary genre as Dorothea Lange and Paul Taylor's *An American Exodus*, or James Agee and Walker Evans's *Let Us Now Praise Famous Men*. The photos, selected by Edwin Rosskam, came from the archive of the Farm Security Administration (and included several taken by Lange and Evans). Wright's text, poetically wrought and composed in the collective "we," drew on the research files of his friend Horace Cayton, Jr., a sociologist whose long-running study of Chicago's South Side was partially funded by the WPA. (When Cayton and St. Clair Drake published their influential *Black Metropolis* in 1945, Wright contributed the foreword.) With the FSA photos, Cayton's WPA-funded research, and Wright's FWP training, the book perfectly exemplified the fruits that sprang, later, from the seeds sown by the New Deal's cultural and documentary activities.

Just about everything Wright published in the forties, though, emerged from his FWP career. He wrote his seminal novel *Native Son* while he was on the project, and his autobiography, *Black Boy*, was essentially an expanded version of "The Ethics of Living Jim Crow" from *American Stuff*. Both of those books became bestsellers and Book-of-the-Month Club selections.

When *Native Son* appeared, federal writers in Chicago began posting review clippings on a bulletin board in the office. Nelson Algren, still on the project, was struck by the book's power. And he was moved by the inscription that Wright had scrawled inside a copy he mailed Algren as a gift: "To my old friend Nelson. Who I believe is still the best writer of good prose in the U.S.A."

"I'm now hoping I can do something—just a little—toward earning that inscription," Algren wrote back. *Never Come Morning*, his unflinching novel about a boxer in Chicago's Polish slum, was the result. (It was so unflinching that the Polish Roman Catholic Union tried to have it withdrawn by the publisher.) Algren didn't have the benefit of an FWP creative unit as did Wright, but he'd been working on his novel while the project kept him alive and circulating through the downcast and overlooked places of Chicago. He'd ride the momentum from that book and write *The Man with the Golden Arm*, which won a National Book Award, and the stories of *The Neon Wilderness* in between. Like Wright, he'd reached the highest plateau of his career, as far as critical acclaim and sales were concerned. Either one of them might have achieved that success without the FWP—they went onto the project with more talent and ambition than you'll find in most aspiring writers. But there is only one way that it happened, and it didn't happen that way.

In 1949, Wright and Algren met for the last time. Algren was visiting Paris with Simone de Beauvoir. (They were in the midst of a romantic affair that, in certain minds, would end up overshadowing Algren's actual writing.) They stopped at Wright's apartment. Wright and his family had been living in Paris for two years; he'd had enough of the pervasive racism that shaped his life in the United States, even as a famous author. By then, too, his long drift away from the Communist Party had become a decisive break: in 1944, he published "I Tried to Be a Communist" in *The Atlantic Monthly*, formalizing the split. (It was a selection from the unpublished second half of *Black Boy*, which didn't appear until 1977, with the title *American Hunger*.) Wright got the impression that Algren was moving to Paris, as he'd done, but Algren corrected him. He could never leave his roots, he said. His work would suffer. Wright replied that some of the best novels were written in exile, but Algren said that it mattered whether a writer had been exiled or *chose* to leave their country. The implication was that Wright had abandoned his relationship with the American land and its people, *his* people, and shut himself off from his richest source. That was the end of their friendship.

A few years later, Algren bundled his assessment of Wright's career arc into *Chicago: City on the Make*. It was both a dig at Wright and a wistful admonition:

> Since the middle twenties the only party of over-average height to stop off here awhile was a Mississippi Negro named Wright. And he soon abandoned his potentialities, along with his people, somewhere along Forty-seventh Street . . . For the artist lucky enough to come up in Chicago there ought to be a warning engraved on the shinbone alley tenement which was once Wright's home: Tough it out, Jack, tough it out.

It was unfair of Algren to suggest that Wright's self-exile was a moral failure—Wright, after all, was trying to escape from racist treatment that Algren would never experience. But Algren's critique of Wright contained the idea that had powered the FWP and, beyond the need to create jobs for the jobless, had given it purpose: that a close engagement with the American scene was not just beneficial to creative artists but, in some vital and unpredictable way, crucial to the direction, and perhaps the lasting value, of their work.

WHEN THE ROAD FORKS

The Federal Writers' Project is remembered, when it's remembered at all, for that need to chart and possess the American scene. Academic scholars have found, in this aspect of the FWP, a rich vein to mine. The project is also remembered for its books, as objects, which continue to exist, of course—either as rare first editions or new editions, repackaged as glimpses into "thirties" America. This is the realm of book collectors and publishers.

Occasionally, though, a lone voice will call upon us—scholars, collectors, publishers, everyone—urging us not only to remember the FWP but to resurrect it. *Let it rise from the thirties dustbin,* they say, *let federal writers roam the land once more.* Such calls typically appear at moments of great economic stress. It happened during the crisis of 2008, which was, at that time, the worst since the Depression. And it happened during the coronavirus pandemic, which is now the worst economic crisis since the Depression—until the next crisis comes along, as it inevitably will. These calls, it seems to me, are less policy proposals than protests against the way creative artists are undervalued and neglected in the United States. Someone who says we need a new FWP is really indicting the entire state of our culture and government, just as those writers and intellectuals who supported the Communist Party candidates for president in 1932 were throwing curses at the whole rotten system. To call for an exceedingly improbable goal, in other words, is to denounce the conditions that make such a thing improbable.

This ought not to be true of the FWP. It wasn't all that long ago when federal writers did their work; other, surviving pieces of the New Deal (such as Social Security) remain vastly popular. And yet astronauts will likely land on Mars before the federal government again pays writers, as writers, to undertake collective cultural projects such as the American Guides.

So: should there be a new Federal Writers' Project? Perhaps the best answer is this: If enough people, by virtue of simply being alive in the United States at this moment, had secure, good-paying jobs, with plenty of free time in which to realize their full potential, then a new FWP might not be necessary. That is, maybe the problem is not the *lack* of an FWP but the underlying conditions that continue to demand one. Maybe calling for a new FWP is both too much and far, far too little.

This conversation focuses on the FWP's legacy as a model of work relief. But there's another side to its legacy that is often overlooked. The FWP, utterly and explicitly, was anti-fascist by design. In 1935, when the FWP was created, Germany was imposing its anti-Semitic Nuremburg Laws and Italy was beginning its brutal invasion of Ethiopia. The Spanish Republic was in turmoil and would descend into civil war a year later. Pro-fascist groups were worming their way into American society, rallying and marching out in the open, growing bolder and aligning with homegrown variants such as the KKK. This was the backdrop against which the FWP was initiated, the fascist upsurge that it sought, through the American Guides and other efforts, to oppose.

It's a weird and unexpected association, but I'm reminded of the FWP's anti-fascist legacy when I think about where the American Guides came from—that is, where they originated for me, in the old and rambling house in Connecticut, where a set of guides were hiding out in a musty attic, inside their antique bookcase, before they fell into my lap. Not because my Old Uncle Fred was a fascist—he was a Republican of the old school. (He once showed me a photo of himself and a man, around the same age, who resembled him a little bit: "Me and George Bush," he said, referring to H.W., "raisin' funds.") But there was another book in that house, resting on a shelf in Fred's private study, that drew my fascination, and a touch of dread, on the few occasions I visited him—and it.

His house was in a sleepy corner of Stamford and it sat at the end of a long private driveway that curved through sloping woods. He and my Aunt Jane were pleasant and distant and had angular faces softened by age and comfort. Their home was well appointed and fusty, the kind that kids find fascinating and unnerving and boring all at once. It had low ceilings—lower than eight feet—and six fireplaces. The rooms were full of antique furniture that had belonged to the people whose portraits hung on the walls. Many of those people were Boards and Brewsters and Kingslands, long dead. (Kingsland is my middle name.) Fred wound their grandfather clocks and sat in their chairs. His study had a country scene painted on one wall. Another room was papered with matchbook covers that Fred and Jane had collected on their trips around the world. (Here was one of their Christmas cards, framed, showing Jane in Timbuktu, holding a machine gun.) If you sat at the head of the dining room table, you could press your toe to a buzzer hidden under the carpet and it would summon a servant. Of course they had no servants—press the buzzer and it sounded into empty rooms—but in the kitchen there was a narrow staircase that led up to what were once the servants' quarters. The house had a dumbwaiter. It had a root cellar where you could touch the cold earth.

And there were books, upon books, upon books: entire rooms filled with nothing but bookcases and desiccated spider plants. I knew about the American Guides only dimly. I was more interested in Fred's massive collection of miniature books: tiny "thumb Bibles," *Snake-Handling Sunday in the Blue Church* (bound in python skin); *Moby-Dick Meets the Pequod* (which folded out like an accordion into a little diorama showing the encounter between leviathan and ship); one from the Eastern Bloc that contained the words to "L'Internationale" in thirty-one languages; *The Compleat Angler* and the complete works of Shakespeare and *Hotsy Totsy in Her Original "Fanny Dance"* (a tiny flipbook for adults only).

The one book, though, that most caught my attention—and that jostles in my brain today alongside the American Guides, triggering disquieting associations—was a family genealogy. It was bound in withered black leather, in two volumes, and compiled by Aunt Jane over many years. That memory is perhaps more jarring than it ought to be. After all, the genealogy revealed some curious nodes on our family tree. There was Elder William Brewster, a religious fanatic who sailed on the *Mayflower*. (I'd think of him on the drive home to New Jersey as we passed the exit for Brewster, New York, heading toward the Tappan Zee Bridge.) There was the first Board in North America, Cornelius, who landed in 1730 on a mission from Lord Sterling to find copper deposits and discovered iron ore instead. He established a mine and foundry that later produced cannonballs for the Continental Army, as well as the massive iron chains that were strung across the Hudson River just south of West Point to deter British warships. (I live today in an old iron-mining district of New Jersey, whose now-dead industry sprang from Cornelius's eighteenth-century discovery.) There were Cornelius Board's descendants who joined the Bergen County Committees of Observation and Correspondence and helped put down the Whiskey Rebellion and fought in the War of 1812. An entire branch or two lived in Boardville, a town in northwest New Jersey that in the twenties was submerged beneath the Wanaque Reservoir. (I have framed near my desk a faded photograph from that drowned village.) There were ministers and Union soldiers and my favorite ancestor: Anna Brewster, known as "Little Aunt Nancy," who died in 1844. I don't know where "Nancy" came from, but she was called "Little" because she was a dwarf. According to her death notice, Nancy once refused George Washington's invitation to visit him in retirement at Mount Vernon: "She, supposing it to proceed from curiosity rather than respect, refused to go. She was very proud and sensitive."

For me, as a kid, the genealogy was more a source of unease than of fascination. To sit in Fred's house and page through it was like visiting a cemetery. It gave me the creeps. What was the genealogy, after all, but a kind of textual mausoleum? Turning those pages was like tiptoeing past the reposeful dead, past each tomb until reaching the empty space at the end and realizing what it was there for. (When Fred died, the genealogy went to my dad, whose task it was to dutifully log Fred's death in the place awaiting him.)

It seems to hold another lesson now, but by comparison. The American Guides are a kind of genealogy, too. They show us different ancestors and an alternative lineal descent—many lines of descent, in fact, tangled and dangling and frequently confounding. There's a philosophy of history at work in the guides, a sense of possibility in how we might relate to the past and sort through the things we've inherited from it—such as a national story or a method of governing. A conventional genealogy, however, can trace only a route of heredity and law, one that is sharply exclusive. It can't be otherwise, of course, and such things are fascinating and worth knowing. (I think of Little Aunt Nancy giving George Washington the brush-off, and I feel proud that she's my ancestor.) But the philosophy that resides in this approach, at its very worst, is blood and soil, the fascist ideal. If the American Guides offer an opposing genealogy, it's one that is open and inclusive, public, multitudinous. It doesn't plug you into a hierarchy and affirm your place in the grand scheme of things; rather, it shows you different routes forking off in many directions and, like the old joke, simply says: take it. They all belong to you.

A NOTE ON SOURCES AND
FURTHER READING

———————◆———————

Much of my account of the Federal Writers' Project is derived from research in two main archives. The National Archives at College Park, Maryland, contain the bulk of the FWP's administrative records and correspondence, as well as some manuscripts, housed there alongside the vast archival holdings from the WPA. The Library of Congress in Washington, DC, contains a great deal of manuscripts and related research material, along with some correspondence, other official documents, and the papers of Katharine Kellock. There are FWP records scattered across the states as well, sometimes in multiple locations. (For instance, I've drawn on material from the Illinois project held by the Abraham Lincoln Presidential Library and Museum in Springfield.) All of these records belong to the public, and they are available for the public to explore. I've also consulted a number of personal archives, including the papers of Jerre Mangione at the University of Rochester, where his research material on the FWP is deposited.

In addition to these archives, I've benefited just as much from the many writers and scholars who, over the past half century, have themselves told the story of the FWP or investigated a particular aspect of it. Below is a limited selection of the books that I've found useful in crafting my own account, and that will reward further reading. (This is to say nothing about the essays, reviews, book catalogs, and unpublished dissertations—and of course, the FWP publications themselves—available for even *further* reading.)

Jerre Mangione's *The Dream and the Deal: The Federal Writers' Project, 1935–1943* (1972) is the first book about the FWP and arguably the most essential. Mangione, the project's former national coordinating editor, combines memoir and history in an indispensable if occasionally meandering account. Monty Noam Penkower's *The Federal Writers' Project: A Study in Government Patronage of the Arts* (1977) is a crisp and detailed administrative history. Both were preceded by William F. McDonald's *Federal Relief Administration and the Arts: The Origins and Administrative History of the Arts Projects of the Works Progress Administration* (1969), which covers all of Federal #1 and is of primary interest to specialists.

Others have considered the FWP as a whole, but from distinct perspectives and in pursuit of different concerns. Christine Bold's *The WPA Guides: Mapping America* (1999) examines and critiques the process through which the guidebooks were created, by way of several case studies. Jerrold Hirsch's *Portrait of America: A Cultural History of the Federal Writers' Project* (2003) delves into the attitudes and ideals of the FWP's key architects. David A. Taylor's *Soul of a People: The WPA Writers' Project Uncovers Depression America* (2009) presents an overview of how a number of federal writers experienced their time on the project; it was published in conjunction with the documentary *Soul of a People: Writing America's Story* (2009), produced and directed by Andrea Kalin. And Wendy Griswold's *American Guides: The Federal Writers' Project and the Casting of American Culture* (2016) takes a sociological approach toward understanding the cultural impact of the guidebooks.

Several studies of individual state projects offer a glimpse of how the FWP operated in local settings: Christine Bold's *Writers, Plumbers, and Anarchists: The WPA Writers' Project in Massachusetts* (2006), Paul Sporn's *Against Itself: The Federal Theater and Writers' Projects in the Midwest* (1995), George T. Blakey's *Creating a Hoosier Self-Portrait: The Federal Writers' Project in Indiana, 1935–1942* (2005), and Marilyn Irvin Holt's *Nebraska During the New Deal: The Federal Writers' Project in the Cornhusker State* (2019).

Two valuable thematic studies are Catherine A. Stewart's *Long Past Slavery: Representing Race in the Federal Writers' Project* (2016), which pays special attention to the narratives of formerly enslaved people, and Sara Rutkowski's *Literary Legacies of the Federal Writers' Project: Voices of the Depression in the American Postwar Era* (2017), which explores the FWP's influence on the development of creative writing in the United States between the Depression and the postwar era.

Quite a few collections of unpublished FWP material have appeared in the decades since the project's demise, and as scholars continue to mine the archives, more are certain to be published. Some noteworthy examples include the testimonials assembled in *First-Person America* (1980), edited by Ann Banks, and *Such As Us: Southern Voices of the Thirties* (1978), edited by Tom E. Terrill and Jerrold Hirsch, as well as the narratives of formerly enslaved people selected for *Lay My Burden Down: A Folk History of Slavery*, edited by Benjamin A. Botkin (1945). The only book devoted to the work of a single federal writer, as far as I can tell, is *Go Gator and Muddy the Water: Writings by Zora Neale Hurston from the Federal Writers' Project* (1999), edited by Pamela Bordelon (who also contributed an illuminating essay). The "America Eats" project, to which Nelson Algren was assigned, has spawned something of a cottage industry: there is *The Food of a Younger Land: A Portrait of American Food—Before the National Highway System, Before the Chain Restaurants, and Before Frozen Food, When the Nation's Food Was Seasonal, Regional, and Traditional—from the Lost WPA Files* (2009), edited and illustrated by Mark Kurlansky; Algren's own posthumous *America Eats* (1992), edited by David E. Schoonover; Pat Willard's tribute to the original, *America Eats! On the Road with the WPA; The Fish Fries, Box Supper Socials, and Chitlin Feasts That Define Real American Food* (2008); and Camille Bégin's scholarly study *Taste of the Nation: The New Deal Search for America's Food* (2016).

Less easy to categorize are Geoffrey O'Gara's enjoyable travelogue *A Long Road Home: In the Footsteps of the WPA Writers* (1989) and Jason Boog's *The Deep End: The Literary Scene in the Great Depression and Today* (2020), the latter of which considers the FWP alongside reflections on the economic struggles of writers past and present. Readers interested in the story of the WPA as a whole would do well to consult Nick Taylor's *American-Made: The Enduring Legacy of the WPA: When FDR Put the Nation to Work* (2008). Another excellent resource for exploring the legacy of the WPA, and much else besides, is the Living New Deal, an ever-expanding, online repository of information and images (livingnewdeal.org). And worthy of special mention is Susan Rubenstein DeMasi's sensitive and thorough biography *Henry Alsberg: The Driving Force of the New Deal Federal Writers' Project* (2016). Of the many secondary sources that examine the culture of the 1930s, three books I found highly valuable for situating and understanding the FWP are

Richard H. Pells's *Radical Visions and American Dreams: Culture and Social Thought in the Depression Years* (1973), William Stott's *Documentary Expression and Thirties America* (1973), and Michael Denning's *The Cultural Front: The Laboring of American Culture in the Twentieth Century* (1997).

Although not *about* the FWP per se, *State by State: A Panoramic Portrait of America* (2008), edited by Matt Weiland and Sean Wilsey, assembles an exceptional group of writers who each contribute an essay on a different state; the collection is both a tribute to the FWP and a demonstration that, well into the twenty-first century, the project continues to inspire.

Finally, for the reader who is curious about my Old Uncle Fred, I direct you to his cameo in Nicholas A. Basbanes's *A Gentle Madness: Bibliophiles, Bibliomanes, and the Eternal Passion for Books* (1995).

NOTES

ABBREVIATIONS

NARA PI57: FWP Records, Record Group 69, National Archives and Records Administration, College Park, MD

NARA PC37: WPA Central Files, Record Group 69, National Archives and Records Administration, College Park, MD

LOC KP: Katharine Kellock papers, Library of Congress, Washington, DC

LOC FWPC: FWP correspondence, Library of Congress, Washington, DC

LOC FWPSS: FWP Special Studies and Projects, 1691–1942, Library of Congress, Washington, DC

LOC FWPF: FWP Folklore Project, 1936–1940, Library of Congress, Washington, DC

LOC FWPG: FWP General Administrative Records, 1935–1940, Library of Congress, Washington, DC

LOC FWPN: FWP Negro Studies Project, 1722–1939, Library of Congress, Washington, DC

EPIGRAPH

vii *"More public good"*: Lewis Mumford, "Writers' Project," *The New Republic*, Oct. 20, 1937.

PROLOGUE

3 *"It is the district"*: Federal Writers' Project, *New York City Guide* (New York: Random House, 1939), 167.

5 *wasn't a huge program*: Jerre Mangione, *The Dream and the Deal: The Federal Writers' Project, 1935–1943* (1972; repr., Philadelphia: University of Pennsylvania Press, 1983), 9; Monty Noam Penkower, *The Federal Writers' Project: A Study in Government Patronage and the Arts* (Urbana: University of Illinois Press, 1977), 62.

5 *"the biggest literary project"*: "WPAccounting," *Time*, Feb. 15, 1943.

5 *"The work we do"*: Henry Alsberg to Waldo Frank, Dec. 28, 1938, NARA PI57, administrative correspondence, box 29, folder "Edward Dahlberg."

6 *"Project? For Writers?"*: quoted in Penkower, *Federal*, 247.

6 *"one of the noblest"*: W. H. Auden, "Introduction," in Anzia Yezierska, *Red Ribbon on a White Horse: My Story* (1950; repr., New York: Persea Books, 1987).

6 *"I went down for my interview"*: Alfred Kazin, *Starting Out in the Thirties* (Boston: Atlantic Monthly Press, 1965), 138–39.

7 *his application letter*: Alfred Kazin to Henry Alsberg, Sept. 30, 1936, and assorted correspondence, NARA PI57, administrative correspondence, box 32, folder "New York City 'K.'" In his memoir, Kazin places this scene in the summer of 1939 and implies that he turned down a job offer. His correspondence, however, is from the fall of 1936 and reveals that no jobs were available. It's possible that the correspondence is from a separate, earlier occasion, but it's also possible that he fudged the details in his memoir for dramatic effect. (The summer of 1939, when the FWP was on the chopping block and Kazin was halfway through writing *On Native Grounds*, seems an unlikely time for him to apply.) His biographer, Richard M. Cook, allows for the idea that Kazin took creative liberties in his autobiographical writing set in the thirties. See Cook, *Alfred Kazin: A Biography* (New Haven: Yale University Press, 2007), 34.

7 *"literature of nationhood"*: Alfred Kazin, *On Native Grounds: A Study of American Prose Literature from 1890 to the Present* (1942; repr., Garden City, NY: Doubleday Anchor Books, 1956), 378.

8 *"The WPA state guides"*: Kazin, *Native*, 392.

9 *envisioned a permanent FWP*: Jerrold Hirsch, *Portrait of America: A Cultural History of the Federal Writers' Project* (Chapel Hill: University of North Carolina Press, 2003), 43.

11 *launch a New New Deal*: The historian Jefferson Cowie argues that the original New Deal emerged from a singular and unrepeatable confluence of historical forces, making a "New New Deal" virtually impossible to achieve; he calls instead for a new political approach. See Jefferson Cowie, *The Great Exception: The New Deal and the Limits of American Politics* (Princeton: Princeton University Press, 2016).

13 *"doubtful if there has ever"*: Robert Cantwell, "America and the Writers' Project," *The New Republic*, Apr. 26, 1939.

14 *American Indians*: Native participation in the FWP deserves further study. For two considerations of this subject, see Mindy J. Morgan, "Constructions and Contestations of the Authoritative Voice: Native American Communities and the Federal Writers' Project, 1935-41," *American Indian Quarterly*, vol. 29, no. 1/2 (winter/spring 2005); and Hartwig Isernhagen, "Identity and Exchange: The Representation of 'The Indian' in the Federal Writers Project and in Contemporary Native American Literature," in Gretchen M. Bataille, ed., *Native American Representations: First Encounters, Distorted Images, and Literary Appropriations* (Lincoln: University of Nebraska Press, 2001).

15 *many possible ways to tell*: The inward-looking nature of the FWP also makes this, in large part, a story about the United States. For an invaluable study of the New Deal in an international context, see Kiran Klaus Patel, *The New Deal: A Global History* (Princeton: Princeton University Press, 2016).

TOUR ONE: HENRY ALSBERG, WASHINGTON, DC

18 *"Dear E.G."*: Henry Alsberg to Emma Goldman, Dec. 26, 1933, Emma Goldman Papers, International Institute of Social History, Amsterdam, The Netherlands, folder 47. Available to view online at https://socialhistory.org/en/collections/emma-goldman.

18 *"He brought with him"*: Emma Goldman, *Living My Life*, vol. 2 (1931; repr., New York: Dover Publications, 1970), 792–95.

18 *"I am passionately interested"*: Henry Alsberg to Emma Goldman, May 13, 1925, Goldman papers, folder 47.

19 *casualty of the 50 percent drop*: Monty Noam Penkower, *The Federal Writers' Project: A Study in Government Patronage of the Arts* (Urbana: University of Illinois Press, 1977), 4–5.

19 *the One Hundred Days*: Ira Katznelson, *Fear Itself: The New Deal and the Origins of Our Time* (2013; repr., New York: Liveright, 2014), 123–24; David M. Kennedy, *Freedom from Fear* (New York: Oxford University Press, 1999), 153–54. For a detailed study of this phase, see Anthony J. Badger, *FDR: The First Hundred Days* (New York: Hill and Wang, 2008).

19 *signaled policies to come*: So began a political trajectory that would be adjusted and clarified during Roosevelt's four terms in office and, more than that, would come to dominate American

political life until well into the 1970s. For a multifaceted discussion of the rise, perseverance, and destruction of a "New Deal order," see Steve Fraser and Gary Gerstle, eds., *The Rise and Fall of the New Deal Order, 1930–1980* (Princeton: Princeton University Press, 1989), and Gary Gerstle, Nelson Lichtenstein, and Alice O'Connor, eds., *Beyond the New Deal Order: U.S. Politics from the Great Depression to the Great Recession* (Philadelphia: University of Pennsylvania Press, 2019).

19 *Gone since 1929*: D. Kennedy, *Freedom*, 162–66.

21 *"not such a terrible carpenter"*: Alsberg to Goldman, Jan. 6, 1934, Goldman papers, folder 47.

21 *Harry Hopkins made no secret*: My account of Hopkins's early life and career relies on Robert Sherwood, *Roosevelt and Hopkins: An Intimate History* (New York: Harper and Brothers, 1948), chapters 1 and 2. For a thorough study of Hopkins and federal relief policy, see Searle F. Charles's *Minister of Relief: Harry Hopkins and the Depression* (Syracuse: Syracuse University Press, 1963).

21 *"the purity of St. Francis"*: quoted in Sherwood, *Roosevelt*, 49.

22 *a field that was newly professionalized*: William F. McDonald, *Federal Relief Administration and the Arts: The Origins and Administrative History of the Arts Projects of the Works Progress Administration* (Columbus: Ohio State University Press, 1969), 10–12.

22 *"an ulcerous type"*: quoted in Sherwood, *Roosevelt*, 29.

22 *a multisided thing*: Josephine Chapin Brown, *Public Relief, 1929–1939* (New York: Henry Holt, 1940). Brown was a social worker and official with the FERA and the WPA who worked closely with Harry Hopkins.

23 *benefits for Civil War veterans*: The sociologist and political scientist Theda Skocpol describes how this sprawling system of Civil War benefits, while more limited in scope and intent, was comparable to or even exceeded the generosity of burgeoning welfare states in Europe and Australasia. And yet, because the system became too much associated with political patronage, it was rejected by many reformers as a basis for permanent social policy legislation. The other half of Skocpol's study considers a wave of legislation designed to protect mothers and children, but, significantly, these policies were implemented at the state level, with one conspicuous exception: federal funding for maternal and infant healthcare delivered by the Sheppard–Towner Act, which was in place for most of the 1920s. See Theda Skocpol, *Protecting Soldiers and Mothers: The Political Origins of Social Policy in the United States* (1992; repr., Cambridge: Belknap Press, 1995).

23 *By one account*: Brown, *Public*, 427–28.

23 *relief system was quickly overwhelmed*: Arthur M. Schlesinger, Jr., *The Age of Roosevelt, Vol. 1: The Crisis of the Old Order, 1919–1933* (Cambridge: Riverside Press, 1957), 248–51; Schlesinger, *The Age of Roosevelt, Vol. 2: The Coming of the New Deal* (Cambridge: Riverside Press, 1959), 263.

23 *Herbert Hoover confronted*: Schlesinger, *Crisis*, 224–47. Hoover was not the laissez-faire absolutist that he would become in the popular imagination. On the issue of direct relief for the poor and the jobless, Hoover's reputation for inaction is well deserved; in general, though, he favored relatively bold government action in a few sharply limited areas. See, for instance, Kenneth Whyte's *Hoover: An Extraordinary Life in Extraordinary Times* (New York: Alfred A. Knopf, 2017), especially chapters 20 to 24. Whyte's portrait of Hoover claims him as a progenitor of both New Deal liberalism and its conservative backlash.

23 *a meager $300 million*: Worse was that the $300 million was initially presented to the states as loans, not grants, although repayment was eventually waived. See McDonald, *Federal*, 15.

24 *Temporary Emergency Relief Administration*: Schlesinger, *Crisis*, 391–93. Initially, Jesse Isidor Straus, president of Macy's department store, chaired the TERA with Hopkins as his deputy, but he resigned after a year and recommended that Hopkins take his place. See Sherwood, *Roosevelt*, 32.

24 *plan for a massive federal relief program*: Schlesinger, *Coming*, 264. The credit for this doesn't belong only to Hopkins: others, including many in Congress, were pushing for such a relief bill.

24 *Hopkins met Roosevelt*: Nick Taylor, *American-Made: The Enduring Legacy of the WPA: When FDR Put the Nation to Work* (2008; repr., New York: Bantam Books, 2009), 102–103. Hopkins quoted on 103.

24 *FERA didn't much change*: Schlesinger, *Coming*, 266–69; Charles, *Minister*, chapter 2.

24 *Civilian Conservation Corps*: N. Taylor, *American-Made*, 106–108.

25 *Civil Works Administration*: Schlesinger, *Coming*, 269–71. Roosevelt was still caught between dueling impulses—in favor of work relief but wary of excessive spending—and so insisted on making the CWA a temporary initiative. See William E. Leuchtenburg, *Franklin D. Roosevelt and the New Deal, 1932–1940* (1963; repr., New York: Harper Perennial, 2009), 122–23.

25 *Around a million workers*: N. Taylor, *American-Made*, 120.

25 *sixteen field investigators*: N. Taylor, *American-Made*, 120–21.

25 *Hickok's letters*: Richard Lowitt and Maurine Beasley, eds., *One Third of a Nation: Lorena Hickok Reports on the Great Depression* (1981; repr., Urbana: University of Illinois Press, 2000).

25 *"I have witnessed"*: quoted in Lowitt and Beasley, *One Third*, 124.

26 *Hopkins refocused his efforts*: Schlesinger, *Coming*, 277–78.

26 *Jacob Baker, an old acquaintance*: Penkower, *Federal*, 20.

26 *the New Dealers*: Schlesinger, *Coming*, 16–20.

26 *"like a darkness"*: Edmund Wilson, *The American Earthquake: A Documentary of the Twenties and Thirties* (1958; repr. New York: Farrar, Straus and Giroux, 1979), 536.

27 *Baker was one*: Penkower, *Federal*, 10; Jerre Mangione, *The Dream and the Deal: The Federal Writers' Project, 1935–1943* (1972; repr., Philadelphia: University of Pennsylvania Press, 1983), 39–40; McDonald, *Federal*, 37–38; oral history interview with Jacob Baker, Sept. 25, 1963, Archives of American Art, Smithsonian Institution.

27 *visited the elderly Kropotkin*: Susan Rubenstein DeMasi, *Henry Alsberg: The Driving Force of the New Deal Federal Writers' Project* (Jefferson, NC: McFarland and Company, 2016), 78, 90.

27 *wore a black shirt*: Penkower, *Federal*, 49.

27 *"an anarchistic sort of a fellow"*: Mangione, *Dream*, 58.

28 *"Has the brains trust"*: Goldman to Alsberg, May 20, 1934, Goldman papers, folder 47.

28 *His first assignment*: Henry G. Alsberg, *America Fights the Depression: A Photographic Record of the Civil Works Administration* (New York: Coward-McCann, 1934). DeMasi, Alsberg's biographer, credits him with the book's inclusive and diverse portrayal of CWA workers. See DeMasi, *Alsberg*, 153.

28 *"a program wholly new"*: "A Vivid Record of CWA Construction," *The New York Times*, Sept. 2, 1934.

28 *1934 midterm elections*: Schlesinger, *Coming*, 506–507. White quoted on 507.

28 *the front rank of New Dealers*: Charles, *Minister*, 92–93.

28 *loaded up a car*: Sherwood, *Roosevelt*, 64–65.

28 *sketching out proposals*: N. Taylor, *American-Made*, 145.

29 *"this is our hour"*: quoted in Sherwood, *Roosevelt*, 65.

29 *recovery was stalling*: Leuchtenburg, *Roosevelt*, 94.

29 *makeup of the relief rolls*: Schlesinger, *Coming*, 272.

29 *"We are now dealing"*: quoted in N. Taylor, *American-Made*, 111.

29 *The FERA and the CWA*: Work relief took on a cultural component, albeit a limited one, even as early as New York State's TERA under Governor Roosevelt and Harry Hopkins. For more on work relief in the arts prior to the WPA, see McDonald, *Federal*, 18–24, chapters 4 and 5, 348–75 for visual art, 487–95 for theater, 592–603 for music, and 650–58 for writing.

29 *"Both the quality of the work"*: Henry Alsberg, "What About the Federal Arts Projects?" *Decision*, May 1941.

29 *Small-scale efforts*: Penkower, *Federal*, 17.

29–30 *project in Connecticut*: Penkower, *Federal*, 23; Mangione, *Dream*, 46.

30 *Public Works of Art Project*: The PWAP was funded with CWA money but administered by the Treasury Department. It was succeeded by the Treasury Section of Painting and Sculpture, later renamed the Section of Fine Arts. During the WPA era, it was briefly joined by the Treasury Relief Art Project, which used WPA funds and ran somewhat in parallel with the WPA's own Federal Art Project. See Richard O. McKinzie, *The New Deal for Artists* (1973; repr., Princeton: Princeton University Press, 1975), chapters 1 to 4; statistics about the artists and their work are on 27. For an interpretative account of the PWAP and the Treasury Section's best-known creations—post office

murals—see Karal Ann Marling, *Wall-to-Wall America: Post Office Murals in the Great Depression* (Minneapolis: University of Minnesota Press, 1982).

30 *"They've got to eat"*: quoted in Sherwood, *Roosevelt*, 57.

30 *"damn good projects"*: quoted in Sherwood, *Roosevelt*, 60.

30 *Pressure came from outside*: Mangione, *Dream*, 34–37; Penkower, *Federal*, 12–15; Franklin Folsom, *Days of Anger, Days of Hope: A Memoir of the League of American Writers, 1937–1942* (Niwot: University Press of Colorado, 1994), 6.

31 *strike at the Macauley Company*: Jason Boog, *The Deep End: The Literary Scene in the Great Depression and Today* (New York: OR Books, 2020), 14–18. Boog highlights another important development in 1934, when the National Recovery Administration issued a code to protect booksellers and publishers from predatory pricing, instigated by department stores such as Macy's selling cut-rate books as a way of drawing in customers. See Boog, *Deep*, 117.

31 *rivalry between Hopkins*: Schlesinger, *Coming*, 282–83, 295, 541–43.

31 *Public Works Administration*: Schlesinger, *Coming*, 285–88.

32 *law began to take shape*: Schlesinger, *The Age of Roosevelt, Vol. 3: The Politics of Upheaval* (Cambridge: Riverside Press, 1960), 343–61; N. Taylor, *American-Made*, 169–74. In devising the WPA's structure, the president created what was nominally a three-part organization, with three equal heads. The first was the Division of Applications and Information, headed by Frank Walker (chosen by FDR to mediate between Ickes and Hopkins), which would receive and filter all the project proposals from state and local governments, federal agencies, and whoever else submitted them. The second was the Advisory Committee on Allotments, headed by Ickes, which convened a large number of government officials and representatives from civil society who would select proposals for the president's approval. The third was the Works Progress Division, headed by Hopkins, which would oversee the projects themselves once approved, and was soon renamed the Works Progress Administration. And yet, because a line in the executive order allowed the WPA to initiate small projects on its own, Hopkins ran away with this authority and turned the WPA into the main engine of activity.

32 *largest single appropriation*: Leuchtenberg, *Roosevelt*, 125. "The law, which permitted Roosevelt to spend this huge sum largely as he saw fit, marked a significant shift of power from Congress to the President."

32 *"Ickes is a good administrator"*: quoted in Schlesinger, *Politics*, 344.

32 *work relief program on a grand scale*: Public works programs were hardly unknown in the United States or in most other countries, yet they were typically carried out at the local level or on a project-by-project basis. With the WPA and its related agencies (such as the PWA and the CCC), the Roosevelt administration launched a national public works regime of unprecedented scope and longevity. See Kiran Klaus Patel, *The New Deal: A Global History* (Princeton: Princeton University Press, 2016), 83. This was distinct from the qualitatively different type of planning then being implemented in the Soviet Union, although Patel suggests that, taken together, developments in the United States, the Soviet Union, and many other countries reflected a global trend toward economic planning during the 1930s. See Patel, *New Deal*, 90–97.

32 *a crucial moment*: For a wider view of the landscape of discontent in 1935, see D. Kennedy, *Freedom*, 218–42.

32 *a chorus of recrimination*: The historian Kim Phillips-Fein explains how this conservative backlash to the New Deal, largely carried out by business leaders, prepared the way for the modern right's rise to power in the United States. See Phillips-Fein, *Invisible Hands: The Making of the Conservative Movement from the New Deal to Reagan* (New York: W. W. Norton, 2009).

32 *trio of figures*: N. Taylor, *American-Made*, 146–53. Townsend was a doctor whose half-baked but well-intentioned scheme for old-age pensions drew tremendous support, especially from the elderly, and spawned an empire of "Townsend Clubs" with significant political muscle. Coughlin was a Catholic priest in Michigan whose populist sermons spilled from the radios in millions of homes, pulling ideas from the left and right into a powerful brew laced with anti-Semitism. Long had consolidated his rule over Louisiana first as governor and then senator, thanks to a

soak-the-rich platform, a record of delivering tangible benefits to the poor (white and Black), and a flamboyant, pugnacious persona. In 1935, two of them would be ushered from the scene—Long assassinated in his state capitol, Townsend undercut by the Social Security Act—while Coughlin's ambivalence toward the New Deal hardened into opposition and his rhetorical incoherence became more recognizably fascist.

32 *conducted a survey*: Lizabeth Cohen, *Making a New Deal: Industrial Workers in Chicago, 1919–1939* (Cambridge: Cambridge University Press, 1990), 281–82.

33 *bored with his FERA assignment*: DeMasi, *Alsberg*, 154.

33 *launched by executive order*: McDonald, *Federal*, 119–32.

33 *"Give it to Alsberg"*: quoted in Penkower, *Federal*, 28. See Penkower, *Federal*, 27–28; oral history interview with Jacob Baker.

33 *a poor administrator*: Penkower, *Federal*, 20–21; Mangione, *Dream*, 58n.

33 *$5 billion appropriation*: Penkower, *Federal*, 29.

34 *He'd seemed destined*: My portrait of Alsberg's early life and career is derived from Susan Rubenstein DeMasi's biography, *Henry Alsberg: The Driving Force of the New Deal Federal Writers' Project*.

34 *an enclave for artistic experimentation*: Daniel Aaron, *Writers on the Left: Episodes in American Literary Communism* (1961; repr., New York: Columbia University Press, 1992), 10–29; John Strausbaugh, *The Village: A History of Greenwich Village* (2013; repr., New York: Ecco, 2014), chapters 6 and 7.

35 *advised officials*: These two officials were Henry Morgenthau, the previous ambassador and a close advisor to Woodrow Wilson, and Felix Frankfurter, then with the War Department. Morgenthau's son, Henry Junior, would become Franklin Roosevelt's only treasury secretary, and Frankfurter himself would become an important advisor to Roosevelt and, eventually, a Supreme Court appointee—as well as Alsberg's friend.

36 *"When the history"*: Henry Alsberg, "The Revolution in Hungary," *The Nation*, May 10, 1919. He also commented on the Hungarian theater: "To old-fashioned eyes, this dictatorship of the proletariat may look oppressive. There is, for instance, no such thing as a free press in Hungary. All the newspapers have been nationalized and write exactly as they are told; all look alike and are alike uninteresting. In the communization of the theatre, however, much has apparently been gained. Schiller, Shaw, Shakespeare, and Molière largely constitute the present programmes. Would not Broadway be much better off for such a dictatorship of the theatre?"

36 *a foreign correspondent*: Emma Goldman describes this period, from her first meeting with Alsberg to his arrest by the Cheka, in *Living My Life*, vol. 2, 794–852.

36 *"The proletariat has the orchestra stalls"*: Alsberg, "Social Reforms in Soviet Russia," *The Nation*, Sept. 18, 1920.

37 *"journalistic conspiracies"*: Alsberg, "Russia: Smoked-Glass vs. Rose-Tint," *The Nation*, June 15, 1921.

37 *downtown theater scene*: Alsberg's dramatic career involved two small theaters: the Provincetown Playhouse in Greenwich Village and the Neighborhood Playhouse on the Lower East Side. The former, once home to the Provincetown Players, now housed a less freewheeling version of the group called the Experimental Theatre, largely under the leadership of Eugene O'Neill. See Strausbaugh, *The Village*, 108, 115–16, and DeMasi, *Alsberg*, chapter 7.

38 *"you are not very grown up"*: Goldman to Alsberg, Jan. 7, 1930, Goldman Papers, folder 47.

38 *"Love is a dead cigarette"*: Alsberg to Goldman, July 6, 1931, and Goldman to Alsberg, Aug. 17, 1931, Goldman Papers, folder 47.

39 *"We worked like mad"*: Hallie Flanagan, *Arena* (New York: Duell, Sloan and Pearce, 1940), 42.

39 *"What is your gripe?"*: quoted in Mangione, *Dream*, 193.

40 *internal WPA proposal*: Penkower, *Federal*, 27.

40 *an old theater*: John DeFerrari, "The Short Happy Life of the Washington Auditorium," Dec. 1, 2014, http://www.streetsofwashington.com/2014/12/the-short-happy-life-of-washington.html.

40 *The theater itself*: Mangione, *Dream*, 70; Penkower, *Federal*, 37.

41 *the journalist Ernie Pyle*: Martha M. Hamilton, "Convention Centers," *The Washington Post*, July 21, 1977.

41 *what to make of their director*: Mangione, *Dream*, 6, 16; Penkower, *Federal*, 20.

41 *Dora Thea Hettwer*: Mangione, *Dream*, 70.

41 *Reed Harris*: Mangione, *Dream*, 59–60; Penkower, *Federal*, 20.

42 *George Cronyn*: Mangione, *Dream*, 59; Penkower, *Federal*, 24; McDonald, *Federal*, 667–68.

42 *belonged to Evalyn Walsh McLean*: Kent Boese, "Lost Washington: The McLean House," *Greater Greater Washington*, https://ggwash.org/view/2176/lost-washington-the-mclean-house; Sarah Booth Conroy, "Hope & Despair: The 'Curse' of the Diamond," *The Washington Post*, Sept. 29, 1997.

42 *drifted through the mammoth rooms*: Mangione, *Dream*, 70–72; Penkower, *Federal*, 37–38.

43 *renting a room*: Jerre Mangione, *An Ethnic at Large: A Memoir of America in the Thirties and Forties* (1978; repr., Syracuse: Syracuse University Press, 2001), 215.

43 *lowly New Deal bureaucrats*: Leuchtenberg, *Roosevelt*, 177.

43 *growing numbers of white-collar workers*: Penkower, *Federal*, 14.

43 *"Don't ever forget"*: quoted in McDonald, *Federal*, 32.

43 *"near writers"*: Mangione, *Dream*, 48.

44 *strict hiring quota*: Penkower, *Federal*, 56–57. The non-relief quota was sometimes expanded temporarily, depending on the needs of a particular state project.

44 *"I finally went on relief"*: Studs Terkel, *Hard Times: An Oral History of the Great Depression* (New York: Pantheon Books, 1970), 422. The speaker is identified as Ward James.

44 Relief Blues: O. Louis Guglielmi, *Relief Blues*, ca. 1938, tempera on fiberboard, Smithsonian American Art Museum, Transfer from General Services Administration, 1971.447.34, https://americanart.si.edu/artwork/relief-blues-9726.

45 *some dubious applicants*: Mangione, *Dream*, 157, 84; Bernard DeVoto, "New England via W.P.A.," *The Saturday Review of Literature*, May 14, 1938; Reed Harris to Leon Pearson, Nov. 1, 1935, NARA PC37, box 0471, folder "211.7 N–Z"; Drew Pearson and Robert S. Allen, "The Washington Merry-Go-Round," Dec. 8, 1935, American University Library, Special Collections.

45 *"if we made it a rule"*: quoted in Mangione, *Dream*, 81.

45 *the poet Marianne Moore*: N. Taylor, *American-Made*, 292.

45 *fielded similar proposals*: Penkower, *Federal*, 18, 23–24; McDonald, *Federal*, 657–58.

46 *the timing was right*: Mangione, *Dream*, 46; Penkower, *Federal*, 22; Wendy Griswold, *American Guides: The Federal Writers' Project and the Casting of American Culture* (Chicago: University of Chicago Press, 2016), 48.

46 *Kellock's job*: assorted field reports, LOC KP, folder "Dept. of Agriculture Resettlement Adm. 1935–36." On the Resettlement Administration, see Schlesinger, *Coming*, 369–76.

46 *commercial publishers*: Reed Harris memo to Oliver Griswold, "The Kellocks," February 15, 1936, NARA PC37, box 0470, folder "Katharine Kellock."

46 *there was a demand*: Griswold, *American*, 73–84, 160.

46 *"Iconography is for the birds"*: quoted in Penkower, *Federal*, 22.

46 *Kellock left*: Mangione, *Dream*, 63–66; Penkower, *Federal*, 22; Christine Bold, *The WPA Guides: Mapping America* (Jackson: University Press of Mississippi, 1999), 67–70. Chapter 4 of Bold's *The WPA Guides* is an extended analysis of Kellock's thinking and the three books issued by the FWP under her direction: *U.S. One*, *The Ocean Highway*, and *The Oregon Trail*.

47 *"small tornado of a woman"*: Mangione, *Dream*, 66. The colleague was Mangione, who worked in DC alongside Kellock as the national coordinating editor.

47 *separate guides*: Penkower, *Federal*, 30.

47 *the goal of a single, massive guide*: The idea persisted in office correspondence and in letters from WPA officials. See, for instance, Joseph Gaer memo to Henry Alsberg, Sept. 14, 1938, NARA PC37, box 0469, folder "211.7 AAAA, 2 of 2."

47 *American Baedeker*: Griswold, *American*, 62–64, 70.

48 *issued a burst of missives*: assorted correspondence, NARA PI57, Alsberg papers, box 1, folders "H. E. Greene" and "Special Contacts in States and Regions."

48 *American Guide Manual*: "The American Guide Manual," Oct. 1935, LOC FWPC, box A7, folder 6.

49 *supplementary instructions*: assorted correspondence, LOC FWPC, box A7, folders 6 to 9, and box A8, folders 1 and 2.

50 *ensnared in a scandal*: Reed Harris memo to Oliver Griswold, "The Kellocks," Feb. 15, 1936, and assorted materials, NARA PC37, box 0470, folder "Katharine Kellock."

50 *a liaison between DC*: McDonald, *Federal*, 675.

50 *recognized by the Roosevelt administration*: For an overview of this development, see Patel, *New Deal*, 139–145.

50 *offered a job*: Harold Kellock clarified this in a letter to Cordell Hull, the secretary of state, asserting that he did not initiate press releases or make any public statements as a spokesperson or publicist but only dealt with incoming material from US sources. See Harold Kellock to Secretary of State [Hull], Sept. 12, 1938, LOC KP, folder "Dies Committee, 1935–44 and U.D."

51 *a select group*: Some of the other editors included Roderick Seidenberg, an architect who'd designed the New Yorker hotel and would handle art and architecture; Waldo Browne, who'd edited *The Dial* and the literary section of *The Nation* and would handle literature; and, later, Morton Royce, a freelance scholar with double PhDs from Columbia who would handle social-ethnic studies. See Mangione, *Dream*, 61–62, 277–78. For more about John Lomax and his replacement as folklore editor by Benjamin Botkin, see chapter 4.

51 *"Differences in Form and Content"*: Kellock memo to Reed Harris, "Differences in Form and Content of Different Types of Books," undated, NARA PI57, Alsberg papers, box 1, folder "H. G. Alsberg, G. W. Cronyn, and Reed Harris."

51 *"It isn't a guidebook"*: Bernard DeVoto, *The Saturday Review of Literature*, Sept. 25, 1937.

52 *"The tour form"*: Alsberg quoted in McDonald, *Federal*, 694.

52 *she envisioned a network*: Kellock memo to Alsberg, "Tour System in State Guides," June 14, 1937, NARA PI57, Gaer papers, box 2, folder "Washington (Folder #3)"; Kellock memo to Alsberg, "Defects in Present Approach to the Guidebook," Feb. 18, 1936, NARA PI57, field reports, box 1, folder "Kellock, Dist. of Col."

52 *one and a half assistants*: Kellock to Grace Kellogg, May 8, 1937, NARA PI57, Alsberg papers, box 2, folder "Miscellaneous (Folder #3)."

52 *"posing as little tin gods"*: Harris memo to Kellock, "Phrasing of Letters and Comments," Feb. 17, 1937, NARA PI57, Cronyn papers, box 2, folder "Instructions (Folder #1)."

53 *"no escaping the conclusion"*: Cronyn memo to McClure and Baker, Sept. 18, 1935, NARA PC37, box 0470, folder "B–C."

53 *"snob appeal"*: Harris memo to Woodward, July 2, 1936, NARA PC37, box 0469, folder "211.7 AAAA, 2 of 2."

53 *"must pay 2600"*: Alsberg and Cronyn phone transcript, Oct. 14, 1935, NARA PI57, Alsberg papers, box 1, folder "H. G. Alsberg, G. W. Cronyn, and Reed Harris."

54 *his dedication to the work*: Mangione, *Dream*, 227.

54 *"I never would have believed"*: Goldman to Alsberg, Nov. 19, 1935, Goldman Papers, folder 47.

54 *Every single sentence*: McDonald, *Federal*, 224.

54 *One particularly insouciant report*: George Beck, weekly report for Mar. 21 [no year], NARA PI57, Cronyn papers, box 2, folder "Instructions (Folder #2)."

55 *expressed her feelings in verse*: Mangione, *Dream*, 138–40.

TOUR TWO: VARDIS FISHER, IDAHO

57 *"representative of his generation"*: Vincent McHugh audio interview, Jerre Mangione papers, D.245, Rare Books, Special Collections, and Preservation, River Campus Libraries, University of Rochester, box 149, folder 34.

57 *Up until that period*: Michael Kammen, *Mystic Chords of Memory: The Transformation of Tradition in American Culture* (New York: Alfred A. Knopf, 1991), chapter 2; Jefferson quoted on 42.

58 *From roughly the 1870s*: Kammen examines this period, c. 1870 to 1915, in great detail in part 2 of *Mystic Chords of Memory*.

58 *continued apace into the 1910s*: For c. 1915 to 1945, see Kammen, *Mystic*, part 3. Many others have taken up aspects of this trend in the context of the thirties: see for instance, see Richard H. Pells, *Radical Visions and American Dreams: Culture and Social Thought in the Depression Years* (New York: Harper and Row, 1973); William Stott, *Documentary Expression and Thirties America* (1973; repr., Chicago: University of Chicago Press, 1986); Michael Denning, *The Cultural Front: The Laboring of American Culture in the Twentieth Century* (1997; repr., London: Verso, 2010); Morris Dickstein, *Dancing in the Dark: A Cultural History of the Great Depression* (New York: W. W. Norton, 2009); and chapter 15 of Alfred Kazin, *On Native Grounds: A Study of American Prose Literature from 1890 to the Present* (1942; repr., Garden City, NY: Doubleday Anchor Books, 1956).

58 *"I have fallen in love"*: Benét's poem was continentally inclusive (or perhaps just sloppy): Medicine Hat is in Canada.

59 *the act of discovering*: "It is difficult to render an accurate account of the frequency with which that ubiquitous word 'discovery' recurred during these two decades," as Michael Kammen put it. See Kammen, *Mystic*, 303.

59 *since at least the 1910s*: For an overview of Brooks, Bourne, Mumford, and Frank, see Casey Nelson Blake, *Beloved Community: The Cultural Criticism of Randolph Bourne, Van Wyck Brooks, Waldo Frank, and Lewis Mumford* (Chapel Hill: University of North Carolina Press, 1990).

59 *joined by another type*: This impulse is the overarching subject of Stott's *Documentary Expression and Thirties America*, but see chapters 10 to 13 in particular, and the excellent concluding section of *Let Us Now Praise Famous Men*. See also Pells, *Radical*, 195–201.

60 *writers were becoming radicalized*: Daniel Aaron, *Writers on the Left: Episodes in American Literary Communism* (1961; repr., New York: Columbia University Press, 1992), 161–98. Alternatively, Richard H. Pells argues for a deeper continuity between the two periods: that writers and intellectuals in the thirties tended to amplify ideas about American cultural and spiritual decay that they'd been working out in the twenties. See Pells, *Radical*, 98–100.

60 *Alsberg, in Paris at the time*: Susan Rubenstein DeMasi, *Henry Alsberg: The Driving Force of the New Deal Federal Writers' Project* (Jefferson, NC: McFarland and Company, 2016), 122.

60 *statement urging a vote*: Aaron, *Writers*, 183, 196–98; Malcolm Cowley, *The Dream of the Golden Mountains: Remembering the 1930s* (1980; repr., New York: Penguin Books, 1981), 112–13; and Franklin Folsom, *Days of Anger, Days of Hope: A Memoir of the League of American Writers, 1937–1942* (Niwot: University Press of Colorado, 1994), 337.

61 *"As the months passed"*: Cowley, *Dream*, 15.

61 *in his 1934 book*: Malcolm Cowley, *Exile's Return: A Literary Odyssey of the 1920s* (1934; repr., New York: Penguin Books, 1994).

61 *Cowley even found himself*: Malcolm Cowley, *—And I Worked at the Writer's Trade: Chapters of Literary History, 1918–1978* (1978; repr., New York: Penguin Books, 1979), 113.

62 *All of these literary trends*: By 1935, the Americana turn, the documentary impulse, and the radical commitment had also converged in the form of the Popular Front; see chapter 3.

62 Puzzled America: Sherwood Anderson, *Puzzled America* (New York: Charles Scribner's Sons, 1935).

62 *a master of regionalist Americana*: For this period of Anderson's career, see Walter B. Rideout, *Sherwood Anderson: A Writer in America*, vol. 2 (Madison: University of Wisconsin Press, 2006).

62 *"I found Sherwood Anderson"*: quoted in Rideout, *Anderson*, 99. To be fair, Anderson was aware of his ignorance and asked Wilson to recommend to him some books.

62 *"Everywhere I go"*: This and subsequent quotations are in Anderson, *Puzzled*, 32–33, 36, 97, 71–72.

64 *gathered the staff*: meeting report, Oct. 11, 1935, NARA PI57, Alsberg papers, box 1, folder "Reports on Conference."

64 *"The first and primary object"*: Alsberg to State Directors of Federal Writers' Projects, Oct. 17, 1935, NARA PI57, Alsberg papers, box 1, folder "Interoffice Correspondence (Folder #2)."

65 *all forty-eight states*: California began as a single state project but, in 1937, it was separated into northern and southern projects when the WPA divided the state into two administrative units. Both North and South collaborated on the single California guidebook. See Katharine Kellock,

"Brief History of the Federal Writers' Project (1935–1939)," LOC KP, folder "WPA, Federal Writers' Project, 'A Brief History of the Federal Writers' Project, July 1, 1935–August 31, 1939,'" 6.

65 *sought out candidates:* Jerre Mangione, *The Dream and the Deal: The Federal Writers' Project, 1935–1943* (1972; repr., Philadelphia: University of Pennsylvania Press, 1983), 73–74; transcript of telephone conversation, Alsberg and Mr. Smith, Oct. 2, 1935, Jerre Mangione papers, D.245, Rare Books, Special Collections, and Preservation, River Campus Libraries, University of Rochester, box 15, folder 1.

65 *fourteen of them:* Mangione, *Dream,* 88.

65 *"far higher":* Katharine Kellock, "The WPA Writers: Portraitists of the United States," *The American Scholar,* vol. 9, no. 4 (autumn 1940), 478.

65 *Twenty-one directors:* Wendy Griswold, *American Guides: The Federal Writers' Project and the Casting of American Culture* (Chicago: University of Chicago Press, 2016), 100–107.

65 *"Anyone who can wet-nurse":* Monty Noam Penkower, *The Federal Writers' Project: A Study in Government Patronage of the Arts* (Urbana: University of Illinois Press, 1977), 41.

65 *some fell short:* Mangione, *Dream,* 76–80.

65 *said to be a former mistress:* Marilyn Irvin Holt treats this episode at length in *Nebraska During the New Deal: The Federal Writers' Project in the Cornhusker State* (Lincoln: University of Nebraska Press, 2019), chapter 1.

66 *"Have you ever seen":* quoted in Mangione, *Dream,* 80.

66 *Merriam ran his project:* Penkower, *Federal,* 41. Merriam was a founder of the regional literary magazine *The Frontier.* When he wrote to Alsberg, *The Frontier* had recently merged with another important regional magazine, becoming *Frontier and Midland.* Its new partner magazine was founded and run by the future director of the Illinois writers' project John T. Frederick.

66 *he'd hired a novelist:* Tim Woodward, *Tiger on the Road: The Life of Vardis Fisher* (Caldwell, ID: Caxton Printers, 1989), 132–33.

66 *an unnerving stare:* Woodward, *Tiger,* 108.

66 *looking for a director:* Merriam actually recommended Margaret Fisher for the directorship, but Vardis told Merriam that Margaret was planning on soon having a baby and wouldn't be available. See Merriam to Margaret and Vardis Fisher, Aug. 26, 1935, and Fisher to Merriam, Sept. 3, 1935, Fisher papers, box 24, folder "Fisher, Vardis to HG Merriam."

67 *according to his student:* Wallace Stegner and Richard W. Etulain, *Stegner: Conversations on History and Literature* (Reno: University of Nevada Press, 1996), 24–25.

67 *"His face was like":* Wallace Stegner, "The View from the Balcony," *Collected Stories of Wallace Stegner* (1990; repr., New York: Penguin Books, 1991) 96. In the early sixties, Fisher was shown the story by Joseph Flora, a young academic. Fisher dismissed Stegner: "He made a father-image of me and wanted to kill me, as sons usually want to do with fathers, both real and image; but I wouldn't know whether this story owes anything to that murderous effort." See Fisher to Joseph Flora, Oct. 6, 1963, Fisher papers, box 26, folder "Flora, Joseph M."

67 *"I have friends":* Fisher, "The Novelist and His Work," *Thomas Wolfe as I Knew Him and Other Essays* (Denver: Alan Swallow, 1963), 103.

67 *"laying aside my writing":* Fisher to Cronyn, Oct. 20, 1935, NARA PI57, administrative correspondence, box 11, folder "Idaho A Vardis Fisher."

67 *telegrammed Fisher:* Mangione, *Dream,* 78. Fisher recounts this episode in his novel *Orphans in Gethsemane* and adds his reaction to Merriam's ("Merrick's") telegram: "Why, the God damn stinker!"

68 *"didn't expect any real literature":* quoted, along with Cronyn, in Ronald Warren Taber, "The Federal Writers' Project in the Pacific Northwest: A Case Study" (PhD diss., Washington State University, 1969), 134–35.

68 *didn't give a damn:* Fisher later said: "By telephone and letter Alsberg told me repeatedly that for Idaho to be first among the forty-eight states would be a dreadful embarrassment. I thought the national office so incompetent and cynical and political that I cared nothing about its embarrassment." See Mangione, *Dream,* 191.

68 *the crisis got there*: Michael P. Malone, "The New Deal in Idaho," *Pacific Historical Review*, vol. 38, no. 3 (Aug. 1969), 294.

69 *drove forty miles*: Fisher to Cronyn, Oct. 6, 1935, NARA PI57, administrative correspondence, box 11, folder "Idaho A Vardis Fisher."

69 *He was a regionalist*: For an overview of regionalism in the thirties as an intellectual pursuit carried out by a diverse crowd of writers, thinkers, and policy makers, see Michael C. Steiner, "Regionalism in the Great Depression," *Geographical Review*, vol. 73, no. 4 (Oct. 1983), 430–46.

69 *He knew Wolfe*: Fisher, "Thomas Wolfe as I Knew Him," *Essays*, 34. Fisher wrote years later: "I felt time and again that he was looking to the bottom of me. It is, then, no less than astonishing that he was able to turn on himself only a reverent gaze that looked through mist and tears."

69 *dismissed Willa Cather*: Fisher to Philip and Mary J. Keeney, Jan. 11, 1933, Fisher papers, box 30, folder "Fisher, V." Fisher was proud of his decision not to spare readers "the sweat and spit and dirt and stink," as he put it, alluding derisively to Cather and Ferber. "Art today is only a bust for the most part," he insisted. "It is below the diaphragm that our ills originate and I'm interested in the whole torso."

69–70 *"detested the Antelope country"*: Fisher, "Hometown Revisited," *Essays*, 117.

70 *As a young man*: Fisher, "The Failure of Public Education in a Democracy," *Essays*, 154; John R. Milton, *Three West: Conversations with Vardis Fisher, Max Evans, Michael Straight* (1970; repr., Vermillion, SD: Dakota Press, 1972), 10.

70 *the Radical Club*: Stegner and Etulain, *Conversations*, 24–25. Wallace Stegner, Fisher's student, attended a few meetings.

70 *he was cautiously optimistic*: Fisher to his parents, [undated] 1933, and Nov. 9, 1933, Fisher papers, box 33, folder "3:2, 1933 July–Oct."; assorted correspondence in folder "3:2, 1933 July–Oct." and folder "3:6, 1935 June–Sept."

70 *"deep but quite unreasonable"*: "Author's Field Day: A Symposium on Marxist Criticism," *New Masses*, July 3, 1934. This single issue contained at least four other future FWP workers: Jack Conroy, who worked on the Missouri and Illinois projects; Edward Dahlberg, on the New York City project; Murray Godwin, an editor on the DC staff; and Merle Colby, who began as the assistant director of the Massachusetts project, then worked as an editor in DC and was responsible for writing the guides to Alaska and Puerto Rico, and then became the project's final director.

71 *journey to the FWP*: My account of Fisher's life draws on Tim Woodward's *Tiger on the Road: The Life of Vardis Fisher* as well as Fisher's essays collected in *Thomas Wolfe as I Knew Him and Other Essays* and the Fisher papers in the Beinecke Library at Yale University. For a short, critical biography that focuses on Fisher's literary work, see Joseph M. Flora, *Vardis Fisher* (New Haven, CT: College and University Press, 1965).

71 *"glad I knew them"*: Fisher, "Hometown Revisited," *Essays*, 127.

71 *close of the frontier*: See Gerald D. Nash, "The Census of 1890 and the Closing of the Frontier," *The Pacific Northwest Quarterly*, vol. 71, no. 3 (July 1980), 98–100, for the circumstances of the census and its historiographic impact, particularly as the impetus for Frederick Jackson Turner's famous "Frontier Thesis."

72 *afraid of the Bible*: Fisher, "My Bible Heritage" *Essays*, 161. Fisher's Mormon background and his lifelong fascination with historical religions has made the question of his belief or disbelief a controversial one. For two views on this subject, see Mick McAllister, "Vardis Fisher's Mormon Heritage Re-Examined: A Critical Response," *At Wanderer's Well*, Nov. 2001, http://www.dancingbadger.com /vfmormonf.htm, and Stephen L. Tanner, "Vardis Fisher and the Mormons," in Joseph M. Flora, ed., *Rediscovering Vardis Fisher: Centennial Essays* (Moscow: University of Idaho Press, 2000), 97–113.

72 *inspired by an uncle*: Fisher to Kenneth Larson, Aug. 19, 1958, Fisher papers, box 24, folder "Fisher, Vardis to Larson, Kenneth."

72 *Their mother's tutoring*: Fisher to Kenneth Larson, Aug. 19, 1958, Fisher papers, box 24, folder "Fisher, Vardis to Larson, Kenneth."

73 *commandeered the school's typewriter*: Fisher to James T. Babb, Jan. 11, 1959, Fisher papers, box 22, folder "Babb, James T."

73 *class of nine*: Rigby high school commencement book, 1915, Fisher papers, box 42.

73 *Fisher revealed that he'd met*: Fisher to his parents, June 4, 1924, Fisher papers, box 31, folder "1:9, 1924 Jan.–Sept."

73 *"Be careful, Irene"*: quoted in Woodward, *Tiger*, 87.

73 *"Just a line to say"*: Leona Fisher to Fisher family, Aug. 31, 1924, Fisher papers, box 31, folder "1:9, 1924 Jan.–Sept."

74 *wore her ring*: Fisher to his parents, Sept. 24, 1924, Fisher papers, box 31, folder "1:9, 1924 Jan.–Sept."; some of the poems he sent home are in folder "1:10 1924 Oct.–Dec." The poems eventually constituted his first book, *Sonnets to an Imaginary Madonna*, issued in five hundred copies by a vanity publisher.

74 *Washington Square College*: In an example of how the FWP knitted together people on the lower rungs of the American literary scene, George Cronyn's sister-in-law had been a student of both Fisher brothers (Vivian taught psychology at NYU) and he became acquainted with Vivian through her. It seems that Cronyn knew Vardis by reputation, although not personally. See Cronyn to Fisher, Oct. 24, 1935, NARA PI57, administrative correspondence, box 11, folder "Idaho A Miscellaneous."

74 *"I see all around me"*: Fisher to his family, Apr. 3, 1931, Fisher papers, box 32, folder "2:8 1930–1931."

75 *Vridar Hunter reflected*: On the veracity of the tetralogy, see, for instance, Woodward, *Tiger*, 99. On the whole, Woodward treats the tetralogy as a thinly fictionalized but basically accurate account of Fisher's life.

75 *Doubleday, Doran worked out*: Houghton Mifflin published Fisher's first two novels but turned down his third because, even though the editorial department had fought for his previous one, *Dark Bridwell*, over objections that it was "over-strong meat for our table," it sold poorly and they decided that a third novel was not worth the risk. See Houghton Mifflin editor [name illegible] to Fisher, Aug. 19, 1931, Fisher papers, box 30, "Vardis Fisher Misc. Corresp. (1 of 3)." A somewhat inaccurate version of this story was used by Doubleday to promote the tetralogy, saying that his last publisher found these books to be "too strong meat for our table" and passed, and thus entered the Fisher lore. See press release: "Doubleday, Doran to Publish Vardis Fisher Tetralogy," undated, Fisher papers, box 23, folder "Doubleday + Co."

75 *commissioned the painter Grant Wood*: R. Tripp Evans, *Grant Wood: A Life* (New York: Alfred A. Knopf, 2010), 228–30. It was the only time that Wood created jacket art for more than one book by a single author.

75 *landed him a literary agent*: Elizabeth Nowell to Fisher, June 20, 1935, Fisher papers, box 28, folder "Nowell, Elizabeth to Fisher, Vardis 1935–39"; Fisher to Nowell, Sept. 13, 1935, Fisher papers, box 25, folder "Fisher, Vardis, Letters to Elizabeth Nowell."

75 *"publishing houses curling up"*: Harry Maule to Fisher, May 11, 1933, Fisher papers, box 23, folder "Doubleday + Co."

75 *the New York Public Library bought*: Rideout, *The Radical Novel in the United States: Some Interrelations of Literature and Society, 1900–1954* (1956; repr., New York: Columbia University Press, 1992), 137.

75 *conditions in the publishing industry*: J. H. Gipson to Margaret Fisher, July 11, 1935, Fisher papers, box 23, "Caxton Printers 1934–39." Whether or not this was statistically true, it reflected the perception among publishing houses in New York.

75 *"throw my typewriter away"*: Fisher to Merriam, Sept. 3, 1935, Fisher papers, box 24, folder "Fisher, Vardis to HG Merriam."

75 *offered him a salary*: Taber, "Federal," 121–22.

76 *"I'm a Roosevelt man"*: Fisher to Merriam, Oct. 15, 1935, Fisher papers, box 24, folder "Fisher, Vardis to HG Merriam."

76 *"I feel absurd"*: Fisher to Elizabeth Nowell, Oct. 10, 1935, Fisher papers, box 25, "Fisher, Vardis, Letters to Elizabeth Nowell."

76 *reshaping the West*: For a full view of federal policies in the region, see Richard Lowitt, *The New Deal and the West* (1984; repr., Norman and London: University of Oklahoma Press, 1993).

76 *"cruel and stupid laws"*: quoted in Lowitt, *New Deal*, 123. The Office of Indian Affairs is today called the Bureau of Indian Affairs.

77 *So it was in Idaho*: Michael P. Malone, "The New Deal in Idaho," *Pacific Historical Review*, vol. 38, no. 3 (Aug. 1969); Lowitt, *New Deal* 112–21.

77 *resigned in a huff*: Christine Bold, *The WPA Guides: Mapping America* (Jackson: University Press of Mississippi, 1999), 39.

77 *frustrated by the WPA*: Taber, "Federal," 122.

77 *organized on three levels*: Searle F. Charles, *Minister of Relief: Harry Hopkins and the Depression* (Syracuse: Syracuse University Press, 1963), 134. Instead of using counties as the smallest administrative unit, the WPA created its own local districts in order to more evenly distribute the relief load.

77 *relationship between state WPA*: William F. McDonald, *Federal Relief Administration and the Arts: The Origins and Administrative History of the Arts Projects of the Works Progress Administration* (Columbus: Ohio State University Press, 1969), 136–46; Mangione, *Dream*, 73.

78 *took it out on Fisher*: Taber, 122–24; Mangione, *Dream*, 73. In later years, Fisher blamed J. L. Hood's WPA underlings for his hassles and had kind words for Hood himself. And while Hood complained about Fisher's temperamental nature and occasionally tried to insert himself in FWP business, he did back Fisher quite forcefully whenever his support was needed. See Mangione's audio interviews with Fisher, June 4, 1968, Mangione papers, box 149, folders 26 and 27.

78 *"I want an office"*: Fisher to Cronyn, Nov. 5, 1935, NARA PI57, administrative correspondence, box 11, folder "Idaho A Employment."

78 *intervened on Fisher's behalf*: Alsberg to Hood, Nov. 8, 1935, NARA PI57, administrative correspondence, box 11, folder "Idaho G–Z"; Baker to Hood, Dec. 30, 1935, NARA PI57, administrative correspondence, box 11, folder "Idaho A Employment."

78 *"dirty little hole"*: Fisher to Cronyn, Nov. 25, 1935, NARA PI57, administrative correspondence, box 11, folder "Idaho A Funds."

78 *moved to an apartment*: Their address was 1415 Franklin Street. See Gipson to Fisher, Nov. 6, 1935, Fisher papers, box 23, folder "Caxton Printers 1934–39."

78 *WPA regulations allowed*: *Final Report on the WPA Program, 1935–43* (Washington, DC: US Government Printing Office, 1946), 17.

78 *she was just as busy*: For instance, Vardis wrote to George Cronyn and said that Margaret spent "the better part of five months" gathering source material for the guide's flora essay. See Fisher to Cronyn, July 18, 1936, NARA PI57, editorial correspondence, box 11, folder "Idaho State Guide Essays"; and assorted correspondence in Fisher papers, boxes 33 and 37.

78 *equally qualified to be*: Margaret Trusler, "The Language of the Wakefield Playwright," *Studies in Philology*, vol. 33, no. 1 (Jan. 1936), 15–39; "Memo to Katy Mead Murphy, 7/18/77" [from Margaret Trusler], Fisher papers, box 42, folder "12:5, Biographical—Family." She went on to a career as an English professor and continued publishing religious lyric poetry. See Trusler's entry in the University of Indiana online database of *Indiana Authors and Their Books*, available at http://webapp1.dlib.indiana.edu/inauthors/.

78 *"an enormous ass"*: Fisher to Philip Keeney, Nov. 9, 1935, Fisher papers, box 30, folder "Fisher, V."

79 *"Idaho is not"*: Fisher to Alsberg, Aug. 15, 1936, NARA PI57, administrative correspondence, box 11, folder "Idaho A E–F."

79 *less-populated states*: Penkower, *Federal*, 58.

79 *Idaho project took shape*: Taber, "Federal," 126–30.

79 *fifteen and twenty people*: Bold, *WPA*, 38. Bold points out that the Historical Records Survey— initially a component of the FWP—lists around two dozen published authors in Idaho during that time, and quotes Harold Merriam's belief that Idaho did have a number of aspiring writers but no one of Fisher's stature.

79 *asking them to copy*: Mangione, *Dream*, 79.

79 *"The preparation of a book"*: Fisher to Alsberg, May 4, 1936, NARA PI57, editorial correspondence, box 11, folder "Idaho State Guide Miscellaneous." Though he praised his typists and

secretary, Fisher was dismissive of just about everyone else in the office and said he was handling all copy, administrative tasks, and tours, working seven days a week, including most evenings.

79 *person who* was *available*: Taber, "Federal," 130–31.

79 *routes by plane*: Maurice Howe, field report, Oct. 1, 1936, NARA PI57, field reports, box 1, folder "Idaho–Howe."

79 *"scouring the hinterlands"*: Fisher to Nowell, Feb. 18, 1936, Fisher papers, box 25, folder "Fisher, Vardis, Letters to Elizabeth Nowell."

79 *rambling all day*: Fisher audio interview, Mangione papers.

79 *the guide's Tour One*: Federal Writers' Project, *Idaho: A Guide in Word and Picture* (Caldwell, ID: Caxton Printers, 1937), 197–215.

81 *"book drunkard"*: Flora, *Fisher*, 20.

81 *poised for early publication*: The guides to Massachusetts, Maine, Vermont, and Rhode Island were published in 1937; Connecticut and New Hampshire appeared in 1938.

82 *Puritanism and its legacy*: See Warren I. Susman, "Uses of the Puritan Past," in *Culture as History: The Transformation of American Society in the Twentieth Century* (New York: Pantheon Books, 1984), and Kammen, *Mystic*, 206–15, 387–92. Kammen shows the amusing frequency with which combatants on both sides of this debate—which was essentially cultural and not historical—struggled with the distinction between Pilgrims and Puritans.

82 *"The story of how"*: Kellock to [Grace] Kellogg, May 8, 1937, NARA PI57, Gaer papers, box 1, folder "Correspondence to Washington, 1937 (Folder #2)."

82 *getting it up and running*: For a detailed account of this particular project, see Christine Bold, *Writers, Plumbers, and Anarchists: The WPA Writers' Project in Massachusetts* (Amherst and Boston: University of Massachusetts Press, 2006).

82 *among the larger projects*: Bold, *Writers*, 21–22; "Employment Quotas by Units of Federal Writers Project from 1937 to July 1939," LOC KP, folder "WPA FWP State Guides 1937–41."

82–83 *Advisors to the project*: Roderick Seidenberg to Alsberg, Mar. 27, 1936, NARA PI57, field reports, box 3, folder "Massachusetts—Roderick Seidenberg."

83 *Ray Billington*: Howard R. Lamar, "Ray Allen Billington," *The Proceedings of the American Antiquarian Society*, vol. 92, pt. 1 (Apr. 1982), 19–23.

83 *"a roaring maelstrom"*: Ray Allen Billington, "Government and the Arts: The W.P.A. Experience," *American Quarterly*, vol. 13, no. 4 (winter 1961), 470–71.

83 *"most of the college graduates"*: Fisher to Alsberg, Mar. 22, 1937, NARA PI57, administrative correspondence, box 11, folder "Idaho A Employment." And yet, on many occasions, Fisher did stick up for his workers facing dismissal because of cutbacks, when he knew they needed the work.

83 *Billington found his reward*: In "Government and the Arts," Billington makes a point of saying that this transformation was especially gratifying to see in "Negroes or representatives of other minority groups" who benefited from the project and realized they were being judged on merit. And yet, as Christine Bold points out, the project had a poor record of including African Americans and Native Americans, both as subjects covered in the publications and as workers on the payroll. See Bold, *Writers*, chapter 4.

83 *"He has been pictured"*: Federal Writers' Project, *Massachusetts: A Guide to Its Places and People* (Cambridge, MA: Riverside Press, 1937), 3.

84 *"a State of tradition"*: *Massachusetts*, 8.

84 *"Many new strands"*: *Massachusetts*, 51.

84 *the poet Conrad Aiken*: Mangione, *Dream*, 105; Frederick J. Hoffman, *Conrad Aiken* (New York: Twayne Publishers, 1962); Pells, *Radical*, 181.

85 *"literary gem"*: Billington, "Government," 475.

85 *"ghost of a town"*: *Massachusetts*, 223.

85 *"dull and inconsequential"*: Gaer memo to [Grace] Kellogg, Mar. 19, 1937, NARA PI57, Gaer papers, box 1, folder "Correspondence—Miscellaneous."

85 *"I do not see how"*: Gaer to Reed Harris, July 2, 1937, NARA PI57, Gaer papers, box 1, folder "Correspondence to Washington, 1937 (Folder #1)," and assorted correspondence in this folder.

86 *"I know you are having"*: Alsberg to Gaer, July 8, 1937, NARA PI57, Gaer papers, box 1, folder "Correspondence to Washington, 1937 (Folder #1)."

86 *The epic task*: Kellock to [Grace] Kellogg, May 8, 1937, NARA PI57, Gaer papers, box 1, folder "Correspondence to Washington, 1937 (Folder #2)."

86 *should belong to Washington*: Taber, "Federal," 141–42, 143.

86 *a team of twenty*: Penkower, *Federal*, 118.

87 *another motive at work*: Wendy Griswold makes this point about the exhaustive nature of the guide being a tool of flattery. See Griswold, *American*, 124.

87 *"book had to be written"*: Federal Writers' Project, *Washington: City and Capital* (Washington, DC: US Government Printing Office, 1937), vi.

87 *"thoroughly at home here"*: FWP, *Washington*, 9.

88 *"exerted a profound influence"*: FWP, *Washington*, 68–90. This essay was the work of the Negro Affairs editor Sterling A. Brown, and among his finest contributions to the project. For more on Brown, see chapter 4.

88 *pushing into new areas*: See McDonald, *Federal*, 678 (for life histories), 704–707 (folklore), 720–21 (slavery narratives), and 725 (social-ethnic studies).

88 *Historical Records Survey*: For an overview of the HRS, see McDonald, *Federal*, chapters 30 and 31. The HRS, while a federal project, dealt only with state and local archives. Federal archives outside of Washington, DC, were inventoried by Federal project #4, which was carried out jointly by the WPA and the National Archives.

89 *"courthouse lofts"*: Nelson Algren, "Federal Art Projects: WPA Literature," *The Chicago Artist*, vol. 1, no. 7 (Dec.–Jan. 1937–1938), 6.

89 *"WHY THE DEVIL"*: Fisher telegram to Cronyn, Nov. 25, [1936], NARA PI57, editorial correspondence, box 11, folder "Idaho State Guide Printing."

89 *remove digs*: Taber, "Federal," 135–36.

89 *"ugliest of the larger"*: Alsberg to Fisher, July 2, 1936, NARA PI57, editorial correspondence, box 11, folder "Idaho State Guide Tours."

89 *argued over Fisher's description*: Penkower, *Federal*, 98.

89 *"What I want is explicit"*: Fisher to Cronyn, Oct. 28, 1935, NARA PI57, administrative correspondence, box 11, folder "Idaho A Miscellaneous."

90 *shoved it into the furnace*: Taber, "Federal," 133–34.

90 *a major flashpoint*: At first, Fisher didn't even want to include the tours—he was more interested in the essays—and added them only at Washington's insistence, as the basic format for the guides developed. See Penkower, *Federal*, 84.

90 *thought this was "absurd"*: Fisher to Alsberg, May 4, 1936, and Alsberg to Fisher, May 12, 1936, NARA PC37, box 1175, folder "651.317 Idaho 1935–1938."

90 *The Massachusetts editors*: Bold, *Writers*, 22.

90 *Fisher tried recruiting*: assorted correspondence, NARA PI57, administrative correspondence, box 11, folder "Idaho G–Z."

90 *"WE WILL DO ALL"*: Fisher to Cronyn, Nov. 13, 1936, NARA PI57, administrative correspondence, box 11, folder "Idaho A E–F."

90 *"This poor fool"*: Fisher to Philip Keeney, Feb. 1, 1936, Fisher papers, box 30, folder "Fisher, V."

90 *boasted to his parents*: Fisher to his parents, [undated but postmarked] Jan. 27 and Feb. 10, 1936, box 33, folder "3.8, 1936 Jan.–March."

91 *divided people who worked*: This is Jerre Mangione's characterization, which he attributed to Alsberg being too long a bachelor. See Mangione, *Dream*, 58.

91 *"inhabitants of these towns"*: Alsberg to Fisher, Aug. 10, 1936, NARA PI57, editorial correspondence, box 11, folder "Idaho State Guide Tours."

91 *drew a firm line*: Alsberg to J. L. Hood, Oct. 30, 1936, NARA PI51, administrative correspondence, box 11, folder "Idaho A E–F."

91 *He admired Fisher*: Alsberg to Fisher, Apr. 25, 1936, NARA PI57, editorial correspondence, box 11, folder "Idaho State Guide Tours."

91 Tours in Eastern Idaho: Katharine Kellock later described this as a publicity publication meant to demonstrate that the FWP was making progress. See Kellock to J. D. Newsom, "Request for Reclassification," undated, LOC KP, folder "WPA, Federal Writers' Project, Reports and Correspondence 1936–42."

91 *first items published*: The first publication issued by the FWP is somewhat of a mystery. Mangione says it was the *Guide to North Little Rock*; Penkower says *3 Hikes Thru the Wissahickon*, and the latter was advertised as such by the Pennsylvania project and two early FWP catalogs. I concur with the FWP experts and booksellers Arthur Scharf and Marc Selvaggio: "We Americans are continuously enthralled by the 'first' of anything. Although we will refrain from granting the Wissahickon pamphlet the title of 'First Project Publication,' we will state that it's a damn early one." See Marc S. Selvaggio, *The American Guide Series: Works by the Federal Writers' Project*, a catalog from Arthur Scharf, Bookseller and Schoyer's Books, Pittsburgh, Pennsylvania, 1990, page 99.

91 *sold five thousand copies*: Alsberg memo to Hopkins, Dec. 9, 1936, NARA PC37, box 0469, folder "211.7 1935–(A)."

91 *"a very poor little thing"*: Alsberg memo, untitled, Mar. 31, 1937, NARA PI57, Alsberg papers, box 2, folder "Miscellaneous (Folder #3)." The colonel's reaction is quoted in Mangione, *Dream*, 89.

92 *Caxton Printers*: Caxton, located in Caldwell, was a regional printer housed in an old skating rink that specialized in local newspapers, county stationery, school supplies, and textbooks. Only in the late twenties did it begin acquiring and publishing trade books. Its publisher, J. H. Gipson, was an ardent fan of Fisher's novels—he once told Fisher that he would sooner suggest edits to Tolstoy or Shakespeare. And though the conservative Gipson was hardly a New Dealer, he congratulated Fisher on taking the FWP job. "Your enterprise is an extremely worthy one," he told Fisher, "and it should have the assistance of every public spirited citizen and of all who love Idaho, whether they are public spirited or not." Gipson's attitude wasn't unusual; across the country, people who were no fans of Roosevelt could choose to see the FWP through the lens of home-state boosterism and support it for that reason. For background on Caxton, see Paul E. Johnston, "Caxton Printers, Ltd., Regional Publishers," *The Pacific Northwest Quarterly*, vol. 48, no. 3 (July 1957), 100–105. On Gipson and Fisher, see assorted correspondence, Fisher papers, box 22, folder "Caxton Printers, 1931–33," and Woodward, *Tiger*, 180–81. On Gipson and the FWP, see Gipson to Fisher, Nov. 6, 1935, Fisher papers, box 23, folder "Caxton Printers 1934–39."

92 *guide would be off press*: Taber, "Federal," 139–42.

92 *Fisher's surprise arrangement*: Mangione, *Dream*, 221–22.

92 *"Let some yokel"*: Mangione, *An Ethnic at Large: A Memoir of America in the Thirties and Forties* (1978; repr., Syracuse: Syracuse University Press, 2001), 217. By an odd coincidence, Mangione had the RA job recommended to him by his friend Elizabeth Nowell, Vardis Fisher's agent.

93 *"Halting this book"*: Fisher to Alsberg, Oct. 17, 1936, NARA PI57, administrative correspondence, box 11, folder "Idaho A E–F."

93 *"shove under the noses"*: Fisher to Alsberg, Oct. 22, 1936, NARA PI57, administrative correspondence, box 11, folder "Idaho A E–F."

93 *"have taught advanced composition"*: Fisher to Alsberg, Nov. 1, 1936, NARA PI57, administrative correspondence, box 11, folder "Idaho A E–F."

93 *cooked up a plan*: Taber, 142; Mangione, *Dream*, 204–206; Penkower, *Federal*, 126. Years later, in his last autobiographical novel, *Orphans in Gethsemane*, Fisher describes this visit and has the Cronyn character—a sniveling, condescending lush who'd never been west of Chicago—belligerently tossing photographs around and succumbing utterly to his hosts' plot. Mangione, Penkower, and Taber—who all interviewed Fisher—present this incident as true. Fisher also repeated the basic story in an interview with John R. Milton in the late sixties (see Milton, *Three West*). But *Orphans in Gethsemane*, published in 1960, is clearly the work of a man who'd become, over the decades, increasingly jaded about his experience with the FWP—and more frustrated in his career and reactionary in his politics—so it can't be trusted entirely. For his part, Cronyn's subsequent letters to Fisher and Gipson suggest that he enjoyed the trip. See Vardis Fisher, *Orphans in Gethsemane: A Novel of the Past in the Present* (Denver: Alan Swallow, 1960), 749–55.

94   *nearly the entire thing*: "Foreword," *Idaho*, 7–8; Bold, *WPA*, 38–39.
94   *"After three centuries"*: *Idaho*, 17.
95   *curiously unpeopled*: As Christine Bold puts it, the guide "refused to conform to the New Deal's cultural vision, implicitly challenging the dominant 1930s' meanings of the frontier, authorizing rugged individualism in a presocial landscape, and thus naturalizing a version of social relations profoundly at odds with the Progressive history critical to New Dealers' faith in social improvement." This argument forms the basis of her analysis of the Idaho guide in *The WPA Guides*, chapter 3.
95   *"But what has happened"*: [Ruth] Crawford, undated, NARA PI57, editorial correspondence, box 11, folder "Idaho State Guide Essays."
95   *"had a constant struggle"*: Alsberg memo to Harry Hopkins, "Idaho State Guide," Jan. 22, 1937, Mangione papers, box 14, folder 2.
95   *larger trim size*: This is pointed out by Griswold, *American*, 128. The guide was published as a sumptuous "library edition," with a planned "tourist edition" to follow at half the price, but it never appeared. See Selvaggio, "American," 27.
96   *met with a wave*: Mangione, *Dream*, 206–207; see also press release and assorted reviews in Mangione papers, box 9, folder 14.
96   *two hundred reviews*: *Publications of the Federal Writers' Project in Idaho*, WPA pamphlet (undated), Fisher papers, box 30, folder "Fisher, V."
96   *"a swell book"*: Alsberg to Fisher, Jan. 26, 1937, NARA PI57, administrative correspondence, box 11, folder "Idaho A E–F."
96   *arrived in April*: Fisher had been in Washington years earlier: while finishing his dissertation, he worked in the Library of Congress, and wrote home about how much he hated the city, and all cities, and life in the East generally. "Every day I see bloated bellied guys with protruding jaws who may be, for all I know, senators, federal judges, or whatnot," he told his parents then. He looked at such figures with contempt and a bit of sardonic sympathy. "It is a safe bet that their legs are weak and have all sorts and kinds of aches from carrying around so much unnecessary garbage in the shape of windbags and bellows." Now, he worked for such politicians and bureaucrats, and he rode into their town something of a hero. See Fisher to family, Jan. 1 and 11, 1925, Fisher papers, box 32, folder "2:1, 1925 Jan.–March." On that early trip to Washington, Fisher carried with him the blithe racism that tinges some of his private correspondence: "Like most cities this is an ugly dump. A beautiful capitol building in the center, surrounded by doby houses filled with coons."
96   *"There she is"*: quoted in Mangione, *Dream*, 208. Six years after this trip, the story about meeting Kellock got around to Fisher. He denied it and claimed that he ignored her during the party. See Fisher to Mary J. Keeney, Apr. 13, 1943, Fisher papers, box 30, folder "Fisher, V."
96   *guide to the District of Columbia*: Mangione, *Dream*, 209.
97   *first copies arrived*: Mangione, *Dream*, 209, 11.
97   *overall response*: The FWP staff kept track of this information in a large document, noting whether someone acknowledged receipt of the guide, had favorable or unfavorable comments, and offered suggestions for improvement. At the top of the list was FDR: "favorable." See "Acknowledgements of 'Washington: City and Capital,'" NARA PI57, Alsberg papers, box 2, folder "Miscellaneous (Folder #3)." For a summary of the positive press reviews, see Mangione, *Dream*, 210.
97   *unprecedented expansion of federal power*: In 1933, there were 604,000 federal civil servants; by 1939, there were 954,000. Federal spending also grew dramatically, from $3.1 billion in 1929 to $8.8 billion in 1939. According to the historian Kiran Klaus Patel, the national government in the United States expanded at a rate greater than those of most other countries: "Overall, the United States seemed to move from the rear to the vanguard of state building, as defined by the European standards of the time." And yet this expansion would soon be eclipsed by even more dramatic growth in the number of federal employees and amount of federal spending during the Second World War. See Patel, *The New Deal: A Global History* (Princeton: Princeton University Press, 2016), 242, 263.
97   *welcomed such an expansion*: I don't mean to suggest that the New Deal involved a simple, top-down imposition of state power that solicited only passive reactions, positive or otherwise, and not other forms of participation. As the historian Meg Jacobs argues, New Deal state building

involved a dynamic interplay between government policies and grassroots activity, most especially among workers, with the broad aim of redistributing economic and political power generally. See Jacobs, "State Building from the Bottom Up: The New Deal and Beyond," in Gary Gerstle, Nelson Lichtenstein, and Alice O'Connor, eds., *Beyond the New Deal Order: U.S. Politics from the Great Depression to the Great Recession* (Philadelphia: University of Pennsylvania Press, 2019). The classic study along these lines is Lizabeth Cohen, *Making a New Deal: Industrial Workers in Chicago, 1919–1939* (Cambridge: Cambridge University Press, 1990).

97–98   *threw themselves a party*: Mangione, *Dream*, 224–25.

98   *just been forced out*: Oral history interview with Jacob Baker, Sept. 25, 1963, Archives of American Art, Smithsonian Institution. Baker joined an official "Inquiry on Cooperative Enterprise in Europe," which Roosevelt initially supported with great enthusiasm. But after a conservative backlash, Roosevelt distanced himself from the inquiry, and its report was recast as a factual description of cooperatives in Europe while avoiding any potentially controversial prescriptions for the United States. See Patel, *New Deal*, 222–28.

98   *emerged from Democratic politics*: Woodward details: "Ellen Woodward (1887–1971)," *The Living New Deal*, https://livingnewdeal.org/glossary/ellen-woodward-1887-1971/.

98   *"thrust into this motley melee"*: *Congressional Record: Third Session of the Seventy-Fifth Congress*, vol. 83, pt. 7, 7367. In *The Dream and the Deal*, Mangione reports that Bilbo had this expunged from the record, but it is there for all posterity to view—although, when Bilbo spoke, it was more than a year after the party. Clearly, this was not a spontaneous outburst but part of his prepared speech.

99   *"I am pleased"*: Harry Shaw to Alsberg, June 3, 1938, NARA PI57, administrative correspondence, box 30, folder "New York City Publicity January–July 1938."

99   *Alsberg opened the bidding*: Penkower, *Federal*, 121–22, 128–30.

99   *carved up among*: Alsberg worried that the big New York publishers would have no interest in acquiring guides to faraway, thinly traveled states. The new national coordinating editor, Jerre Mangione, suggested bundling states into packages that combined the potentially lucrative ones with others that were not so appealing. That is how they proceeded, and the response was tremendous. See Mangione, *Dream*, 230–32.

99   *professional copy marker*: Joseph Gaer to Alsberg, May 1, 1937, NARA PI57, Gaer papers, box 1, folder "Correspondence to Washington, 1937 (Folder #2)."

99   *"unquestionable triumph"*: Bernard DeVoto, "New England via W.P.A.," *The Saturday Review of Literature*, May 14, 1938. His review was otherwise quite critical of the essays and some other aspects of the guides.

100   *wrecked from the outset*: Bold, *Writers*, chapters 1 and 3; Mangione, *Dream*, 216–20; Penkower, *Federal*, 101–107. Bold details how the Massachusetts guide was eventually—and quietly—censored for subsequent printings. Alsberg initially opposed this but acquiesced and allowed the publisher, the state, and the Massachusetts project to tone down the guide's perceived radicalism by rewriting the essay on labor and making subtle changes throughout. By then, Billington and Loewenberg had left the project and Colby was working out of DC. See Bold, *Writers*, chapter 3.

100   *"take care of Merle Colby"*: Mangione, *Dream*, 101.

101   *Roosevelt was unfazed*: Mangione, *Dream*, 220.

101   *took up new tasks*: Taber, "Federal," 145–52. *The Idaho Encyclopedia* was meant to be the first in a series of state encyclopedias but none were published, ostensibly because they too much resembled the "made work" that administrators wanted to avoid. See McDonald, *Federal*, 734.

101   *"If you drop"* and *"Insanity"*: *Idaho Lore* (Caldwell, ID: Caxton Printers, 1939), 203, 212. There is also this cure for bed-wetting: "Cook a mouse, preferably by boiling, and make the flesh into a sandwich and feed to the child."

101   *"pop Mr. Pugmire"*: In this instance, Fisher seemed to be in the right. Even the strenuously diplomatic Reed Harris shared his frustration, and wrote, "Mr. Pugmire seems to be an amazing person. Perhaps I will join you on your 'pop in the eye' expedition." See Fisher to Harris, May 21,

1937, and Harris to Fisher, June 4, 1937, and assorted correspondence, NARA PI51, administrative correspondence, box 11, folder "Idaho G–Z," as well as correspondence in NARA PC37, box 1175, folder "651.317 Idaho 1935–1938."

101 *permission to work*: Fisher to Alsberg, June 29 1937, NARA PI57, administrative correspondence, box 11, folder "Idaho A Employment."

101 *"Modern Rousseau"*: Fred T. Marsh, "Vardis Fisher, Modern Rousseau," *The New York Times*, Mar. 8, 1936. See also John Peale Bishop, "The Strange Case of Vardis Fisher," *The Southern Review* (autumn 1937), 348–59.

101 *"the homeliest girl"*: Vardis Fisher, *April: A Fable of Love* (Caldwell, ID, and Garden City, NY: Caxton Printers and Doubleday, Doran, 1937), 6. See also Woodward, *Tiger*, 150.

102 *irritated that the Idaho guide*: Fisher to Philip and Mary J. Keeney, [undated] 1937, Fisher papers, box 30, folder "Fisher, V."

102 *"digging under the dirty"*: Wallace Stegner, "Forgive Us Our Neuroses," *Rocky Mountain Review*, vol. 2, no. 4 (spring 1938). See also Woodward, *Tiger*, 151.

102 *book-length Marxist polemic*: David Rein, *Vardis Fisher: Challenge to Evasion* (Chicago: Normandie House, 1938). *Evasion* was a key word in Fisher's philosophy, and though admiring of Fisher's work, Rein argued that the novels "evaded" basic questions of socioeconomic oppression by focusing instead on the psychological makeup of individual characters. In his preface, Fisher clarified his point of view, denied that he was a Freudian, and took a dig at Malcolm Cowley, then the literary editor of *The New Republic*, for ignoring his books.

102 *diaries of Mormon pioneers*: Penkower, *Federal*, 245.

102 *effect on Fisher's career*: Woodward, *Tiger*, 147–50. He dedicated the novel to J. H. Gipson of Caxton Printers, publisher of all the Idaho project books.

103 *"Margaret will soon have"*: Fisher to Philip and Mary J. Keeney, [undated] 1937, Fisher papers, box 30, folder "Fisher, V."

103 *"that period of chaos and dark"*: Margaret Fisher to Vardis Fisher, Oct. 9, 1938, Fisher papers, box 30, folder "Vardis Fisher Misc. Corresp. (2 of 3)." See also Woodward, *Tiger*, 143–45.

103 *editor to Nevada and Utah*: Taber, "Federal," 153.

103 *arrested for speeding*: Alsberg to Fisher, Mar. 8, 1939, LOC FWPC, box A3, folder 3; Alsberg to Mary Isham, May 19 1939, and attached clippings and correspondence, NARA PC37, box 0474, folder "211.712 A–Z."

TOUR THREE: NELSON ALGREN, CHICAGO

105 *Nelson Algren*: Biographical details about Algren throughout this chapter are derived mostly from Bettina Drew, *Nelson Algren: A Life on the Wild Side* (New York: G. P. Putnam's Sons, 1989); Colin Asher, *Never a Lovely So Real: The Life and Work of Nelson Algren* (New York: W. W. Norton, 2019); and Mary Wisniewski, *Algren: A Life* (Chicago: Chicago Review Press, 2017).

106 *"All these scenes"*: H. E. F. Donohue, *Conversations with Nelson Algren* (1963; repr., New York: Berkley Medallion Books, 1965), 52–54.

106 *"typewriter is the only"*: quoted in Drew, *Algren*, 68.

106 *a deserter from*: Wisniewski, *Algren*, 55.

107 *"So Help Me"*: At the first American Writers' Congress, James T. Farrell singled out this story in his talk: it "should classify as one assessing the cost of capitalistic society, bringing before our eyes some of the lineaments, as it were, of contemporary American life, and re-creating a sense of the meaning of life, the feel, the atmosphere, of it amongst the lower strata of our 'dollar casualties.'" It was not a bad summation of Algren's work to come. See Farrell, "The Short Story," *American Writers' Congress*, ed. Henry Hart (New York: International Publishers, 1935), 110.

107 *"Whenever he thought"*: Algren, *Somebody in Boots* (1935; repr., New York: Berkley Medallion Books, 1965), 230.

107 *"In every chapter"*: quoted in Martha Heasley Cox and Wayne Chatterton, *Nelson Algren* (Boston: Twayne Publishers, 1975), 33.

108 *churning out proletarian literature*: For an overview, see Michael Denning, *The Cultural Front: The Laboring of American Culture in the Twentieth Century* (1997; repr., London: Verso, 2010), 200–229; Walter B. Rideout, *The Radical Novel in the United States: Some Interrelations of Literature and Society, 1900–1954* (1956; repr., New York: Columbia University Press, 1992), chapters 7 and 9; and Daniel Aaron, *Writers on the Left: Episodes in American Literary Communism* (1961; repr., New York: Columbia University Press, 1992), passim.

108 *hard-boiled style*: For a consideration of this type of fiction in the context of the New Deal—including the careers of two federal writers, Jim Thompson and Chester Himes—see Sean McCann, *Gumshoe America: Hard-Boiled Crime Fiction and the Rise and Fall of New Deal Liberalism* (Durham, NC: Duke University Press, 2000).

108 *"delighted in hitting back"*: Alfred Kazin, *On Native Grounds: A Study of American Prose Literature from 1890 to the Present* (1942; repr., Garden City, NY: Doubleday Anchor Books, 1956), 294.

108 *"She wanted to strike out"*: Algren, *Somebody*, 189.

108 *lumpenproletariat who had*: Later in Algren's career, his attachment to the dispossessed gave some critics reason to dismiss him as the "bard of the stumblebum," in Leslie Fiedler's well-known appellation.

109 *"capitalist system crumbles"*: "Call for an American Writers' Congress," *New Masses*, Jan. 22, 1935, 20.

109 *a liberal professor*: Aaron, *Writers*, 194–95, 282.

110 *including Theodore Dreiser*: Dreiser was one of the congress's boldface names but at this moment he was facing charges of anti-Semitism for comments about Jews that some regarded as insensitive and ignorant and others regarded as fascist. The issue of *New Masses* published to coincide with the congress had as its cover story "Dreiser Replies: I Am Not Anti-Semitic" and carried a brief statement by Dreiser to that effect, along with a longer account of the affair by the editors that sharply reprimanded Dreiser, called his statement inadequate, and suggested that he'd betrayed his honorable reputation but could still redeem himself. (Nonetheless, the following issue carried a stinging polemic against Dreiser by Michael Gold.) See *New Masses*, Apr. 30, 1935, and Aaron, *Writers*, 276–78.

110 *Dos Passos contributed*: Denning, *Cultural*, 166.

110 *Writers' Congress convened*: Proceedings from the congress were edited and compiled in *American Writers' Congress*, ed. Henry Hart (New York: International Publishers, 1935). My description also draws on Malcolm Cowley, *The Dream of the Golden Mountains: Remembering the 1930s* (1980; repr., New York: Penguin Books, 1981), chapter 23; and Malcolm Cowley, Kenneth Burke, Granville Hicks, William Phillips, and Daniel Aaron, "Symposium: Thirty Years Later: Memories of the First American Writers' Congress," *The American Scholar*, vol. 35, no. 3 (summer 1966).

110 *first such gathering*: Hart makes this claim in the introduction to his volume of congress proceedings; so does the literary critic Newton Arvin in his speech to the second congress, "The Democratic Tradition in American Letters," *The Writer in a Changing World*, ed. Henry Hart (n.p.: Equinox Cooperative Press, 1937), 34; see also Denning, *Cultural*, 442.

110 *rows of folding chairs*: Cowley, *Dream*, 123.

111 *"story of middle-class"*: Waldo Frank, "Values of the Revolutionary Writer," *New Masses*, May 7, 1935, 18–20. On his friendship with Alsberg, see Alsberg to Harold Strauss, Dec. 3, 1938, NARA PI57, administrative correspondence, box 29, folder "Edward Dahlberg."

111 *"We do not want"*: Earl Browder, "Communism and Literature," *Communism in the United States* (New York: International Publishers, 1935), 311–15. Browder's speech contained a line about putting writers in "uniforms," which attendees would have understood as a reference to Max Eastman's book *Artists in Uniform*, an account of cultural repression in the Soviet Union published the year before. Eastman was by now a fierce critic of the Communist Party and a supporter of Trotsky, and his book was attacked by the party. See Aaron, *Writers*, 446n12.

111 *an incident involving*: Cowley, "Symposium," 506–507. Burke's talk, "Revolutionary Symbolism in America," appears in *American Writers' Congress*, 87–94.

111 *"Particularly to those"*: Kenneth Burke, "The Writers' Congress," *The Nation*, May 15, 1935.

112 *a major shift*: For two accounts of the Third Period and the Popular Front, see Harvey Klehr, *The Heyday of American Communism: The Depression Decade* (New York: Basic Books, 1984), and Irving Howe and Lewis Coser, *The American Communist Party: A Critical History* (1957; repr., New York: Da Capo Press, 1974), 177–88, 230–32, 319–86. For extended studies of the cultural ramifications of the Popular Front, see Denning, *Cultural*; Aaron, *Writers*; and Richard H. Pells, *Radical Visions and American Dreams: Culture and Social Thought in the Depression Years* (New York: Harper and Row, 1973).

112 *disrupted a socialist meeting*: Aaron, *Writers*, 350. "The Socialist Party had called the mass meeting to honor the Socialist victims of Chancellor Dollfuss, whose soldiers had shot down Viennese workers and bombarded their apartment houses." Communist Party members attempted to seize the meeting and instead set off a melee.

112 *"back where he came from"*: Joseph North, "Earl Browder: A Profile," *New Masses*, Apr. 30, 1935, 13–15. North was blunt: "The location of the birthplace of one of America's leading revolutionaries is an apt commentary on the charge that Communism is an importation—an un-American idea disseminated by furtive Slavs and Semites who pop up in our industrial centers distributing fiery handbills calling for uprising before midnight."

113 *Algren was elected*: Drew, *Algren*, 90–97.

113 *seemed to be unraveling*: After the congress, James T. Farrell tried to calm Algren and arranged for him to spend time at the Yaddo artists' retreat upstate. (Algren went but left the next day.) Farrell was in his early thirties and enjoying the success of the first two volumes of his Studs Lonigan trilogy, with a third on the way. He was already regarded as a successor to Theodore Dreiser and Upton Sinclair—an example of what Algren hoped to be. But their relationship was fraught. Farrell was a reader for *Somebody in Boots* and pressed for substantial changes to the manuscript, which Algren resented. Farrell was also embroiled in a feud with Jack Conroy, in which Algren participated, including by staging a boisterous play that mocked Farrell. And Farrell's increasingly vocal criticism of the Communist Party line (and association with Trotskyists) made him suspect in Algren and Conroy's view. Their relationship is covered in the Algren biographies; on Farrell's reputation, see Robert Morss Lovett, "James T. Farrell," *The English Journal*, vol. 26, no. 5 (May 1937), 347–54.

113 *number of new books*: Rideout, *Radical*, 137. This refers to the total copies of new books printed each year, not new titles published.

114 *"You'll know it's the place"*: Algren, *Chicago: City on the Make* (1951; repr., Chicago: University of Chicago Press, 2011), 73.

114 *city during the Depression*: Lizabeth Cohen, *Making a New Deal: Industrial Workers in Chicago, 1919–1939* (Cambridge: Cambridge University Press, 1990), chapter 5.

115 *project's first home*: The project's changing addresses are reflected in NARA PI57, administrative correspondence, boxes 11 and 12. For the Illinois project joining Federal #1, see Gaer memo to Alsberg, June 18, 1936, NARA PI57, field reports, box 2, folder "Illinois–Joseph Gaer."

115 *"one of the most promising"*: Orrick Johns to Reed Harris, June 10, 1936, NARA PI57, administrative correspondence, box 12, folder "Illinois A–D." See attached correspondence for the circumstances of Algren's hiring, as well as Drew, *Algren*, 100.

115 *same revitalizing effect*: Before Algren finally landed on the FWP, he developed an idea for a tetralogy of novels that would form a composite portrait of Chicago, with each based in a different ethnic neighborhood. He seems to have written some of the first installment but his work tapered off as he focused on the FWP. In a sense, the books would have been a fictional counterpart to the social-ethnic studies that the FWP was undertaking across the country, including in Illinois. See Asher, *Never*, 136.

115 *"WPA provided a place"*: Donohue, *Conversations*, 61–62.

115 *observed correlation*: Feijun Luo et al., "Impact of Business Cycles on US Suicide Rates, 1928–2007," *American Journal of Public Health*, vol. 101, 6 (2011), 1139–46. Health data show that the suicide rate tends to rise during recessions and fall during expansions; the Great Depression triggered an exceptionally high rate.

115 *descended from recent immigrants*: Denning makes this observation about what he calls "the CIO working class," which was composed of migrants from agricultural peripheries in specific parts of Europe, Asia, Mexico, and the southern United States, who found work in industrial centers in the Midwest and Northeast, and whose children not only played an outsize role in the CIO but became "the creators of a new militant working-class culture that was no longer marginalized in the 'foreign' ghettos." See Denning, *Cultural*, 7 and passim.

116 *an eccentric Swede*: Algren said his grandfather was named Nels, and other writers have followed him, but his biographer Colin Asher makes a convincing case for "Nils."

116 *"Can pseudo-intellectualism"*: quoted in Cox, *Algren*, 18.

118 *"We want to print"*: Michael Gold, "Write for Us!," *New Masses*, July 1928, 2, and "Go Left, Young Writers!," *New Masses*, Jan. 1929, 3–4. See also Aaron, *Writers*, 202–13, and Denning, *Cultural*, 203–205.

118 *went through eleven*: Rideout, *Radical*, 151.

119 *college enrollment stayed*: Rideout, *Radical*, 137.

119 *work selling papers*: Cox, *Algren*, 20.

119 *"a man representing"*: Algren, "Preface," *Somebody*, 8–9.

120 *director was Clark Slover*: Cronyn to Slover, Apr. 2, 1936, NARA PI57, editorial correspondence, box 12, folder "Illinois Chicago, The Vacation City"; Reed Harris memo to Lawrence Morris, Jan. 27, 1937, and assorted correspondence, NARA PI57, administrative correspondence, box 12, folder "Illinois S–T."

120 *died in 1939*: "Mystery Seen in Death of Writer," *The Wilkes-Barre Times Leader*, Dec. 26, 1939.

120 *"I have a sincere"*: James Phelan to Alsberg, Jan. 26, 1937, NARA PI57, administrative correspondence, box 12, folder "Illinois K–P."

120 *asked Jay Du Von*: Alsberg memo to Ellen Woodward, Apr. 20, 1937, NARA PI57, administrative correspondence, box 12, folder "Illinois A–D."

121 *DC's first choice*: Cronyn to John T. Frederick, Oct. 21, 1935, NARA PI57, administrative correspondence, box 12, folder "John T. Frederick." See also Brian Dolinar, "Editor's Introduction," *The Negro in Illinois: The WPA Papers* (Urbana: University of Illinois Press 2013), xxi.

121 *considered the most effective*: Mangione, *Dream*, 119.

121 *best known for editing*: John T. Frederick was born in Iowa (three years after Harry Hopkins) and raised on his family's farm. By the time he was hired to direct the Illinois project, he'd published textbooks and edited anthologies and, in the twenties, wrote two novels, *Druida* and *Green Bush*. See Sargent Bush, Jr., "The Achievement of John T. Frederick," *Books at Iowa*, no. 14 (1971), 8–30, and Philip A. Greasley, ed., *Dictionary of Midwestern Literature*, vol. 1, *The Authors* (Bloomington: Indiana University Press, 2001), 203–204.

121 *merged with* The Frontier: "Aggressive Regionalism: Commentary," Center for the Study of the Pacific Northwest, University of Washington, http://www.washington.edu/uwired/outreach/cspn /Website/Classroom%20Materials/Reading%20the%20Region/Aggressive%20Regionalism /Commentary/6.html.

121 *"part of the government's"*: John T. Frederick, "Federal Writers' Project Activities as Planned for the Future," text of a speech given Oct. 18, 1938, at a regional conference in Chicago, NARA PC37, box 0470, folder "D–F."

122 *called it "brain erosion"*: quoted in McDonald, *Federal*, 96n.

122 *note-taking habit*: Douglas Wixson, *Worker-Writer in America: Jack Conroy and the Tradition of Midwestern Literary Radicalism, 1898–1990* (Urbana: University of Illinois Press, 1994), 434. Algren was spending time with a group of unsavory characters he'd met through Jack Conroy, led by a CIO organizer and pseudo-aspiring writer named Bud Fallon. Algren was not as chummy with the "Fallonites" as Conroy, and Fallon wrote a poem mocking Algren's habit of keeping "a pocketful of notes." Fallon, a cruel prankster, also enjoyed sending abusive and anti-Semitic letters with false signatures, including ones he mailed, signed by "Algren," to the editor of *Esquire*— and to Henry Alsberg. See also Asher, *Never*, 156.

122   *churning out the raw material*: Records from the Illinois project, including a selection of Algren's work, are held by the Abraham Lincoln Presidential Library and Museum in Springfield, Illinois. Some of these documents are attributed to Algren; others are attributed to "N. Abraham," who is almost certainly Algren as well. His legal name was still "Nelson Algren Abraham" while he worked for the FWP, and although he did not use it often, he didn't change his name until 1944, when he was in the army and trying to get deployed overseas. (See Asher, *Never*, 101, 194). I thank Colin Asher for his expertise on this matter and for kindly reviewing the FWP documents.

122   *"Midwestern Literature"*: Algren, "Midwestern Literature: Its Origins and Tendencies, 1848–1865," Dec. 1, 1936, Federal Writers' Project Records, 1935–1944, Abraham Lincoln Presidential Library, Springfield, IL, box 77, folder 12.

123   *was among the largest*: "Employment Quotas by Units of Federal Writers Project from 1937 to July 1939," LOC KP, folder "WPA FWP State Guides 1937–41."

123   *spun off into topics*: Undated Chicago office roster, Jerre Mangione papers, D.245, Rare Books, Special Collections, and Preservation, River Campus Libraries, University of Rochester, box 9, folder 18.

123   *a catalog of items*: "Guides, Dictionaries, and Bibliographies," [undated], NARA PC37, box 1236, folder "Ill. 651.3117 June–Dec. 1942."

124   *a guide to Galena*: Federal Writers' Project, *Galena Guide* (City of Galena, 1937). The cover and illustrations were by Robert Delson of the Federal Art Project, who would eventually transfer to the FAP in Florida and contribute head and tail pieces to the Florida guide. See Carita Corse to Alsberg, Mar. 29, 1939, NARA PC37, box 1108, folder "Fla. 651.3172 Jan. 1939–Jan. 1941."

124   *patron saint of local guides*: Kammen, *Mystic Chords of Memory: The Transformation of Tradition in American Culture* (New York: Alfred A. Knopf, 1991), 272.

124   *editor in Rockford*: Rollins to Alsberg, Dec. 30, 1936, NARA PI57, editorial correspondence, box 12, folder "Illinois Galena Guide."

124   *project was planning*: Rollins to Alsberg, Mar. 1, 1937, NARA PI57, editorial correspondence, box 12, folder "Illinois Galena Guide."

125   *"the inherent dignity"*: "Galena Summary Criticism," Apr. 14, 1937, NARA PI57, box 13, editorial correspondence, folder "Ill. April 36–June 37." See also in this folder, "Editorial Report on State Copy" for Galena, Mar. 29, 1937.

125   *Alsberg read both*: Jay Du Von to Alsberg, May 26, 1937, NARA PI57, editorial correspondence, box 12, folder "Illinois Galena Guide."

125   *"seems at first glance"*: "Galena Summary Review," May 27, 1937, NARA PI57, editorial correspondence, box 12, folder "Illinois Galena Guide." This review is unsigned but is almost certainly by Cronyn: his initials are handwritten at the top, he handled much of this type of correspondence, and it sounds like him. Also, he had a pedantic streak that explains the following overlong criticism of Algren's use of the word *antiquity*: "This word gives a false quantity to Galena's age which, placed at the beginning is apt to effect [sic] the reader's point of view throughout the manuscript. Funk & Wagnall's Standard Dictionary defines antiquity, 'Ancient times, people, or Civilization especially, before the disappearance of the Western Roman Empire from history.' A ruling of the United States Treasury allows any article made before 1700 to be admitted duty free, as an 'antique.' The word should only be used to indicate great age, far beyond Galena's brief history and the fact that careless newspaper writers and chamber of commerce blubbers continuously misuse the word does not excuse its false application in what ought to be an authentic document. Surely a synonym can be found to characterize Galena's dignified old-age more accurately."

125   *raved to WPA officials*: Henry Horner to Robert McKeague, Aug. 3, 1937, and to Charles Miner, July 29, 1937, NARA PC37, box 1251, folder "Illinois, 651.317 1935–Jan. 1937." Horner contributed a signed essay on Lincoln to *Illinois: A Descriptive and Historical Guide*, which appeared in 1939.

125   *mayor of Galena*: I. L. Gamber to Alsberg, July 10, 1937, NARA PI57, editorial correspondence, box 12, folder "Illinois Galena Guide."

125   *"read a dozen biographies"*: Robert Cantwell, "America and the Writers' Project," *The New Repub-lic*, Apr. 26, 1939.

125   *sold 1,500 copies*: Lawrence Morris memo to Ellen Woodward, July 24, 1937, NARA PC37, box 0471, folder "211.7 L–M." *Somebody in Boots* sold 762 in one year. See Drew, *Algren*, 87.

125   *Algren was promoted*: Mary Gillette Moon to Charles E. Miner, Aug. 9, 1937, NARA PI57, admin-istrative correspondence, box 11, folder "Illinois A Employment 1937."

126   *joined the union's shop*: Charles Novak to Alsberg, July 8, 1937, with report attached, NARA PI57, administrative correspondence, box 12, folder "Illinois S–T."

126   *"We move in a world"*: quoted in Drew, *Algren*, 104–105.

126   *become the chapter secretary*: Asher, *Never*, 146.

126   *a 1919 emergency convention*: Irving Howe and Lewis Coser, *The American Communist Party: A Critical History* (1957; repr., New York: Da Capo Press, 1974), 37–40. Regarding this tumultuous conference, the authors conclude that information about "who, if anyone, punched whom is more difficult to discover than almost anything else in the buried history of American radicalism."

126   *408 demonstrations*: Asher, *Never*, 61n.

126   *"For it was here"*: Algren, *Chicago*, 85.

126   *"the new man"*: Orrick Johns, "The John Reed Clubs Meet," *New Masses*, Oct. 30, 1934, 25–26. Johns would become a director of the NYC project.

126   *unusual overture toward*: For an overview of the party's stance toward intellectuals in the thirties, see Klehr, *Heyday*, chapters 4 and 18.

127   *issued an open letter*: *An Open Letter to All Members of the Communist Party: Adopted by the Ex-traordinary National Conference of the Communist Party of the U.S.A., held in New York City, July 7–10, 1933* (New York: Central Committee, Communist Party U.S.A., 1933).

127   *Five years after*: On the John Reed Clubs, see Denning, *Cultural*, 205–11. The JRC, like *New Masses*, officially affiliated with the International Union of Revolutionary Writers at a conference held in Kharkov, Ukraine, in 1930. The IURW was, as Walter Rideout puts it, "a literary coun-terpart of the Comintern," and it no doubt placed demands on Communist Party members in America. But how that influence trickled down to the more informal JRC rank and file was more complicated. See Rideout, *Radical*, 145–46.

128   *"I listened to poets"*: Mangione, *Dream*, 33. See also Mangione, *An Ethnic at Large: A Memoir of America in the Thirties and Forties* (1978; repr., Syracuse: Syracuse University Press, 2001), 121–23.

128   *Cowley visited the same*: Cowley, *Dream*, 134–35. See chapter 13 for more on the JRC.

128   *stood a better chance*: Denning, *Cultural*, 207.

128   *One was Abe Aaron*: Drew, *Algren*, 51–52.

128   *joined the Illinois project*: Wisnewski, *Algren*, 76; Hazel Rowley, *Richard Wright: The Life and Times* (New York: Henry Holt, 2001), 109. Lipton was the father of the writer, actor, and TV host James Lipton.

129   *Dorothy Farrell*: Undated Chicago office roster, Mangione papers, box 9, folder 18. On her separa-tion from James T., see Edgar M. Branch, *James T. Farrell* (Minneapolis: University of Minnesota Press, 1963), 7.

129   *taken his name*: Studs Terkel, *Touch and Go: A Memoir* (New York: New Press, 2007), 104.

129   *a law school graduate*: Alan Wieder, *Studs Terkel: Politics, Culture, but Mostly Conversation* (New York: Monthly Review Press, 2016), 28–33. Terkel acted in productions of two of the era's most important political plays, an adaptation of Sinclair Lewis's anti-fascist novel *It Can't Happen Here* and Clifford Odets's Popular Front sensation *Waiting for Lefty*.

129   *project's radio division consisted*: Terkel, *Touch*, 99, 101; Terkel, John de Graaf, and Alan Harris Stein, "The Guerrilla Journalist as Oral Historian: An Interview with Louis 'Studs' Terkel," *The Oral History Review*, vol. 29, no. 1 (winter/spring 2002), 95.

129   *Terkel's scripts dealt*: See LOC FWPSS, box A867, folder "Radio Scripts Illinois Terkel, Louis." In "The Amazing Mister Nutmeg," a letter carrier, Mr. Nutmeg, has his secret exposed when everyone's mail is interrupted, and the anxious townspeople finally spot him in the home of

NOTES [333]

Mr. Pickle, holding a razor to Mr. Pickle's throat—and giving him a shave. Mr. Nutmeg admits, "Ever since I was a little boy I've wanted to be a barber, to give people haircuts and to shave them. Mr. Pickle is the only person in the village who understood me." This was apparently a true story from Cornwall, England; it was sponsored by Local 1 of the National Federation of Postal Clerks and the radio station WCFL.

129 *"dull guys won"*: Terkel, *Touch*, 193–94. See also David A. Taylor, *Soul of a People: The WPA Writers' Project Uncovers Depression America* (Hoboken, NJ: John Wiley and Sons, 2009), 53.

129 *noticed him cashing*: Drew, *Algren*, 118. It was Jack Conroy who noticed this.

130 *first was Richard Wright*: Hazel Rowley, *Richard Wright: The Life and Times* (New York: Henry Holt, 2001), 108.

130 *Bontemps's literary credentials*: Charles L. James, "Arna Bontemps," *New Crisis*, vol. 109, no. 5 (Sept./Oct. 2002); Steven C. Tracy, "Introduction," *Writers of the Black Chicago Renaissance* (Urbana: University of Illinois Press, 2011), 5.

130 *watch Algren flirt*: Mangione, *Dream*, 127.

130 *"Women liked him"*: Terkel, *Touch*, 196.

130 *hovered around ten*: Dolinar, *Negro*, xi–xii. For overall employment numbers, see "Employment Quotas by Units of Federal Writers Project from 1937 to July 1939," LOC KP, folder "WPA FWP State Guides 1937–41."

130 *Richard Durham*: Patrick Naick, "Richard Durham," *Writers of the Black Chicago Renaissance*, 185–92. In the late forties, Durham created three innovative radio shows that celebrated the African American experience: *Democracy USA*, *Here Comes Tomorrow* (the only Black serial on the air), and *Destination Freedom*.

130 *Fenton Johnson*: James C. Hall, "Fenton Johnson," *Writers of the Black Chicago Renaissance*, 218–32. Bontemps did include some of the WPA poems in an anthology he edited in the mid-sixties.

130 *Willard Motley*: Alan M. Wald, "Willard Motley," *Writers of the Black Chicago Renaissance*, 250–73.

130 *Frank Yerby*: James L. Hill, "Frank Yerby," *Writers of the Black Chicago Renaissance*, 386–412.

131 *Katherine Dunham*: Mangione, *Dream*, 127; Dolinar, *Negro*, xxii; Mangione papers, notes from an interview with Nathan Morris, Jan. 7, 1968, box 13, folder 7.

131 *paid no heed to Saul Bellow*: Mangione, *Dream*, 123.

131 *"Fundamentally his approach"*: Saul Bellow, "Sherwood Anderson," Jan. 19, 1939, FWP records, Lincoln Library, box 144, folder 40.

131 *"a story of American* bezprizorni": Jack Conroy, "The Hunted and Booted," *New Masses*, Apr. 16, 1935, 21–22.

131 *"fresh and sizzling"*: H. W. Boynton, "'Somebody in Boots' and Other Recent Works of Fiction," *The New York Times*, Apr. 7, 1935.

132 *Conroy was born*: My account of Conroy's early life and career is drawn from Douglas Wixson, *Worker-Writer in America: Jack Conroy and the Tradition of Midwestern Literary Radicalism, 1898–1990* (Urbana: University of Illinois Press, 1994).

133 *"Depression started early"*: quoted in Wixson, *Worker-Writer*, 72.

134 *activists like Michael Gold*: Gold was so enthused by *The Disinherited* that, instead of writing a conventional book review, he published a letter to Conroy in *New Masses* that was full of praise for the author, along with some gentle criticism of Conroy's weak characterization. See Michael Gold, "A Letter to the Author of a First Book," *New Masses*, Jan. 9, 1934, 25–26.

135 *"section of venerable"*: Conroy, "Writers Disturbing the Peace," *New Masses*, Nov. 17, 1936, 13.

135 *encountered a familiar face*: Wixson, *Worker-Writer*, 422–25.

135 *Jack Balch*: Balch would publish a novel about his FWP experience, *Lamps at High Noon*, and in it describe a character based on Conroy: "A more pacific and gentle person than Hennessey he had never met. The big fellow burlesqued pugnacity by the command of a robust and blasphemous vocabulary and often an ultra-menacing attitude. He fooled people with this mannerism sometimes, occasionally to his cost." At one point, Hennessey gets drunk and weeps over the suffering of workers; at another he threatens to punch a goon who is harassing a union meeting

and is himself immediately knocked out. But the protagonist, a stand-in for Balch, never wavers in his admiration. See Balch, *Lamps at High Noon* (1941; repr., Urbana: University of Illinois Press, 2000), 305.

135 *Alsberg's first choice*: Mangione, *Dream*, 76.

135 *Pendergast political machine*: David McCullough, *Truman* (New York: Simon and Schuster, 1992), 151–61, 194–200, 211–16. Truman's opponent in the race claimed that he would grow calluses on his ears from listening so often to orders from his boss over the phone; indeed, Pendergast's parting instructions to Truman were "Work hard, keep your mouth shut, and answer your mail."

135 *hired on his recommendation*: Mangione, *Dream*, 103–104.

135 *"I think these people"*: Alsberg to Geraldine Parker, July 7, 1936, NARA PI57, Cronyn papers, box 2, folder "Editorial Material (Other than Cronyn's) (Folder #1)."

135 *Parker revealed herself*: Mangione, *Dream*, 194–95.

136 *"I wouldn't hang him"*: quoted in Mangione, *Dream*, 195.

136 *Tensions finally exploded*: Mangione, *Dream*, 195–98; Penkower, *Federal*, 162–65.

136 *"Does the administration"*: Conroy, "Writers Disturbing the Peace," *New Masses*, Nov. 17, 1936, page 13.

136 Lamps at High Noon: Dora Thea Hettwer, for one, thought the novel offered a distorted view of the project. She wrote to Alsberg: "Though it is not a truthful picture of the project it nevertheless has much of truth in it, and therefore very misleading." See Dora Thea Hettwer to Alsberg, June 17, 1941, Alsberg/Hettwer correspondence, Bienes Museum of the Modern Book, box 1, folder 10.

136 *one in the public sector*: On the thorny issue of public sector workers organizing and striking during the New Deal, and Roosevelt's often misinterpreted attitude toward such activity, see Joseph A. McCartin, "An Embattled New Deal Legacy: Public Sector Unionism and the Struggle for a Progressive Order," in Gary Gerstle, Nelson Lichtenstein, and Alice O'Connor, eds., *Beyond the New Deal Order: U.S. Politics from the Great Depression to the Great Recession* (Philadelphia: University of Pennsylvania Press, 2019).

137 *"The government saves"*: Balch, *Lamps*, 309.

137 *"That is an absolute"*: Transcript of meeting in Alsberg's office, Nov. 10, 1936, Mangione papers, box 14, folder 1.

137 *Reed Harris concluded*: Years later, Harris insisted that Barker was indeed guilty of using the project photo lab to develop obscene photos he'd taken in the brothels of East St. Louis, and even hung the photos up. But Jack Balch, who knew Barker well, denied this strenuously and believed that Barker was fired as a power play against the project's radical contingent. See Jerre Mangione's interviews with Harris and Balch, Mangione papers, box 149, folders 32 (Harris) and 3 and 4 (Balch).

137 *stayed with the project*: Wixson, *Worker-Writer*, 428, 436–38.

137 *drafting guidebook copy*: For more on Conroy and Balch's project work, see Christine Bold, *The WPA Guides: Mapping America* (Jackson: University Press of Mississippi, 1999), 168–73; Conroy quoted on 169. Bold treats this episode in detail and considers it emblematic of the fundamental conflict between local knowledge being produced in the states and the centralizing, standardizing impulse of the DC office, whose editors sought to absorb all the copy into a New Deal master narrative.

138 *Conroy quit*: Wixson, *Worker-Writer*, 437–48.

138 *in the Algrens' bed*: Drew, *Algren*, 106.

138 *installed a new director*: Mangione, *Dream*, 338–39.

138 *they knew each other*: Wixson, *Worker-Writer*, 220, 310, 438.

138 The New Anvil: Wixson, *Worker-Writer*, 440–43.

139 *passed over for a job*: Wisnewski, *Algren*, 76.

139 *"If you're stopped"*: This was Orrick Johns speaking to *The New York Times*, quoted in Jerrold Hirsch, *Portrait of America: A Cultural History of the Federal Writers' Project* (Chapel Hill: University of North Carolina Press, 2003), 47.

140 *Henry Mayhew*: Ann Banks, "Preface," *First Person America* (1980; repr., New York: W. W. Norton, 1991), xxi.

140 *pulp magazines were stuffed*: William Stott, *Documentary Expression and Thirties America* (1973; repr., Chicago: University of Chicago Press, 1986), 199–201.

140 *Mass Observation movement*: Caleb Crain, "Surveillance Society," *The New Yorker*, Sept. 11, 2006, and http://www.massobs.org.uk/. Eventually, its three charismatic founders drifted away, and Mass Observation devolved into a market research company, and then dissolved completely. In 1981, a new iteration, the Mass Observation Project, was launched by the archive that holds records of the old M-O, and it persists to this day.

140 *an important prelude*: Hirsch takes up the significance of the FWP's life histories in *Portrait*, chapter 6, and argues that, because the FWP had a limited impact on the academic world, it can't properly be considered the overlooked, "real" originator of oral history in the United States.

141 *W. T. Couch*: For an overview of Couch's FWP work, see Hirsch, *Portrait*, chapter 7. Couch was originally associate director of the North Carolina project and then became regional director in order to carry out the collection of life histories from a higher perch. For more on the North Carolina project and a perceptive critique, see Bold, *WPA*, chapter 6.

141 *"The criteria to be observed"*: "Instructions to Writers," ed. W. T. Couch, *These Are Our Lives: As Told by the People and Written by Members of the Federal Writers' Project of the Works Progress Administration in North Carolina, Tennessee, Georgia* (1939; repr., New York: W. W. Norton, 1975), 418. Years later, more collections of these life histories appeared: in 1978, *Such As Us: Southern Voices of the Thirties*, ed. Tom E. Terrill and Jerrold Hirsch, and, in 1980, *First-Person America*, ed. Ann Banks. Additional collections continue to appear, some of them thematic and some state-specific. The Library of Congress maintains a large collection of digitized life histories on its website: https://www.loc.gov/collections/federal-writers-project/.

141 *"The people, all"*: W. T. Couch, "Preface," *These Are Our Lives*, xiii–xiv.

142 *"I'll admit there's some"*: "Them that Needs," *These Are Our Lives*, 366. Couch included the names of federal writers who collected the pieces and, where applicable, the editors; this was collected by Della Yoe and edited by Jennette Edwards.

142 *applied this task*: The FWP's second folklore editor, Benjamin Botkin, was the driving force behind efforts to collect folklore that was more expansively and inclusively conceived, especially material derived from industrial and urban settings. For more on Botkin, see chapter 4.

142 *into the Chicago streets*: Wixson, *Worker-Writer*, 438–39; Drew, *Algren*, 108–109, 111.

142 *"You see the way"*: These three extracts are from assorted reports in LOC FWPF, box A587, folder "Chicago Occupational Lore (Jack Conroy)."

143 *"Some of the waste"*: Banks, *First-Person*, 84. See also Banks, "Introduction," *First-Person*, xvii.

143 *"One day I tore"*: Abe Aaron, "Post Office workers—(Carriers)," June 22, 1939, and assorted reports, LOC FWPF, box A707, folder "Chicago Abe Aaron."

144 *"When a girl got nobody"*: Nelson Algren, "When You Live Like I Done," LOC FWPF, box A707, folder "Chicago Nelson Algren." See this folder for the Davey Day testimonial as well. Both are available on the LOC website; "When You Live Like I Done" appears in Banks's *First-Person America*, under the name Ellen O'Connor, 177–80.

144 *O'Connor's statement*: Sara Rutkowski, "Nelson Algren's *Personalism*: The Influence of the Federal Writers' Project," *Studies in American Naturalism*, vol. 9, no. 2 (winter 2014), 208.

144 *"Men at Work"*: LOC FWPSS, box A852, folder "'Men At Work' Draft (Folder 1 of 2)" and folder "'Men At Work' Draft (Folder 2 of 2)." A version of this manuscript was eventually published as *Men at Work: Rediscovering Depression-Era Stories from the Federal Writers' Project*, edited and introduced by Matthew L. Basso (Salt Lake City: University of Utah Press, 2012).

145 *"hillbilly from way"*: Banks, *First-Person*, "Highpockets," 90–92. For the idea that Conroy wrote some of Algren's narratives, see Wixson, *Worker-Writer*, 439, 570n63, 64. The other narrative is "Hank the Freewheeler," which appears in Benjamin Botkin's 1944 *Treasury of American Folklore*, attributed to Algren.

145 *wasn't gathering testimonials*: audio interview with Studs Terkel, Mangione papers, box 149a, folder 7. Terkel doesn't say it outright, but this interview contains hints that he wasn't much in contact with office life. He suggests that Mangione speak with supervisors for stories about work-place conflicts, and he wasn't aware that Arna Bontemps, whom he knew, worked for the project.

145 *"lucky to be alive"*: Terkel interview, *Soul of a People: Writing America's Story*, dir. Andrea Kalin, 2009, DVD deleted scenes.

146 *"I was an editor"*: Donohue, *Conversation*, 61.

146 *downplayed his own experience*: See, for instance, Mangione, *Dream*, 121; Penkower, *Federal*, 170; and Wisnewski, *Algren*, 78. Algren seems to have told similar stories to Mangione and Pen-kower, and to the filmmakers of the 1976 German documentary *The New Deal for Artists*, which is quoted in Wisnewski and excerpted in the 2015 documentary *Nelson Algren: The End Is Nothing, the Road Is All*, dir. Denis Mueller, Ilko Davidov, and Mark Blottner.

146 *"The truth is that"*: Algren to Erling Larsen, Mar. 19, 1964, in "The 1930's, a Symposium (with Poems, a Story, and Reviews)," *The Carleton Miscellany*, vol. 6, no. 1 (winter 1965), 104. Algren conti-nued: "The great fallacy of the era of Proletarian literature was that, with the single exception of Rich-ard Wright, it was conducted by intellectuals. Whatever I may have contributed was accidental since I was neither a proletarian nor an intellectual. All the right-thinking people I know are drug addicts."

146 *carried heavy traces*: For the literary scholar Sara Rutkowski, Algren's writing developed in a way that is representative of the FWP's broader influence on the shape of American literature: from an emphasis on social critique and documentary methods in the thirties to a postwar style of inward-looking, psychological fiction (or "personalism," as Malcolm Cowley put it in an essay). For an expanded treatment of this idea, see Rutkowski, "Nelson Algren," as well as Rutkowski's *Literary Legacies of the Federal Writers' Project: Voices of the Depression in the American Postwar Era* (New York: Palgrave Macmillan, 2017).

146 *"Men who may otherwise"*: Algren, "Federal Art Projects: WPA Literature," *The Chicago Artist*, vol. 1, no. 7 (Dec.-Jan. 1937-38), 6, 10. This obscure piece was brought to my attention by a reference in Drew, *Algren*, 105.

147 *held a staff meeting*: "Staff Conference in Industrial Folklore," July 13, 1939, LOC FWPF, box A707, folder "Chicago Administrative Materials."

147 *promoted to supervisor*: Conroy, "Memories of Arna Bontemps: Friend and Collaborator," *Ameri-can Libraries*, vol. 5, no. 11 (Dec. 1974), 602. According to Conroy, they became supervisors after John T. Frederick resigned and a new director instituted a testing system for promotions, which they both passed. Other sources seem to suggest that Algren became a supervisor earlier.

147 *"Listen to what"*: "I'm a Could-Have-Been," collected by Hyde Partnow of the NYC project, was published in *Direction* magazine under the title "I'm a Might-Have-Been," and was seemingly re-arranged. The original quoted here is available from the Library of Congress online, https://www .loc.gov/item/wpalh001505/. See also Mangione, *Dream*, 272-73.

TOUR FOUR: ZORA NEALE HURSTON, FLORIDA

149 *before she was*: "Statement of Katharine A. Kellock," undated, LOC KP, folder "Dies Committee, 1935-44 and U.D."; "A Red 'Baedeker'" advertisement, NARA PC37, box 0470, folder "Katha-rine Kellock." Kellock was a field representative for about six weeks. In mid-February, the "Red Baedeker" episode compelled Alsberg to reassign her to the less visible but vastly more important job as national tours editor. See chapter 1.

149 *Kellock was dismayed*: assorted reports, LOC KP, folder "WPA, Federal Writers' Project, Reports and Correspondence 1936-42." See also Jerre Mangione, *The Dream and the Deal: The Federal Writers' Project, 1935-1943* (1972; repr, Philadelphia: University of Pennsylvania Press, 1983), 65-66, and Christine Bold, *The WPA Guides: Mapping America* (Jackson: University Press of Mississippi, 1999), 127-28.

150 *"skilled city editor"*: quoted in Bold, *WPA*, 126.

150 *"Manuals are like"*: Kellock to Alsberg, Jan. 20, 1936, NARA PI57, field reports, box 1, folder "Florida–Kellock."

150 *"One person of writing"*: Alsberg to Kellock, Jan. 22, 1936, NARA PI57, field reports, box 1, folder "Florida–Kellock."

150 *impoverished in a deep*: Ira Katznelson, *Fear Itself: The New Deal and the Origins of Our Time* (2013; repr., New York: Liveright, 2014), 158, 170–72. See Katznelson's chapter 5 for a longer discussion of the political impact of southern backwardness on the New Deal.

151 *commissioned a study*: For an overview of the report, see David L. Carlton and Peter A. Coclanis, "1938 Economic Report on the South," *The New Encyclopedia of Southern Culture*, vol. 20, *Social Class* (Chapel Hill: University of North Carolina Press, 2012), 415–17. This episode only deepened the rift that, by 1938, was growing between the New Dealers and the bloc of conservative Southern Democrats.

151 *Florida was no exception*: Pamela G. Bordelon, "The Federal Writers' Project's Mirror to America: The Florida Reflection" (PhD diss., Louisiana State University and Agricultural and Mechanical College, 1991), 32–34.

151 *"Throughout more than"*: Federal Writers' Project, *Florida: A Guide to the Southernmost State* (New York: Oxford University Press, 1939), 3.

151 *a tragic start*: Nick Taylor, *American-Made: The Enduring Legacy of the WPA: When FDR Put the Nation to Work* (2008; repr., New York: Bantam Books, 2009), 203–204. Another Florida debacle was the WPA's attempt to build a cross-state shipping canal: it was underfunded from the start, opposed by farmers worried about salt water contaminating the aquifer, and then killed by Congress because Roosevelt had bypassed them without a specific appropriation for such a large project. See N. Taylor, *American-Made*, 205–207.

152 *"Wind and waves"*: FWP, *Florida*, 330. This passage puts the estimated victims at 800; earlier, on 61, it gives a Red Cross estimate of 425 dead and missing, which seems closer to the consensus.

152 *"You found them"*: Ernest Hemingway, "Who Murdered the Vets?" *New Masses*, Sept. 17, 1935, 9–10.

152 *project's main office*: The office seemed to be in the Roberts Building, while the state WPA offices were in the Exchange Building. Both appear on FWP correspondence, but, in every state, letters were often routed through the WPA office—see, for instance, a comment by the field supervisor Darel McConkey, who said the FWP was in the Roberts Building, not the Exchange Building, just as the DC staff was at 1500 I Street, the McLean mansion, and not 1734 New York Avenue, the Walker-Johnson Building and national headquarters for the WPA. Darel McConkey, field report, Sept. 19, 1936, NARA PI57, field reports, box 1, folder "McConkey–Florida."

152 *sent Alsberg favorable reports*: Kellock to Alsberg, Oct. 29, 1935, NARA PI57, field reports, box 1, folder "Florida–Kellock"; Kellock to Alsberg, Nov. 17, 1935, NARA PI57, field reports, box 1, folder "Kellock, Dist. Of Col."

152 *"heard gruesome details"*: Kellock to Alsberg, Jan. 23, 1936, NARA field report, box 1, folder "Florida–Kellock."

152 *"Can I talk"*: Kellock and Alsberg phone transcript, Jan. 22, 1936, Jerre Mangione papers, D.245, Rare Books, Special Collections, and Preservation, River Campus Libraries, University of Rochester, box 15, folder 3.

152 *"Broken bluffs beribboned"*: quoted in Bordelon, "Mirror," 72.

153 *"the ladies' club"*: Kellock to "My dearest" [Harold Kellock], Jan. 23, [1936,] LOC KP, folder "WPA, Federal Writers' Project, Reports and Correspondence 1936–42."

153 *"don't feel too worried"*: Kellock and Alsberg phone transcript, Feb. 3, 1936, Mangione papers, box 15, folder 3.

153 *very first copy*: Monty Noam Penkower, *The Federal Writers' Project: A Study in Government Patronage of the Arts* (Urbana: University of Illinois Press, 1977), 79. According to a field report, Mundo was a journalist who attained the rank of brigadier-general while fighting alongside Lee Christmas, the Louisiana-born mercenary, in three campaigns in Latin America. See McConkey

field report, Oct. 21, 1935–Nov. 1, 1935, NARA PI57, field reports, box 1, folder "Kentucky–Darel McConkey."

153 *"Negro Units," existed*: Bordelon, "Mirror," 133–35. The Louisiana Negro Unit was directed by Lawrence Reddick, the professor who'd initiated the interviews of formerly enslaved people under the FERA, which were continued by the FWP.

154 *"Ph.D's doing ditch-digging"*: Kellock to Alsberg, Jan. 23, 25, and 26, 1936, NARA PI57, field reports, box 1, folder "Florida–Kellock."

154 *took it for granted*: Typical was this statement from a field representative visiting the Georgia project: "They say that there is a law in Georgia prohibiting Negroes from working in the same office with white people. Even if this were not so I feel that as a matter of policy it would be best to keep Negroes out of the office." See Darel McConkey, "Field Report on Georgia, South Carolina, and North Carolina," Dec. 26, 1935, NARA PI57, field reports, box 1, folder "McConkey–Georgia."

154 *"This knowledge would"*: Carita Corse to Alsberg, Oct. 30, 1935, NARA PI57, administrative correspondence, box 9, folder "Florida A Miscellaneous."

154 *had someone in mind*: Corse to Alsberg, Oct. 19, 1935, NARA PI57, administrative correspondence, box 9, folder "Florida A Miscellaneous"; Corse to Kellock, Mar. 24, 1936, NARA PI57, editorial correspondence, box 8, folder "Florida Editorial 1935–1936."

154 *Alsberg gave Corse permission*: Alsberg to Corse, Feb. 20, 1936, NARA PI57, administrative correspondence, box 9, folder "Florida Employment 1936, 1935."

155 *following this same template*: At the same time, Horace Cayton, a sociologist at the University of Chicago, was overseeing a massive WPA-funded study of African Americans in Chicago, using mostly Black graduate students and some federal writers to compile the data; the federal writers in turn drew on some of that group's findings as they put together "The Negro in Illinois." Cayton's study became the basis for his 1945 book with St. Clair Drake, *Black Metropolis*. See Brian Dolinar, "Editor's Introduction," *The Negro in Illinois: The WPA Papers* (Urbana: University of Illinois Press 2013), xvii–xviii.

155 *"toothy and gracious"*: Jack Conroy, "Memories of Arna Bontemps: Friend and Collaborator," *American Libraries*, vol. 5, no. 11 (Dec. 1974), 604.

155 *The Florida unit*: For details about the Florida Negro Unit, see Stetson Kennedy, "Working with Zora," *All About Zora! Proceedings of the Academic Conference of the First Annual Zora Neale Hurston Festival of the Arts, January 26–27, 1990, Eatonville, Florida* (Winter Park, FL: Four-G Publishers, 1991), 122, 127; Catherine A. Stewart, *Long Past Slavery: Representing Race in the Federal Writers' Project* (Chapel Hill: University of North Carolina Press, 2016), 177–83; and *The Florida Negro: A Federal Writers' Project Legacy*, ed. Gary W. McDonogh (Jackson: University Press of Mississippi, 1993).

156 *Carita Corse appeared*: S. Kennedy, "Working," 121.

156 *"Maitland is Maitland"*: FWP, *Florida*, 361–62.

157 *Hurston was back in Florida*: My account of Hurston's life draws on Valerie Boyd, *Wrapped in Rainbows: The Life of Zora Neale Hurston* (New York: Scribner, 2003), and Robert E. Hemenway, *Zora Neale Hurston: A Literary Biography* (1977; repr., Urbana: University of Illinois Press, 1980), as well as Hurston's autobiographical *Dust Tracks on a Road*, collected in *Folklore, Memoirs, and Other Writings*, ed. Cheryl A. Wall (New York: Library of America, 1995).

157 *finished a grueling trip*: See Boyd, *Wrapped*, chapters 25 and 26, for an account of this journey and the genesis of *Their Eyes Were Watching God*.

158 *novel's fine reviews*: Not all the reviews were positive. Richard Wright famously attacked the book (see chapter 5), and Alain Locke wrote a mixed review that deeply perturbed Hurston, who'd seen Locke as a mentor. See Boyd, *Wrapped*, 306–309.

158 *"The bees are humming"*: Hurston to Carl Van Vechten, Feb. 21, 1938, in ed. Carla Kaplan, *Zora Neale Hurston: A Life in Letters* (2002; repr., New York: Anchor Books, 2003), 413.

158 *found a house for rent*: Pamela G. Bordelon, "Zora Neale Hurston: A Biographical Essay," *Go Gator and Muddy the Water: Writings by Zora Neale Hurston from the Federal Writers' Project* (New York: W. W. Norton, 1999), 22.

158 *"stillness on a calm day"*: Paul Diggs, "To the House by the Lake," in appendix B of McDonogh, *Florida*, 147. Diggs dated this piece Sept. 22, 1938, so he likely visited Hurston after she was already on the project.

158 *grandparents had been enslaved*: It is likely that one or more of Hurston's biological ancestors on her paternal side were white slaveowners, including, possibly, her grandfather. See Boyd, *Wrapped*, 15.

159 *"no discrete nuances"*: Hurston, *Dust*, 599–601. Clarke was the one who'd been elected marshal of Maitland and then became a founder of Eatonville.

159 *"seemed as she died"*: Hurston, *Dust*, 618.

160 *"Negro farthest down"*: Hurston, *Dust*, 689. Hurston here is paraphrasing Charlotte Mason, "Godmother," but she is in full sympathy with the idea of defining her life's work in such a way.

160 *"I found out too"*: Hurston, *Dust*, 664.

161 *Arna Bontemps*: Robert Bone, "Richard Wright and the Chicago Renaissance," *Callaloo*, no. 28 (summer 1986), 447.

161 *"My typewriter is clicking"*: Hurston to Annie Nathan Meyer, May 12, 1925, in Kaplan, *A Life*, 55.

162 *groundbreaking anthropologist*: For a thorough account of Boas and his students, including Hurston, see Charles King, *Gods of the Upper Air: How a Circle of Renegade Anthropologists Reinvented Race, Sex, and Gender in the Twentieth Century* (New York: Doubleday, 2019).

162 *Boas's thinking would have*: Jerrold Hirsch, *Portrait of America: A Cultural History of the Federal Writers' Project* (Chapel Hill: University of North Carolina Press, 2003), 5, 38. For Boas's specific if limited connection with the FWP, see Penkower, *Federal*, 149.

163 *"spy-glass of Anthropology"*: Hurston, *Mules and Men*, collected in Wall, *Folklore, Memoirs, and Other Writings*, ed. Cheryl A. Wall (New York: Library of America, 1995), 9.

163 *heavily plagiarized article*: The article was about Cudjo Lewis, a man believed to be the last enslaved African brought to the United States. Hurston did interview him but plagiarized a substantial portion of her article from an old history book. (Perhaps it was sloppiness, or resentment toward her assignment, or an impulse to sabotage her academic career that compelled her to pad out the meager material she'd gathered in person.) This episode was uncovered by the linguist William Stewart in 1972 and made public in Hemenway's 1977 biography; Hurston's longer manuscript about Lewis was finally published as *Barracoon: The Story of the Last "Black Cargo"* in 2018.

164 *Her advance for* Jonah's Gourd Vine: King, *Gods*, 211.

164 *"Every phase of Negro life"*: Hurston, "Characteristics of Negro Expression," in Wall, *Folklore, Memoirs, and Other Writings*, 830–31. This, along with five other essays, originally appeared in the 1934 book *Negro: An Anthology*, edited by Nancy Cunard.

164 *With the FTP*: William F. McDonald, *Federal Relief Administration and the Arts: The Origins and Administrative History of the Arts Projects of the Works Progress Administration* (Columbus: Ohio State University Press, 1969), 496–583. For a fine narrative account of the FTP, see also Susan Quinn, *Furious Improvisation: How the WPA and a Cast of Thousands Made High Art out of Desperate Times* (New York: Walker and Company, 2008).

164 *Hallie Flanagan*: Quinn, *Furious*, 30, 37, 39–40.

165 *"small, quietly decisive woman"*: John K. Hutchens, "Vassar's Hallie Flanagan," *The New York Times*, Sept. 22, 1935.

165 *"The newest adventure"*: Brooks Atkinson, "'The Revolt of the Beavers,' or Mother Goose Marx, Under WPA Auspices," *The New York Times*, May 21, 1937.

165 *Negro Unit in Harlem*: John Houseman, *Run-Through: A Memoir* (New York: Simon and Schuster, 1972), 173–210.

166 *"scandalized both Left and Right"*: Houseman, *Run-Through*, 205. In September 1936—six months after Hurston left the FTP—the Seattle Negro Unit staged a version of *Lysistrata* set in Africa, which was subsequently shut down by the state WPA. It's unclear if this was anything more than a coincidence. See Quinn, *Furious*, 206.

166 *"New York is not"*: Hurston to Edwin Osgood Grover, Dec. 29, 1935, in Kaplan, *A Life*, 363.

166 *offered her a job*: Bordelon, "Biographical," 14–15.

166 *had to go on relief*: It isn't entirely clear if Hurston went on relief when she joined the Federal The-
     ater Project. Like the FWP, the FTP set aside a percentage of jobs for non-relief technical experts.
     In the project's early days, when Hurston joined, it often exceeded its non-relief quota by a great
     deal (see McDonald, *Federal*, 524). So Hurston would have had the opportunity to join the project
     without going on relief; her peripatetic lifestyle may have made her ineligible, anyway, because
     of the residency requirement. Hurston's experience of going on relief is always discussed in the
     context of her FWP work.

167 *"something about poverty"*: Hurston, *Dust*, 635.

167 *"When I left Florida"*: Darel McConkey, field report, Apr. 22, 1938, NARA PI57, field reports,
     box 1, folder "McConkey–Florida."

167 *most published Black woman*: This is the judgment of Pamela Bordelon in "New Tracks on *Dust
     Tracks*: Toward a Reassessment of the Life of Zora Neale Hurston," *African American Review*,
     vol. 31, no. 1 (spring 1997), 19; and Boyd, *Wrapped*, 349, regarding the years immediately after
     Hurston's work for the FWP.

167 *saw a robust woman*: Nancy Williams, "An Interview with the State Director of the Federal Writ-
     ers' Project in Florida, Dr. Carita Doggett Corse," New Smyrna Beach, FL, 1976 (George A. Sma-
     thers Libraries, Special and Area Studies Collections, University of Florida, Gainesville), 11.

167 *Corse had directed*: For a description of Corse, see Bordelon, "Mirror," 41–43, 56–57.

167 *Pepper was a personal friend*: Claude Pepper to Alsberg, Dec. 18, 1937, NARA PI57, administrative
     correspondence, box 10, folder "Florida M–Z."

168 *woman running the project*: Lafayette McLaws to Alsberg, Jan: 9, 1937, NARA PI57, administra-
     tive correspondence, box 10, folder "Florida M–Z"; Bordelon, "Mirror," 43.

168 *"Her point of view"*: Kellock to Alsberg, Oct. 29, 1935, NARA PI57, field reports, box 1, folder
     "Florida–Kellock."

168 *"Corse is a Florida 'lady'"*: Kellock to Alsberg, Jan. 21, 1936, and Kellock, field report, Jan. 22,
     1936, NARA PI57, field reports, box 1, folder "Florida–Kellock." Corse's possible misspending
     aside, Kellock's investigation did discover that the state WPA was hitting the Florida project with
     unauthorized charges, likely motivated by hostility toward the arts projects in general. See Borde-
     lon, "Mirror," 51.

168 *admired Corse's prose*: Kellock to Corse, Apr. 10, 1936, NARA PC37, box 1107, folder "Florida
     651.317 1935 + 1936."

168 *Corse once insisted*: See assorted correspondence, NARA PI57, editorial correspondence, box 8,
     folder "Florida Editorial Miscellaneous 1937–1938."

168 *"Chamber of Commerce line"*: Alsberg untitled memo, Mar. 31, 1937, NARA PI57, Alsberg papers,
     box 2, folder "Miscellaneous (Folder #3)."

168 *project initially employed*: Bordelon, "Mirror," 36, 46–47.

169 *Only Corse and two others*: Corse to Alsberg, Nov. 7, 1935, NARA PI57, administrative correspon-
     dence, box 9, folder "Florida A Miscellaneous."

169 *No other workers on the Florida project*: Stetson Kennedy said that Hurston was the only published
     author, but this doesn't seem to be true. (See S. Kennedy, "Working," 121.) Before Hurston's time,
     the Florida project did hire a writer named Carl Lester Liddle, the co-author of a 1933 novel,
     Tunchi, about an American explorer dodging "head hunters" in a South American jungle. Corse
     fired him for inactivity, which seems to have had the opposite effect: as Bordelon put it, "Liddle,
     who was somewhat unbalanced, wrote so many letters to Washington questioning his dismissal
     that his file was soon an inch thick." See Bordelon, "Mirror," 60–61.

169 *cited her as an authority*: Alsberg to Corse, Jan. 28, 1938, NARA PI57, administrative correspon-
     dence, box 9, folder "Florida Tampa Guide."

169 *friends of a friend*: Hurston to Fannie Hurst, Jan. 22, 1937, in Kaplan, *A Life*, 392; see note 2.

169 *Corse invited Hurston*: Bordelon, "Biographical," 20.

169 *visit a Black storefront church*: Williams, Corse interview, 11–12.

169 *"It is putting back"*: Hurston, "The Sanctified Church," *Go Gator*, 97.

170 *Hurston's role on the project*: Alsberg to Corse, June 21, 1938, and Corse to Alsberg, June 27, 1938, NARA PI57, administrative correspondence, box 9, folder "Florida Employment"; see also Bordelon, "Biographical," 15–16. Accommodating Jim Crow seems the most likely explanation for why Corse would not make Hurston a supervisor, despite her excuse about the quota. Later that year, she made the white, twenty-two-year-old Stetson Kennedy a supervisor in charge of life histories, folklore, and social ethnic studies—a position for which Hurston was clearly more than qualified. See Corse to Alsberg, Dec. 9, 1938, NARA PI57, administrative correspondence, box 9, folder "Florida Employment."

170 *"Anybody heard from Zora?"*: S. Kennedy, "Working," 120–21. Hurston apparently kept a PO box in Maitland and had her paychecks sent there, so it's possible that, despite Kennedy's recollection, she sent FWP material from there, too, not Eatonville. See Bordelon, "New Tracks," 16.

170 *"Folk-lore is not"*: Hurston, *Mules*, 10.

171 *memories of her first trips*: See Boyd, *Wrapped*, chapters 16 to 19 for an account of this period, which largely formed the basis for Hurston's book *Mules and Men*. Hurston also recalls the attack and her time in New Orleans in *Dust*, 689–700.

171 *"carefully accented Barnardese"*: Hurston, *Dust*, 687.

171 *two of her nieces*: Bordelon, "New Tracks," 14–17. They were the daughters of her older brother Bob, a doctor, who'd died in 1935. Wilhelmina married a man named John Hamilton, a citrus picker and one of Hurston's sources.

172 *rested on three visible pillars*: David M. Kennedy, *Freedom from Fear* (New York: Oxford University Press, 1999), 117.

172 *collaboration with the racial structure*: Katznelson, *Fear*, chapter 5, 241–42, 260, 270–72; and Roger Biles, *The South and the New Deal* (Lexington: University Press of Kentucky, 1994), 111–17.

173 *symbol of this collaboration*: Katznelson, *Fear*, 83–92. In 1946, Bilbo was investigated by a Senate special committee over charges that he intimidated and threatened Black voters during his primary campaign—which he had—but the committee's majority of three southern Democrats ruled that he did nothing illegal. He died the next year, facing accusations of campaign finance misdeeds involving war contractors. He was eulogized in the Senate.

173 *wasn't purely an instrument*: Harvard Sitkoff, "The New Deal and Race Relations," *Toward Freedom Land: The Long Struggle for Racial Equality in America* (Lexington: University Press of Kentucky, 2010). This is Sitkoff's addendum to his 1978 study *A New Deal for Blacks*, which traces the modern civil rights movement back to the shortcomings of, and struggles over, the New Deal. For a view of how this complexity played out in the cultural realm, see Lauren Rebecca Sklaroff, *Black Culture and the New Deal: The Quest for Civil Rights in the Roosevelt Era* (Chapel Hill: University of North Carolina Press, 2009).

174 *"the term 'Civil War'"*: Mary Branham to Corse, Aug. 6, 1938, and Alsberg to Corse, Aug. 18, 1938, NARA PI57, editorial correspondence, box 8, folder "Florida State Guide Miscellaneous"; Stewart, *Long*, 47.

174 *FWP's race problem*: Penkower, *Federal*, 67; Stewart, *Long*, 124.

175 *weren't entirely acquiescent*: They initially had in mind for this position Mary Church Terrell, the prominent educator and activist. See Cronyn memo to Baker, Nov. 30, 1935, NARA PI57, Cronyn papers, box 2, folder "Instructions (Folder #2)." More pressure to act came from John Preston Davis, head of the Joint Committee on National Recovery, a broad African American coalition formed to push back against discrimination in New Deal programs. Davis also insisted that they hire someone to oversee the project's Negro Affairs and pushed for greater Black employment in state offices. See Stewart, *Long*, 49–50.

175 *"I feel that it would"*: Alsberg memo to Aubrey Williams, Dec. 16, 1935, NARA PI57, Alsberg papers, box 1, folder "H. G. Alsberg, G. W. Cronyn, and Reed Harris."

175 *oversee the "Negro Affairs" division*: For an overview of Brown and the work of the Negro Affairs division, see Sklaroff, *Black Culture*, chapter 3.

175 *highest-ranking African American*: Sklaroff, *Black Culture*, 83.

175 *had thrown a banquet at Howard*: Cronyn memo to Jacob Baker, Nov. 30, 1935, NARA PI57, Cronyn papers, box 2, folder "Instructions (Folder #2)."

175 *fusing Black vernacular culture*: Charles H. Rowell and Sterling A. Brown, "'Let Me Be with Ole Jazzbo': An Interview with Sterling A. Brown," *Callaloo*, vol. 21, no. 4 (autumn 1998), 789–809. This special issue of *Callaloo* devoted to Brown offers an expansive treatment of his life and work.

176 *poems somewhat in parallel*: Brown's first collection, *Southern Road*, would be published several years after Hughes's *Weary Blues*. But Brown's collection was highly praised and carried a glowing introduction by James Weldon Johnson. For the contemporary reception, see Hirsch, *Portrait*, 118–20.

176 *homecoming for Brown*: Joanne V. Gabbin, *Sterling A. Brown: Building the Black Aesthetic Tradition* (Charlottesville: University Press of Virginia, 1985), 15.

176 *Hurston may have met*: Boyd has Brown attending Stylus meetings at Howard but it's not clear if they met or even if they would have recalled it; both were present at the *Opportunity* awards ceremony but may not have spoken (see Boyd, *Wrapped*, 84, 97). They did meet later, according to a letter Hurston wrote to Mason on Sept. 16, 1932, in Kaplan, *A Life*, 272.

176 *to see* The Great Day: Hemenway, *Hurston*, 181.

176 *an impressive figure*: Hurston to Alain Locke, Mar. 24, 1934, in Kaplan, *A Life*, 294.

176 *"exploitation and terrorism"*: Sterling A. Brown, "Old Time Tales," *New Masses*, Feb. 25, 1936, 24–25. On the context of Brown's review, see Hemenway, *Hurston*, 220–21.

176 *small editorial team*: Brown was assisted by Glaucia B. Roberts, an editorial assistant and Howard graduate, and two other Black scholars, Ulysses Lee of Lincoln University and Eugene Holmes of Howard. See Stewart, *Long*, 51.

176 *immensity of their task*: Rowell, "Let Me Be," 801–802; Stewart, *Long*, 51–52.

176 *intervening in cases*: Cases of discrimination weren't confined to the deep South. In Oklahoma, Brown had to intervene when white workers stopped a Black colleague from using the water fountain. In New York, a less cut-and-dried situation involved Ted Poston (just beginning his career as a pathbreaking Black journalist), who was fired and blamed racial discrimination. The director, Travis Hoke, denied it strenuously, seemed hurt by the accusation, and said that other Black workers had started a petition in his defense. See Rowell, "Let Me Be," 801, and Hoke to Brown, Jan. 8, 1937, NARA PI57, Negro Studies, box 1, folder "letters from State Directors."

177 *particularly in the South*: There were problems in northern offices, of course. In NYC, before Brown came on board, a supervisor was fired for "grossly and inexcusably" discriminating against Black workers, as Alsberg put it. Van Olinda, the director at the time, blamed the situation on "white agitators and malcontents," and even cast some resentment at Alsberg for pushing him to hire African Americans who he believed were unqualified. Alsberg was firm when he reported the incident to Hopkins: "If there is one thing I have done in New York City that I think worthwhile it is removing Moran," the supervisor in question. See Alsberg memo to Harry Hopkins, Jan. 6, 1936, NARA PC37, box 2124, folder "651.317 New York City"; W. K. Van Olinda to Alsberg, Dec. 9, 1935, NARA PI57, administrative correspondence, box 33, folder "New York City 'N.'"

Norman Macleod's *You Get What You Ask For*, his novel about the project, includes a managing editor named Morrison who is unambiguously a racist:

In the meantime, Morrison was discriminating against the Negro workers, making them stand with cap in hand waiting for hours. I don't know what to do with those dinges, Morrison would confide in Gordon. They can't go interviewing borough presidents.
What's wrong with their working in Harlem? Gordon asked.
What can they write about Harlem? Morrison asked.

177 *"no apologia for slavery"*: Myrtle Miles to Alsberg, Mar. 4, 1937, and Miles to Cronyn, Aug. 17, 1937, NARA PI57, Negro Studies, box 1, folder "Incoming Letters by State"; Stewart, *Long*, 53–55.

177 *In North Carolina*: Bold, *WPA*, 133–35. "SOB Brown" is in Jerrold Hirsch's MA thesis "Culture on Relief: The Federal Writers' Project in North Carolina, 1935–42" (University of North Carolina, 1973) and is quoted in Bold, *WPA*, 135.

177 *Mississippi was his most trying*: Stewart, *Long*, 55–56.

177 *"Our faith is in God"*: Federal Writers' Project, *Mississippi: A Guide to the Magnolia State* (New York: Viking Press, 1938), 8; subsequent quotations on 22, 30, 431.

178 *"The Portrait of the Negro as American"*: Stewart, *Long*, 58–59. The book was never published.

178 *testimonials of formerly enslaved people*: One of these original scholars was Charles S. Johnson, who taught sociology at Fisk University. (As editor of *Opportunity*, Johnson published Zora Neale Hurston's early stories and encouraged her to move to New York.) Lawrence D. Reddick was a research assistant on the Fisk study, and he subsequently initiated the first federally funded project under the FERA, supervising twelve Black researchers who conducted 250 interviews with formerly enslaved people in Indiana and Kentucky. With the formation of the WPA, the FWP continued similar research (sporadically, at first) and eventually expanded it to other states. Johnson, meanwhile, became an advisor to the FWP. See Stewart, *Long*, 62–63. More than two thousand of these narratives are available to view online through the Library of Congress website. See also Norman R. Yetman's accompanying online essay, "An Introduction to the WPA Slave Narratives," and his more comprehensive "The Background of the Slave Narrative Collection," *American Quarterly*, vol. 19, no. 3 (autumn 1967), 534–53.

178 *raised some tricky questions*: Stewart, *Long*, 5, 34, 60–90.

178 *"The general run"*: quoted in Stewart, *Long*, 138.

179 *about sixty workers*: Corse to Alsberg, "Bi-Monthly Employment Report," July 6, 1938, NARA PI57, administrative correspondence, box 9, folder "Florida Employment 1938 1937."

179 *good portion of the tours*: McConkey to Alsberg, Mar. 1, 1938, and McConkey, field report, Florida, Apr. 22, 1938, NARA PI57, field reports, box 1, folder "McConkey–Florida."

179 *thought the Florida copy was weak*: Cronyn to Corse, May 26, 1937, NARA PI57, editorial correspondence, box 8, folder "Florida State Guide Essays"; see also assorted correspondence in this folder and folder "Florida State Guide Miscellaneous."

179 *"The Florida Negro"*: A version of "The Florida Negro" edited by Gary W. McDonogh was finally published in 1993, using manuscript selections from the earliest complete draft created in 1937, before Hurston joined the project—so it includes none of her work.

179 *unit had been gathering*: Bordelon, "Biographical," 25–27, 29, 30; Bordelon, "Mirror," 138.

180 *"There is still an opportunity"*: Hurston, "Proposed Recording Expedition into the Floridas," *Go Gator*, 67.

181 *"Obviously, leading citizens of towns"*: "Supplement #9-A (Replacing Part A of #9, March 12, 1936), Folklore and Folk Customs, July 27, 1936," LOC FWPG, box A7, folder 8.

181 *As a folklorist, Lomax*: For an overview of Lomax's early life and career, see John Szwed, *Alan Lomax: The Man Who Recorded the World* (2010; repr., New York: Penguin Books, 2011), chapters 1 to 3. Lomax was also known as the person who "discovered" and managed Leadbelly, the folksinger and former prisoner. Their relationship was fraught and continues to be a source of controversy.

182 *worked under the auspices*: Szwed, *Lomax*, 51–52, 54.

182 *Lomax spotted a tale*: George T. Blakey, *Creating a Hoosier Self-Portrait: The Federal Writers' Project in Indiana, 1935–1942* (Bloomington: Indiana University Press, 2005), 83–84.

182 *he gleefully reported*: Lomax to Alsberg, Oct. 6, 1936, NARA PI57, Alsberg papers, box 1, folder "H. G. Alsberg, G. W. Cronyn, and Reed Harris."

182 *who became the obstacle*: Hirsch, *Portrait*, 30; Stewart, *Long*, 101–103; "Sterling Brown: 1901–1989," in William Ferris, ed., *The Storied South: Voices of Writers and Artists* (Chapel Hill: University of North Carolina Press, 2013), 106.

182 *when they corresponded*: See, for instance, the letters in Kaplan, *A Life*, 333, 356–57, 359–61.

182 *recruited for a collecting trip*: Szwed, *Lomax*, 77–86.

183 *Alsberg replaced Lomax*: Mangione, *Dream*, 276. In *Portrait of America*, Jerrold Hirsch argues that Botkin, along with Sterling Brown and the social-ethnic studies editor Morton Royse, best embodied the FWP's spirit of romantic nationalism fused with cultural pluralism.

183 *Botkin belonged to a scholarly*: Mangione, *Dream*, 269–77.
183 *poems by Sterling Brown*: Robert G. O'Meally, "An Annotated Bibliography of the Works of Sterling A. Brown," *Callaloo*.
183 *"The folk movement must come"*: quoted in Mangione, *Dream*, 270.
184 *Hurston's contributions mixed*: Her known contributions are collected in Pamela Bordelon, *Go Gator and Muddy the Water: Writings by Zora Neale Hurston from the Federal Writers' Project*.
184 *"Folklore is the boiled-down"*: Hurston, "Go Gator and Muddy the Water," *Go Gator*, 68–88.
185 *question came up in every*: For instance, a field representative reported that, in Michigan, the director and head editor believed "that anything which belongs to Michigan must be good. So that workers in a Ford factory, according to their copy, leave work as clean as [if] they came out of a dry cleaning plant and as fresh as the proverbial daisies. They have a staff of good writers who resent this attitude in the Guide, accounting greatly for the friction in the office." See Joseph Gaer to Alsberg, field report, June 6, 1936, NARA PI57, field reports, box 4, folder "Gaer, Michigan."
185 *"palm trees and bathing beauties"*: Stetson Kennedy described the conflict in these terms. See David A. Taylor, *Soul of a People: The WPA Writers' Project Uncovers Depression America* (Hoboken, NJ: John Wiley and Sons, 2009), 173. For details about this rift, see S. Kennedy, "Working," 128–29; Bordelon, "Mirror," 89–91; and Bob [Robert Cornwall] to Stetson [Kennedy], Mar. 22, 1939, folder 14, Stetson Kennedy Papers, #4193, Southern Historical Collection, Wilson Library, University of North Carolina at Chapel Hill.
185 *project's two chief editors*: biographical statements, NARA PI57, field reports, box 1, folder "Florida–Kellock"; Darel McConkey, field report, Sept. 19, 1936, NARA PI57, field reports, box 1, folder "McConkey–Florida."
185 *Kennedy grew up*: D. Taylor, *Soul*, 162–67.
185 *"Aren't we going to have"*: Robert Cornwall to Stetson Kennedy, May 31, 1938, Stetson Kennedy papers, Broward County archives, box 7, folder 7.
185 *downplaying the two fatal hurricanes*: Alsberg to Corse, June 21, 1938, with McConkey memo attached, NARA PI57, editorial correspondence, box 8, folder "Florida State Guide Cities."
186 *Hunter and Phillips in charge*: Darel McConkey, field report, Apr. 22, 1938, NARA PI57, field reports, box 1, folder "McConkey–Florida."
186 *they were summoned to DC*: Phil [Roland Phillips] to Corse, Oct. 22, 1938, and Phillips to Dubie [Moselle DuBose], Oct. 24, 1938, folder 1, Kennedy papers, UNC; and assorted correspondence in folders 1 and 2; Bordelon, "Mirror," 92.
186 *"small dull offices"*: Flanagan, *Arena*, 285.
186 *"Uncle Henry wandering"*: Hunter to Corse, Dec. 1, 1938, and assorted correspondence from Hunter, Zora Neale Hurston Papers, Special and Area Studies Collections, George A. Smathers Libraries, University of Florida, Gainesville, Florida, box 13, folder 8.
186 *"from a Marxian perspective"*: Anonymous and undated "Memorandum" in folder 3, in Kennedy Papers, UNC. The memo's missing page appears to be in L1979-37_1514_35, Stetson Kennedy Papers, Southern Labor Archives, Special Collections and Archives, Georgia State University, Atlanta.
187 *"skimpy and patchy"*: Alsberg to Corse, Oct. 12, 1938, NARA PI57, editorial correspondence, box 8, folder "Florida State Guide Essays."
187 *sent for Hurston herself*: Bordelon, "Biographical," 28.
187 *1920 massacre in Ocoee*: S. Kennedy, "Working," 129–30; his notes and fragments of "No Race Champion" are in the Kennedy papers, GSU, as well as in the Hurston papers, UF; he also confirms the details of this episode involving Hurston in McDonogh, *Florida*, xx–xxi. For a historical account of the massacre, see Paul Ortiz, *Emancipation Betrayed: The Hidden History of Black Organizing and White Violence in Florida from Reconstruction to the Bloody Election of 1920* (Berkeley: University of California Press, 2005), 220–24 (cited in King, *Gods of the Upper Air*).
187 *Hurston had known Du Bois*: Hurston had been acquainted with Du Bois since she arrived in Harlem. They were sometimes collaborators: she joined the Krigwa players, a theater group he organized, and later, in the mid-thirties, contributed to his prospective *Encyclopedia Africana*. But

Hurston was a co-founder of the magazine *Fire!!* which was intended as a rebuke to the old-guard figures epitomized by Du Bois, their Victorian sensibilities, and their fixation on the race problem. Du Bois never spoke of *Fire!!* publicly but, so the rumor went, he took the attack personally and became sad and quiet whenever someone mentioned it. See Hemenway, *Hurston*, 47–50; Boyd, *Wrapped*, 135; Hurston to Du Bois, July 3, 1926, and Apr. 1936, in Kaplan, *A Life*, 86, 374.

188 *"Being poor myself":* Hurston to William Stanley Hoole, Mar. 7, 1936, in Kaplan, *A Life*, 367.

188 *had not been an eyewitness*: In his biography of Hurston, Hemenway points out that she does not include information about the Ocoee massacre in *Mules and Men*, even though it was close to Eatonville and the events would have entered the local lore. This, for Hemenway, was indicative of her "strategic and philosophic" approach to handling racism and Black resentment. See Hemenway, *Hurston*, 220.

188 *interviewing some of the townspeople*: Bordelon also notes that Hurston visited Ocoee and based her essay on interviews she conducted there, but leaves out or rejects the circumstances described by Kennedy. She does, however, acknowledge that "the Ocoee incident was not something that one would expect Zora Neale Hurston to chronicle, considering the vehement charges of contemporaries that she did not concern herself with racial injustice in her writings." And yet she does not suggest why Hurston did, in fact, write this unexpected account. See Bordelon, *Go Gator*, 146–47.

188 *a long paragraph*: FWP, *Florida*, 457.

188 *this is Kennedy's explication*: Kennedy was so dismayed by this episode (along with some of Hurston's other work) that he wrote an essay, "No Race Champion," castigating her for, he believed, soft-pedaling racism. But he never published it.

189 *"You might have been"*: Hurston to Corse, Dec. 3, 1938, in Kaplan, *A Life*, 417–18.

189 *relatively liberal on racial matters*: Stewart, *Long*, 175, 177–78.

189 *"Living in an all-colored town"*: Sterling Brown, review of *Their Eyes Were Watching God*, *The Nation*, Oct. 16, 1937.

190 *"no Negro exists as an individual"*: Hurston, "Art and Such," *Go Gator*, 142.

190 *probably wrote this essay*: Bordelon, "Biographical," 32.

190 *he drew up a list*: Brown to Daniel [Darel] McConkey, May 25, 1936, NARA PI57, Negro Studies, box 1, folder "General Letters File." Brown suggested Hurston alongside Mary McLeod Bethune, who supported the Florida Negro Unit from the start. (She and Bethune would clash after Hurston left the FWP and briefly worked at Bethune's college.) In this letter, Brown seems to think that Hurston was working for the FWP in Jacksonville already, although he wasn't sure if she'd left—which suggests that she did make some kind of arrangement with Corse, two years before she did officially join the project in early 1938.

190 *thinking of leaving the FWP*: Hurston to Van Vechten, Feb. 19, 1939, in Kaplan, *A Life*, 420–21.

190 *one unexpected development*: Boyd, *Wrapped*, 325.

190 *Both of them passed*: Stewart, *Long*, 188.

190 *appeared that year*: The guide included head and tail pieces by Robert Delson of the Federal Art Project, who'd also illustrated the Galena guide that Nelson Algren worked on. See Carita Corse to Alsberg, Mar. 29, 1939, NARA PC37, box 1108, folder "Fla. 651.3172 Jan. 1939–Jan. 1941."

191 *granted as much space*: The essay does include a few long sections on works of historical value, such as Inca Garcilaso de la Vega's account of the de Soto expedition—but those are different.

191 *"In older people"*: Williams, Corse interview, 9; see also Bordelon, "Biographical," 36–37.

191 *a recording machine*: Corse took Hurston's earlier request seriously and wrote to Alsberg, but they got no equipment until the following year. See Hurston to Corse, June 16, 1938, in Kaplan, *A Life*, 415.

191 *recorded directly onto acetate*: Herbert Halpert, "Coming into Folklore More Than Fifty Years Ago," *The Journal of American Folklore*, vol. 105, no. 418 (autumn 1992), 448–51.

191 *made Hurston the advance scout*: For more on the project's audio recordings and the trip into the turpentine camp, see Bordelon, "Biographical," 39–44; S. Kennedy, "Working with Zora," 123–24; and D. Taylor, *Soul*, 179–81.

192   *Her white colleagues*: This is Stetson Kennedy's account, which has him and Robert Cook meeting
       Hurston at the camp. Pamela Bordelon names another editor, William Duncan, as the one who trav-
       eled with Cook and met Hurston. All four of them—Hurston, Kennedy, Duncan, and Cook—visited
       the camp; some of Kennedy and Cook's recordings are available online from the Library of Congress.
       But the exact circumstances are somewhat unclear. For Robert Cook's FWP report on one visit, see
       "Photographing the Turpentine Industry at Cross City, Fla.," Hurston papers, UF, box 12, item 5.

192   *"Dear Lord," she said*: S. Kennedy, "Florida Folklife and the WPA," an introduction to *A Reference
       Guide to Florida Folklore from the Federal WPA Deposited in the Florida Folklife Archives* (Florida
       Division of Historical Resources, 1990), 18.

192   *"ambulatory repositories"*: S. Kennedy, "A Florida Treasure Hunt," Library of Congress website,
       https://www.loc.gov/collections/florida-folklife-from-the-works-progress-administration/articles
       -and-essays/a-florida-treasure-hunt/; see also S. Kennedy, "Working with Zora," 124.

192   *sang more than a dozen*: Bordelon, "Biographical," 45–46; "The Jacksonville Recordings," *Go
       Gator*, 157–77. These recordings are available online from the Library of Congress, https://www
       .loc.gov/collections/florida-folklife-from-the-works-progress-administration/. They're also in-
       cluded on a CD that accompanies the lavish scrapbook *Speak, So You Can Speak Again* by Lucy
       Anne Hurston and the Estate of Zora Neale Hurston (New York: Doubleday, 2004).

193   *interviewer was Herbert Halpert*: Halpert may or may not have realized that Hurston had helped to
       inspire his own career. He'd been a student of Mary Barnicle at NYU, and after listening to record-
       ings Barnicle had made with Alan Lomax—including some from their ill-fated expedition through
       the South with Hurston—he decided to become a folklorist. See Halpert, "Coming Into," 442–47.

193   *discarded by the white editors*: Bordelon, "Biographical," 35. Catherine Stewart makes the im-
       portant point that Hurston's colleagues on the Negro Unit might very well have agreed with
       the decision to drop her contributions, because her writing differed so markedly in tone and
       perspective—regarding racial progress and the value of folk customs—from what they had already
       written. See Stewart, *Long*, 174.

TOUR FIVE: RICHARD WRIGHT, NEW YORK CITY

195   *WPA's forty-ninth state*: Nick Taylor, *American-Made: The Enduring Legacy of the WPA: When
       FDR Put the Nation to Work* (2008; repr., New York: Bantam Books, 2009), 187.

195   *would have six directors*: Jerre Mangione, *The Dream and the Deal: The Federal Writers' Project,
       1935–1943* (1972; repr, Philadelphia: University of Pennsylvania Press, 1983), 83*n*.

196   *nation's literary capital*: The FWP's essay "Market Place for Words," in *New York Panorama*
       (New York: Random House, 1938), is a good summary, although oddly reluctant to assign the city
       any more importance beyond being an accidental cluster of literary commerce. See also Susan Ed-
       miston, "Literature," *The Encyclopedia of New York City*, 2nd ed., ed. Kenneth T. Jackson (New
       Haven: Yale University Press, 2010), 753–57.

196   *"Whether or not it may"*: FWP, *Panorama*, 162.

196   *more jobless writers and editors*: This was a constant note in criticism of the project from a variety
       of groups. For instance, the journalist George Creel, serving as president of the Authors' League
       Fund, sent Harry Hopkins a scathing letter: "The means test, together with the stupid arrange-
       ment by which each state has been given a certain amount of money regardless of whether that state
       has writers or not, has defeated your purposes and our hope. As you must know, writers are largely
       grouped in various centers. As a consequence, three-quarters of the states are utterly unable to
       find writers to fill their quotas, while in a city like New York, the quota is utterly inadequate to take
       care of the professional writers in need of work." He had a point, although there was an underlying
       meaning in the FWP's decision not merely to prop up pockets of professional writers but instead
       to stretch out across the country, reach into every county, and mobilize ordinary citizens far away
       from Manhattan.

197   *"hectic camaraderie among us"*: Anzia Yezierska, *Red Ribbon on a White Horse: My Story* (1950;
       repr., New York: Persea Books, 1987), 165.

197 *an example of both*: Reed Harris to Travis Hoke, July 30, 1936, and attached correspondence, NARA PI57, editorial correspondence, box 8, folder "Florida State Guide Essays"; Hoke to Harris, Nov. 9, 1936, and attached correspondence, NARA PI57, editorial correspondence, box 8, folder "Florida Editorial 1935–1936." Rose Silverman and Angelica Bastar were the Middle Spanish–speaking workers.

197 *"The Boondoggle and The Fact"*: Magraw to Harris, Jan. 6, 1936, NARA PI57, administrative correspondence, box 30, folder "New York City A Publicity 1935–1936."

197 *"We are here to write"*: Arthur Halliburton memo to staff, "Notes on Style for Rewrite Staff of Guide," May 4, 1936, NARA PI57, administrative correspondence, box 30, folder "New York City A Project Procedure."

197 *"vast psychodrama"*: Mangione, *Dream*, 155.

197 *"Although my reaction"*: Joseph Gaer to Alsberg, "Field Trip to Pennsylvania, Massachusetts, Connecticut, New Jersey and New York, December 27–31 [no year]," NARA PI57, field reports, box 1, folder "Gaer, Conn." In this report, he also recognizes the high level of talent among NYC project workers.

197 *bigness of the project*: The FWP undermined itself by not formally separating editorial and administrative duties within each state project, a structural flaw that was especially visible in NYC. Smaller offices found ways to get around this—for instance, Vardis Fisher maintained such a tiny staff that he could handle both, and Carita Corse tended to focus on editorial matters, while her assistants covered day-to-day administration. But New York was operating on a different scale; it was beset by administrative troubles while generating a vast amount of copy that required constant editorial attention.

197 *Communist Party had an official*: At the lowest level, the party was organized into shop units within workplaces and street/town units within certain geographic spaces, the latter being for members who did not belong to formal workplaces. Working in parallel to these units were party "fractions" within unions and other organizations. Units composed a section, sections composed a district, and districts fell under the national leadership. Above the national leadership was the international: the Comintern. This structure changed somewhat in 1935 with the Popular Front: street units were replaced by larger neighborhood branches (which eventually contained the most members), and industrial units, comprising members in the same industry or union, were formed alongside shop units. At the same time, the party experimented with other types of local formations, the better to participate in electoral politics and outside organizations. See J. Peters, *The Communist Party: A Manual on Organization* (New York: Workers Library Publishers, 1935), for a contemporary schematic, and for changes after 1935, see Harvey Klehr, *The Heyday of American Communism: The Depression Decade* (New York: Basic Books, 1984), 369–70.

198 *had its own newsletter*: Shaw to Alsberg, Apr. 12, 1938, NARA PI57, administrative correspondence, box 33, folder "New York City 'Ra–Ri.'" Shaw mentioned a similar publication, now defunct, for the music project but not the title.

198 *"Our workers were not"*: Orrick Johns, *Time of Our Lives: The Story of My Father and Myself* (New York: Stackpole Sons, 1937), 343–44. Johns was at that time the director of the New York City Reporters' Project, a short-lived operation that ran parallel to the FWP and covered WPA efforts in general.

198 *case of Norman Macleod*: Van Olinda to Alsberg, Jan. 31, 1936, NARA PI57, administrative correspondence, box 33, folder "New York City 'Mc'"; Mangione, *Dream*, 177–78. Years later, when he was an established poet and teacher, Macleod told Mangione a tamer version of this story, but the correspondence seems to contradict it.

198 *ended Macleod's career*: The Macleod story does not end there. Thanks to some friendly string-pulling, he got a job on the New Mexico project. He tore up no more guidebook copy but did get thrown in jail after a night of drinking, and had to ask the project director, Inez Cassidy, to bail him out. She agreed but threatened to let him rot next time. Eventually, he quit and wrote a novel, *You Get What You Ask For*, about his time on the project.

199 *"We were lousy"*: quoted in Mangione, *Dream*, 158. For the early days in the office, see Samuel Duff McCoy to George Cronyn, Dec. 6, 1935, NARA PI57, editorial correspondence, box 35, folder "NYC Guide Essays."

199 *"We could never find"*: Johns, *Time*, 345.

199 *hit with a petition*: Federal Writers Project Employees to Alsberg, "A Petition," Nov. 13, 1935, NARA PI57, administrative correspondence, box 29, folder "New York City A Employment 1935." It was signed by twenty-six workers, including Maxwell Bodenheim, Philip Rahv, and the future Dies Committee witness Edwin Banta.

199 *On a visit from DC*: Olinda to Alsberg, Nov. 8, 1935, NARA PI57, administrative correspondence, box 29, folder "New York City A Employment 1935."

199 *recalled spending 90 percent*: audio interview with Jimmy McGraw, Jerre Mangione papers, D.245, Rare Books, Special Collections, and Preservation, River Campus Libraries, University of Rochester, box 149, folder 43.

199 *"They picketed in our laps"*: audio interview with Vincent McHugh, Mangione papers, box 149, folder 34.

199 *Workers' Alliance was among*: Klehr, *Heyday*, 254–300. By 1939, roughly 75 percent of Workers' Alliance members were WPA workers.

200 *"Tom Girdler and Jimmy McGraw"*: audio interview with Jimmy McGraw, Mangione papers, box 149, folder 43.

200 *"The banners they carry"*: "The Federal Writer, Local 1700" newsletter, attached to Johns to Alsberg, June 9, 1936, NARA PI57, administrative correspondence, box 30, folder "New York City A Publicity 1935–1936."

200 *Hopkins once even intervened*: Hopkins memo to Woodward, July 13, 1938, NARA PC37, box 2125, folder "651.317 NYC July 1938."

201 *First was Walter K. Van Olinda*: Mangione, *Dream*, 161.

201 *resituated him in Washington*: According to Katharine Kellock's notes on the Washington staff, Van Olinda remained as a national editor until 1939. See her notes, LOC KP, folder "WPA Federal Writers' Project, Personnel records, 1969."

201 *Alsberg thought highly of Johns*: "Report on the McCoy Case," Feb. 14, 1936, NARA PC37, box 2124, folder "651.317 New York City." On Johns's politics, see Johns, *Time*, 342.

201 *bizarre and potentially damaging episode*: For an overview, see Mangione, *Dream*, 161–63; Alsberg's account is in his "Report on the McCoy Case," Feb. 14, 1936, and his memo to Baker, Feb. 17, 1936, NARA PC37, box 2124, folder "651.317 New York City."

201 *Samuel Duff McCoy*: Excerpt from *Who's Who of 1932*, attached to Grace H. Gosselin to Alsberg, Sept. 5, 1935, NARA PI57, administrative correspondence, box 33, folder "New York City 'Mc.'"

201 *"the unfit, the unruly"*: Lucas to Alsberg, Feb. 8, 1936, NARA PC37, box 2124, folder "651.317 New York City."

202 *Project workers whispered*: Mangione, *Dream*, 161n.

202 *"Is there any way"*: William Nunn and Baker telephone transcript, Feb. 11, 1936; see also transcripts for Feb. 10 and 12; as well as Baker and McCoy telephone transcript, Feb. 11, 1936, NARA PC37, box 2124, folder "651.317 New York City." Nunn, the WPA's Federal #1 administrator in New York City, made his feelings clear in his Feb. 11 conversation with Baker: "I have just had a long talk with Lucas," the right-wing agitator. "I told him in no uncertain terms where to get off. He is a white Russian, identified with the Fascists."

202 *press framed the blowup*: "M'Coy is Dismissed in WPA Writer Row," *The New York Times*, Feb. 13, 1936; "M'Coy Says Fight on Reds Cost Job," *The New York Times*, Feb. 14, 1936.

202 *Lucas's mutiny was hollow*: Alsberg memo to Baker, Feb. 15, 1936, NARA PC37, box 2124, folder "651.317 New York City."

202 *"Everybody hated them"*: audio interview with Donald Thompson and Jimmy McGraw, Mangione papers, box 149a, folder 8.

202 *parody telegram ostensibly dropped*: "Federal Writer," attached to Johns to Alsberg, June 9, 1936, NARA PI57, administrative correspondence, box 30, folder "New York City A Publicity

1935–1936." Lucas was said to have dropped his telegram from the *Hindenburg*, which was still in regular operation that summer, before its final voyage.

203 *a Communist Party member*: Johns, *Time*, 322. According to his memoir, Johns left the party around the time he left the FWP, although the exact timeline isn't clear.

203 *"Roosevelt-fostered national-chauvinist art"*: Orrick Johns, "The John Reed Clubs Meet," *New Masses*, Oct. 30, 1934, 25–26.

203 *"Orrick was a man"*: Vincent McHugh audio interview, Mangione papers, box 149, folder 33. McHugh also corroborated the story of Johns using his wooden leg in bar fights.

203 *after being run over*: Johns, *Time*, 119–20.

203 *"Every payday he would"*: Oral history interview with Jacob Baker, Sept. 25, 1963, Archives of American Art, Smithsonian Institution.

203 *"If one could have"*: "Activities of Writers' Projects," Aug. 21, 1936, NARA PI57, box 36, editorial correspondence, folder "NYC Editorial Miscellaneous 1936."

204 *"It is afflicted"*: Cronyn to Johns, Aug. 25, 1936, and Johns to Alsberg, Aug. 26, 1936, NARA Alsberg papers, box 2, folder "Miscellaneous (Folder #2)."

204 *"Henry, I don't know"*: transcript of telephone conversation, Alsberg and Nunn, Apr. 26, 1936, Mangione papers, box 15, folder 6.

204 *Fate intervened before*: Johns, *Time*, 348; Mangione, *Dream*, 83; "WPA Executive Hurt," *The New York Times*, Oct. 24, 1936.

204 *"exaggerated ideas of Mr. Johns'"*: James Hopper to Harris, Dec. 1, 1936, NARA PI57, administrative correspondence, box 32, folder "NYC Orrick Johns Personal."

205 *"The project is being made"*: Johns to Alsberg, Dec. 4, 1936, NARA PI57, administrative correspondence, box 32, folder "NYC Orrick Johns Personal." Further, he called Alsberg's attempt to transfer him "a surrender to reactionary forces," the faction led by W. O. Lucas, "and their systematic campaign of calumnies, lies and frauds, culminating in the instigation to personal violence to gain their ends."

205 *"swell chap and a fine writer"*: Alsberg to Adelaide Schulkind, Oct. 24, 1935, NARA PI57, box 32, administrative correspondence, folder "NYC Travis Hoke Personal"; see also transcript of telephone conversation, Alsberg and Nunn, Apr. 26, 1936, Mangione papers, box 15, folder 6.

205 *"his nerves were plainly"*: Lawrence Morris to Ellen Woodward, Mar. 27, 1937, NARA PC37, box 2125, folder "651.317 New York City–January 1937."

205 *As Hoke unraveled*: Mangione, *Dream*, 182. Hoke stayed on as a member of the Guilds Committee, the entity that sponsored the NYC guidebook, so he could remain connected to the FWP. See also Hoke to Alsberg, July 2, 1937, and Alsberg to Hoke, July 9, 1937, NARA PI57, administrative correspondence, box 32, folder "NYC Travis Hoke Personal."

205 *Rather than hiring*: It seems that, at one point, the writer and editor Harold Loeb was poised to take over the NYC project, but this must have fallen through. Loeb "headed the group that published *The Chart of Plenty*, has published two novels, and was editor of *The Broom*." See Alsberg memo to Woodward, May 26, 1937, NARA PC37, box 2125, folder "651.317 New York City June 1937."

205 *trio of editors took over*: These were Donald Thompson, Hoke's assistant, who became acting director, along with an editor, Vincent McHugh, and a supervisor, Jimmy McGraw. See Mangione, *Dream*, 182. He calls them a "troika."

205 *McHugh restructured the office*: Mangione, *Dream*, 169–75.

205 *wrote most of the opening essay*: Christine Bold, *The WPA Guides: Mapping America* (Jackson: University Press of Mississippi, 1999), 96.

205 *"All the rays of force"*: FWP, *Panorama*, 4.

206 *strikes on the NYC project*: Mangione, *Dream*, 164–66.

206 *"A MERRY CHRISTMAS"*: Edward F. Gahan telegram to Roosevelt, Dec. 31, 1936, NARA PC37, box 2125, folder "651.317 New York City–January 1937."

206 *possessed two warring instincts*: William E. Leuchtenburg, *Franklin D. Roosevelt and the New Deal, 1932–1940* (1963; repr., New York: Harper Perennial, 2009), 243–46; N. Taylor, *American-Made*, 345–50.

206 *biggest cut yet to the WPA*: Mangione, *Dream*, 167; William F. McDonald, *Federal Relief Administration and the Arts: The Origins and Administrative History of the Arts Projects of the Works Progress Administration* (Columbus: Ohio State University Press, 1969), 223.

206 *mood of labor*: For the broader labor movement context, see David M. Kennedy, *Freedom from Fear* (New York: Oxford University Press, 1999), chapter 10. On the complex and sometimes contentious relationship between the labor movement and the Roosevelt administration, see Steve Fraser, "The 'Labor Question,'" in *The Rise and Fall of the New Deal Order, 1930–1980*, ed. Steve Fraser and Gary Gerstle (Princeton: Princeton University Press, 1989). For a consideration of how New Deal labor law was limited in terms of gender and race, see Eileen Boris, "To Live Decently: New Deal Labor Standards, Feminized Work, and the Fight for Worker Dignity," in *Beyond the New Deal Order: U.S. Politics from the Great Depression to the Great Recession* ed. Gary Gerstle, Nelson Lichtenstein, and Alice O'Connor (Philadelphia: University of Pennsylvania Press, 2019).

207 *their own sit-down strike*: Mangione, *Dream*, 167–69.

207 *"Of course, the first thing"*: "Shaw Scores Cut in WPA Projects," *The New York Times*, June 25, 1937.

207 *brought in an outside firm*: The firm was the venerable social welfare organization and publisher Survey Associates, and the investigator was Robert W. Bruere, whose day job was with the Department of Labor. See Paul Kellogg to Alsberg, Apr. 18, 1937, NARA PI57, administrative correspondence, box 32, folder "New York City 'K.'"

207 *"Almost from the start"*: Robert W. Bruere memo to Paul U. Kellogg, "Appraisal of the Federal Writers' Project in New York City," June 23, 1937, NARA PC37, box 2125, folder "1 of 2 651.317 New York City–August 1937." Bruere applauded the strikes but he didn't approve of them aping the sit-down tactics of steelworkers and autoworkers. His recommendations included that they immediately hire a strong director but also restructure the project so that administrative and editorial duties were handled separately, among other changes.

208 *point to some accomplishments*: Donald Thompson to Alsberg, Oct. 8, 1937, "Federal Writers' Project Publications, New York City," NARA PI57, editorial correspondence, box 34, folder "NYC Editorial Miscellaneous 1937."

208 *New York Times Book Fair*: Thompson to Alsberg, Dec. 8, 1937, NARA PI57, administrative correspondence, box 33, folder "NYC New York Times Nat'l. Book Fair." The DC office used the photos of Hurston and Hurst for publicity purposes.

208 *Richard Wright quit the Illinois project*: Wright's biographical details are drawn from Hazel Rowley, *Richard Wright: The Life and Times* (New York: Henry Holt, 2001), and Michael Fabre, *The Unfinished Quest of Richard Wright*, trans. Isabel Barzun, 2nd ed. (1973; repr., Urbana: University of Illinois Press, 1993), as well as Wright's own autobiographical *Black Boy (American Hunger)*, collected in *Later Works* (New York: Library of America, 1991).

209 *"I sensed that Negro life"*: Wright, *Black Boy*, 254–55.

209 *a delegate to the first*: Rowley, *Wright*, 105–107.

209 *demise of the John Reed Club*: Douglas Wixson, *Worker-Writer in America: Jack Conroy and the Tradition of Midwestern Literary Radicalism, 1898–1990* (Urbana: University of Illinois Press, 1994), 377–81.

210 *forged a friendship*: On Wright and Algren, see, for instance, Colin Asher, *Never a Lovely So Real: The Life and Work of Nelson Algren* (New York: W. W. Norton, 2019), 104–105; and Wright, *Black Boy*, chapter 18.

210 *"grossly sectarian"*: Jerre Mangione, *An Ethnic at Large: A Memoir of America in the Thirties and Forties* (1978; repr., Syracuse: Syracuse University Press, 2001), 124.

210 *tone of the gathering had modulated*: The proceedings are collected in Henry Hart, ed., *The Writer in a Changing World* (n.p.: Equinox Cooperative Press, 1937).

210 *to hear Eugene Holmes*: Eugene Clay [Holmes], "The Negro in Recent American Literature," *American Writers' Congress*, ed. Henry Hart (New York: International Publishers, 1935), 145–53; Holmes, *Changing World*, "A Writer's Social Obligations," 172–79.

210 *"a man who has been associated"*: Holmes, *Changing World*, 241–49. See also "Writers' Vote Spurns 'Gone With the Wind,'" *The New York Times*, June 7, 1937.

212 *case hadn't gone unnoticed*: See assorted correspondence, NARA PI57, administrative correspondence, box 30, folder "New York City Richard Wright." Paul Edwards, the WPA administrative officer in NYC, understood completely that Wright was qualified and capable, but he insisted, fairly, that NYC residents be given preference because there had been so many dismissals at that time. See, in the above folder, Edwards to Woodward, Sept. 28, 1937.

212 *writing for the* Daily Worker: Rowley, *Wright*, 127–29. Wright's pieces are collected in *Byline Richard Wright: Articles from the Daily Worker and New Masses*, ed. Earle V. Bryant (Columbia: University of Missouri Press, 2015).

212 *almost unrecognizable as the place*: On the idea of contrasting Wright's *Daily Worker* articles with the more celebratory work of the Harlem Renaissance, see Bryant, "Introduction: Arrival," *Byline*, 1–4.

212 *"This isn't fiction"*: [Wright], "Negro, with 3-Week-Old Baby, Begs Food on Streets," *Daily Worker*, Aug. 4, 1937, in *Byline*, 58.

213 *"I gritted my teeth"*: Wright, *Black Boy*, 342.

213 *pushed forward with his own writing*: Rowley, *Wright*, 131–37.

213 *"Hurston seems to have"*: Wright, "Between Laughter and Tears," *New Masses*, Oct. 5, 1937, 22–25.

214 *had failed the challenge*: One reader of Wright's "Blueprint for Negro Writing" was Stetson Kennedy, who was so impressed that he sent Wright a letter. The essay also shaped Kennedy's opinion of Zora Neale Hurston, and he quotes from it in his unpublished critique of her, "No Race Champion." See David A. Taylor, *Soul of a People: The WPA Writers' Project Uncovers Depression America* (Hoboken, NJ: John Wiley and Sons, 2009), 173; and Kennedy, "No Race Champion," Zora Neale Hurston Papers, box 12, Special and Area Studies Collections, George A. Smathers Libraries, University of Florida, Gainesville, Florida.

214 *it was a question*: For more on the FWP's creative endeavors, or lack of them, see Mangione, *Dream*, 241–55; Monty Noam Penkower, *The Federal Writers' Project: A Study in Government Patronage of the Arts* (Urbana: University of Illinois Press, 1977), 165–77, and McDonald, *Federal*, 696–704.

214 *"Works Progress Administration took shape"*: Katharine Kellock, "The WPA Writers: Portraitists of the United States," *The American Scholar*, vol. 9, no. 4 (autumn 1940), 477.

215 *major part of his speech*: Hart, *Changing World*, 247. Alsberg cast some of the blame on his audience: "If those of you who are in the Authors League had put on the heat," he said, "we probably would have had a magazine. But the gap is such between you and me and the project that I do not get any support from you and you do not even know what I am doing." He also described the very real problem of how to handle ownership rights of creative work produced by FWP workers: technically, anything they wrote on the project was property of the federal government, and if a book was a bestseller, the profit would go to the US Treasury while the author received the normal salary. It was hard to motivate creative writers under these conditions, Alsberg admitted.

215 *Field representatives sent word*: See, for instance, "Field Report general on Calif., Nev., Utah, Mont.," July 22, 1937, NARA PI57, field reports, box 1, folder "Harris–Cal–Field."

215 *"We know that you agree"*: David Rosenberg to Alsberg, July 15, 1936, NARA PI57, administrative correspondence, box 34, folder "New York City 'Ro–Ry.'"

215 *talk of absorbing Jack Conroy's*: Anvil editorial board to Alsberg, July 15, 1937, NARA PC37, box 0469, folder "211.7 1935–(A)."

216 *stand-alone volume of creative work*: *American Stuff: An Anthology of Prose and Verse by Members of the Federal Writers' Project with Sixteen Prints by the Federal Art Project*, ed. Henry G. Alsberg (New York: Viking Press, 1937). A follow-up to *American Stuff* appeared as a special issue of *Direction* magazine in 1938, the closest the FWP came to issuing a national creative magazine of its own.

216 *"Apparently these young artists"*: Alsberg, "Foreword," *American Stuff*, viii. Alsberg is quite transparent when he discusses the failure of the FWP to formally support creative writing; much of the foreword lays out the many obstacles (although this can be read as excuse-making).

217 American Stuff *editorial group*: "An Editorial Conference," *Conversations with Richard Wright*, ed. Keneth Kinnamon and Michel Fabre (Jackson: University Press of Mississippi, 1993), 6–7. Jerre Mangione later wrote that he personally "persuaded" Alsberg to include the essay in *American Stuff*, but it's hard to imagine Alsberg needing much persuading—unless he foresaw the controversy that was yet to come. See Mangione, *Ethnic*, 263.

218 *"My grandmother was as nearly"*: Wright, *Black Boy*, 39.

219 *"the first experience"*: Wright, *Black Boy*, 40.

220 *"my first baptism"*: Wright, *Black Boy*, 48.

221 *Reviewers noticed the essay's*: Eda Lou Walton, "A Federal Writers' Anthology," *The New York Times*, Aug. 29, 1937; Stephen Vincent Benét, "A Vigorous Anthology of Mixed Americana," *New York Herald Tribune*, Sept. 5, 1937; Jack Conroy, "Review and Comment," *New Masses*, Sept. 14, 1937. It was a significant measure of the FWP's reputation that a negative review of *American Stuff*, by the poet Horace Gregory in *The Nation*, still praised the FWP and even argued for making it permanent, albeit with an emphasis on folklore. "It must be regarded as a first step toward recognizing the responsibility of a civilization to its writers," Gregory wrote. See Horace Gregory, "F.W.P. Homework," *The Nation*, Sept. 11, 1937.

221 *contest for federal writers*: Rowley, *Wright*, 138–39; Alsberg to Whit Burnett, Nov. 27, 1936, and assorted correspondence, NARA PI57, administrative correspondence, box 34, folder "New York City Story Magazine." In an embarrassing slip, one of the runners-up, Richard Greenleaf of Florida, turned out to have not worked for the project since late 1935.

221 *quit the* Daily Worker: Bryant, *Byline*, 249, 253. Wright did contribute to the *Daily Worker* again the following year—a piece on the Louis-Schmeling boxing match—but not again, despite requests.

221 *"Sixty-Third and Stoney Island"*: quoted in Roy Wilder, "Wright, Negro Ex-Field Hand, Looks Ahead to New Triumphs," *New York Herald Tribune*, Aug. 17, 1941, in *Conversations*, 36.

222 *"wave of dust struck their eyes"*: This novel is *Lawd Today!*, which Wright first titled "Cesspool." It was published in 1963, after his death. The passage is in *Lawd Today!* collected in *Early Works* (New York: Library of America, 1991), 116–17.

222 *pushed burial insurance*: By his own account of the insurance job, Wright freely took advantage of the poor women who were willing to trade sex for their ten-cent premium. Whether the arrangement shamed him or whether he was embarrassed by the women is less clear. See Wright, *Black Boy*, 275–80.

222 *submitted a report*: Wright, "Ethnographical Aspects of Chicago's Black Belt," Sept. 29, 1936, Federal Writers' Project Records, 1935–1944, Abraham Lincoln Presidential Library, Springfield, IL, box 199, folders 4 and 5.

224 *detour into the Federal Theater Project*: Rowley, *Wright*, 113–15, 118. In *Black Boy (American Hunger)*, Wright describes joining the FWP and being told by "the administrator of the project" that his Black critics at the FTP were encouraged by his enemies in the Communist Party who wanted to get him fired. This may be written for dramatic effect. Ted Ward, Wright's friend who joined the Negro Unit at his behest, believed that the Black actors were manipulated by anti-left forces, possibly conservative whites, not by CP enemies of Wright. See Wright, *Black Boy*, 358–59, and Alan M. Wald, "Theodore Ward," *Writers of the Black Chicago Renaissance* (Urbana: University of Illinois Press, 2011), 324.

224 *"You get the hell off"*: Wright, *Black Boy*, 348.

224 *editing essays for the Illinois guide*: Wright to Harris, May 22, 1937, NARA PI57, administrative correspondence, box 30, folder "New York City Richard Wright."

224 *He outlined a book*: Rollins to Brown, Mar. 2, Mar. 8, and Apr. 23, 1937, NARA PI57, Negro Studies, box 1, folder "Letters from State Directors"; Brown to Rollins, Mar. 6 and Apr. 21, 1937, NARA PI57, Negro Studies, box 2, folder "Negro Books."

224 *"spoiled by the author's faults"*: "Illinois Negro Material General Criticism," Apr. 22, 1937, NARA PI57, editorial correspondence, box 13, folder "Ill. April 36–June 37."

225 *South Side Writers' Group*: For an overview of the group, see Robert Bone and Richard A. Courage, *The Muse in Bronzeville: African American Creative Expression in Chicago, 1932–1950* (New Brunswick, NJ: Rutgers University Press, 2011), 161–67.

225 *Frank Marshall Davis*: Davis is sometimes included among federal writers in Chicago, but this is wrong: he never joined the FWP. During these years, he was employed by the Associated Negro Press. He did join the South Side Writers' Group and the League of American Writers, and through these organizations got to know federal writers including Wright, Walker, Conroy, and Algren. See Frank Marshall Davis, *Livin' the Blues: Memoirs of a Black Journalist and Poet* (Madison: University of Wisconsin Press, 1992), 238–49. On p. 245, Davis says he did not work for the WPA.

225 *Walker had arrived in Chicago*: Maryemma Graham, "Margaret Walker," *Writers of the Black Chicago Renaissance*, 297–319.

225 *put her in touch with Wright*: Margaret Walker, *Richard Wright, Daemonic Genius: A Portrait of the Man, a Critical Look at His Work* (New York: Warner Books, 1988), 71–72. Walker covers this period of her life in chapter 13.

225 *gained admission with a lie*: Mangione, *Dream*, 124.

225 *Whenever she visited*: Walker, *Daemonic*, 72–73.

226 *She was fond of*: John Griffin Jones interview with Walker, "A Mississippi Writer Talks," Mar. 13, 1982, in *Conversations with Margaret Walker*, ed. Maryemma Graham (Jackson: University Press of Mississippi, 2002), 75.

226 *didn't know Saul Bellow*: Jones, "Mississippi Writer," 75.

226 *Conroy was wonderful*: Kay Bonetti, "An Interview with Margaret Walker Alexander," 1991, in *Conversations*, 128. Walker discusses Algren in this interview as well.

226 *"food was always the same"*: Walker, *Daemonic*, 80. For her impressions of the project's general atmosphere, see 69–70, 78–80.

226 *three hundred poems*: Margaret Walker, "My Creative Adventure," *On Being Female, Black, and Free: Essays by Margaret Walker, 1932–1992*, ed. Maryemma Graham (Knoxville: University of Tennessee Press, 1997), 13.

226 *her style began to change*: D. Taylor, *Soul*, 48.

226 *"Here in the fish picture"*: Margaret Walker, "WPA Tour Art Institute: An Illustrated Lecture of the Expressionists' School of Artists," Feb. 3, 1938, Lincoln Library, box 75, folder 8.

227 *so was Nelson Algren*: Jones, "Mississippi Writer," 81; Walker, *Daemonic*, 297. According to Franklin Folsom, who'd been the league's executive secretary, Black federal writers who became members included Walker, Wright, Arna Bontemps, Ralph Ellison, Frank Yerby, Eugene Holmes, and (briefly) Claude McKay; other prominent Black members included Langston Hughes, Gwendolyn Brooks, Countee Cullen, Jessie Fauset, and Alain Locke. See Folsom, *Days of Anger, Days of Hope: A Memoir of the League of American Writers, 1937–1942* (Niwot: University Press of Colorado, 1994), 75.

227 *published Walker's first short story*: Wixson, *Worker-Writer*, 441.

227 *"Let the martial songs"*: Margaret Walker, "For My People," *Poetry*, Nov. 1937. Later versions of this poem break its lines in different places and drop the concluding exclamation point.

227 *Benét chose her for the prize*: "Margaret Walker, Stephen Vincent Benét, and the Yale Series of Younger Poets," Oct. 9, 2019, https://beinecke.library.yale.edu/article/margaret-walker-stephen-vincent-benet-and-yale-series-younger-poets.

227 *Wright said he'd be leaving*: Walker, *Daemonic*, 103–104.

228 *walked into the NYC project*: Donald Thompson to Alsberg, Jan. 6, 1938, NARA PI57, administrative correspondence, box 30, folder "New York City Richard Wright."

228 *more than 200,000 people*: "Idle Total Highest in New York State," *The New York Times*, Jan. 3, 1938. A census of the unemployed found nearly a million in the state of New York who were either out of work or on a work relief program that fall; nationwide, it was 7,822,912 people.

228 *appointment of yet another*: Alsberg to Shaw, Jan. 20, 1938, and H. A. Watt to Alsberg, Dec. 11, 1937, NARA PI57, administrative correspondence, box 34, folder "NYC Harry L. Shaw";

Lawrence Morris memo to Aubrey Williams, Dec. 30, 1937, NARA PC37, box 2125, folder "1 of 2 651.317 New York City—August 1937."

228 *"The fact remains that"*: "An Editorial Conference," *Conversations with Richard Wright*, 8.

228 Panorama *essay was begun*: Rowley, *Wright*, 543n82. Wright was helped with the material by another worker, Arnold DeMille.

228 *literary reputation was well established*: Wayne F. Cooper, "Introduction," *The Passion of Claude McKay: Selected Prose and Poetry, 1912–1948* (New York: Schocken Books, 1973).

228 *inhabited the same world*: Alsberg's biographer suggests that they could have met during this time and identifies them as friends later in life, during the FWP years, but doesn't provide any specifics. McKay did write to Alsberg in 1935 when he was trying to get on the NYC project; he hoped that Alsberg could put in a good word but his letter doesn't suggest that they were close. See Susan Rubenstein DeMasi, *Henry Alsberg: The Driving Force of the New Deal Federal Writers' Project* (Jefferson, NC: McFarland and Company, 2016), 96, 181; and McKay to Alsberg, Oct. 22, 1935, NARA PI57, administrative correspondence, box 33, folder "New York City 'Mc.'"

229 *they didn't get along*: Arnold Rampersad, *Ralph Ellison: A Biography* (New York: Alfred A. Knopf, 2007), 111–12.

229 *McKay as a relic*: In 1940, McKay published his last book, *Harlem: Negro Metropolis*, which drew on material collected by the FWP—critics weren't impressed, and, after years of declining health and a conversion to Catholicism, he died in 1948.

229 *"verve and frankness"*: Alsberg to James D. Hart, Apr. 28, 1939, LOC FWPC, box A5, folder 1.

229 *response was excellent*: Robert Van Gelder, "Four Tragic Tales," *The New York Times*, Apr. 3, 1938; May Cameron, "Author! Author!: Prize-Winning Novelist Talks of Communism and Importance of 'Felt Life,'" *New York Post*, Mar. 12, 1938, in *Conversations with Richard Wright*, 3.

230 *"I had a most unhappy time"*: Eleanor Roosevelt, "My Day," Apr. 1, 1938, Eleanor Roosevelt Papers Digital Edition. For clarification, see Toru Kiuchi and Yoshinobu Hakutani, *Richard Wright: A Documented Chronology, 1908–1960* (Jefferson, NC: McFarland and Company, 2014), 72. Fabre and Rowley seem to mistake the latter phrase for a piece of Roosevelt's column, but it appeared only in her separate letter.

230 *"a book about hatreds"*: Zora Neale Hurston, "Stories of Conflict," *The Saturday Review*, Apr. 2, 1938.

230 *"I consider Richard Wright"*: Alsberg to Wright, Apr. 9, 1938, and Alsberg to Hopkins, Apr. 13, 1938, NARA PI57, administrative correspondence, box 30, folder "New York City Richard Wright."

231 *launching the magazine* New Challenge: [Wright], "Negro Writers Launch Literary Quarterly," *Daily Worker*, June 8, 1937, in *Byline*, 237–38; see also 215–22.

231 *West was a field worker*: For an overview of Dorothy West's experience on the NYC project, considered alongside those of Wright, Hurston, and Walker, see Sara Rutkowski, *Literary Legacies of the Federal Writers' Project: Voices of the Depression in the American Postwar Era* (New York: Palgrave Macmillan, 2017), chapter 5.

231 *"definitely psychopathic"*: Harry Shaw to Alsberg, May 10, 1939, NARA PI57, administrative correspondence, box 29, folder "Edward Dahlberg." Dahlberg seems to have spent an early stint on the project working on the NYC guide, and then returned to join the creative unit. Alsberg knew Dahlberg could be difficult but believed it was worth bringing a writer of his stature and promise on board. See assorted correspondence, NARA PI57, administrative correspondence, box 29, folder "Edward Dahlberg."

231 *"quiet but determined"*: Travis Hoke to Reed Harris, Jan. 19, 1937, NARA PI57, administrative correspondence, box 33, folder "New York City 'P.'"

231 *Kenneth Fearing and May Swenson*: For more on Fearing and Swenson, see Jason Boog, *The Deep End: The Literary Scene in the Great Depression and Today* (New York: OR Books, 2020), chapter 6 and 94–100.

231 *the project's fiercest Trotskyists*: For his biography and experiences on the project, see Harry Roskolenko, *When I Was Last on Cherry Street* (New York: Stein and Day, 1965). According to

Roskolenko, James P. Cannon, a leading American Trotskyist, drew a paycheck from the FWP—although he was signed up under a false name and didn't, in fact, do anything.

232 *Roskolenko asked a speaker*: Hart, *Changing World*, 225, 228; see also Malcolm Cowley, Kenneth Burke, Granville Hicks, William Phillips, and Daniel Aaron, "Symposium: Thirty Years Later; Memories of the First American Writers' Congress," *The American Scholar*, vol. 35, no. 3 (summer 1966), 509.

232 *favorite target of* Red Pen: "Red Pen Exposes Secret Campaign of Trotskyite Attacks on Project Unity," *Red Pen*, Jan. 1938, NARA PI57, administrative correspondence, box 33, folder "New York City 'Ra–Ri'"; Roskolenko, *When*, 153.

232 *Wright got along*: Roskolenko, *Cherry*, 153–54.

232 *Wright promised that*: According to Roskolenko, when Wright said this, they were sitting in a cafeteria on Third Avenue drinking coffee with John Cheever, Lionel Abel, Philip Rahv, and Claude McKay. See Roskolenko, *Cherry*, 153.

232 *Roskolenko thought of it*: Roskolenko, *Cherry*, 150–55.

233 *Yezierska was a full generation*: For Yezierska's biography, see Louise Levitas Henriksen, with assistance from Jo Ann Boydston, *Anzia Yezierska: A Writer's Life* (New Brunswick, NJ: Rutgers University Press, 1988). Yezierska's own account of her life, *Red Ribbon on a White Horse*, is essentially a fictional reworking of real events and people; her description of the NYC project is half invented and shouldn't be taken literally.

234 *"From an author in Hollywood"*: Yezierska, *Red*, 219.

234 *"Their waiting was no longer"*: Yezierska, *Red*, 156, 161–62.

234 *"calm smile of a young Buddha"*: Yezierska, *Red*, 157.

234 *Joe Gould, the peerless eccentric*: Mangione, *Dream*, 178–81.

235 *"My own book"*: quoted in Jill Lepore, *Joe Gould's Teeth* (New York: Alfred A. Knopf, 2016), 103.

235 *He was fired*: For this episode, see Alsberg to Harold Strauss, Feb. 2, 1939, LOC FWPC, box A2, folder 4; Alsberg to Joe Gould, Feb. 11, 1939, LOC FWPC, box A2, folder 5; Alsberg to E. E. Cummings, Mar. 7, 1939, LOC FWPC, box A3, folder 3; James Magraw to Alsberg, Feb. 16, 1939, and Gould to Alsberg, Feb. 10 and 12, 1939, NARA PI57, administrative correspondence, box 29, folder "New York City Employment E–H."

235 *Cheever first wrote*: John Cheever to Alsberg, Sept. 25, 1935, NARA PI57, administrative correspondence, box 31, folder "New York City 'Ca–Cl.'"

235 *recommendation of Saxe Commins*: DeMasi, *Alsberg*, 123–24, 210.

235 *staying in the apartment of Walker Evans*: For an account of Cheever during this period, see Blake Bailey, *Cheever: A Life* (New York: Alfred A. Knopf, 2009), chapters 6 and 7.

236 *"There is also an old lady"*: Cheever to Elizabeth Ames, *The Letters of John Cheever*, ed. Benjamin Cheever (1988; repr., New York: Simon and Schuster, 2009), 45.

236 *Cheever decamped to Manhattan*: Bailey, *Cheever*, 96–97.

236 *contributing some prose*: Bold, *WPA*, 110.

236 *"twisting into order"*: quoted in Bailey, *Cheever*, 96.

236 *sent Cheever other assignments*: Alsberg to Cheever, Nov. 26, 1938, NARA PI57, administrative correspondence, box 28, folder "New York City"; Alsberg to Cheever, Jan. 19, 1939, LOC FWP, box A2, folder 2.

236 *Cheever again tried*: Alsberg to Cheever, Jan. 7, 1939, LOC FWPC, box A1, folder 6; Alsberg to Cheever, May 19, 1939, Cheever to Alsberg, May 19, 1939, and Alsberg to Cheever, June 2, 1939, NARA PC37, box 0474, folder "211.711 A–Z."

237 *Ellison's path to the FWP*: For a biographical account of Ellison, see Arnold Rampersad, *Ralph Ellison*.

237 *"These rich bastards"*: quoted in Rampersad, *Ellison*, 111.

237 *As a federal writer*: Rampersad, *Ellison*, 110–16, 154. See also J. J. Butts, "Ralph Ellison and the Federal Writers' Project," *American Studies*, vol. 54, no. 3 (2015), 35–49. Sara Rutkowski examines more textual and thematic links between the FWP and Ellison's writing—particularly the central place of oration and orality in *Invisible Man*—in *Literary Legacies*, chapter 4.

238 *"It proves that anyone"*: James Baldwin, preface to *The Negro in New York: An Informal Social History, 1626–1940*, edited by Roi Ottley and William J. Weatherby," in *The Cross of Redemption: Uncollected Writings*, ed. Randall Kenan (New York: Pantheon Books, 2010), 227.

238 *Ellison's research could be tedious*: list of assignments, LOC FWPN, box A885, folder "New York City Administrative List of Worker Assignments."

238 *Halpert spent several months*: Herbert Halpert, "Coming into Folklore More Than Fifty Years Ago," *The Journal of American Folklore*, vol. 105, no. 418 (autumn 1992), 451.

238 *"Sweet-the-Monkey"*: Ellison, "Leo Gurley," *First Person America*, ed. Ann Banks (1980; repr., New York: W. W. Norton, 1991), 243.

238 *he was training himself*: Banks, "Introduction," *First Person America*, xx.

239 *creative writing unit*: It seems that there were other instances of federal writers being permitted to do creative work away from the office, although New York had the only organized unit. Margaret Walker, for instance, said that, for a time, she turned in chapters of a novel as her project assignment. See Walker, *Daemonic*, 77, and Penkower, *Federal*, 167.

239 *their own self-selected creative assignments*: On the formation of this unit, see assorted correspondence, NARA PI57, editorial correspondence, box 35, folder "NYC Creative Assignments." Johns is quoted from Johns to Alsberg, Aug. 25, 1936. See also Mangione, *Dream*, 245, and Penkower, *Federal*, 166–67. Documentation about this unit is sketchy, and the details in Mangione's and Penkower's brief accounts don't completely align.

239 *"I feel that everyone"*: Robert W. Bruere memo to Paul U. Kellogg, "Appraisal of the Federal Writers' Project in New York City," June 23, 1937, NARA PC37, box 2125, folder "1 of 2 651.317 New York City–August 1937."

240 *used the time to bundle*: Cooper, "Introduction," 36–37.

240 *"Suddenly I was a poet"*: Roskolenko, *Cherry*, 155.

240 *followed his usual procedure*: See assorted letters from Alsberg, LOC FWPC, box A1, folder 5.

240 *"written without a single drink"*: Harry Kemp to Alsberg, undated, NARA PI57, administrative correspondence, box 32, folder "New York City 'K'"; see also Penkower, *Federal*, 167.

240 *"an insult to the intelligence"*: James Magraw to Alsberg, Feb. 7, 1939, NARA PI57, administrative correspondence, box 29, folder "New York City Employment E–H." That editor was Harold Rosenberg.

240 *Bodenheim initially seemed*: Mangione, *Dream*, 160.

240 *who took up the constant picket*: audio interview with Jimmy McGraw, Mangione papers, box 149, folder 43.

240 *Bodenheim read his poems*: Fabre, *Quest*, 114–15.

241 *living in Brooklyn with a couple*: Rowley, *Wright*, chapter 8.

241 *if she would handle some research*: Walker, *Daemonic*, 122–25. Walker's relationship with Wright ended in the summer of 1939, after he left the FWP and *Native Son* was being revised. Walker was visiting him in New York and he severed their connection; the circumstances are somewhat murky, but their relationship had always been complicated. Walker treats this at length in Richard Wright, *Daemonic Genius*, 127–46.

241 *"When I went into news offices"*: Walker, *Daemonic*, 122.

242 *"Only my deep interest"*: Bennett Cerf to Alsberg, June 16, 1938, NARA PI57, editorial correspondence, box 35, folder "NYC Guide Sponsorship & Publication Arrangements."

242 *passed the gas station on Lexington*: Alsberg to Harold Strauss, Feb. 20, 1939, NARA PI57, editorial correspondence, box 35, folder "NYC Guide Tours." On another occasion, Alsberg wrote to Strauss about the New York City guide and said, "I want to give it the once-over myself." See Alsberg to Strauss, Feb. 20, 1939, LOC FWPC, box A3, folder 2.

242 *appeared in September*: "WPA Guide to City Is Due Wednesday," *The New York Times*, Sept. 11, 1938, and "WPA City Guide Out June 21," *The New York Times*, June 11, 1939.

242 *"It is hard to believe"*: Ralph Thompson, "Books of the Times," *The New York Times*, Sept. 14, 1938, and "Briefly Noted," *The New Yorker*, Sept. 17, 1938.

242 *"useful, broadly informative"*: Katherine Woods, "Here Is All New York," *The New York Times*, July 23, 1939, and Charles Poore, "Books of the Times," *The New York Times*, July 1, 1939.

242 *"one of the finest books"*: Cerf to NYC project, May 31, 1939, NARA PC37, box 0474, folder "211.72 Jan. 1939."

242 *unexpectedly harsh response*: Marshall also said that this line—that her pages "less consistently" maintained a reputation for liberalism than Cowley's pages—was one she'd seen before in Communist Party and CP-aligned literature and implied that FWP radicals were responsible. See Marshall to Shaw, Sept. 21, 1938, NARA PI57, box 33, administrative correspondence, folder "New York City The Nation."

242 *directorial churn continued*: Shaw to Alsberg, Sept. 22, 1938, and Alsberg to Shaw, Sept. 23, 1938, NARA PI57, administrative correspondence, box 34, folder "NYC Harry L. Shaw." For a while, Shaw stayed on as a consultant.

242 *appointed Harold Strauss*: He was an acting director for the beginning of his term, and then hung around for a few months as a consultant after he resigned the directorship. In March 1939, Carl Mamberg became the next temporary director, until he was replaced by Frederick Clayton that September. See Alsberg memo to Lawrence Morris, Mar. 20, 1939, and Strauss to Alsberg, Oct. 18, 1937, NARA PI57, administrative correspondence, box 34, folder "New York City Harold Strauss."

243 *"Several of the project boys"*: Wright to Alsberg, Aug. 22, 1938, and Mar. 27, 1939, NARA PI57, administrative correspondence, box 34, folder "New York City 'Wh–Wy.'" The poet Kenneth Fearing, who'd already left the project, was awarded a fellowship that year, too. See Alsberg telegram to Clair Laning, Mar. 27, 1939, NARA PI57, administrative correspondence, box 30, folder "New York City Publicity Jan to July 1939."

243 *cranked out a press release*: Lawrence Morris to Roscoe Wright, Mar. 27, 1939, NARA P37, box 0470, folder "G–H."

243 *"country's best known writers"*: "America Learns of Negro from Books of the Federal Writers' Project," Mar. 6, 1939, NARA Negro Studies, box 1, folder "Releases and Information on Federal Writers' Project."

243 *"feather in the cap of WPA"*: Edward Aswell to Harry Shaw, June 1, 1938, NARA PI57, administrative correspondence, box 30, folder "New York City Richard Wright."

244 *quit the project altogether*: Mangione, *Dream*, 289–90.

244 *"All workers on Federal Project"*: "Special Bulletin No. 88," Aug. 4, 1938, NARA PI57, administrative correspondence, box 28, folder "New York City A Miscellaneous 1937–1938."

TOUR SIX: HENRY ALSBERG AND MARTIN DIES, JR., WASHINGTON, DC

245 *"When Roosevelt was elected"*: Martin Dies, Jr., *Martin Dies' Story* (New York: Bookmailer, 1963), 138. For his attitude toward the New Deal, see Dies, *Story*, 58, 101, and William Gellerman, *Martin Dies* (1944; repr., New York: Da Capo Press, 1972), 40.

246 *southern populist who looked the part*: Gellerman, *Dies*, 72–73.

246 *hostile to concentrated wealth*: Gellerman, *Dies*, 32–39.

246 *introduced on his second day*: Walter Goodman, *The Committee: The Extraordinary Career of the House Committee on Un-American Activities* (New York: Farrar, Straus and Giroux, 1968), 20.

246 *His father, Martin Dies, Sr.*: Gellerman, *Dies*, 16–30.

246 *congressional nativists passed*: This type of legislation wasn't unique to the United States; it belonged to a worldwide surge of exclusionary and often xenophobic immigration laws during the first decades of the twentieth century. See Kiran Klaus Patel, *The New Deal: A Global History* (Princeton: Princeton University Press, 2016), 21–23, 171–76.

246 *majority of Communist Party members*: Harvey Klehr, *The Heyday of American Communism: The Depression Decade* (New York: Basic Books, 1984), 5, 162–63, 381. In 1929, readership of the *Daily*

Worker was less than one tenth the combined readership of the party's foreign-language papers. Party leaders worried that having too few native-born members isolated them from the US working class; even the Comintern admonished the American party for this imbalance.

246 *passed Dies's version*: August Raymond Ogden, *The Dies Committee: A Study of the Special House Committee for the Investigation of Un-American Activities, 1938–1943* (Washington: Catholic University of America Press, 1943), 31–32.

247 *"the great alien invasion"*: Martin Dies, Jr., "The Immigration Crisis," *The Saturday Evening Post*, Apr. 20, 1935.

248 *inimical to the portrait of America*: Jerrold Hirsch's *Portrait of America: A Cultural History of the Federal Writers' Project* (Chapel Hill: University of North Carolina Press, 2003) makes the case that the FWP's key architects were motivated by a sensibility that combined romantic nationalism and cultural pluralism. On Dies's contrasting ideology and why he saw the FWP as a threat, see 199–201.

248 *welcoming of immigrants*: During the New Deal, the exclusionary immigration legislation from the 1920s was left in place—making the FWP perhaps among the most overtly pro-immigrant elements of the entire New Deal apparatus. The historian Jefferson Cowie argues that these immigration restrictions led to a sense of white, working-class cohesion that in fact helped make the New Deal possible. See Cowie, *The Great Exception: The New Deal and the Limits of American Politics* (Princeton: Princeton University Press, 2016), 130–32.

248 *break with the Roosevelt administration*: Dies, *Story*, 139.

248 *"Free silverites, single taxers, Socialists"*: Dies, *Story*, 29–30, 130–31.

249 *court-packing scheme*: Dies, *Story*, 139–40.

249 *Senate launched investigations*: Ogden, *Dies*, 14–18.

249 *"The worst of it is"*: quoted in Ogden, *Dies*, 18. On another occasion, London was excoriated for his socialist politics in a lengthy floor speech by none other than Martin Dies, Sr. See Gellerman, *Dies*, 25–28.

249 *committee led by Representative Hamilton Fish*: Ogden, *Dies*, 23–32; Goodman, *Dies*, 6–9.

250 *"They do not seem to know"*: Edmund Wilson, *The American Earthquake: A Documentary of the Twenties and Thirties* (1958; repr. New York: Farrar, Straus and Giroux, 1979), 187.

250 *begat the McCormack Committee*: Goodman, *Committee*, 3–4, 10–12; Ogden, *Dies*, 32–37.

250 *He paid attention when*: Dies, *Story*, 59–60; Goodman, *Committee*, 14–20; Ogden, *Dies*, 45.

251 *members were appointed in June*: Goodman, *Committee*, 24; Ogden, *Dies*, 46.

251 *Dies's statements leading up*: Ogden, *Dies*, 47–51.

251 *signaled the onslaught*: Ogden, *Dies*, 48; "Theatre Project Faces an Inquiry," *The New York Times*, July 27, 1938. See also "J. Parnell Thomas, Anti-Red Crusader, Is Dead," *The New York Times*, Nov. 20, 1970.

251 *"obviously absurd"*: "Defends Theatre Project," *The New York Times*, July 28, 1938.

252 *a cauldron of accusation*: See, for instance, Jerre Mangione, *The Dream and the Deal: The Federal Writers' Project, 1935–1943* (1972; repr, Philadelphia: University of Pennsylvania Press, 1983), 290–92; Monty Noam Penkower, *The Federal Writers' Project: A Study in Government Patronage and the Arts* (Urbana: University of Illinois Press, 1977), 181–86; and Hirsch, *Portrait*, 51. Easley's attack was part of a bigger campaign against the WPA and indeed a longer pattern of anti-left activism; see "Easley Says Reds Rule WPA Writers," *The New York Times*, July 19, 1937.

252 *none other than W. O. Lucas*: "Sit-in Groups Win ERB Concessions," *The New York Times*, July 22, 1937.

252 *Alsberg demolished Easley's charges*: "Defends Writings of WPA Authors," *The New York Times*, July 22, 1937.

252 *"It was the fashion"*: Hallie Flanagan, *Arena* (New York: Duell, Sloan and Pearce, 1940), 335.

252 *Formal hearings began*: For a blow-by-blow summary, see Ogden, *Dies*, 51–100. The Online Books Page has compiled a helpful set of links to Dies Committee documents available online; see http://onlinebooks.library.upenn.edu/webbin/metabook?id=diescommittee.

253 *"Man of the Week"*: Goodman, *Committee*, 30.

253 *another highly visible committee*: Michael Denning suggests that La Follette's and Dies's commit- tees were bookends to the crest of Popular Front enthusiasm in the 1930s, and even argues that the Dies Committee was intended to draw attention away from the findings of La Follette's committee. See Denning, *The Cultural Front: The Laboring of American Culture in the Twentieth Century* (1997; repr., London: Verso, 2010), 13, 23, 104. See also Leo Huberman, *The Labor Spy Racket* (New York: Modern Age Books, 1937).

253 *the distinction between them*: Ogden, *Dies*, 102.

254 *"It is easy to 'smear'"*: Quoted in Ogden, *Dies*, 51.

254 *A cautious Roosevelt administration*: Regarding clashes with the administration, see Ogden, *Dies*, 66–67, 74–88; Roosevelt quoted on 80, 86.

254 *called Dies an "ass"*: quoted in Goodman, *Committee*, 52, 54n7.

255 *"It is grand to see"*: Van Wyck Brooks to Alsberg, Sept. 18, 1938, NARA PC37, box 0470, folder "B–C." Alsberg, it so happened, had helped to get Brooks's son Charles a job on the DC staff. Af- ter receiving this letter, he passed it up the WPA chain to other officials, and during her testimony, Ellen Woodward read it to the Dies Committee—leaving out the final line.

255 *formal investigation into the arts projects*: For the transcript, see *Investigation of Un-American Propaganda Activities in the United States: Hearings Before a Special Committee on Un-American Activities, House of Representatives, Seventy-Fifth Congress, Third Session, Seventy-Eighth Con- gress, Second Session, on H. Res. 282*, vol. 1 (Washington, DC: US Government Printing Office, 1938), 775–868.

255 *"One of the weirdest collections"*: Ogden, *Dies*, 62–63.

255 *first witness was Edwin P. Banta*: Dies hearings, vol. 2, 981–1017, and vol. 4, 2433–34.

256 *"incompetence and crackpotism"*: quoted in Mangione, *Dream*, 293–94.

257 *Banta seemed to become confused*: When Representative Joe Starnes, who did the questioning, asked what the NYC project had produced, Banta replied, "A couple of almanacs." Starnes, to his credit, reminded Banta of other publications—and even stuck up for them. The whole thing reached a bizarre crescendo as Banta described an incident when, before the hearings, he was detained and interrogated by Communist Party members who'd found out that he was leaking information to newspapers. They stuck a camera in his face, snapped a photo, and then published it in the *Daily Worker* alongside an article, "Workers' Enemies Exposed," labeling Banta a "stool pigeon" and "traitor to the working class" who'd joined the party for "his own slimy purposes."

257 *"It is our purpose to curtail"*: "Banta Sentenced; Called a Traitor," *The New York Times*, Dec. 1, 1944.

257 *committee heard Ralph De Sola*: Dies hearings, vol. 2, 1021–26, and vol. 3, 2396–415; see also Mangione, *Dream*, 295–301.

257 *made him a pariah*: This point was made by Vincent McHugh, the editor in NYC. See audio interview with McHugh, Jerre Mangione papers, D.245, Rare Books, Special Collections, and Preservation, River Campus Libraries, University of Rochester, box 149, folder 34.

258 *people passed in and out*: Klehr, *Heyday*, 154–55.

258 *"A good many people:"* De Sola testimony, Dies hearings, vol. 3, 2406.

258 *their intended audience*: In later testimony before a subcommittee of the House Appropriations Committee, Ralph De Sola affirmed this idea: his activities on the project involved publishing *Red Pen* and distributing it to project workers. See *Investigation and Study of the Works Progress Administration: Hearings Before the Subcommittee of the Committee on Appropriations, House of Representatives, Seventy-Sixth Congress, First Session, Acting Under House Resolution 130, Di- recting the Committee on Appropriations of the House to Conduct an Investigation and Study of the Works Progress Administration as a Basis for Legislation*, part 1 (Washington, DC: US Govern- ment Printing Office, 1939), 255–56.

259 *a typical dustup*: Mangione, *Dream*, 173.

259 *"They used to say"*: McHugh audio interview, Mangione papers, box 149, folder 34.

259 *"The Communists were out"*: George Willison interview typescript, Nov. 24, 1967, Mangione papers, box 13, folder 10.

259 *shared aesthetic and political sensibility*: This sensibility is the subject of Michael Denning's *The Cultural Front*, in which he gives priority of place to the CIO and argues that the Communist Party was a significant but not central actor.

260 *brought in three FWP workers*: For Lazell's, Shreve's, and Tax's testimonies, see Dies hearings, vol. 4, 3109–39.

261 *becoming a dangerous propaganda machine*: She blamed Alsberg and Joseph Gaer, the field representative and editor. "Did Mr. Gehr [*sic*] ever make any statement to you to lead you to believe that he was a member of the Communist Party?" Dies asked. "No," she said. "He only fights me on every point in which I endeavor to smooth things out." "Has he ever made any radical or revolutionary statements to you?" "No, indeed. The only statement that I understood he made was that I was a dangerous Nazi. I happen to be a niece of Gen. Zachary Taylor, once President of the United States, and I am about as much of a Nazi as he was."

262 *"the underprivileged Negro"*: As Jerrold Hirsch points out, in 1938, it was a legal fact that African Americans did not enjoy the same privileges as whites and were therefore precisely "underprivileged." See Hirsch, *Portrait*, 206.

262 *followed by Jeremiah Tax*: After serving in Europe with the US Army during the Second World War, Tax became a sportswriter and editor who worked at *Sports Illustrated* for a quarter century, eventually becoming its executive editor.

263 *"A handful of damn fool"*: Hunter to Corse, Dec. 1, 1938, Zora Neale Hurston Papers, box 13, folder 8, Special and Area Studies Collections, George A. Smathers Libraries, University of Florida, Gainesville, Florida.

263 *Woodward decided to spare them*: For Woodward's testimony, see Dies hearings, vol. 4, 2729–838. Flanagan later wrote: "Henry Alsberg and I pointed out with a good deal of heat that we had been silenced for months, while our projects were being subjected to attack, always on the promise of a day in court. We felt that Mrs. Woodward, with the best intentions in the world, would not be able to answer technical questions." See Flanagan, *Arena*, 339.

266 *"Eight thousand people"*: Flanagan, *Arena*, 342.

267 *committee called Henry Alsberg*: For Alsberg's testimony, see Dies hearings, vol. 4, 2886–908. See also Mangione, *Dream*, 314.

268 *if Alsberg had bungled the question*: Mangione, *Dream*, 318.

269 *the hearings ended*: Mangione, *Dream*, 320–21; Susan Rubenstein DeMasi, *Henry Alsberg: The Driving Force of the New Deal Federal Writers' Project* (Jefferson, NC: McFarland and Company, 2016), 211.

269 *correspondence through the final weeks*: See assorted correspondence, LOC FWPC, box A1, folders 3, 4, and 5.

270 *new secretary of commerce*: Robert Sherwood, *Roosevelt and Hopkins* (New York: Harper and Brothers, 1948), 92–99, 105–10.

270 *results were impressive*: Nick Taylor, *American-Made: The Enduring Legacy of the WPA: When FDR Put the Nation to Work* (2008; repr., New York: Bantam Books, 2009), 359, 547.

270 *"Don't kid me"*: quoted in Sherwood, *Roosevelt*, 105.

271 *took stock of the FWP*: Alsberg to Robert Cantwell, Jan. 19, 1939, LOC FWPC, box A2, folder 2; Alsberg to Peter Neumann, Feb. 6, 1939, LOC FWPC, box A2, folder 5; Alsberg memo to Florence S. Kerr, "Progress Report for period from January 1 to January 31, 1939, Federal Writers' Project," Feb. 1, 1939, LOC FWPC, box A2, folder 4.

272 *triggered in the Golden State*: Mangione, *Dream*, 68–69; William F. McDonald, *Federal Relief Administration and the Arts: The Origins and Administrative History of the Arts Projects of the Works Progress Administration* (Columbus: Ohio State University Press, 1969), 659–60.

272 *effectively reset and reoriented*: For an overview of the California project, see Mangione, *Dream*, 131–41, and David A. Taylor, *Soul of a People: The WPA Writers' Project Uncovers Depression America* (Hoboken, NJ: John Wiley and Sons, 2009), chapter 7, which focuses on Rexroth and Partch. See also David Kipen's fine introductions to the new editions of FWP guides that have

been retitled and published by the University of California Press: *California in the 1930s, Los Angeles in the 1930s, San Francisco in the 1930s*, and *San Diego in the 1930s*.

273 *total number of copies*: Wendy Griswold, *American Guides: The Federal Writers' Project and the Casting of American Culture* (Chicago: University of Chicago Press, 2016), 156.

273 *By 1941, there would be*: Merle Colby, "Presenting America to All Americans," *Publishers Weekly*, May 3, 1941.

274 *expressive of the New Deal moment*: Arthur M. Schlesinger, *The Age of Roosevelt*, vol. 2, *The Coming of the New Deal* (Cambridge: Riverside Press, 1959), 520–28, 558–63, 571; Roosevelt quoted on 525.

274 *This was a president*: David M. Kennedy, *Freedom from Fear* (New York: Oxford University Press, 1999), 95, 112–13; Tugwell quoted on 112. William Stott also describes Roosevelt as having a "documentary imagination" that epitomized this aspect of the New Deal and the broader documentary approach in the thirties. See William Stott, *Documentary Expression and Thirties America* (1973; repr., Chicago: University of Chicago Press, 1986), 93–102.

275 *"I wish in some way"*: Alsberg to Roosevelt, June 18, 1937, and Roosevelt to Alsberg, June 22, 1937, NARA PC37, box 0471, folder "211.7 Q–R."

275 *appeared in early January*: *Investigation of Un-American Activities and Propaganda: Report of the Special Committee on Un-American Activities Pursuant to H. Res. 282*, Seventy-Fifth Congress (Washington, DC: US Government Printing Office, 1939). The arts projects are covered on 31–39.

276 *hung on to this lie*: Dies, *Story*, 67. In the book, Dies cites his own committee hearings as the source of "one third," although the record plainly shows that this claim was, at best, highly misleading. On the same page, he asserts, wrongly, "Our evidence was so complete that the predominantly Liberal Congress abolished both projects." Only the FTP was abolished in 1939, by a Congress that was moving in a markedly conservative, anti–New Deal direction.

276 *"a splendid vehicle"*: As the historian Jerrold Hirsch puts it, "Dies's assessment of the Writers' Project stands in sharp contrast to that of virtually every historian who has written about either him or the FWP." See Hirsch, *Portrait*, 198.

276–77 *the committee would live on*: Ogden, *Dies*, 101–102, 113.

277 *Evalyn Walsh McLean*: Dies, *Story*, 124. Dies says that McLean used her social contacts to pass the committee information.

277 *left the FWP behind*: That spring, Dies made *The New Yorker*'s "Talk of the Town" section with a report that he'd tempered his views while recovering from an illness at home: "When Mr. Dies made the astounding statement that many of the institutions which he had at first thought ill of were really O.K. and American, in spite of a Communistic element in their membership, the reporter ventured to remark that he seemed to have changed some of his opinions. The legislator laughed modestly, and waved his hand toward a pile of books on a nearby table. 'Books!' he said. 'While I was in bed I read every book I could get my hands on.'" See "Changed Man," *The New Yorker*, Apr. 8, 1939, 12.

277 *"So you are one of our lousy"*: Anonymous to Alsberg, Feb. 21, 1939, Alsberg/Hettwer correspondence, Bienes Museum of the Modern Book, box 1, folder 1.

277 *wrote to the state directors*: assorted correspondence, LOC FWPC, box A3, folder 3.

277 *discussing a guidebook to Hawaii*: Rockwell Kent to Alsberg, May 19, 1939, and Alsberg to Ernest Gruening, May 24, 1939, LOC FWPC, box A5, folder 5.

277 *balance of power in Congress shifted*: William E. Leuchtenburg, *Franklin D. Roosevelt and the New Deal, 1932–1940* (1963; repr., New York: Harper Perennial, 2009), 252–74.

277–78 *trend that only intensified*: Alan Brinkley, *The End of Reform: New Deal Liberalism in Recession and War* (1995; repr., New York: Vintage Books, 1996), 140–43.

278 *"Are you just making"*: N. Taylor, *American-Made*, 418.

278 *appointed Colonel Francis C. Harrington*: N. Taylor, *American-Made*, 420; Mangione, *Dream*, 329.

278 *phase two of the congressional assault*: Mangione, *Dream*, 321–26; N. Taylor, *American-Made*, 431–34.

278 *reheated charges of communist domination*: Testimony from various witnesses appears in *Investigation and Study of the Works Progress Administration: Hearings Before the Subcommittee of the Committee on Appropriations, House of Representatives, Seventy-Sixth Congress, First Session, Acting Under House Resolution 130, Directing the Committee on Appropriations of the House to Conduct an Investigation and Study of the Works Progress Administration as a Basis for Legislation*, part 1 (Washington, DC: US Government Printing Office, 1939). De Sola is on 249-61; the "demoted supervisor," Joseph Thomas Barrett, is on 261-68.

279 *Forty-four publishers*: "44 Publishers Ask WPA Writing to Go On," *The New York Times*, May 22, 1939.

279 *"The affection with which"*: Mangione, *Dream*, 3-12. Mangione wasn't invited as a representative of the FWP but because an author he knew from his days in publishing was close with the Roosevelts and arranged the invitation.

279 *Alsberg sent instructions*: Alsberg to Carita Corse, July 21, 1939, NARA PC37, box 1108, folder "Fla. 651.3172 Jan. 1939-Jan. 1941."

280 *Congress abolished the FTP*: Flanagan, *Arena*, 363-65.

280 *were fundamentally altered*: McDonald, *Federal*, 309-15.

280 *achieved what Alf Landon*: "Landon's Plan for Relief," *The New York Times*, Oct. 14, 1936.

280 *best workers*: Penkower, *Federal*, 223.

280 *director did not*: For one account of Alsberg's termination, see DeMasi, *Alsberg*, 217-20.

280 *key target of the investigation*: For the discussion of Alsberg, see *Further Additional Appropriation for Work Relief and Relief, Fiscal Year 1939: Hearings Before the Subcommittee of the Committee on Appropriations, House of Representatives, Seventy-Sixth Congress, First Session, on H.J. Res 209 and 246, Making Further Additional Appropriation for Work Relief and Relief, Fiscal Year 1939* (Washington, DC: US Government Printing Office, 1939), 211-14.

281 *"I'm not discussing it"*: Oral history interview with Florence Kerr, Oct. 18-Oct. 31, 1963, Archives of American Art, Smithsonian Institution. Penkower alludes to rumors about Alsberg's homosexuality playing a role in his dismissal; DeMasi, Alsberg's biographer, discovered no additional information aside from the editor Vincent McHugh mentioning such rumors years later. See Penkower, *Federal*, 212, and DeMasi, *Alsberg*, 229.

281 *Alsberg refused to resign*: According to a letter Clair Laning wrote to Reed Harris, who was no longer on the project, Alsberg was open to the idea of retiring if they replaced him with John T. Frederick or someone equally competent, and then allowed him to gradually bow out. Colonel Harrington, instead, was determined to get rid of Alsberg immediately. "They intend to kill off the Writers' Project by silent treatment," Laning wrote. "At the present moment WPA is probably the most anti-New Deal agency going." See Laning to Harris, Aug. 14, 1939, Mangione papers, box 37, folder 6.

281 *detractors within the FWP*: Mangione, *Dream*, 14.

281 *"The dismissal looks too much"*: untitled editorial, *The Nation*, Aug. 19, 1939; see also "Killing the Writers' Project," *The New Republic*, Aug. 23, 1939; Walter White to Alsberg, Aug. 10, 1939, Mangione papers, box 14, folder 7; Barnet Nover, "Farewell Presents," *The Washington Post*, Aug. 20, 1939.

281 *"You were the guiding star"*: Dora Thea Hettwer to Alsberg, Aug. 15, 1939, Mangione papers, box 14, folder 7.

282 *"Dismay, dissension, and that private"*: Malcolm Cowley, —*And I Worked at the Writer's Trade: Chapters of Literary History, 1918-1978* (1978; repr., New York: Penguin Books, 1979), 154-55.

282 *perhaps the quintessential liberal*: Daniel Aaron, *Writers on the Left: Episodes in American Literary Communism* (1961; repr., New York: Columbia University Press, 1992), 363.

282 *a veteran communist*: Audio interview with Vincent McHugh, Mangione papers, box 149, folder 34.

282 *speeded up his break*: Bettina Drew, *Nelson Algren: A Life on the Wild Side* (New York: G. P. Putnam's Sons, 1989), 117.

282 *"great step toward peace"*: Angelo Herndon, "Negroes Have No Stake in This War, Wright Says," in *Conversations with Richard Wright*, 25–27. This was published in February 1940, after war in Europe had already begun.

282 *new structure of the Writers' Program*: For a full account of the Writers' Program, successor to the FWP, see Mangione, *Dream*, chapter 9, and Penkower, *Federal*, chapter 11.

283 *FWP left behind 128*: Katharine Kellock, "Brief History of the Federal Writers' Project (1935–1939)," 23, LOC KP, folder "WPA, Federal Writers' Project, 'A Brief History of the Federal Writers' Project, July 1, 1935–August 31, 1939.'"

283 *Six editors were initially dispatched*: Dora Thea Hettwer to Alsberg, Mar. 19, 1941, Alsberg/Hettwer correspondence, box 1, folder 10.

283 *Newsom had been director*: For Newsom's biographical details, see "J. D. Newsom, Headed U.S. Writers Group," *The New York Times*, Apr. 27, 1954, and Mangione, *Dream*, 331.

283 *"Says he with an efficient snap"*: "WPAchievement," *Time*, Aug. 12, 1940.

283 *"PERPETUATION OF FORMER PRACTICES"*: Newsom telegram to Charles D. Wood, Nov. 27, 1939, NARA PC37, box 0473, folder "211.7 (writers) J. D. Newsom."

284 *required workers to sign an affidavit*: N. Taylor, *American-Made*, 495–96. See also "Bodenheim Dropped in WPA Red Inquiry," *The New York Times*, Aug. 2, 1940.

284 *questioned by a WPA investigator*: Report attached to Roy C. Jacobson memo to Malcolm J. Miller, Jan. 14, 1941, NARA PC37, box 2126, folder "NYC 651.3171 A–Z." See also Bold, *WPA*, 105.

284 *"The accusation has been made"*: Burton J. Barnett to Franklin Roosevelt, Jan. 14, 1938, NARA PC37, box 1253, folder "651.3179 Ill. A–B."

284 *Only two states*: Mangione, *Dream*, 330.

285 *Idaho project disappeared*: E. M. Wilson to C. E. Triggs, Mar. 13, 1940, NARA PC37, box 1175, folder "651.317 Idaho 1935–1938." A WPA official in Idaho wrote to DC and said the project would end on Mar. 15, 1940. "We are confronted with another situation in Idaho which makes it difficult to operate the project and that is the loss of Vardis Fisher, who acted as Director. We do not seem to have, at the present time, in Idaho, a person of sufficient talent to supervise the project."

285 *subject to the new rule*: Stetson Kennedy was laid off for the same reason, although he managed to continue recording folk songs by getting a new job with the music project in Florida. See Carita Corse to Newsom, Jan. 6, 1940, PC37, box 1108, folder "Fla. 651.3173 A–Z."

285 *project rolls went from*: "Report on WPA Writers' Program," Mar. 1, 1940, NARA PC37, box 0473, folder "211.7 (writers) J. D. Newsom"; Katharine Kellock, "Brief History of the Federal Writers' Project (1935–1939)," 23, LOC KP, folder "WPA, Federal Writers' Project, 'A Brief History of the Federal Writers' Project, July 1, 1935–August 31, 1939.'"

285 *Corse continued to direct*: Stella Bloch Hanau, Florida field report, Nov. 17, 1941, and Corse memo to Rolla Southworth, "Highlights Report December 1, 1941–February 1, 1942," NARA PC37, box 1107, folder "Fla. 651.317 Jan 1941–Jan 1942."

285 *no Black workers*: Maurice Howe, field report, Aug. 3–13, 1941, NARA PC37, box 0472, folder "H 1941."

285 *"American cookery and the part"*: Kellock, "General Notes to Regional Editors of America Eats," LOC KP, folder "WPA Federal Writers' Project America Eats 1952–62 and UD." See also *The Food of a Younger Land*, ed. Mark Kurlansky (New York: Riverhead Books, 2009) 14–22, 200–273; and Algren, *America Eats* (Iowa City: University of Iowa Press, 1992). Kurlansky's book collects material from the whole of the "America Eats" archive at the Library of Congress, while Algren's is a version of his manuscript dealing with the Midwest only (including original recipes and updated variations by the chef Louis Szathmary, who purchased the manuscript from Algren and arranged for its publication after Algren's death).

286 *"These are the blue plate"*: Algren, *America Eats*, 79.

286 *"Nebraskans Eat the Weiners"*: quoted in Kurlansky, *Food*, 202.

286 *"Mrs. Hanau's recommendations"*: Newsom memo to Walter M. Kiplinger, Dec. 10, 1941, with attachment, "Report on a Field Visit to Oklahoma, December 3–5, 1941, Stella Bloch Hanau,

Technical Consultant, WPA Writers' Program," NARA PC37, box 0472, folder "H 1941." On the Oklahoma guide, see Mangione, *Dream*, 337n.

286   *Writers Unit of the War Services*: Mangione, *Dream*, 347–48.

286   *staff had shrunk down*: Katharine Kellock to J. D. Newsom, "Request for Reclassification," undated, LOC KP, folder "WPA, Federal Writers' Project, Reports and Correspondence 1936–42."

286   *"Not a soul here"*: Kellock, untitled notes, Mar. 26 [1942], LOC KP, folder "WPA, Federal Writers' Project, Reports and Correspondence 1936–42."

286   *she would hear the booms*: Kellock to Harold Coy, May 14, 1942, LOC KP, folder "WPA, Federal Writers' Project, Reports and Correspondence 1936–42."

287   *"A rueful smile"*: Kellock, "The Writers' Project, Morituri," Mar. 25, 1942, LOC KP, folder "WPA, Federal Writers' Project, Reports and Correspondence 1936–42."

287   *subsumed by the war mobilization*: Merle Colby, "Writers Program, 1942 Re-direction Suggestions," Jan. 1942, NARA PC37, box 0472, folder "211.7 M–Z."

287   *submitted to the Office of Censorship*: N. R. Howard to G. F. Willison, Feb. 9, 1942, NARA PC37, box 0472, folder "211.7 M–Z."

287   *"It seemed inadvisable"*: Kellock to "Mrs. Evans," undated, LOC KP, folder "WPA Federal Writers' Project <u>America Eats</u> 1952–62 and UD."

287   *Margaret Mead landed*: Charles King, *Gods of the Upper Air: How a Circle of Renegade Anthropologists Reinvented Race, Sex, and Gender in the Twentieth Century* (New York: Doubleday, 2019), 314.

287   *the project was at an end*: Kellock to Harold Coy, May 14, 1942, LOC KP, folder "WPA, Federal Writers' Project, Reports and Correspondence 1936–42."

288   *Merle Colby and a few others*: Merle Colby, "Final Report on Disposition of Unpublished Materials of WPA Writers' Program," Apr. 8, 1943. This is reprinted, along with several ancillary reports, in Marc S. Selvaggio, *The American Guide Series: Works by the Federal Writers' Project*, a catalog from Arthur Scharf, Bookseller, and Schoyer's Books, Pittsburgh, Pennsylvania, 1990, 169–74.

288   *"high standards of excellence"*: See assorted correspondence, NARA PC37, box 0474, folder "211.71 Jan. 1939."

288   *"If one is honest"*: Alsberg to Dora Thea Hettwer, Sept. 18, 1939, Alsberg/Hettwer correspondence, box 1, folder 9.

289   *he was also relieved*: For an account of Alsberg's post-FWP life and career, see DeMasi, *Alsberg*, chapter 12.

289   *mourned Emma Goldman*: For a brisk survey of Goldman's later years, see Vivian Gornick, *Emma Goldman: Revolution as a Way of Life* (New Haven, CT: Yale University Press, 2011), part 3.

289   *one-volume guide to America*: *The American Guide: A Source Book and Complete Travel Guide for the United States*, ed. Henry Alsberg (New York: Hastings House, 1949). See also DeMasi, *Alsberg*, 233–34.

289   *several FWP alumni*: Of the authors mentioned in the literature essay, only Conrad Aiken, Richard Wright, and Claude McKay were federal writers. Vardis Fisher does rank a mention in the introduction to the mountain states. So does Zora Neale Hurston in the introduction to the South, along with Wright. (The two of them are included in a list of southern Black writers, which, in its entirety, also includes Booker T. Washington and James Weldon Johnson.) There's no mention of Algren, although perhaps he did not notice—that same year, he published *The Man with the Golden Arm*, which would win the National Book Award.

290   *"a great Newfoundland"*: "Their Own Baedeker," *The New Yorker*, Aug. 20, 1949.

290   *Walt Whitman's*: As Richard Poirier put it, "The production of mess, of puzzle, might be called his [Whitman's] method if not his métier. Mess, like America itself, is infinitely expansive, and, because of that, it can endlessly postpone the finality of any answer as to what and where it is or will be." See Richard Poirier, "In Praise of Mess," *London Review of Books*, vol. 20, no. 11 (June 4, 1998). I'm grateful to Ken Bleeth for bringing this piece to my attention.

EPILOGUE

291 *might have become permanent*: For an overview of this legislation, see Richard D. McKinzie, *The New Deal for Artists* (Princeton: Princeton University Press, 1973), 151–55.

291 *"I regard Congress as"*: quoted in Richard O. Boyer, "Boy Orator Grows Older," *The New Yorker*, Nov. 5, 1938.

292 *"literally laughed out of existence"*: Mangione, *The Dream and the Deal: The Federal Writers' Project, 1935–1943* (1972; repr, Philadelphia: University of Pennsylvania Press, 1983), 254n.

292 *Sirovich tried again*: Cedric Larson, "The Cultural Projects of the WPA," *The Public Opinion Quarterly*, vol. 3, no. 3 (July 1939), 492.

292 *"The work in Washington"*: "Dr. Sirovich Dies; a Representative," *The New York Times*, Dec. 18, 1939.

292 *The Office of War Information*: Sydney Weinberg, "What to Tell America: The Writers' Quarrel in the Office of War Information," *The Journal of American History*, vol. 55, no. 1 (June 1968), 73–89; Denning, *The Cultural Front*, 81–82.

293 *a comprehensive study of Japan*: Charles King, *Gods of the Upper Air: How a Circle of Renegade Anthropologists Reinvented Race, Sex, and Gender in the Twentieth Century* (New York: Doubleday, 2019), 318–31. Benedict was criticized for never setting foot in Japan but, as King points out, she was denied her request to travel there by her superiors.

293 *"hack work"*: Alsberg to Dora Thea Hettwer, Nov. 13, 1942, Alsberg/Hettwer correspondence, Bienes Museum of the Modern Book, box 1, folder 9.

293 *abolished it*: David M. Kennedy, *Freedom from Fear* (New York: Oxford University Press, 1999), 783.

293 *anti-institutional mood*: A striking example of this is a review by Harold Rosenberg, who'd been an editor on the DC staff and went on to become a well-regarded art critic. Writing about Jerre Mangione's book *The Dream and the Deal*, Rosenberg praised the American Guides but judged the overall project a misguided failure because of its very nature. See Harold Rosenberg, "Anyone Who Could Write English," *The New Yorker*, Jan. 20, 1973.

293 *from the end of the war*: For a study of the post-WPA era, leading up to the creation of the National Foundation for the Arts and Humanities, see Gary O. Larson, *The Reluctant Patron: The United States Government and the Arts, 1943–1965* (Philadelphia: University of Pennsylvania Press, 1983).

293 *National Defense Education Act*: This period, from 1945 to 1975, is considered the Golden Age of American higher education, which Louis Menand attributes, in part, to a "gravy train" of federal funding. See Louis Menand, *The Marketplace of Ideas: Reform and Resistance in the American University* (New York: W. W. Norton, 2010), 64–68. See also Arthur S. Flemming, "The Philosophy and Objectives of the National Defense Education Act," *The Annals of the American Academy of Political and Social Science*, Jan. 1960, vol. 327, 132–38. Flemming was Eisenhower's secretary of health, education, and welfare when the act was passed.

294 *Others found succor*: For an overview of CIA activities in the cultural sphere, see Frances Stonor Saunders, *The Cultural Cold War: The CIA and the World of Arts and Letters* (New York: New Press, 2000). For two more targeted accounts of how these activities involved writers, see Eric Bennett, *Workshops of Empire: Stegner, Engle, and American Creative Writing During the Cold War* (Iowa City: University of Iowa Press, 2015), and Joel Whitney, *Finks: How the CIA Tricked the World's Best Writers* (New York: OR Books, 2016).

294 *"The difference now"*: Pepper quoted in *Reluctant Patron*, 215.

295 *"old French gentleman poodle"*: John Steinbeck, *Travels with Charley: In Search of America* (1962; repr., New York: Penguin Books, 1986), 8, 134.

295 *"a college town"*: Federal Writers' Project, *California: A Guide to the Golden State* (New York: Hastings House, 1939), 375.

296 *"haven't read der 'Steinbeck's' 'Charlie,'"*: Alsberg to Dora Thea Hettwer, Jan. 10, 1963, Alsberg/Hettwer correspondence, box 1, folder 8.

296 *continued his un-American crusade*: Walter Goodman, *The Committee: The Extraordinary Career of the House Committee on Un-American Activities* (New York: Farrar, Straus and Giroux, 1968), 161–62, 167–69; "Ex-Rep. Martin Dies, 71, Is Dead; Led Un-American Activities Unit," *The New York Times*, Nov. 15, 1972.

296 *the junior senator from Wisconsin*: Martin Dies, Jr., *Martin Dies' Story* (New York: Bookmailer, 1963), 176–77.

297 *"chronic mental indigestion"*: Fisher, *Thomas Wolfe as I Knew Him and Other Essays* (Denver: Alan Swallow, 1963), 67.

297 *in touch with Benjamin Botkin*: Carla Kaplan, ed., *Zora Neale Hurston: A Life in Letters* (2002; repr., New York: Anchor Books, 2003), 623n3.

297 *"That dear, departed"*: Kaplan, *A Life in Letters*, 534. See also 535 for her opinion of New Dealers.

297 *"In my philosophy"*: Fisher to Mary J. Keeney, Apr. 13, 1943, Vardis Fisher Papers, Yale Collection of American Literature, Beinecke Rare Book and Manuscript Library, box 30, folder "Fisher, V."

297 *Later in life*: John R. Milton, *Three West: Conversations with Vardis Fisher, Max Evans, Michael Straight* (1970; repr., Vermillion, SD: Dakota Press, 1972), 10.

298 *whether his death was accidental*: Fisher had always had a fondness for mordant talk; when he was in DC celebrating the Idaho guide, he delivered a long monologue to Jerre Mangione about the philosophical advantages of suicide and proposed that they form a national organization promoting it, like Alcoholics Anonymous. Mangione didn't know if it was the bourbon talking or if Fisher was a little serious—then again, in all his dealings with the DC office as they assembled the guide, Fisher was often a little serious and a little bit joking. See Jerre Mangione, *An Ethnic at Large: A Memoir of America in the Thirties and Forties* (1978; repr., Syracuse: Syracuse University Press, 2001), 230.

298 *Horace Cayton, Jr.*: For an overview of Cayton and St. Clair Drake's work, see Mitchell Duneier, *Ghetto: The Invention of a Place, the History of an Idea* (New York: Farrar, Straus and Giroux, 2016), chapter 2.

299 *struck by the book's power*: Colin Asher, *Never a Lovely So Real: The Life and Work of Nelson Algren* (New York: W. W. Norton, 2019), 164–67.

299 *met for the last time*: Bettina Drew, *Nelson Algren: A Life on the Wild Side* (New York: G. P. Putnam's Sons, 1989), 206.

300 *"Since the middle twenties"*: Nelson Algren, *Chicago: City on the Make* (1951; repr., Chicago: University of Chicago Press, 2011), 53–54.

ACKNOWLEDGMENTS

I'm grateful to the archivists and librarians and their colleagues at multiple institutions whose work made my research for this book possible; my debt goes beyond what is reflected in the citations. Thanks, in particular, to Eugene Morris at the National Archives in College Park, Maryland, who helped me navigate the extensive WPA holdings; and to Florence M. Turcotte and Terrence Phillips at the University of Florida Smathers Libraries, for their crucial remote assistance during the coronavirus pandemic. The wonderful staff of the Montclair Public Library made my life as an independent researcher much easier as well.

Thank you to Deena Vecchiollo, who ably and professionally carried out research on the ground for me in Illinois; to Colin Asher, who kindly discussed ideas and lent his expertise on Nelson Algren; and to Susan Rubenstein DeMasi and Brent McKee, who generously shared photo-research advice and photographs during the lockdown.

A hearty thanks to James Sheehan and Teresa Biagioni for their hospitality and camaraderie during my visits to DC. I'm indebted to Ken Bleeth and Ian Blair for offering thoughtful, valuable comments on an early draft of the manuscript (although any remaining errors and shortcomings are, of course, my own). Susie Linfield, as always, was generous with her support at critical moments. My years spent working in the publishing industry have helped me to tell the story of the FWP, and I'm grateful to my past colleagues, especially Martin Paddio and Amanda Moon, from whom I learned a great deal about the making of books.

Thank you to my agent, Edward Orloff of McCormick Literary, for his early enthusiasm for this project and for his keen insight into how to clarify and organize my ideas. I'm lucky to have benefited from such an excellent team at FSG, including Ian Van Wye, whose incisive comments were complemented by his deft oversight; Scott Auerbach, Nina Frieman, and Gretchen Achilles, who did meticulous work inside the book; and Alexis Nowicki, who tirelessly spread the word. My editor, Alex Star, by way of his example, helped to shape this book before I even knew I wanted to write it, and it has been my good fortune to rely on his expert instincts, wise counsel, and generous intellect.

To my family (on both sides, including the newest generation) and my friends (near and far), for their enthusiasm and overall support, I offer a great collective thank-you. I owe a special thanks to the late Fred Board, whose FWP collection, which he spent years assembling, eventually became the catalyst for this project, and whose bibliophilia, I suspect, informed it in one way or another.

This book is dedicated to my parents, Susan and Neil Borchert, who have encouraged me to write for as long as I've been able to do so, and probably longer; in so many ways, they made this book possible, and not just by passing that FWP collection on to me. It's also dedicated to Addie Borchert, who has been my partner in the creation of this book, for which I'm deeply grateful, and in everything else, too—for which no expression of gratitude will suffice.

INDEX

California, 10, 79, 82, 204, 216, 254, 272, 295, 317*n*
Calumet Baking Powder Company, 122
Cambridge University, 283
Cannon, Clarence, 279
Cantwell, Robert, 13, 125
Cather, Willa, 69, 319*n*
Catton, Bruce, 96
Caxton Printers, 75, 92–93, 101, 324*n*
Cayton, Horace, Jr., 298
Central Intelligence Agency (CIA), 294
Cerf, Bennett, 99, 242
Chaucer, Geoffrey, 117
Cheever, John, 235–37, 242, 269, 355*n*
Chemistry, US Bureau of, 34
Chicago, 45, 108, 115, 117, 121, 124–25, 138, 175, 231, 350*n*; Algren in, 105–108, 113–17, 119–20, 122–23, 125–26, 129–32, 138, 142–46, 159, 208, 238; Black writers in, 130–31, 172, 208–209, 212, 221–26, 230, 237, 239, 241; cluster of writers in, 73, 79; CWA projects in, 29; Federal Theater Project in, 224; Great Migration to, 218, 225; Haymarket massacre in, 289; industry in, 114, 122, 207; racial strife in, 226, 241; radicals in, 27, 126, 133, 201, 212, 240, 284; University of, 67, 73, 78, 120, 128, 131
Chicago: City on the Make (Algren), 146, 200, 300
Chicago Defender, 130
Chicago Tribune, 129
Children of God (Fisher), 102
Christensen, Hans, 286
CIA (Central Intelligence Agency), 294
CIO, 116, 126–27, 173, 207, 253, 259, 296, 330*nn*, 360*n*
Civilian Conservation Corps (CCC), 5, 24–25, 62, 106, 122, 165, 252, 273, 313*n*; segregation of, 172–73
civil rights, 154, 173–74, 341*n*
Civil Service, 174
Civil War, 23, 57–58, 119, 123, 153

Civil Works Administration (CWA), 25–26, 28–32, 45–46, 62, 256, 312*n*
Clara White Mission, 192
Clarke, Joe, 159, 161, 339*n*
Clark University, 83
Clemens, Samuel, 135
Coast, The, 215
Coffee-Pepper Bill (1938), 291–92, 294
Colby, Merle, 100, 113, 287–28, 319*n*
Cold War, 294
Collier, John, 76
Collier's magazine, 236
Colonial Dames of America, 86
Colorado, 10, 27, 103
Columbia University, 34, 42, 47, 162, 167, 183; Center for Oral History Research, 140; Teachers College, 233
Commerce, US Department of, 270, 279
Coming of Age in Samoa (Mead), 162, 164
Comintern, 36, 112, 198, 229, 258, 332*n*, 347*n*, 358*n*
Communist Party, 139, 210, 220, 246, 299, 301, 329*nn*, 332*n*, 347*n*; accusations of membership in, 100; in Chicago, 126, 222, 352*n*; Conroy's avoidance of, 134–35; Dies Committee hearings on, 249–50, 256–59, 275–76, 360*n*; in New York, 197–99, 203, 213, 229–32, 235, 282, 284, 329*n*, 359*n*; platform and line of, 61, 109–12, 242; presidential candidate of, 109; recruitment in South for, 188; writers' organizations involved with, 109–12, 199, 328*n*
communists, 127, 176, 183, 234, 240, 263–67; in Chicago, 223, 241; government employees accused of supporting, 50, 85, 241, 252–53, 255–59; magazine publishing stories by, 118, 268; *see also* Communist Party, Soviet Union
Confederacy, 105, 150
Congress, US, 77, 93, 200, 245, 283, 284, 294; FWP opposed in, 9, 13, 206–208,

A NOTE ABOUT THE AUTHOR

Scott Borchert is a writer and editor based in New Jersey, and a former assistant editor at Farrar, Straus and Giroux. He holds a master's degree in cultural reporting and criticism from the Arthur L. Carter Journalism Institute at New York University, and his work has appeared in *Southwest Review*, *Monthly Review*, *The Rumpus*, *PopMatters*, *Brooklyn Magazine*, and other publications.